UNDERSTANDING THE TIMES

THE RELIGIOUS WORLDVIEWS
OF OUR DAY AND THE SEARCH FOR TRUTH

ABRIDGED EDITION

DAVID A. NOEBEL

Published By

ASSOCIATION OF CHRISTIAN SCHOOLS INTERNATIONAL AND **SUMMIT MINISTRIES**

ACSI • P.O. Box 35097 • Colorado Springs • Colorado 80935
Summit Ministries • P.O. Box 207 • Manitou Springs • Colorado 80829

http://www.christiananswers.net/summit/sumhome.html

Understanding The Times
Copyright © 1995 by David A. Noebel
ISBN # 0-936163-22-4
Printed in the United States of America

INTRODUCTION

Every human being bases his thoughts, decisions and actions on a worldview. A person may not be able to identify his worldview, and it may lack consistency, but his most basic assumptions about the origin of life, purpose, and the future guarantee adherence to some system of thought.

Because worldviews are pertinent to every person's life—the way we think and the way we act—and because virtually all worldviews promise salvation or utopia, the study of worldviews is of critical importance. It is for this reason that Dr. Noebel wrote Understanding The Times. Too many Christians are ill-prepared to formulate, articulate and defend a Biblical worldview. Dr. Noebel believes that a comprehensive knowledge of the Biblical Christian worldview and its rivals will provide today's students with the understanding and motivation to become Christian leaders in all areas of life (families, education, church, jobs, government).

Years of conscientious research have gone toward presenting each worldview accurately in the words of its own proponents. In this way the internal inconsistencies and fatal assumptions of Secular Humanism, Marxism/Leninism, and the New Age movement are exposed. These worldviews, in turn, are compared to Biblical Christianity.

After studying this text, all concerned Christians will. . .

- gain a deeper appreciation for God's truth, beauty and goodness
- be ready to give a positive Biblical defense on controversial ideas and issues
- cultivate wisdom and discernment about viewpoints that oppose Christian values

This new understanding will help believers become more established in the Christian faith (Colossians 2:7), take captive every idea for Christ (II Corinthians 10:5), and not be deceived by "vain and deceitful philosophy" (Colossians 2:8).

Dr. Paul Kienel
Founder, President Emeritus
ACSI

CONTENTS

FOUR WESTERN WORLDVIEW MODELS

SOURCES	SECULAR HUMANISM HUMANIST MANIFESTOS I AND II	MARXISM/ LENINISM WRITINGS OF MARX AND LENIN	COSMIC HUMANISM WRITINGS OF SPANGLER, FERGUSON, ETC.	BIBLICAL CHRISTIANITY BIBLE
THEOLOGY	Atheism	Atheism	Pantheism	Theism
PHILOSOPHY	Naturalism	Dialectical Materialism	Non-Naturalism	Supernaturalism
ETHICS	Relativism	Proletariat Morality	Relativism	Absolutes
BIOLOGY	Darwinian Evolution	Darwinian/Punctuated Evolution	Darwinian/Punctuated Evolution	Creation
PSYCHOLOGY	Self-Actualization	Behaviorism	Collective Consciousness	Mind/Body
SOCIOLOGY	Non-Traditional Family	Abolition of Home, Church and State	Non-Traditional Home, Church and State	Traditional Home, Church and State
LAW	Positive Law	Positive Law	Self-Law	Biblical and Natural Law
POLITICS	World Government (Globalism)	New World Order (New Civilization)	New Age Order	Justice, Freedom and Order
ECONOMICS	Socialism	Socialism	Universal Enlightened Production	Stewardship of Property
HISTORY	Historical Evolution	Historical Materialism	Evolutionary Godhood	Historical Resurrection

CHAPTER 1

The Battle for Hearts and Minds

"Nothing short of a great Civil War of Values rages today throughout North America," say James Dobson and Gary Bauer. "Two sides with vastly differing and incompatible worldviews are locked in a bitter conflict that permeates every level of society."[1]

This book is an in-depth account of this "Second Great Civil War"—an account of the war for our children and grandchildren. The war, as Dobson and Bauer put it, is a struggle "for the hearts and minds of people. It is a war over ideas."[2]

To be more precise, it is a battle between worldviews. On one side is the Christian worldview. On the other is the Humanist worldview divided into three easily definable branches: Secular Humanism, Marxism/Leninism, and Cosmic Humanism (the New Age movement). While the latter three don't agree in every detail, there is one point on which they unanimously concur—their opposition to Biblical Christianity. It is in this context that we will seek to understand all three while presenting a strong, honest, truthful, intelligent defense of the Biblical Christian worldview.

"Someday soon," Dobson and Bauer say, "a winner [in the battle for our children's hearts and minds] will emerge and the loser will fade from memory. For now, the outcome is very much in doubt."[3] In order to emerge victorious, Christians must quickly arrive at an understanding of the times and "know what they ought to do" (1 Chronicles 12:32).

1

THE HEART OF A WORLDVIEW

The term *worldview* refers to any ideology, philosophy, theology, movement, or religion that provides an overarching approach to understanding God, the world, and man's relations to God and the world. Specifically, a worldview should contain a particular perspective regarding each of the following ten disciplines: theology, philosophy, ethics, biology, psychology, sociology, law, politics, economics, and history.

If Biblical Christianity contains a specific attitude toward all ten disciplines it is, by our definition, a worldview. And, since it contains a theology, it is by implication a religious worldview.

Secular Humanism and Marxism/Leninism are also religious, as this study will show. Both have theologies. There is a Secular Humanist theology; there is a Marxist/Leninist theology. Further, both are worldviews, because they speak directly to each of the other nine disciplines. The New Age movement (Cosmic Humanism) is a less tightly-organized worldview.

> **Worldview: Any ideology, philosophy, theology, movement, or religion that provides an overarching approach to understanding God, the world, and man's relations to God and the world.**

Each worldview offers a particular perspective from which to approach each discipline. Conversely, each discipline is value-laden with worldview implications. Christian students must understand that these various disciplines are not value-free. Each discipline demands basic assumptions about the nature of reality in order to grant meaning to specific approaches to it.

This text analyzes the four worldviews' perspectives on each of the ten disciplines, but it does so without losing sight of how each system of thought integrates its various presuppositions, categories, and conclusions. We are not out to "over-analyze." Rather, we are attempting to understand each discipline and how it fits into each worldview. Dissecting is artificial; integration is the real world. No discipline stands alone. Each affects all others in one way or another. The line separating theology and philosophy is fragile; the line separating theology, philosophy, ethics, law, and politics is more so. In fact, there is no ultimate line, only a difference in emphasis and perspective.

Thus, the arrangement of the categories is, to some degree, arbitrary; but we have tried to place them in their most logical sequence. It is clear that theological and philosophical assumptions color every aspect of one's worldview and that disciplines such as sociology and psychology are related; but other relations and distinctions are less recognizable. Therefore, one reader may feel that we have done law an injustice by distancing it from ethics, and another may feel history to be almost as foundational to a worldview as philosophy. There is no correct order according to which these chapters must be read. Our format is a logical suggestion; it is not binding. Readers are encouraged to adhere to any study method or outline with which they feel comfortable.

Regardless of the approach you choose, keep in mind that you are studying the four worldviews that exert the most influence over Western man. Other worldviews exist, but they wield much less power; Confucianism, for example, may profoundly influence some Eastern countries, but hardly phases the West. The major ideas of the West are contained in the following four worldviews.

THE CHRISTIAN WORLDVIEW

This text will focus on Christianity because it is the only worldview that provides a consistent explanation of all the facts of reality with regard to theology, philosophy, ethics, economics, or anything else. As Carl F.H. Henry says, "The Christian belief system, which the Christian knows to be grounded in divine revelation, is relevant to all of life."[4]

This relevance results from the fact that Christianity is, we believe, the one worldview based on truth. "Christianity is true," says George Gilder, "and its truth will be discovered anywhere you look very far."[5] Gilder (who is not only an outstanding economic philosopher but also a sociologist) found Christ while seeking sociological truth.

Philosopher C.E.M. Joad found Christ and Christianity because he was seeking ethical truth. "I now believe," he wrote, "that the balance of reasoned considerations tells heavily in favour of the religious, even of the Christian view of the world."[6] Joad recognized the need for absolute truth, rather than a truth that evolves with each new discovery: "A religion which is in constant process of revision to square with science's ever-changing picture of the world might well be easier to believe, but it is hard to believe it would be worth believing."[7]

Christianity is the embodiment of Christ's claim that he is "the way, the truth, and the life" (John 14:6). When we say "this is the Christian way," we mean "this is the way Christ would have us act in such a situation." It is no small matter to think and act as Christ instructs. The Christian agrees with Humanist Bertrand Russell's admission that "What the world needs is Christian love or compassion."[8]

America is often described as a Christian nation. Over one hundred and fifty years ago, Alexis de Tocqueville wrote, "There is no country in the whole world, in which the Christian religion retains a greater influence over the souls of men than in America; and there can be no greater proof of its utility, and of its conformity to human nature, than that its influence is most powerfully felt over the most enlightened and free nation of the earth."[9] Unfortunately, however, America—and the rest of Western Civilization—are turning away from their heritage. Western nations are eradicating large chunks of Christianity from the public square.

> "I now believe that the balance of reasoned considerations tells heavily in favour of the religious, even of the Christian view of the world."
>
> C.E.M. Joad

We contend that America should be moving in the opposite direction—embracing the Christian worldview rather than pushing it away. Francis Schaeffer blames America's drift toward secularism and injustice on the Christian community's failure to apply its worldview to every facet of society: "The basic problem of the Christians in this country in the last eighty years or so, in regard to society and in regard to government, is that they have seen things in bits and pieces instead of totals."[10] He goes on to say that Christians have very gradually "become disturbed over permissiveness, pornography, the public schools, the breakdown of the family, and finally abortion. But they have not seen this as a totality—each thing being a part, a symptom of a much larger problem. They have failed to see that all of this has come about due to a shift in the world view—that is, through a fundamental change in the overall way people think and view the world and life as a whole."[11]

This study is a wake-up call for America. A country seeking to promote human rights and liberty must adhere to the only worldview that can account for their existence. Unfortunately, countless Americans are embracing other worldviews—most notably, Secular Humanism, Marxism/Leninism, and Cosmic Humanism.

THE MARXIST/LENINIST WORLDVIEW

Marxism/Leninism is a well-developed atheistic worldview. It is more consistent than either Cosmic or Secular Humanism. Marxist/Leninists have developed a perspective regarding each of the ten disciplines—usually in great detail. Often, Marxism produces a "champion" of its perspective in the various fields (for example, I.P. Pavlov in psychology or T.D. Lysenko in biology). All these things make Marxism worthy of study—but the main reason it is crucial for Christians to understand Marxism is that Marxism is one of Christianity's most vocal detractors.

This fact becomes all the more sinister when one realizes that some Christian groups have attempted to combine their Christianity with Marxism. Evangelical voices often referred to as the "Christian Left" have been known to support the Marxist

4

position. The World Council of Churches saw no inconsistency in holding its meetings behind the Iron Curtain before it disintegrated. The editors of *National Review* note that "Substantial parts of various American churches . . . have been active on the side of communist insurrection. The Maryknoll priests, the liberation theologians, Episcopal and Methodist groups and Jesuits have placed themselves in direct alliance with totalitarianism. . . . With an enormous Christian rebirth taking place in Eastern Europe, it is ironic that so much of the American church is decadent."[12]

The liberal American churches' position regarding Marxism does not, of course, take into account the profound incompatibility of their faith with the Marxist worldview. Alexander Solzhenitsyn, before the fall of the Iron Curtain, described this incompatibility in concrete terms:

> The Soviet Union [under Marxist rule] is a land where churches have been leveled, where triumphant atheism has rampaged uncontrolled for two-thirds of a century, where the clergy is utterly humiliated and deprived of all independence, where what remains of the Russian Orthodox Church as an institution is tolerated only for the sake of propaganda directed at the West, where even today, people are sent to labor camps for their faith, and where, within the camps themselves, those who gather to pray at Easter are clapped into punishment cells.[13]

Obviously, there is a need for a text that delineates the insurmountable differences between Marxism and Christianity. This study, by addressing both worldviews, highlights their incompatibility.

Some might raise the objection that the Marxist/Leninist worldview has already been proved to be a failure and completely incompatible with reality, as witnessed by the downfall of communist countries all over the world. Why, in light of these events, need one study the Marxist/Leninist perspective? Isn't Marxist ideology dead?

Two words should suffice: Tiananmen Square. While Marxism has crumbled in many countries, it still embraces others in its death grip. And if even one country is held sway by Marxism, people somewhere are suffering. Marxism/Leninism hates resistance, and will crush believers in rival worldviews any way possible, even with tanks.

Today, Marxism is the dominant view in some African and Latin American countries (under the guise of Liberation Theology) and, incredibly, on many American university campuses. In an article titled "Marxism in U.S. Classrooms,"[14] *U.S. News and World Report* reported that there are ten thousand Marxist professors on America's campuses. Georgie Anne Geyer says that "the percentage of Marxist faculty numbers can range from an estimated 90 percent in some midwestern universities."[15]

Arnold Beichman says that "Marxist academics are today's power elite in the universities."[16]

"The strides made by Marxism at American universities in the last two decades are breathtaking," says New York University's Herbert London. "Every discipline has been affected by its preachment, and almost every faculty now counts among its members a resident Marxist scholar."[17] Duke University Slavic Languages professor Magnus Krynski described increasing Marxist presence on his campus—a presence actively encouraged by the university administration, which, he says, is "faddishly" luring Marxist literary critics to Duke with large salaries. In March 1987 Duke University hosted the Southeast Marxist Scholars Conference. Dr. Malcolm Gillis, former vice provost of Duke University, thanked some one hundred Marxist professors, graduate students, and activists for gathering at Duke and said, "When I left this campus twenty years ago, there were very few Marxists here. When I returned in 1984, I saw Marxists in many parts of the social science faculty."[18] The conference was sponsored by the Marxist Educational Press (based at the University of Minnesota) and Duke's own Program on Perspectives in Marxism and Society.

The Marxist influence (or, as it is now preferred: the "Politically Correct") has reached its most alarming heights in American universities' humanities departments. "With a few notable exceptions," says former Yale professor Roger Kimball, "our most prestigious liberal arts colleges and universities have installed the entire radical menu at the center of their humanities curriculum at both the undergraduate and the graduate level."[19] Kimball provides more evidence that Duke University is in the forefront of academia's move toward Marxism, noting that it has "recently conducted a tireless—and successful—campaign to arm its humanities department with the likes of the Marxist literary critic Frederic Jameson, Barbara Herrnstein Smith, Frank Lentricchia, Stanley Fish (and his pedagogically like-minded wife, Jane Tompkins), and other less well known souls of kindred intellectual orientation."[20]

The Marxist worldview is alive and well in the American classroom. As Dr. Fred Schwarz says, "The colleges and universities are the nurseries of communism."[21] Christian students must not get caught up in these nurseries.

THE SECULAR HUMANIST WORLDVIEW

Marxism, however, is not the only worldview that threatens to take the classroom hostage. Secular Humanism also vies for total control of education.

In fact, Secular Humanism is the dominant worldview in our secular colleges and universities. It has also made gains in many Christian colleges and universities. Christians considering a college education must be well versed in the Humanistic worldview or risk losing their own Christian perspective by default. Why? Because Humanist professors are unwilling to present the Christian perspective accurately, while many Christian educators feel duty-bound to give fair representation to the Humanist viewpoint.

Humanists recognize the classroom as a powerful context for indoctrination. They understand that many worldviews exist and they believe Humanists must use the classroom to flush out "unenlightened" worldviews and encourage individuals to embrace their worldview. Christianity has been deliberately, some would say brilliantly, erased from America's educational system. The direction of America's education can be seen as a descent from Jonathan Edwards (1750) and the Christian influence, through Horace Mann (1842) and the Unitarian influence, to John Dewey (1933) and the Humanist influence.

But we contend that Jonathan Edwards has more to say than John Dewey, and that Christianity should get back into the public square and influence educational policy. The Christian worldview is a fitting competitor to Dewey's religious view (as summarized in *A Common Faith*). But since most Christian teenagers accept their older, "wiser" professors' teachings uncritically and may therefore find themselves subject to Humanistic viewpoints, this study becomes necessary to equalize the battle for the mind. Hosea's statement, "My people are destroyed for lack of knowledge" (4:6), applies in spades to Christian college-bound students. Many never recover from their educational befuddlement, lapsing instead into atheism, materialism, new morality, evolutionism, globalism, etc. Others suffer for years from their near loss of faith. Those prepared, however, survive and flourish.

> **Jonathan Edwards has more to say than John Dewey … Christianity should get back into the public square and influence educational policy.**

America's colleges and universities are not the only areas of Secular Humanist influence, however. The mass media continually publish and broadcast the Humanist worldview. The 1990 Humanist of the Year was Ted Turner, chief executive officer of Turner Broadcasting System, which now owns TBS SuperStation, CNN, CNN Headline News, and Turner Network Television (TNT). In 1985 Turner founded the Better World Society; presently he is willing to present $500,000 to anyone able to invent a new worldview suitable for the new, peaceful earth. According to Turner, Christianity is a "religion for losers" and Christ should not have bothered dying on the cross. "I don't want anybody to die for me," said Turner. "I've had a few drinks and a few girlfriends, and if that's gonna put me in hell, then so be it."[22] Turner also maintains that the Ten Commandments are "out of date." He wants to replace them with his Ten

Voluntary Initiatives, which include the statements: "I promise to have love and respect for the planet earth and living things thereon, especially my fellow species— humankind. I promise to treat all persons everywhere with dignity, respect, and friendliness. I promise to have no more than two children, or no more than my nation suggests. I reject the use of force, in particular military force, and back United Nations arbitration of international disputes. I support the United Nations and its efforts to collectively improve the conditions of the planet."[23]

Still another reason for examining the Humanist worldview is that many Humanists besides Turner have gained positions of considerable influence in our society. B.F. Skinner, Abraham Maslow, Carl Rogers, and Erich Fromm, all former Humanists of the Year, have powerfully affected psychology. Carl Sagan, another Humanist of the Year, preached his Humanism on a widely heralded television series. Norman Lear has produced and otherwise influenced a number of the shows on television today. Ethical decisions are made for our young people by Humanist of the Year Faye Wattleton, former director of Planned Parenthood. Humanist Isaac Asimov wrote tirelessly for his cause. Clearly, Humanists are willing to support their worldview—often more faithfully than Christians.

COSMIC HUMANISM

In recent years, a fourth worldview has begun to gain visibility. Commonly referred to as the New Age movement, it is more accurately described by the term *Cosmic Humanism*. Because it is still in its formative stages and professes a marked disdain for dogma, this worldview is more vaguely defined than the other three. Indeed, some members of the New Age movement go so far as to claim that their worldview "has no religious doctrine or teachings of its own."[24]

This attitude results from the New Age belief that truth resides within each individual and, therefore, no one can claim a corner on the truth or dictate truth to another. "The New Age," explains Christian writer Johanna Michaelsen, "is the ultimate eclectic religion of self: Whatever you decide is right for you is what's right, as long as you don't get narrow-minded and exclusive about it."[25]

By assuming that truth resides within each individual, however, one lays the cornerstone for a worldview. Granting oneself the power to discern all truth is a facet of theology, and this theology has ramifications that many members of the New Age movement have already discovered. Some have grudgingly begun to consider their movement a worldview. Marilyn Ferguson, author of *The Aquarian Conspiracy* (a book referred to as "The New Age watershed classic"), says the movement ushers in a "new mind—the ascendance of a startling worldview."[26] This worldview is summed up in its skeletal form, agreeable to virtually every Cosmic Humanist, by Jonathan Adolph: "In its broadest sense, New Age thinking can be characterized as a form of utopianism, the desire to create a better society, a 'New Age' in which humanity lives in harmony with itself, nature, and the cosmos."[27]

While the New Age movement still appears to be fragmented and without strong leadership, it has grown at a remarkable rate. The Stanford Research Institute estimates that "the number of New Agers in America could be as high as 5 to 10 percent of the population—12 million or more people."[28] Others have put the figure as high as 60 million, although this includes people who merely believe in reincarnation and astrology. John Randolph Price, a world leader of the New Age movement, says, "there are more than half a billion New Age advocates on the planet at this time, working among various religious groups."[29]

Further, people adhering to the Cosmic Humanist worldview are gaining power in our society and around the world. Malachi Martin lists dozens of organizations that are either New Age or New Age sympathetic. Barbara Marx Hubbard, a spokeswoman for the New Age, made a bid for the 1984 Democratic vice presidential nomination. Clearly, Cosmic Humanism is becoming a "fourth force" in the Western hemisphere.

CONCLUSION

Throughout this study, it should become clear that Marxism and Secular Humanism are similar in a number of ways. The body of this work will demonstrate that this relationship is not casual or peripheral. The two are family. Secular Humanism is the mother (Humanists trace their heritage to the Greeks four hundred years before Christ), and Marxism is the daughter. Secular Humanism is the root, Marxism the branch. At the heart of both worldviews are atheism, materialism, spontaneous generation, evolution, and moral relativism. From a comprehensive point of view, their differences are minor. Both Karl Marx and Humanist Paul Kurtz recognize the truth of these assertions. Marx said it like this: "Communism, as fully developed naturalism, equals humanism."[30] And Kurtz says Marx "is a humanist because he rejects theistic religion and defends atheism."[31]

Further, Cosmic Humanism and Secular Humanism are close kin. The New Age movement is little more than spiritualized Secular Humanism. Take the Secular Humanist's exaltation of self and hatred for Christ, sprinkle in some meditation, reincarnation, and anti-rationalism, and Presto! You've created another worldview. Cosmic Humanism claims to meet man's spiritual needs—something Marxism and Secular Humanism cannot claim—but it is stuck with an impersonal, unjust god (there is little difference between claiming no god exists and claiming everything is god). At bottom, the New Age movement is as bankrupt as all other anti-Christian worldviews.

The significance of the similarities between these three anti-Christian views cannot be overstated. While we watch Marxism crumble in Eastern Europe, and while men and women in India suffer horribly because of their society's acceptance of a version of Cosmic Humanism, America's public schools are immersed in these same values, under a different name and with a slight change in emphasis. Only when the emphasis has completely shifted to a Christian perspective can young people flourish in light of the true worldview. And this dramatic shift in emphasis can be brought about best through the leadership of a few well-grounded, confident Christian students.

This, then, is our fundamental reason for preparing *Understanding the Times*: too many Christian young people are ill-prepared to lead. The vast majority have no concept of the components of their worldview and stand intellectually naked before left-wing professors. Henry says that evangelical students know more about God than their secular counterparts, but "with some few gratifying exceptions, neither home nor church has shaped a comprehensive and consistent faith that stands noon-bright amid the dim shadows of spiritual rebellion and moral profligacy."[32]

Christ's teachings impart just such a noon-bright faith to all Christians who master their worldview, who "understand the times." This book's foundational verse, 1 Chronicles 12:32, announces that just two hundred individuals who "understood the times" provided the leadership for an entire nation. We believe that a comprehensive knowledge of the Christian worldview and its rivals will provide today's young people with the understanding necessary to become Christian leaders.

CHAPTER 2

Religious Worldviews in Conflict

Many people believe that when Christians confront other worldviews and attempt to speak to such "worldly" disciplines as politics, economics, biology, and law, they are overstepping their bounds. "Mind your own business," we are told. Jesus taught His followers, "you do not belong to the world, but I have chosen you out of the world" (John 15:19).

How, then, can the Christian justify his claim to a worldview that speaks to every facet of life? Shouldn't he stick to spiritual matters and allow non-Christians to concentrate on the practical matters of running the world?

In short, isn't there a difference between the secular and the sacred?

Not according to Dietrich Bonhoeffer, who says we should not distinguish between the two: "There are not two realities, but only one reality, and that is the reality of God, which has become manifest in Christ in the reality of the world."[1]

From the Biblical Christian perspective, the ten disciplines addressed in this text reflect various aspects of God and His creative or redemptive order. God created mankind with theological, philosophical, ethical, biological, etc. dimensions. We live and move and have our being (our very essence and existence) within and about these categories. Why? Because that is the way God created us.

Such being the case, these categories are, from the Christian perspective, sacred and not secular. They are sacred because they are imprinted in the creative order.

Both the early record of Genesis and the life of Jesus Christ reflect this truth.

For example, Genesis 1:1—"In the beginning God created the heavens and the earth"—is value-laden with theological and philosophical ramifications. Genesis 2:9—"knowledge of good and evil"—contains ethical ramifications; Genesis 1:21—"after their kind"—biological; Genesis 2:7—"a living soul"—psychological; Genesis 1:28—"be fruitful, and multiply, and fill the earth"—sociological and ecological; Genesis 3:11—"I commanded thee"—legal; Genesis 9:6—"whoso sheddeth man's blood"—political and legal; Genesis 1:29—"it shall be for food"—economic; Genesis 3:15—"enmity between thee and the woman"—historical. All ten disciplines are addressed in just the first few chapters of the Bible because they manifest and accent certain aspects of the creative order.

Further, God manifests Himself in the form of Christ in such a way as to underline the significance of each discipline. In theology, for example, Jesus Christ is "the fullness of the Godhead" (Colossians 2:9); in philosophy, Christ is the Logos of God (John 1:1); in ethics, Christ is "the true light" (John 1:9, 3:19-20); in biology, Christ is "the life" (John 1:4, 11:25; Colossians 1:16); in psychology, Christ is "Savior" (Luke 1:46-47; Titus 2:13); in sociology, Christ is "Son" (Luke 1:30-31; Isaiah 9:6); in law, Christ is lawgiver (Genesis 49:10; Isaiah 9:7); in politics, Christ is "King of kings and Lord of lords" (Revelation 19:16; 1 Timothy 6:15; Isaiah 9:6; Luke 1:33); in economics, Christ is Owner of all things (Psalm 24:1; 50:10-12; 1 Corinthians 10:26); and in history, Christ is the Alpha and Omega (Revelation 1:8). The integration of these various categories into society has come to be known as Western Civilization.

The Bible and the life of Jesus Christ provide the Christian with the basis for a complete worldview. Indeed, the Christian gains a perspective so comprehensive that he is commanded to "take captive every thought to make it obedient to Christ" (2 Corinthians 10:5).

Once we have captured all thoughts and made them obedient to Christ, we are to use these thoughts to "demolish arguments and every pretension that sets itself up against the knowledge of God" (2 Corinthians 10:4-5). When nations and men forget God (see Psalm 2) they experience what mankind has experienced in the twentieth century. Nazism and communism, two major movements bereft of the knowledge of God, cost the human race millions of lives. Whittaker Chambers says that communism's problem is not a problem of economics, but of atheism: "Faith is the central problem of this age."[2] Alexander Solzhenitsyn echoes him: "Men have forgotten God."[3]

> **"Faith is the central problem of this age."**
>
> *Whittaker Chambers*

14

The Apostle Paul insists in Colossians 2 that those who have "received Christ Jesus the Lord" (Colossians 2:6) are to be rooted and built up in him, strengthened in the faith as they were taught (Colossians 2:7). While the Christian works to strengthen his faith or worldview, he must see to it that no one takes him "captive through hollow and deceptive philosophy, which depends on human tradition and the basic principles of this world rather than on Christ" (Colossians 2:8). From the Christian point of view Secular, Cosmic and Marxist Humanism fall within the confines of "the basic principles of this world." They are based on the wisdom of this world, and not upon Christ.

This wasn't mere doctrine for Paul. He practiced what he preached. In Acts 17, Paul confronted the vain and deceitful philosophies of the atheistic Epicureans and pantheistic Stoics—the professional Humanists of his day. The Apostle countered their ideas with Christian ideas, he reasoned and preached, and he accented three Christian truths—the resurrection of Jesus Christ (Acts 17:18), the creation of the universe by God (Acts 17:24), and the judgment to come (Acts 17:31).

Can we do less? We, too, must fearlessly proclaim the good news of the gospel (God created the universe and all things in it, mankind rebelliously smashed the image of God by sin, Jesus Christ died for our sin, was raised from the dead, and is alive forevermore [1 Corinthians 15:1-4]), and we must stand fast in the context of the same worldview as Paul—creation, resurrection, and judgment.

THE RELIGION OF MARXISM/LENINISM

Paul recognized that man cannot compartmentalize aspects of his life into boxes marked "sacred" and "secular." He understood not only that Christianity was both a worldview and a religion, but also that all worldviews are religious by definition. Indeed, he went so far as to tell the Epicureans and Stoics that they were religious—they just worshiped an "Unknown God."

Most people have no problem recognizing that certain non-Christian worldviews are religious. Cosmic Humanists talk about god, so they must practice a religion. But how can the "religious" label apply to atheists like the Marxists or Secular Humanists?

It applies because all worldviews contain a theology—that is, all begin with a religious declaration. Christianity begins with "In the beginning God." Marxism/Leninism and Secular Humanism begin with "In the beginning no God." Cosmic Humanism begins with the declaration "Everything is God."

The Marxist view demonstrates itself to be religious in a number of other ways, as well. Marxism's philosophy of dialectical materialism grants matter god-like attributes, as Gustav A. Wetter acknowledges in *Dialectical Materialism:*

[T]he atheism of dialectical materialism is concerned with very much more than a mere denial of God.... [I]n dialectical materialism ... the higher is not, as such, denied; the world is interpreted as a process of continual ascent, which fundamentally extends into infinity. But it is supposed to be matter itself which continually attains to higher perfection under its own power, thanks to its indwelling dialectic. As Nikolai Berdyaev very rightly remarks, the dialectical materialist attribution of "dialectic" to matter confers on it, not mental attributes only, but even divine ones.[4]

We will discuss this further in the Marxist philosophy chapter. For now, it is enough to understand that Wetter perceives communism as religious in character.

Even Secular Humanists such as Bertrand Russell recognize the religiosity of Marxism: "The greatest danger in our day comes from new religions, communism and Nazism. To call these religions may perhaps be objectionable both to their friends and to their enemies, but in fact they have all the characteristics of religions. They advocate a way of life on the basis of irrational dogmas; they have a sacred history, a Messiah, and a priesthood. I do not see what more could be demanded to qualify a doctrine as a religion."[5]

THE RELIGION OF SECULAR HUMANISM

Secular Humanism is even more openly religious than Marxism. Charles Francis Potter, a signatory of the first *Humanist Manifesto,* wrote a book in 1930 entitled *Humanism: A New Religion.* Potter claimed to have organized a religious society— the First Humanist Society of New York.

The first *Humanist Manifesto* (1933) describes the agenda of "religious" Humanists. The 1980 preface to the *Humanist Manifestoes I & II,* written by Paul Kurtz, says, "Humanism is a philosophical, religious, and moral point of view."[4] John Dewey, a signatory of the 1933 *Manifesto,* wrote *A Common Faith*, in which he said, "Here are all the elements for a religious faith that shall not be confined to sect, class or race.... It remains to make it explicit and militant."[6]

While the *Humanist Manifesto II* (written primarily by Kurtz and published in 1973) drops the expression "religious humanism," it nevertheless contains religious implications and even religious terminology, including the statement that "no deity will save us; we must save ourselves."[7]

Lloyd L. Morain, a past president of the American Humanist Association, wrote a book with his wife Mary entitled *Humanism as the Next Step* (1954). In this work the authors describe Humanism as the fourth religion. The Morains were co-winners of the 1994 Humanist of the Year award.

The U.S. Supreme Court, in its decision in *Torcaso v. Watkins* (June 19, 1961), declared that "Among religions in this country which do not teach what would generally be considered a belief in the existence of God are Buddhism, Taoism, Ethical Culture, Secular Humanism and others."[9] A few years later (1965) the Supreme Court allowed Daniel Seeger conscientious objector status because of his religious beliefs. He claimed to be a Secular Humanist.

Auburn University's current Student, Faculty and Staff Directory contains a section entitled "Auburn Pastors and Campus Ministers." Included in the listing is a Humanist Counselor, Delos McKown, who also happens to be the head of Auburn's philosophy department. This is not an isolated example. The University of Arizona also lists Humanism under religious ministries. Harvard University has a Humanist chaplain who is one of 34 full- or part-time chaplains that comprise the United Ministry at Harvard and Radcliffe. He is sponsored by the American Humanist Association, the American Ethical Union, the Fellowship of Religious Humanists, and "generous gifts from Corliss Lamont."

In fact, the American Humanist Association "certifies humanist counselors who enjoy the legal status of ordained priests, pastors, and rabbis."[10] In its preamble, the Association states that one of it functions is to extend its principles and operate educationally. Toward this end it publishes books, magazines, and pamphlets; engages lecturers; selects, trains, and "accredits humanistic counselors as its ordained ministry of the movement."[11]

Kurtz—who has written a book that denies that Humanism is a religion throughout its first half and, in the second half, encourages the establishment of Humanist churches, calling them Eupraxophy Centers—admits that the organized Humanist movement in America is put in a quandary over whether

John Dewey, author of *A Common Faith* and signatory of *Humanist Manifesto I*, influenced American public school educational theory more profoundly than anyone.

Snapshots In Time

The American public school system was not a unique concept developed in the 20th century. Thomas Jefferson, Benjamin Rush, and other founding fathers called for free public education for all citizens immediately after the American Revolution. As early as 1647, the state of Massachusetts passed a law requiring towns to sponsor elementary schools.

These early efforts to create a public school system failed largely because funds were limited and there was no centralized bureaucracy to support the schools. Many parents showed little interest in supporting these school systems voluntarily or with their tax dollars, either because these parents viewed education as a luxury or chose to educate their children at home or in private schools.

Such concerns and choices were largely swept away by the Common School Movement, led by Unitarian Horace Mann, in the 19th century. Mann believed that the moral education of students could be better orchestrated by a public school system than by local schools and parents. By 1860, a majority of the states had established public school systems, and more than half of America's children were entrenched in these schools.

Humanism is a religion. Why? Simply because "the Fellowship of Religious Humanists (300 members), the American Ethical Union (3,000 members), and the Society for Humanistic Judaism (4,000 members) consider themselves to be religious. Even the American Humanist Association," says Kurtz, "has a [501(c)3] religious tax exemption."[12]

Kurtz's recent denial that Secular Humanism is a religion is not based on truth; it is a calculated political manuever. Kurtz seeks to dodge the all-important question: If Secular Humanism is a religion, then what is it doing in the public schools? If Christianity is thrown out of secular schools under the guise of separation of church and state, why shouldn't we banish Secular Humanism as well? Kurtz understands this, admitting that if Secular Humanism is a religion, "then we would be faced with a violation of the First Amendment to the United States Constitution."[13]

Christians who have seen their worldview effectively eliminated from the public schools are rightfully outraged by the Humanists' violations of the present interpretation of the First Amendment. They are angered that a mere 7.3 million Humanists can control the content of American public schooling while the country's Christians provide the lion's share of the students and bear the majority of the cost through their tax dollars.

Humanists attempt to downplay their violation of the present interpretation of the First Amendment by claiming that they present a neutral viewpoint. But no educational approach is neutral, as Richard A. Baer notes: "Education never takes place in a moral and philosophical vacuum. If the larger questions about human beings and their destiny are not being asked and answered within a predominantly Judeo-Christian framework [worldview], they will be addressed with another philosophical or religious framework—but hardly one that is 'neutral.' "[14]

Clearly, both Humanism and Marxism are religious worldviews. Trying to separate the sacred from the secular is like trying to sever the soul from the body—a deadly experiment. Thus, in order to provide a just educational system for our young people, we must recognize that all worldviews have religious implications and that it is discriminatory to bar some worldviews and not others from the classroom.

EVEN-HANDED APPROACH

After many years of study, contemplation, and teaching, we believe that the Biblical Christian worldview is spiritually, intellectually, emotionally, and practically far superior to all other worldviews. Christianity is something that, as C.S. Lewis said, mankind "could not have guessed," but that, once revealed, is recognizable as indisputable truth. Therefore, we believe that if students are given the opportunity to study and seriously think through creation versus evolution, for example, the vast majority will choose the creationist or Christian position.

This book represents an effort to allow individuals such opportunities by comparing the doctrines of four dominant worldviews. We have presented these views and their approach to the ten disciplines as accurately as possible. We have not represented non-Christians as either stupid or insane, despite their tendency to describe Christians in such unflattering terms. While Humanists such as Albert Ellis call Christians "emotionally disturbed: usually neurotic but sometimes psychotic,"[15] this text resists such name-calling and treats Secular Humanists, Marxists, and New Agers simply as individuals who have not yet recognized the inconsistent and erroneous nature of their worldviews.

No Marxist or Humanist (Cosmic or Secular), upon reading this text, should feel that we misrepresented his position. We quote the exact words of adherents to each worldview in their corresponding chapters, so that Cosmic Humanists describe the New Age position, Marxists the Marxist position, etc. When we say Secular Humanism is atheistic, we believe the student should hear what the Secular Humanists say about the issue themselves. When we contend that Marxism/Leninism relies biologically on punctuated equilibrium, the student should hear that from the Marxist. Further, no quote has purposely been taken out of context. We have, in the best tradition of Christian scholarship, allowed the competing non-Christian worldviews to have their say as they wish to say it.

> **Christianity explains the facts of reality better than any other worldview because it relies upon divine inspiration.**

We contend that by seeing the worldviews contrasted, the student will understand his own worldview and the alternatives better and be able to enunciate and defend his position more persuasively and intelligently. Many young people don't have the foggiest notion what they believe; it is the Christian's duty to share his faith with such a spiritually and intellectually rootless generation. The Apostle Peter says as much when he exhorts believers in Jesus Christ to "be prepared to give an answer to everyone who asks you to give the reason for the hope that you have" (1 Peter 3:15).

A WORD ABOUT SOURCES

There is no lack of sources or resources for each worldview we have chosen to analyze, and we have focused on the best of these materials. When we describe the Marxist position, for example, we will quote its ideological leaders, not a small band of neo-Marxists from Duke.

The primary publishing house of the Secular Humanists is Prometheus Books, located in Buffalo, New York. Their leaders include John Dewey, Roy Wood Sellars, Corliss Lamont, Paul Kurtz, Isaac Asimov, Sidney Hook, Carl Sagan, Julian Huxley, and Erich Fromm. The list of signatories of the *Humanist Manifestoes* includes scores of men and women who endorse that position. Those chosen as "Humanist of the Year" also provide a rich source of Humanistic viewpoints, as do contributing authors in *The Humanist* and *Free Inquiry* magazines. Through strict adherence to these resources, we are able to describe Secular Humanism without distortion.

Marxism/Leninism is even easier to document. None deny the major roles Karl Marx, Frederick Engels, V.I. Lenin, and Joseph Stalin have played in formulating the Marxist position. International Publishers, in New York City, prints and distributes hundreds of books from the Marxist/Leninist point of view. English translations of works published in the former Soviet Union are easily accessible, thanks to various distribution centers located in the United States.

The New Age worldview fills entire bookstores in America today. Cosmic Humanist leaders include Shirley MacLaine, David Spangler, Shakti Gawain, Joseph Campbell, John Denver, and Robert Muller. Many feminist leaders, including Marianne Williamson and Gloria Steinem, have begun to embrace the New Age movement. Many publishers woo New Age authors; the Bantam Doubleday Dell Publishing Group has a special New Age Books imprint.

The Bible, of course, is the primary source for the Christian worldview. Christianity explains the facts of reality better than any other worldview because it relies upon divine inspiration. If the Bible is truly God's special revelation to man, as we believe it is, then the only completely accurate view of the world must be founded on Scripture.

The divine inspiration of Scripture explains not only its miraculous coherency but also the incredible power of the figure of Christ. Atheist historian W.E.H. Lecky admits that the character of Jesus "has been not only the highest pattern of virtue but the strongest incentive to its practice; and has exercised so deep an influence that it may be truly said that the simple record of three short years of active life has done more to regenerate and to soften mankind than all the disquisitions of philosophers, and all the exhortations of moralists."[16] We believe the reason for this is that when Christ told the woman who spoke of the Messiah, "I who speak to you am he" (John 4:26), He was telling her the most fundamental truth of all. What Christ said concerning life and death, the saved and lost condition of mankind, body and soul, and truth constitutes the central precepts of the Christian worldview. Christ is its cornerstone. He is the way, the truth, and the life (John 14:6).

When presenting the Christian worldview, then, we take the Bible at face value. Call it "literal" interpretation if you wish, but it is difficult to see how else the writers of the Old and New Testaments meant to be taken. Figures of speech, yes; typologies, yes; analogies, yes; but overall they wrote in simple, straightforward terms. When a writer says, "In the beginning God created the heavens and the earth," we understand him to say that there is a God, there was a beginning to creation, that heaven and earth exist, and that God made them.

It does not take a Ph.D. or a high IQ to comprehend the basic message of the Bible. God's special revelation is open to everyone. There is no room for an "intellectual elite" in Christianity; only one "high priest" need intercede between God and man—Jesus Christ. For this reason, every man may "approach the throne of grace with confidence" (Hebrews 4:14-16).

This text will also rely on Christian men and women to describe the Christian worldview; however, these men and women's words must always conform to the truth of Scripture. "We accept man's testimony, but God's testimony is greater because it is the testimony of God, which he has given about his Son" (1 John 5:9). The Christian worldview stands or falls on the accuracy of the Bible.

Perhaps after reading this text, however, the student will decide that the Bible is not right, and that another worldview most conforms to the truth. If the facts support such a conclusion, personal integrity demands that the student adopt that view. But we contend that such a conclusion is not possible. We have examined the facts and wrestled with the possibilities, and we have found that intellectual integrity demands adherence to Biblical Christianity.

Most social ills, problems, and sins are ultimately matters of the mind, soul, and spirit. Materialistic and pantheistic worldviews are unable to solve these ills; instead they contribute more problems. Only the worldview based on Jesus Christ—a worldview that promotes and sustains the proper attitudes toward family, church, and state—can effectively speak to these areas. However, we cannot force this conclusion on others. All we can do is encourage individuals to "Taste and see that the Lord is good." We believe the Lord is good and His ways are good, and His teachings form a consistent, truthful, well-rounded Christian worldview.

STUDY PROCEDURES

Students wishing to build a foundation for approaching this text would do well to read James Orr's *A Christian View of God and the World*, along with James W. Sire's *The Universe Next Door* and four significant manifestoes: *A Christian Manifesto* by Francis Schaeffer, the *Communist Manifesto* by Karl Marx and Frederick Engels, and

Humanist Manifestoes I and II by Roy Wood Sellars and Paul Kurtz respectively. These works make a fitting introduction to this study by preparing the student to think in terms of worldviews and enforcing the notion that ideas have consequences—even logical consequences that proceed from prior beliefs.

However, reading such books is not mandatory for the student approaching this text—nor does the student need to be well-versed in worldview study. This work paints the various categorical positions of each worldview with broad and general strokes, adhering to Albert Einstein's dictum: Everything should be made as simple as possible, but not simpler. Each chapter of a section, we know, could consume thousands of pages by itself. Millions of pages and billions of words have been written on Christian theism alone. We have attempted, therefore, not to address every subtlety of each approach, but rather to capture the "kernel" of each worldview's perspective on each discipline. We follow C.S. Lewis's formula, striving to capture "mere Christianity," as well as mere Cosmic Humanism, etc. For example, the heart of Christian theology will always be theism, just as the heart of Humanist ethics will always be relativism and the heart of Marxist biology will always be evolution. Thus, we examine the core, the foundational approach, of each worldview. In this way, we assure the reader a text that will never become outdated.

There are two possible approaches to this text. A student could focus on one section at a time, thereby concentrating on each discipline, or he could focus on a specific worldview and examine its approach to each of the ten disciplines before moving on to study a second worldview and then a third. Whichever approach he chooses, the final result will be the same—the student will have gained insight by contrasting the various ideas central to each point of view. He or she will have engaged in comparative analysis.

A few decades ago (1925), evolutionists were bemoaning the fact that they were not given the opportunity to teach their viewpoint to American students. Dudley Field Malone, John Scopes's attorney, argued, "For God's sake, let the children have their minds kept open—close no doors to their knowledge; shut no door from them."[17] Today the situation is completely reversed. Creationism is barred, by law, from public school classrooms. Christianity rarely receives a fair hearing in the public square.

But how can a person seeking truth determine truth, if certain worldviews are hidden from him? How can people develop a worldview unless they compare and contrast worldviews?

This course of study is based on the belief that by learning to contrast worldviews, the student improves his overall conceptual skills. Perhaps some people feel that Christians should be shielded from non-Christian views. We disagree. Such studies are essential to prepare Christians to face the real world, including the university.

FACING THE CHALLENGE

As the Apostle Paul faced the religious humanists of his day, so the faithful and aware Christian must, if he is truly to follow Christ, face the religious Humanists of our day. In the West this means facing the Secular, Cosmic, and Marxist varieties. It also means—a lot of hard work.

This study requires work. But the student need not be disheartened by the effort required. The ideas of theism, atheism, supernaturalism, teleology, naturalism, materialism, dialectics, spontaneous generation, evolution, biblical morality, class morality, new morality, freedom, totalitarianism, private property, socialism, globalism, mind, soul, spirit, self-actualization, sin, and law make the world turn. Those willing to struggle with such ideas earn an invaluable reward: "an all-encompassing belief system, grander than the individual and larger than the family, to explain disparate facts and to furnish meaning in life."[18]

We believe the Christian worldview is the only proper "all-encompassing belief system"—larger than both the individual and the family, but destroying neither. Christianity furnishes meaning in life and best fits the facts of experience.

"The greatest question of our time is not communism versus individualism, not Europe versus America, not even the East versus the West," says Humanist Will Durant, "it is whether man can live without God."[19s] This text attempts to demonstrate the impossibility of survival on such terms by delineating a theistic worldview so comprehensive that it renders all questions of atheism obsolete. Christianity is so consistent and so faithful to the truth that we should ask instead why man would want to live without God.

It is our prayer that this study will assist each Christian student to see the value, truthfulness, and superiority of the Christian worldview, as he grows in the grace and knowledge of his Lord and Savior, Jesus Christ.

FOUR WESTERN WORLDVIEW MODELS

SOURCES	SECULAR HUMANISM — HUMANIST MANIFESTOS I AND II	MARXISM/LENINISM — WRITINGS OF MARX AND LENIN	COSMIC HUMANISM — WRITINGS OF SPANGLER, FERGUSON, ETC.	BIBLICAL CHRISTIANITY — BIBLE
THEOLOGY	Atheism	Atheism	Pantheism	Theism
PHILOSOPHY	Naturalism	Dialectical Materialism	Non-Naturalism	Supernaturalism
ETHICS	Relativism	Proletariat Morality	Relativism	Absolutes
BIOLOGY	Darwinian Evolution	Darwinian/Punctuated Evolution	Darwinian/Punctuated Evolution	Creation
PSYCHOLOGY	Self-Actualization	Behaviorism	Collective Consciousness	Mind/Body
SOCIOLOGY	Non-Traditional Family	Abolition of Home, Church and State	Non-Traditional Home, Church and State	Traditional Home, Church and State
LAW	Positive Law	Positive Law	Self-Law	Biblical and Natural Law
POLITICS	World Government (Globalism)	New World Order (New Civilization)	New Age Order	Justice, Freedom and Order
ECONOMICS	Socialism	Socialism	Universal Enlightened Production	Stewardship of Property
HISTORY	Historical Evolution	Historical Materialism	Evolutionary Godhood	Historical Resurrection

CHAPTER 3

Secular Humanist Theology

"Humanism cannot in any fair sense of the word apply to one who still believes in God as the source and creator of the universe."[1]

—Paul Kurtz

INTRODUCTION

After thinking about religion and the supernatural for three years, Bertrand Russell abandoned the notion of God. He later admitted, "I believed in God until I was just eighteen."[2] Russell, one of Secular Humanism's international voices, maintained that the whole idea of God was a conception derived from the ancient Oriental despotisms, and therefore concluded, "I am not a Christian . . . I do not believe in God and in immortality; and, . . . I do not think that Christ was the best and wisest of men, although I grant Him a very high degree of moral goodness."[3]

While eighteen may seem a tender age to determine whether or not God exists, Miriam Allen deFord, an American Humanist, had by age thirteen already concluded that there was sufficient evidence for denying the existence of all gods. Furthermore, she was convinced that man possessed no soul and that immortality (life after death) was a hoax. "To put it bluntly and undiplomatically," deFord says, "Humanism, in my viewpoint, must be atheistic or it is not Humanism as I understand it."[4]

According to nearly fifty years of *The Humanist* magazine and numerous articles and books by recognized Humanists, deFord's understanding of Humanism accurately describes the beliefs of most Humanists. The weight of evidence is so overwhelmingly in favor of atheism as the theological foundation of Secular Humanism that whatever nonatheistic Humanists there may be must be viewed as anomalies, even self-contradictions.

Corliss Lamont, author of *The Philosophy of Humanism*, insists that Humanism, "rejecting supernaturalism" and "seeking man's fulfillment in the here and now of this world," has a long and honored tradition of atheism, beginning with Democritus in ancient Greece and Lucretius in ancient Rome and continuing through history to John Dewey and Bertrand Russell in the twentieth century.

THEOLOGICAL BELIEFS OF LEADING HUMANISTS

The theology of the Humanist is surprisingly unshakeable in its dogmatism: the supernatural, including God, Satan, angels, demons, souls, and consciences, does not exist. This theology is spelled out in all its certitude by various Humanist leaders.

Lamont believes that the fundamental principle of Humanism, the principle that distinguishes it from all other worldviews, is that "Humanism . . . considers all forms of the supernatural as myth."[5] The supernatural—that is, anything outside nature, "does not exist."[6] "Humanism," says Lamont, "in its most accurate philosophical sense, implies a worldview in which Nature is everything, in which there is no supernatural."[7]

Lamont asserts that "intellectually, there is nothing to be gained and much to be lost for philosophy by positing a supernatural Creator or First Cause behind the great material universe."[8] There is no place in the Humanist worldview for God and, insists Lamont, instead of the gods creating the cosmos, "the cosmos, in the individualized form of human beings giving rein to their imagination, created the gods."[9]

> "Without God, what is left? Man and the Universe. That should be enough. That has to be enough because that is all there is."
>
> *Peter Angeles*

Some years earlier than Lamont's first edition of *The Philosophy of Humanism* (1949), many Humanists, including Dewey, Roy Wood Sellars, John H. Randall, Jr., E. A. Burtt, and Edwin H. Wilson, published *Humanist Manifesto I* (1933). It described the universe as "self-existing and not created." Further, the *Manifesto* declared, "the time has passed for theism. . . ."[10]

Forty years after the 1933 *Manifesto*, the Humanists published *Humanist Manifesto II* and reiterated, "We find insufficient evidence for belief in the existence of a supernatural; it is either meaningless or irrelevant to the question of the survival and fulfillment of the human race. As non-theists, we begin with humans not God, nature not deity." Again, ". . . we can discover no divine purpose or providence for the human species. While there is much that we do not know, humans are responsible for what we are or will become. No deity will save us; we must save ourselves."[11] Hundreds of Humanists signed this declaration of atheism.

Isaac Asimov served as the director of the American Humanist Association from 1989 to 1992. Writing in *Free Inquiry,* Asimov leaves no doubt regarding his personal theology: "I am an atheist, out and out. It took me a long time to say it. I've been an atheist for years and years, but somehow I felt it was intellectually unrespectable to say one was an atheist, because it assumed knowledge that one didn't have. Somehow it was better to say one was a humanist or an agnostic. I finally decided that I'm a creature of emotion as well as reason. Emotionally I am an atheist. I don't have the evidence to prove that God doesn't exist, but I so strongly suspect he doesn't that I don't want to waste my time."[12]

> **"No deity will save us; we must save ourselves."**
>
> *Humanist Manifesto II*

Bold atheism is proclaimed by every orthodox Humanist, including Paul Kurtz. He declares, "Humanism cannot in any fair sense of the word apply to one who still believes in God as the source and creator of the universe. Christian Humanism would be possible only for those who are willing to admit that they are atheistic Humanists. It surely does not apply to God-intoxicated believers."[13]

For Kurtz, "God himself is man deified."[14] Such theology, of course, is quite close to the Marxist point of view. In fact, Kurtz refers to Marx as "one of history's great humanist thinkers." Kurtz says Marx is a Humanist because "he rejects theistic religion and defends atheism."[15]

Julian Huxley said, "I disbelieve in a personal God in any sense in which that phrase is ordinarily used." He went on to say, "For my own part, the sense of spiritual relief which comes from rejecting the idea of God as a supernatural being is enormous."[16]

Norman Mailer admits, "I suppose that I would have to list myself under 'atheistic humanism.' "[17]

Harold H. Titus says that Humanism is a "religion without God,"[18] adding, "Humanistic naturalists regard the universe as 'self-existing and not created.' They have abandoned all conceptions of a supernatural and all forms of cosmic support."[19]

JOHN DEWEY: GURU TO THE PUBLIC SCHOOLS

One leading Humanist's atheism had such an impact on American culture that it requires more intense scrutiny. Because of John Dewey's status as an educator, and especially because he had such a profound influence on America's public school system, his theological views must be understood by everyone seeking to understand modern education.

In his work *A Common Faith*, Dewey distinguishes between the words *religion* and *religious*. He reserves the term *religion* for the supernatural while maintaining the term *religious* for the world of the natural (especially as it involves human relations, welfare, and progress). Dewey rejects the supernatural and the supernatural God. He accepts only evolving nature, with all of its "religious" ramifications: "I cannot," says Dewey, "understand how any realization of the democratic ideal as a vital moral and spiritual ideal in human affairs is possible without surrender of the conception of the basic division to which supernatural Christianity is committed."[20] For Dewey, democracy cannot ingest the Christian notions of *saved* and *lost, sheep* and *goats,* etc. He considers such notions "spiritual aristocracy" and contrary to the ideals of democracy. A democratic church must include believer and unbeliever.

A Brief Look At: John Dewey (1859-1952)

1884: Career as a college professor begins at the University of Michigan

1904: Assumes the chair of education at Columbia University

1915: Elected first president of the American Association of University Professors

1920: Helps establish the American Civil Liberties Union

1921: Joins the newly-formed League for Industrial Democracy

1930: Retires from Columbia University

1933: Signs the *Humanist Manifesto*

1934: Publishes *A Common Faith*

Dewey makes it clear that he believes science has largely discredited Biblical Christianity. "Geological discoveries," he says, "have displaced Creation myths which once bulked large."[21] Biology, says Dewey, has "revolutionized conceptions of soul and mind which once occupied a central place in religious beliefs and ideas."[22] He also says that biology has made a "profound impression" on the ideas of sin, redemption, and immortality. Anthropology, history, and literary criticism have furnished a "radically different version of the historic events and personages upon which Christian religions have built."[23] And psychology is already opening up "natural explanations of phenomena so extraordinary that once their supernatural origin was, so to say, the natural explanation."[24] For Dewey, science and scientific method have exiled God and the supernatural to the dustbins of history.

HUMANISTIC THEOLOGICAL LITERATURE

Secular Humanism's primary publishing arm is Prometheus Books, located in Buffalo, New York. Among other things, Prometheus publishes atheistic children's books, including *What About Gods?* by Chris Brockman. This book is designed to indoctrinate children with dogmatic atheistic sentiments like, "Many people say they believe in a god. Do you know what a god is? Do you know what it means to believe in a god? A god is a mythical character. Mythical characters are imaginary, they're not real. People make them up. Dragons and fairies are two of many mythical characters people have made up. They're not real. . . ."[25]

Prometheus also publishes atheistic literature geared toward adult audiences. Paul Blanshard's *Classics of Free Thought* was published "to keep atheism before the public." *Critiques of God*, edited by Peter Angeles, contains 371 pages supporting Humanist theology's denial of the existence of God.

In *Critiques,* Angeles explains that belief in the supernatural has all but vanished from our culture. He says that God has lost His spatial location as a monarch in heaven and His temporal precedence to the universe as its Creator *ex nihilo*. "It is not that God is being relegated to a remote region," Angeles insists. "It is not that God has become a bodiless abstraction (a sexless It). It is the realization that there is no God left to which to relate. Without God, what is left? Man and the Universe. That should be enough. That has to be enough because that is all there is."[26]

CONCLUSION

The Secular Humanists' latest declaration (1980) does not diverge significantly from their orthodox theological views. Written by Kurtz and published in *Free Inquiry,* it contends that "Secular Humanists may be agnostics, atheists, rationalists, or skeptics, but they find insufficient evidence for the claim that some divine purpose exists for the universe. They reject the idea that God has intervened miraculously in history or revealed himself to a chosen few, or that he can save or redeem sinners."[27]

Humanist theology, start to finish, is based on the denial of God and the supernatural. This denial, however, leads the Humanist to another necessary theological conclusion: man is the Supreme Authority (of course, it is possible that Humanism's deification of man may have preceded its atheistic assumptions, since the existence of God becomes a decided nuisance after one has declared one's self sovereign).

At bottom, it is of little importance whether atheism or the deification of man was Humanism's first theological presupposition; the crux of their theology remains anti-God. This is the heart and soul of Secular Humanism: man setting himself in place of God. Unfortunately for the Humanist, this theology often strips him of all sense of purpose. As Ernest Nagel explains, atheism "can offer no hope of personal immortality, no threats of divine chastisement, no promise of eternal recompense for injustices suffered, no blueprints to sure salvation. . . . A tragic view of life is thus an uneliminable ingredient in atheistic thought."[28]

Theology
At A Glance

Secular Humanist

Atheism

CHAPTER 4

Marxist/Leninist Theology

"Religion is opium for the people. Religion is a sort of spiritual booze. . . ."[1]
—V.I. Lenin

INTRODUCTION

"We Communists are atheists,"[2] declared Chou En-lai at the Bandung Conference in April, 1955. This Chinese communist leader captured the fundamental theological ingredient of Marxism/Leninism in one word: *atheism.* Today, Marxist/Leninists prefer two words: *scientific atheism.*

From the university days of Karl Marx to the present, official spokesmen for Marxism have been consistent about the content of their theology—God, a Supreme Being, a Creator, a Ruler, does not, can not, and must not exist.

God is considered an impediment, even an enemy, to a scientific, materialistic, socialistic world outlook. The idea of God, insists Lenin, encourages the working class (the proletariat) to drown its terrible economic plight of slavery and misery "in a sort of spiritual booze" of some mythical heaven ("pie in the sky by and by"). Even a single sip of this intoxicant decreases the revolutionary fervor necessary to exterminate the oppressing class (the bourgeois), thus causing the working class to forfeit their only chance of creating a truly human heaven on earth: global communism.

A Brief Look At: Karl Marx (1818-1883)

1836: Joins the Young Hegelians at the University of Berlin

1848: Co-authors the *Communist Manifesto* with Frederick Engels

1849: Exiled from Prussia and France

1852: Begins contributing articles to the *New York Daily Tribune*

1864: Helps found the First International, a communist "Workingmen's Association"

1867: Publishes *Das Kapital*

1881: Jenny, his wife and childhood sweetheart, dies

1883: Six people attend his funeral

MARX'S THEOLOGICAL BELIEFS

Religion as the opium of the masses, however, was a later development in the mind of Karl Marx. His atheism was conceived in the heady arena of philosophy, not economics or sociology. When Marx became an atheist at the University of Berlin, he was not thinking about surplus value or the dictatorship of the proletariat. He was thinking about the philosophies of Prometheus, Georg W. F. Hegel, Bruno Bauer, David Strauss, and Ludwig Feuerbach.

"Philosophy makes no secret of it," said Marx. "Prometheus's admission: 'In sooth all gods I hate' is its own admission, its own motto against all gods, heavenly and earthly, who do not acknowledge the consciousness of man as the supreme divinity. There must be no god on a level with it."[3]

In a circle of radical Young Hegelians that included Ludwig Feuerbach, Arnold Ruge, Max Stirner, Moses Hess, and eventually Frederick Engels, Marx became an atheist. Atheism was embraced by the group, with Feuerbach proclaiming, "It is clear as the sun and evident as the day that there is no God; and still more, that there can be no God."[4]

Accepting Feuerbach's conclusion that God is a projection of man writ large, Marx boasted, "Man is the highest being for man." Indeed, Marx explains that this view signals the demise of all religion: "The criticism of religion ends with the teaching that man is the highest being for man. . . ."[5]

For Marx, then, man is God. Man created God in his own image. Man created religion in order to worship himself. The notion that God is merely a projection of man is contained in Marx's assertion that man "looked for a superhuman being in the fantastic reality of heaven and found nothing there but the reflection of himself."[6]

Since Marx believes man is God, he also believes man must seize control of reality and shape it to his specifications. "The philosophers have only interpreted the world, in various ways;" says Marx, "the point, however, is to change it."[7] Since the institutions of society rested on a foundation of theism, Marx determined to change all social institutions and re-establish them on atheistic foundations. To this end, Marx and Engels, in the *Communist Manifesto,* called for the "forcible overthrow" of all existing social conditions.

It is important to note that this call was based on Marx's dogmatic atheism, and not on dispassionate societal observation. Marx's economic theories—and, indeed, his entire worldview—were tailored to fit his theology.

SIGNIFICANCE OF THEOLOGY IN MARXIST THEORY

While some attempts have been made to minimize atheism's role in Marxist theory (especially in recruiting naive Christians and other religious people to participate in Marxist/Leninist activity—such as the Liberation Theology movement), Marxists are privately aware of their fundamental need for an atheistic foundation.

Marx's search for "scientific truths" to bolster his atheism led him to conclusions that shaped his communist theory. As he moved from the philosophical basis for his atheism into the socioeconomic realm, he reached the conclusion (based upon his atheistic assumptions) that religion is merely an anti-depressant for the oppressed working class. His summary of this explanation has

Karl Marx co-authored the Communist Manifesto with his close friend and financial supporter Frederick Engels in 1848.

Snapshots In Time

People supported some form of communism in France, Germany, Belgium and England years before Karl Marx burst on the scene. Why, then, is Marx regarded as the founder of the communist movement?

The answer lies in the *Communist Manifesto.* Before Marx and Frederick Engels collaborated to create this *Manifesto,* communist groups did not have "an integrated philosophical basis for their views." The *Manifesto* provided this basis. Though no more than 13,000 words, this work describes communism not just as a political or economic movement, but as a complete worldview.

Marx would go on to write thousands of pages developing his worldview, but none of them are as lucid, or as inspiring, as his *Manifesto* (perhaps indicating that Engels, not Marx, was most responsible for systematizing the Marxist worldview). Some critics, including A.J.P. Taylor, consider the *Manifesto* to be "a holy book, in the same class as the Bible or the Koran."

been quoted throughout the world, even though it was not his original basis for atheism. "Religion," said Marx, "is the sigh of the oppressed creature, the sentiment of a heartless world, as it is the spirit of spiritless conditions. It is the opium of the people."[8]

Marx's friend and fellow atheist, Engels, declared, "We want to sweep away everything that claims to be supernatural and superhuman, for the root of all untruth and lying is the pretension of the human and the natural to be superhuman and supernatural. For that reason we have once and for all declared war on religion and religious ideas and care little whether we are called atheists or anything else."[9]

As with Marx, Engels foresaw a time when all religion would cease. He contended that when society adopts socialism, i.e., when society takes possession of all means of production and uses them on a planned basis (thus eliminating the working class's economic bondage), religion itself will vanish.

LENIN'S THEOLOGICAL CONTRIBUTIONS TO MARXISM

Some years later, V. I. Lenin affirmed the conclusions of Marx and Engels: "The philosophical basis of Marxism, as Marx and Engels repeatedly declared, is dialectical materialism . . . a materialism which is absolutely atheistic and positively hostile to all religion."[10] Elsewhere, Lenin made it clear that fighting religion was an essential ingredient in a materialistic reality. "We must combat religion," he said, "that is the ABC of all materialism, and consequently of Marxism."[11]

> "...we have once and for all declared war on religion and religious ideas and care little whether we are called atheists or anything else."
>
> *Frederick Engels*

In his "Socialism and Religion" address, Lenin insists that the communist program is based on the scientific, materialistic world outlook and therefore "our propaganda necessarily includes the propaganda of atheism."[12] Lenin went on to urge his fellow communists to follow Engels' advice and translate and widely disseminate the atheistic literature of the eighteenth-century French Enlightenment.

Lenin made it clear that any idea of God was taboo, claiming, "Every religious idea, every idea of God, even flirting with the idea of God, is unutterable vileness . . . vileness of the most dangerous kind, 'contagion' of the most abominable kind. Millions of sins, filthy deeds, acts of violence and physical contagions . . . are far less dangerous than the subtle, spiritual idea of a God decked out in the smartest 'ideological' customes. . . . Every defense or justification of the idea of God, even the most refined, the best intentioned, is a justification of reaction."[13]

Clearly, Lenin's theology unerringly corresponds with that of Marx and Engels. Together they established the foundations for future communist declarations of atheism.

ATHEISM IN THE FORMER SOVIET UNION

Marxist theology has remained consistent throughout the history of communism. From Marx's time to the present, communists everywhere have vehemently denied the existence of God. This becomes especially obvious when one considers the theological stance of the former U.S.S.R. *The Great Soviet Encyclopedia*, published in Moscow in 1950, called on the Communist Party to oppose religion and "to fight for the 'full victory' of atheism."[14] The Young Communist League's list of Ten Commandments contains the declaration "If you are not a convinced atheist, you cannot be a good Communist. . . . Atheism is indissolubly bound to Communism."[15]

In 1955, Soviet premier Nikita Khrushchev said, "Communism has not changed its attitude of opposition to religion. We are doing everything we can to eliminate the bewitching power of the opium of religion."[16]

The Atheist's Handbook was published in Moscow in 1959 in conjunction with Khrushchev's campaign to eliminate the remaining traces of religion in the U.S.S.R. This text attacks the Bible, the Koran, Christianity and Islam. "Science," says the *Handbook,* "has long since established that Jesus Christ never existed, that the figure of the alleged founder of Christianity is purely mythical."[17] The Apostle Paul, too, turns out to be "a mythical figure."[18]

THE MARXIST ASSAULT ON THE CHURCH

This Marxist hatred of anything supernatural—and especially anything Christian—is most often vented on religious peoples and institutions in Marxist countries.

Although the July 10, 1918 Constitution of the former U.S.S.R. recognized freedom of both "religious and anti-religious propaganda" as the right of every citizen, the Soviet state constantly worked to suppress theistic religion. Article 65 of the 1918 Constitution declared priests and clerics to be "servants of the bourgeoisie" and disfranchised. This meant, among other things, that priests were denied ration cards and their children were barred from schools above the elementary grade. Paul Kurtz, a Secular Humanist, points out that from 1918 to 1921 "religious persecution continued unabated. . . . All church property was nationalized, and it is estimated that tens of thousands of bishops, clerics, and laymen were killed or imprisoned."[19]

In the former Soviet Union, church after church was declared counter-revolutionary and shut down. Churches were turned into cinemas, radio stations, granaries, museums, machine repair shops, etc. Before the revolution Moscow had 460 Orthodox churches. On January 1, 1930, the number was down to 224, and by January 1, 1933, the figure was about 100.

Even though the 1936 Soviet Constitution again guaranteed "freedom of religion," Marxist attacks on religious peoples continued unabated. In the days following the new Constitution, some Christians attempted to conform to laws by registering with the government. The Soviet government required these believers to collect fifty signatures. When the Christians presented the signatures to the government officials, all fifty "conspirators" would be deemed "members of a secret counter-revolutionary organization"[20] and arrested.

Such persecution will continue as long as the Marxist worldview rules any country. Modern times have not made Marxists more tolerant of religion. In 1993 in the People's Republic of China, Marxist leaders tore down an Islamic mosque, ostensibly because it was not "government sanctioned." The Marxist government can sanction only one religion: the religion of atheism—the "ABC of Marxism."

Theology At A Glance

Secular Humanist	Marxist/Leninist
Atheism	Atheism

CONCLUSION

In theory and practice, Marxism/Leninism reflects its atheistic base. To be a Marxist/Leninist demands adherence to atheism. To be a good Marxist/Leninist entails being a propagator of atheism. To be the best Marxist/Leninist is to see atheism as part of the scientific, materialistic, socialistic world outlook and to strive to eradicate all religious sentiment.

Theists everywhere recognize, as did Feodor Dostoevski, that "The problem of Communism is not an economic problem. The problem of Communism is the problem of atheism."[21]

CHAPTER 5

Cosmic Humanist Theology

"What is God? God is the interlinking of yourself with the whole."[1]

—Kevin Ryerson

INTRODUCTION

Like every other worldview, Cosmic Humanism's theology forms the foundation for all other aspects of its worldview. However, Cosmic Humanism (the New Age movement) differs from Christianity and the secular worldviews in that it embraces neither theism nor atheism.

Cosmic Humanism begins by denying the preeminence of any purported special revelation over any other. That is, Cosmic Humanists believe that the Bible is no more the word of God than is the Koran, or the words of Confucius. David Spangler, who has been described as the "Emerson of the New Age," says, "We can take all the scriptures, and all the teachings, and all the tablets, and all the laws, and all the marshmallows and have a jolly good bonfire and marshmallow roast, because that is all they are worth."[2]

Obviously, if the Bible is valuable only as fuel, this nullifies the significance of the life, death, and resurrection of Jesus Christ. The Cosmic Humanist sees Christ's life as

41

important only in the sense that it showed man to be capable of achieving perfection, even godhood. An article in the New Age publication *Science of Mind* states, "The significance of incarnation and resurrection is not that Jesus was a human like us but rather that *we are gods like him*—or at least have the potential to be."[3] This interpretation of Christ allows the New Age theologian to postulate, as John White does, that "The Son of God . . . is not Jesus but our combined Christ consciousness."[4] Jesus is looked on as one of a select company, having achieved Christ consciousness. Every person is encouraged to acquire this same level of consciousness.

How can anyone hope to achieve such a divine consciousness? Because everyone is a part of God. Cosmic Humanists believe that man and God are ontologically one.

A Brief Look At: Joseph Campbell (1904-1987)

1921: Begins questioning his Catholicism at Dartmouth College

1927: Receives MA from Columbia University

1934: Joins faculty at Sarah Lawrence College, an experimental women's school

1941: Begins writing *The Hero with a Thousand Faces*

1954: Travels to India

1985: First of a series of interviews with Bill Moyers

1988: *The Power of Myth* is published

EVERY PERSON IS GOD

"Each of us has access to a supraconscious, creative, integrative, self-organizing, intuitive mind whose capabilities are apparently unlimited," says John Bradshaw. "This is the part of our consciousness that constitutes our God-likeness."[5]

Most Cosmic Humanists state the case more forcefully. Ruth Montgomery supposedly channeled a spirit that spoke through her, claiming, "We are as much God as God is a part of us . . . each of us is God . . . together we are God . . . this all-for-one-and-one-for-all . . . makes us the whole of God."[6] White states that "sooner or later every human being will feel a call from the cosmos to ascend to godhood."[7] Meher

Baba declares, "There is only one question. And once you know the answer to that question there are no more to ask. . . . Who am I? And to that question there is only one answer—I am God!"[8] Shirley MacLaine recommends that every person should begin each day by affirming his or her own godhood. "You can use *I am God* or *I am that I am* as Christ often did, or you can extend the affirmation to fit your own needs."[9]

Special revelation need not exist in books or in any other form outside of man, because each man has his own special revelation in his higher consciousness, his ability to get in touch with the part of him that is God. Inner soul-searching becomes the only significant means of discovering truth. By asserting that man is God, the Cosmic Humanist grants each individual the power of determining reality by creating or co-creating truth.

ALL IS ONE

It is important to understand that the belief that every individual is God and God is every individual is tied inextricably to the concept of consciousness. Because the Cosmic Humanist has this "all is one" mentality, he necessarily believes that humanity can become attuned to all the powers of its godhood by achieving unity of consciousness. "Once we begin to see that we are all God," says Beverly Galyean, "that we all have the attributes of God, then I think the whole purpose of human life is to reown the Godlikeness within us; the perfect love, the perfect wisdom, the perfect understanding, the perfect intelligence, and when we do that, we create back to that old, that essential oneness which is consciousness."[10] Robert Muller says, "Only the unity of all can bring the well-being of all."[11]

The belief that everything is God and God is everything is known as *pantheism.*

The concept of mankind's unity, the idea that all is one, tends to support the theological concept of reincarnation. Virtually every "orthodox" adherent of the New Age movement believes that each individual's soul was present in other material forms earlier in history and that it will manifest itself in still other forms after its present body dies. The body may pass away, but the soul will continue its quest for godhood in other bodies. This belief in reincarnation caused MacLaine, when recalling her daughter's birth, to muse, "When the doctor brought her to me in the hospital bed on that afternoon in 1956, had she already lived many many times before, with other mothers? Had she, in fact, been one herself? Had she, in fact, ever been *my* mother? Was her one-hour-old face housing a soul perhaps millions of years old?"[12]

In order to understand oneself (and one's path to godhood), a person must be cognizant of at least some of his past lives. Gary Zukav explains:

> If your soul was a Roman centurion, an Indian beggar, a Mexican mother, a nomad boy, and a medieval nun, among other incarnations, for example, . . . you will not be able to understand your proclivities, or interests, or ways of responding to different situations without an awareness of the experiences of those lifetimes.[13]

Reincarnation can serve little purpose unless people can know about and learn from their past lives.

EVERYTHING IS GOD

Reincarnation, however, is not the only logical consequence of a theology based on the unity of God and man and the concept that all is one. If one cannot delineate between God and man, how can one be certain that he can delineate between other living or dead things and God? Indeed, if all is one, perhaps everything that exists is God.

And so it is. Stars are God, water is God, plants are God, trees are God, the earth is God, whales and dolphins are God, everything is God. Cosmic Humanists worship the creation and the creator at the same time. For them, there is no difference.

The belief that everything is God and God is everything is known as *pantheism*. This ancient concept forms the theological foundation of the New Age movement. "Everything has divine power in it," says Roman Catholic New Ager Matthew Fox, and this divine force is what gives the planet its "sacredness."[14] Shakti Gawain puts her pantheism in plainer language, proclaiming the "great trust I now have in the higher power of the universe [a synonym for God] that is within me and within everyone and everything that exists."[15]

The most blatant example of pantheistic theology occurs in a New Age children's book entitled *What is God?*: "There are many ways to talk about God. Does that mean that everything that everybody ever says about God is right? Does that mean that God is everything? Yes! God is everything great and small! God is everything far away and near! God is everything bright and dark! And God is everything in between! If everything is God, God is the last leaf on a tree, If everything is God, God is an elephant crashing through the jungle."[16]

Theology At A Glance

Secular Humanist	Marxist/Leninist	Cosmic Humanism
Atheism	**Atheism**	**Pantheism**

CONCLUSION

One thing this God is not, however, is personal. The New Age God is cosmic force. There is no transcendent God "out there" apart from His creation. God is the creation. Says Marilyn Ferguson, "In the emergent spiritual tradition God is not the personage of our Sunday School mentality. . . . God is experienced as flow, wholeness . . . the ground of being. . . . God is the consciousness that manifests as *Lila,* the play of the universe. God is the organizing matrix we can experience but not tell, that which enlivens matter."[17]

Unlike the Marxist/Leninist and the Secular Humanist, the Cosmic Humanist believes in a supernatural realm consisting of spiritual relationships. However, the New Age version of God differs infinitely from the Christian concept of God. While the Christian believes that God created mankind and all that exists and that man can know His will only through the general revelation of nature and conscience and the special revelation of the Bible, the Cosmic Humanist believes that every person and all reality *is* God, and therefore that any "truth" our inner selves discover is God's truth. If we fail to realize our godhood in this lifetime, never fear! We'll soon have another incarnation and another chance at achieving Christ consciousness.

Ultimately, every person will achieve godhood, and total unity will be restored. New Age theology, like fairy tales, guarantees a happy ending.

CHAPTER 6

Biblical Christian Theology

"Theism, the belief that God is, and atheism, the belief that God is not, are not simply two beliefs. They are two fundamental ways of seeing the whole of existence. The one, theism, sees existence as ultimately meaningful, as having a meaning beyond itself; the other sees existence as having no meaning beyond itself."[1]

—Stephen D. Schwarz

INTRODUCTION

Christian theism rests primarily on two foundations: special revelation (the Bible) and general revelation (the created order). While the Bible reveals the character and personality of God page after page, the "whole workmanship of the universe," according to John Calvin, reveals and discloses God day after day.

James Orr explains that the theistic position is established not by any single clue or evidence, but by "the concurrent forces of many, starting from different and independent standpoints."[2] Christians see evidences of God everywhere. It is the Christian position that history, theology, philosophy, science, mathematics, logic, and experience all point to the existence of a Creator and Redeemer.

SPECIAL REVELATION

Christian theists believe that God has revealed Himself to mankind in a general way through creation and in a special (personal) way evidenced by His divine words and acts contained in the Bible and especially in the person of Jesus Christ. Millard Erickson defines the two forms of revelation this way: "On the one hand, general revelation is God's communication of Himself to all persons, at all times, and in all places. Special revelation on the other hand, involves God's particular communications and manifestations which are available now only by consultation of certain sacred writings."[3]

General revelation has been viewed consistently throughout church history by a variety of Christian theists as a necessary but insufficient means for providing knowledge about the Creator and His character. It is better theology and philosophy to begin with the God of the Bible to explain the universe than to begin with the universe to explain God.

According to the Christian view, the destiny of created mankind involves both salvation and judgment. It is not general revelation but special revelation (the Bible) that answers such questions as: How can mankind be saved? From what must mankind be saved? Why will judgment occur? Special revelation, then, is "special" because it is the key that opens the door to both heaven and earth.

One of the most basic tenets of Christian belief is the divine inspiration of the Bible. When the individual accepts Scripture as the Word of God, the teachings and events described in the Bible become the most important basis for understanding all reality. Without faith that the Bible is God's Word, mankind is left floundering— forced to trust his own (unfounded) thought processes as his ultimate criteria for discerning truth. No one can deny the Bible's divine inspiration and still claim to be a Biblical Christian, for the simple reason that Scripture proclaims itself to be God-breathed (2 Timothy 3:16-17). If one believes the Bible to be a true and accurate document, then one must accept its claim to be divinely inspired.

The evidence for the Christian's belief in the divine inspiration of the Bible is convincing. For example, the unity of teaching in the Bible is startling in light of the fact that its books were authored by different men faced with very different circumstances. Further, the astounding ability of the Bible to metamorphose the lives of individuals (for the better) who accept its authority strengthens its claim to be special revelation from God. The degree of moral truth contained in the Bible also supports its divine inspiration. All these arguments support the belief that the Bible is God's Word; however, the most convincing witness for divine inspiration is the Bible itself. Those hesitant to accept Scripture as God's special revelation are most often convinced by a thorough, open-minded study of the Bible.

In studying the Bible, the reader meets God's most direct form of special revelation: the person of Jesus Christ. "In Jesus of Nazareth," writes Carl F.H. Henry, "the divine source of revelation and the divine content of that revelation converge and coincide."[4] Christ's teachings and actions as revealed in the Bible provide the cornerstone for special revelation and a solid foundation for Christian theism.

A Brief Look At: St. Augustine (354-430)

373: Converts to the Persian religion of Manichaeism

383: Travels to Rome to teach rhetoric

387: Converts to Christianity after reading Romans 13:13

391: Becomes a priest and founds a religious community in Hippo

396: Becomes a bishop

400: Writes his most influential book, *Confessions*

420: Finishes writing *City of God*, a work he had begun in 413

The purpose of divine revelation lies in its communication to the Christian of the significance of Christ's teachings and actions. The third member of the Trinity, the Holy Spirit, plays an important role in this dialogue. Henry explains: "Scripture itself is given so that the Holy Spirit may etch God's Word upon the hearts of his followers in ongoing sanctification that anticipates the believer's final, unerring conformity to the image of Jesus Christ, God's incarnate Word."[5] This is the ultimate reason God chose to reveal Himself and His plan for mankind in the Bible.

For this reason, the Christian's reliance on the Bible should be profound and constantly renewed—the Christian doesn't read the Bible once and set it aside; rather, he studies it as the Word of God and works constantly to conform himself to its teachings. He spends his life seeking to understand the powerful message of the Bible.

DESIGN AND GENERAL REVELATION

Special revelation, then, is the linchpin of Christianity, while general revelation serves as a prod that encourages man to recognize the ultimate truths set down in Scripture and embodied in Jesus Christ.

Although God's revelation through nature, in and of itself, fails to bring men to a saving knowledge of God, it is capable of bringing men to a general knowledge of God. A great majority of intellectuals agree that the concepts of purpose and design, for example, have validity in regard to the question of the existence of God.

Anglican clergyman William Paley argued in *Natural Theology* (a book about which Charles Darwin admitted, "I do not think I hardly ever admired a book more . . .")[6] that a man chancing upon a watch in the wilderness could not conclude that the watch had simply always existed; rather, the obvious design of the watch—not only its internal makeup but also the fact that it clearly exists for a *purpose*—would necessarily imply the existence of its designer. Paley went on to substitute the universe for the watch and contended that a mechanism so obviously designed as the universe necessitated the existence of a grand Designer. This is an excellent example of the way in which the created order reveals the existence of God.

The universe forces its sense of design (and thus a Designer) on all men open to such a possibility. Many discover God through the general revelation of a structured universe; many more encounter God in the general revelation of the purposeful nature of reality. C.E.M. Joad, who was an atheist for much of his professional career, wrote a book entitled *The Recovery of Belief* shortly before his death. This book traces his gradual advance toward God and Jesus Christ. Joad was largely convinced by his observation of human nature—his realization that a moral law exists, and that men often flaunt that law.

Still another twist on the argument for the general revelation of God's existence is presented by C.S. Lewis. Suppose there were no intelligence behind the universe, says Lewis. In that case nobody designed my brain for the purpose of thinking. Thought is merely the by-product of some atoms within my skull. "But if so, how can I trust my own thinking to be true?" asks Lewis. "But if I can't trust my own thinking, of course, I can't trust the arguments leading to atheism, and therefore have no reason to be an atheist, or anything else. Unless I believe in God, I can't believe in thought; so I can never use thought to disbelieve in God."[7]

The evidence points to what Christians believe—that a personal God has revealed Himself through a created world, and that He has a plan and ultimate destiny for that world.

WHAT DOES REVELATION TELL US ABOUT GOD?

The Christian is concerned not only with the existence of God in general, but also with the relationship that exists between God and man, and particularly with the redemption of all mankind. While Humanists declare in the *Humanist Manifesto II* that no God can save us—"we must save ourselves"—Christian theism echoes Thomas, who referred to Jesus as "My Lord and My God" (John 20:28), and Peter, who said to Jesus, "You alone have the words of eternal life" (John 6:68). God, as revealed throughout the Bible and especially in the person of Christ, is clearly knowable and desires to be known.

> **Each created thing has an appointed destiny—God has a plan for His world, and nothing takes Him by surprise.**

To say that God is knowable is also to say that God "relates" or has personality—that He is "personal." God's self-awareness, His emotions, and His self-determining will make up the core of His divine personality. The Bible is emphatic in describing God as a person aware of Himself. In Isaiah 44:6, God says, "I am the first and I am the last, and there is no God besides me." In Exodus 3:14, God says to Moses, "I Am Who I Am."

Besides possessing a sense of self-awareness, the God of the Bible (like man) has sensibilities. At times God is portrayed as being sorrowful (Genesis 6:6), angry (Deuteronomy 1:37), compassionate (Psalm 111:4), jealous (Exodus 20:5), and able to show satisfaction (Genesis 1:4). Theologians do not feel that such scriptures suggest that God is limited, but rather that God is willing to reveal Himself in an anthropomorphic, personal way to mankind.

CHARACTERISTICS OF THE PERSONAL GOD

Besides believing that God is a personal God and has communicated His nature to mankind, Christians believe that God is self-determining—that is, sovereign in regard to His will. God's self-determination is described in Daniel 4:35: "And all the inhabitants of the earth are accounted as nothing, but he does according to His will in the host of heaven and among the inhabitants of the earth; and no one can ward off His hand or say to Him, 'what hast Thou done?' "

In addition to being self-determining, the God of the Bible is moral. Proverbs 15:3 warns us that God distinguishes between good and evil, and that He is concerned with our morality (see also Proverbs 5:21). God's uncompromisingly moral character is one of the most crucial aspects of His being. A true understanding of God's absolute goodness leads the individual unerringly to the conclusion that every man has an acute need for a Redeemer.

Long-suffering patience and faithfulness are also personality traits of God. God's willingness to delay His judgment upon the Israelites when they worshipped the golden calf (Exodus 32:11-14) and His faithful promise to save the believer from eternal judgment (John 10:28) are prime examples of His patience and faithfulness.

Perhaps the most astounding characteristic of God's personality is that He is triune. The Christian believes that God is three co-existent, co-eternal persons in one, who are equal in purpose and in essence, but differ in function.

Christ's teachings and actions as revealed in the Bible provide the cornerstone for special revelation and a solid foundation for Christian theism.

The God of the Christian is also a God of power, evidenced by His works in creation and providence. Hebrews 1:10 declares, "In the beginning, O Lord, you laid the foundations of the earth, and the heavens are the works of your hands." Christian theology asserts that God is the source of all things and that He created the cosmos out of His own mind, according to His plan.

God also demonstrates His power by moving His world to its purposeful end. Each created thing has an appointed destiny—God has a plan for His world, and nothing takes Him by surprise. The Bible is emphatic on this point. Romans 9:25-26 says, "I will call those who were not my people, My people, and her who was not beloved, beloved. And it shall be that in the place where it was said to them 'you are not my people,' there they shall be called sons of the living God." Scripture makes it clear that God manifests His power by a sovereign and holy plan—a plan which generally collides with the plans of men.

GOD AS JUDGE

The judgment of God is not a popular subject—even among Christians. A great majority of people abhor the thought that the "God of love" could also be the "God of wrath." However, one cannot read the Bible without encountering the judgment of God.

The holiness of God necessitates the judgment of God. Christian theists agree that God must be a judge because His holy nature is antithetical to sin. Such acts in the Bible as the great flood (Genesis 6:17-7:24), the destruction of Sodom and Gomorrah (Genesis 19), the smiting of Nadab and Abihu (Leviticus 10:1-7), the fall of the Canaanites (Leviticus 18-20), and indeed the fall of Israel (2 Kings 17) and Judah (2 Chronicles 36) are all demonstrations of God's judgment as motivated by His holy nature.

Christianity teaches that God is fair and always right, because His nature is perfect. God is not a giant bully or a cosmic killjoy brooding in the heavens, waiting for every opportunity to spoil man's fun. The Bible teaches that God is truly interested in good winning over evil, and in holiness being the victor over moral depravity. In short, God is the judge of men because men are sinners. The Bible is clear in communicating that God does not take pleasure in the judgment of the wicked (Ezekiel 33:11), but the wicked must be judged because God is holy (Jude 15).

GOD AS REDEEMER

Only one thing can protect men from God's justice on the Day of Judgment: God's mercy. In His mercy, God has provided an advocate for every individual—an advocate so righteous that He washes away the sin that should condemn man. God as the Redeemer, in the person of Christ, saves mankind from His wrath.

The central theme of redemption is the love of God. John 3:16 tells us, "God so loved the world, that He gave His only begotten Son, that whoever believes in Him should not perish, but have eternal life." Using John 3:16 as a text for portraying God's love, theologian Floyd Barackman points out the following characteristics of this love:

1. *God's love is universal.* God loves every nation, tribe, race, class, and gender equally. There were no social prejudices when God offered His Son. Christ died for the rich and for the poor; for the free and for the enslaved; for the old and for the young; for the beautiful and the ugly.

2. *God's love is gracious.* God loves sinners even when they hate Him and are undeserving of His love. Romans 5:8 clearly outlines the nature of God's love: "But God demonstrates His own love toward us, in that while we were yet sinners, Christ died for us." How could God love the sinner? This question is answered by the Christian doctrine of grace. Christianity declares that God's love and mercy are so awesome that He can love the sinner while hating the sin.

3. *God's love is sacrificial.* God did not send His only Son to earth just to be a good example or simply to be a teacher, but to be a perfect and atoning sacrifice for sin. Christ's substitutionary death was sacrificial and closely resembles the Old Testament concept of atonement. The main difference between the Old Testament concept of atonement and the New Testament concept is that atonement in the Old

Testament was temporary, whereas in the New Testament Christ atoned for sins once and for all. Through the death of Christ, God has reconciled the world to Himself, and offered a way for His wrath to be appeased (Colossians 1:20)—man now must be reconciled to God through faith in Christ (2 Corinthians 5:20).

4. ***God's love is beneficial.*** For all those who receive Christ (John 1:12), for all those who are born from above (John 3:3), for all those who believe (John 3:16), there await certain eternal benefits given by God. Scripture declares that through God's grace, the believer will not be condemned (Romans 3:24) and will not be captive to sin (Romans 6:11). Further, the believer is a new creation (2 Corinthians 5:17) who has been declared righteous (2 Corinthians 5:21), redeemed (1 Peter 1:18), forgiven (Ephesians 1:7) and the recipient of the gift of eternal life (John 3:16).

CONCLUSION

Christian theology is Christ-centered. The God who "so loved the world that He gave His only Son" has allowed for a personal relationship between Himself and fallen man. Theoretical atheistic possibilities belittle the God who has revealed Himself propositionally through His creation and His word and has sacrificed His incarnate and holy Son. If the story be true, then the world that lives in unbelief should be fearful, for it sits under the judgment of God until it recognizes and experiences the ever-faithful promise of Jesus: "Behold, I stand at the door and knock; if anyone hears My voice and opens the door, I will come in to him, and will dine with him, and he with Me" (Revelation 3:20).

FOUR WESTERN WORLDVIEW MODELS

SOURCES	SECULAR HUMANISM HUMANIST MANIFESTOS I AND II	MARXISM/LENINISM WRITINGS OF MARX AND LENIN	COSMIC HUMANISM WRITINGS OF SPANGLER, FERGUSON, ETC.	BIBLICAL CHRISTIANITY BIBLE
THEOLOGY	Atheism	Atheism	Pantheism	Theism
PHILOSOPHY	Naturalism	Dialectical Materialism	Non-Naturalism	Supernaturalism
ETHICS	Relativism	Proletariat Morality	Relativism	Absolutes
BIOLOGY	Darwinian Evolution	Darwinian/Punctuated Evolution	Darwinian/Punctuated Evolution	Creation
PSYCHOLOGY	Self-Actualization	Behaviorism	Collective Consciousness	Mind/Body
SOCIOLOGY	Non-Traditional Family	Abolition of Home, Church and State	Non-Traditional Home, Church and State	Traditional Home, Church and State
LAW	Positive Law	Positive Law	Self-Law	Biblical and Natural Law
POLITICS	World Government (Globalism)	New World Order (New Civilization)	New Age Order	Justice, Freedom and Order
ECONOMICS	Socialism	Socialism	Universal Enlightened Production	Stewardship of Property
HISTORY	Historical Evolution	Historical Materialism	Evolutionary Godhood	Historical Resurrection

CHAPTER 7

Secular Humanist Philosophy

"Humanism is naturalistic and rejects the supernaturalistic stance with its postulated Creator-God and cosmic Ruler."[1]

—Roy Wood Sellars

INTRODUCTION

Humanists are hesitant to label their philosophy, since specifically defining the Humanist position would imply that they believe absolute truth exists. Instead, Humanists list a variety of philosophical positions that fit their worldview: materialism, naturalism, organicism or other theories "based upon science." But this choice is not as broad as it sounds—each doctrine listed holds the same basic tenet: the material world is all that exists. In fact, each option presented is really little more than a synonym for naturalism, which is the philosophical view Secular Humanists must hold.

This dogmatic position is summarized in *Humanist Manifesto II*: "Nature may indeed be broader and deeper than we now know; any new discoveries, however, will but enlarge our knowledge of the natural."[2] This belief is the essence of naturalism: whatever exists can be explained by natural causes; the supernatural cannot exist. This belief is foundational for Humanism, regardless of the terminology describing it. Some Humanists prefer to call themselves organicists or materialists (or "scientific" materialists)—the name makes little difference. As Corliss Lamont notes, "Materialism denotes the same general attitude toward the universe as Naturalism."[3]

DENIAL OF THE SUPERNATURAL

The key tenet of naturalism is its denial of the supernatural. People either believe that only the supernatural exists, or that some supernatural things and some natural things exist, or that only natural things exist. By "supernatural," philosophers generally mean things that are not material, such as the soul, personality, or God. Naturalists deny everything that is not made up of matter, that does not exist in nature.

This current of thought runs throughout Humanist beliefs. Sellars writes, "Christianity, for example, had a supernaturalistic framework in a three-tier universe of heaven, earth and hell. . . . The Humanist argues that the traditional Christian outlook has been undercut and rendered obsolete by the growth of knowledge about man and his world."[4] Humanists rely on this "growth of knowledge" to provide a more accurate worldview. Naturalism calls for the object to be observable and measurable to be believable.

> **Worldview: Any ideology, philosophy, theology, movement, or religion that provides an overarching approach to understanding God, the world, and man's relations to God and the world.**

Naturalists are especially unwilling to believe in a universe that exudes too much design, because this design could be construed as evidence for a Designer. The naturalist can accept no Designer and no personal First Cause. Henry Miller plainly states, "To imagine that we are going to be saved by outside intervention, whether in the shape of an analyst, a dictator, a savior, or even God, is sheer folly."[5]

Naturalistic Humanism, then, is the denial of the supernatural. But it is more than that—it is a complete philosophy. Lamont puts it this way: "To define naturalistic Humanism in a nutshell: it rejects all forms of supernaturalism, pantheism, and metaphysical idealism, and considers man's supreme aim as working for the welfare and progress of all humanity in this one and only life, according to the methods of reason, science and democracy."[6] This definition is important from a philosophical perspective because it outlines both the metaphysics and epistemology of naturalism. This chapter will focus on the metaphysics (specifically the cosmology) of naturalism first, and then explore naturalism's epistemology.

COSMOLOGY/METAPHYSICS

Cosmology refers to the philosophical study of the universe, especially its origin. Secular Humanists believe that the physical universe came to exist by accident and that it is all that exists. Obviously, this belief relies on their denial of God and the supernatural. Instead, eternal matter must have spontaneously generated life and ultimately the human mind through evolution.

The cosmology of naturalism is best summed up by Carl Sagan, 1981 Humanist of the Year: "The Cosmos is all that is or ever was or ever will be."[7] For the Humanist, no personal First Cause exists; only the cosmos. "Nature is but an endless series of efficient causes. She cannot create but she eternally transforms. There was no beginning and there can be no end."[8] Of course, there is no need for a God to explain a beginning that didn't happen.

Humanists assign a different basis for reality, a non-sequential group of first causes, to the universe to avoid God as the First Cause. Lamont calls these the "ultimate principles of explanation and intelligibility."[9] For the Humanist, these ultimate principles are a sufficient cause for the rest of reality.

EPISTEMOLOGY

Epistemology refers to one's theory of knowledge. That is, epistemology answers the question, "How much can one know about reality, and how does one obtain this knowledge?" Naturalism answers that everything in the physical world (which means *everything*) is knowable, and science is the proper means of knowing it. Roy Wood Sellars goes so far as to state, "The spirit of naturalism would seem to be one with the spirit of science itself."[10]

Most Humanists agree with Sellars. *The Humanist Manifesto II* states, "Any account of nature should pass the tests of scientific evidence,"[11] which, of course, supernatural explanations could never do, since they are not measurable or observable. The Humanist calls for a god that can be seen and poked and prodded to discover his characteristics; i.e., a god that is not supernatural. Naturalists, those who ground their epistemology in science, will only believe what they see with their eyes—that is, the physical—and so anything supernatural cannot exist.

Humanists' epistemology shapes their metaphysics. Because Humanists believe that science tells us we are products of chance and have evolved over billions of years, they must act on that knowledge and formulate a worldview consistent with it—a worldview in which the universe is all that exists and ever will exist, because science (according to their view) has no means of obtaining knowledge about the supernatural (and therefore the supernatural must not exist). But doesn't this grounding of belief in science as the ultimate means of perception require faith, just as the supernatural does? Doesn't Sagan's statement that "science has itself become a kind of religion"[12] admit that very self-contradiction?

Lamont acknowledges the charge as valid and answers it this way:

It is sometimes argued that since science, like religion, must make ultimate assumptions, we have no more right to rely on science in an analysis of the idea of immortality than on religion. Faith in the methods and findings of science, it is said, is just as much a faith as faith in the methods and findings of religion. In answer to this we can only say that the history of thought seems to show that reliance on science has been more fruitful in the progress and extension of the truth than reliance on religion.[13]

For the naturalist, science is the ultimate means of perception, and therefore the ultimate means of gaining knowledge, and it should be applied to every aspect of life (including the social and moral) so that we can have a better understanding of our world. The epistemology of the naturalist is inseparable from science and, indeed, requires faith in science as the only means of knowing the world around us.

THE MIND-BODY PROBLEM

The epistemology and metaphysics of naturalism present a very specific problem for the Humanist philosophy. This dilemma is traditionally referred to as the mind-body problem, because it asks, "Does the mind exist solely within nature, just as the body does, or is the mind more than matter?"

Cosmology refers to the philosophical study of the universe, especially its origin.

Naturally, Humanists believe that the mind (or consciousness, or personality, or soul—for the sake of continuity we shall refer to this phenomenon as the mind) is simply a manifestation of the brain—just an extension of the natural world, and easily explainable in purely physical terms. This belief arises from their epistemology in the sense that science is our best way of obtaining knowledge, and the knowledge it has obtained (according to Humanists) supports their metaphysical belief that life arose spontaneously and has evolved to its present state. Since this view of the cosmos allows only for the existence of matter, the mind must somehow be a strictly physical phenomenon. This view is commonly referred to as monism, while the opposing view—the belief that mind is more than a conglomeration of matter—is called dualism.

According to the naturalist philosophy, the amazingly complex human mind is the result of evolutionary processes. Lamont says, "naturalistic Humanism .. .take[s] the view that the material universe came first and that mind emerged in the animal man only after some two billion years of biological evolution upon this material earth."[14]

60

IMPLICATIONS OF THE MONISTIC VIEW

Just as the naturalistic epistemology and metaphysics necessitate a monistic view, this view, in turn, implies two more necessary conclusions for the Humanist. The first answers the question, "Is man immortal?" Lamont recognizes this question, accepting the only conclusion open to the naturalist: "If, on the other hand, the monistic theory of psychology is true, as Naturalism, Materialism, and Humanism claim, then there is no possibility that the human consciousness, with its memory and awareness of self-identity intact, can survive the shock and disintegration of death. According to this view, the body and personality live together; they grow together; and they die together."[15]

For the Humanist, there can be no life after death. In fact, the denial of the after-life is inherent to the Humanist worldview, so much so that the belief in mortality is seen by Lamont as the first step in becoming a Humanist. He writes, "The issue of mortality versus immortality is crucial in the argument of Humanism against super-naturalism. For if men realize that their careers are limited to this world, that this earthly existence is all that they will ever have, then they are already more than half-way on the path toward becoming functioning Humanists. . . ."[16]

The second necessary conclusion for Humanists results from their belief that mind evolved through natural processes. According to this view, there is no guarantee that mind is anything special at all—some better mutation of mind could occur any

A Brief Look At: Roy Wood Sellars (1880-1973)

1905: Begins teaching philosophy at the University of Michigan

1922: Publishes *Evolutionary Naturalism*

1928: Publishes *Religion Coming of Age*

1933: As primary author, publishes *Humanist Manifesto I*

1955: Honored as Humanist Pioneer by the American Humanist Association

1955: Elected president of New York chapter of AHA

day. In truth, some Humanists believe this more efficient mind is being created today. Victor J. Stenger, author of *Not By Design*, claims, "Future computers will not only be superior to people in every task, mental or physical, but will also be immortal." He believes it will become possible to save human "thoughts which constitute consciousness" in these computer memory banks, as well as program computers in such a way as to give them the full range of human thought. After all, he says, "If the computer is 'just a machine,' so is the human brain. . . ." So why shouldn't the computer become the next step in the evolutionary chain, the new, higher consciousness? Stenger sees this as a real possibility, and concludes, "Perhaps, as part of this new consciousness, we will become God."[17]

Sound like science fiction? Not for the Humanist. In a naturalistic, monistic worldview, it is not only a logical possibility, but a likely one. Evolution created the human mind strictly out of matter; evolution and natural selection are still at work to improve that mind; and the computer is really nothing more than an incredibly efficient material mind, perhaps the inevitable next step in the evolutionary chain of being.

Philosophy **At A Glance**

Secular Humanist

Naturalism

CONCLUSION

Naturalism, with its denial of the supernatural and its reliance on science as its source of knowledge, necessitates not only specific conclusions about the mind and mortality, but also implies a distinct worldview. This view, as adopted by the Humanists, tends to elevate man in terms of his abilities to control his fate, but at the same time has immense difficulty in overcoming pessimism. E.A. Burtt believes "the ultimate accommodation necessary in a wise plan of life is acceptance of a world not made for man, owing him nothing, and in its major processes quite beyond his control."[18]

This attitude is voiced more eloquently by Clarence Darrow: "The purpose of man is like the purpose of the pollywog—to wiggle along as far as he can without dying; or, to hang to life until death takes him."[19]

CHAPTER 8

Marxist/Leninist Philosophy

"The real unity of the world consists in its materiality, and this is proved . . . by a long and protracted development of philosophy and natural science. . . . But if the . . . question is raised: what then are thought and consciousness, and whence they come, it becomes apparent that they are products of the human brain and that man himself is a product of nature, which has been developed in and along with its environment."[1]
—Frederick Engels

INTRODUCTION

Virtually every individual professing to be a Marxist/Leninist believes dialectical materialism is the proper philosophy for understanding and changing the world. Many of the attributes Christians ascribe to God—eternal, infinite, uncreated, indestructible, lawgiver, life, mind—Marxists assign to dialectical matter. This philosophy affirms matter as ultimately real and denies the reality of God. It is a "sort of godless theology."

Karl Marx, in a letter to Frederick Engels, wrote, "as long as we actually observe and think, we cannot possibly get away from materialism."[2] Along this same epistemological line, Engels wrote, "The materialist world outlook is simply the conception of nature as it is. . . . "[3] In other words, what you see of nature is all there is, and because nature appears to be made up of matter of some sort, that is all there is to the real world. This perspective has been maintained by Marxists throughout their history. It is imperative that one believe in the materialistic interpretation of the world if one is

65

to be a Marxist/Leninist in the true sense of the word.

"Matter is," wrote Lenin, "primary nature. Sensation, thought, consciousness, are the highest products of matter organized in a certain way. This is the doctrine of materialism, in general, and Marx and Engels, in particular."[4] Elsewhere, Lenin contended that matter is a philosophical category denoting objective reality—i.e., people, plants, animals, stars, etc. "Matter is the objective reality given to us in sensation."[5] Our seeing the physical world, the material world, was proof enough for Lenin that only matter existed, that it was eternal, uncreated, indestructible, and dialectical.

When Lenin says that matter is primary, he is saying that matter is eternal and uncreated and that billions of years into this eternity life spontaneously emerged from non-living, non-conscious matter. He is also stating that not only life but also mind, thinking, and consciousness developed or evolved out of this matter.

MARXIST EPISTEMOLOGY

Science plays a crucial role in the Marxist theory of knowledge. "The fundamental characteristic of materialism," says Lenin, "arises from the objectivity of science, from the recognition of objective reality, reflected by science."[6]

Like Humanism, Marxist epistemology professes faith in science and just as much faith that all religious claims are untrue. This faith in science as a virtually infallible source of all knowledge results from Marxism's ideas about reality. Writes Lenin, "Perceptions give us correct impressions of things.—We directly know objects themselves."[7] These objects, of course, are strictly material: "Matter is . . . the objective reality given to man in his sensations, a reality which is copied, photographed, and reflected by our sensations."[8] Of course, since something supernatural is not an objective, materialist reality, according to Marxism, then we have no means of perceiving it and, therefore, no means of obtaining knowledge about it.

For this reason, Marxists deny the supernatural. They distinguish between knowledge and what they term *true belief* in an attempt to allow for scientific speculation while ignoring speculation about God: "What we call 'knowledge' must also be distinguished from 'true belief.' If, for example, there is life on Mars, the belief that there is life on Mars is true belief. But at the same time we certainly, as yet, know nothing of the matter. True belief only becomes knowledge when backed by some kind of investigation and evidence. Some of our beliefs may be true and others false, but we only start getting to know which are true and which are false when we undertake forms of systematic investigation. . . . For nothing can count as 'knowledge' except in so far as it has been properly tested."[9] Therefore, we can never know belief in the supernatural to be "true belief," because it can never be properly (i.e., empirically, scientifically) tested.

66

Only speculations about the material can ever be found to be true beliefs, since only they can be investigated systematically. Knowledge can apply only to the material world.

Marxists believe that *practice,* that is, testing knowledge throughout history, is a valuable aid to gaining knowledge. They think we can test knowledge by applying it to our lives and to society and that this application will eventually determine the truth or falsity of that knowledge. Therefore, by examining history, we can determine better which knowledge is correct and which is not.

Marxist epistemology is inextricably tied to the Marxist dialectic. In fact, it is virtually impossible to separate Marxist materialism, dialectics, and epistemology. This is true largely because Marxists claim that dialectics operates in the place of metaphysics in their philosophy.

MARXIST DIALECTICS

The notion of dialectical process was modified and polished into a broad-based philosophy by Georg Wilhelm Friedrich Hegel, who died when Marx was thirteen years old. The dialectical process was not a creation of Marxist philosophy. Rather the Marxist use of it in conjunction with materialism creates a unique hybrid philosophy. Marx and Engels simply adopted Hegel's ideas, which were built on an idealistic foundation (that is, the dialectic was thought to be a mental construct), and redesigned them to fit into a materialistic scheme of reality. Thus Lenin could write of "The great Hegelian dialectics which Marxism made its own, having first turned it right side up."[10]

> The dialectic . . . views all of life as a constant evolving process resulting from the clash of opposing forces.

Gustav A. Wetter summarizes the Hegelian dialectic as follows: "In Hegel's sense of the term, dialectic is a process in which a starting-point [a thesis, e.g., Being] is negated [the antithesis, e.g., Non-Being], thereby setting up a second position opposed to it. This second position is in turn negated i.e., by negation of the negation, so as to reach a third position representing a synthesis [e.g., Becoming] of the two preceding, in which both are 'transcended,' i.e., abolished and at the same time preserved on a higher level of being. This third phase then figures in turn as the first step in a new dialectical process [i.e., a new thesis], leading to a new synthesis, and so on."[11]

The fundamental perspective with regard to dialectics is best summed up by Engels: "The world is not to be comprehended as a complex of ready-made [created] things, but as a complex of [evolutionary] processes."[12] This notion is inherent to the dialectic, which views all of life as a constant evolving process resulting from the clash of opposing forces.

67

In the dialectical process, the thesis must always attract an antithesis, and this tension must always result in a synthesis, which in turn becomes a new thesis. This new thesis is always more advanced than the last thesis, because dialectics perceives the developmental process as an upward spiral. To simplify: dialectics sees change or process due to conflict or struggle as the only constant—bearing in mind that this change and conflict always lead to more advanced levels.

Marxists believe the proof for dialectics is all around us. Engels notes, "When we reflect on Nature, or the history of mankind, or our own intellectual activity, the first picture presented to us is an endless maze of relations and interactions."[13] These interactions, of course, are always in the process of thesis/antithesis/synthesis. This constant development, or process, or evolution implies that the world (indeed, the universe) is always in motion—always moving, always changing.

> "The philosophers have only interpreted the world in various ways; the point, however, is to change it."
>
> *Karl Marx*

Now we can begin to see how dialectics affects the materialist view. For the Marxist, matter can only be understood when one understands that it is constantly going through an eternal process. This idea is best illustrated in the theory of evolution—for, according to this theory, life on earth underwent changes throughout time beginning with simple living forms and evolving onward and upward to achieve their more advanced states of existence. "Nature is the proof of dialectics,"[14] Engels writes.

Marxists have fixed evolutionary theory into a universal law for the whole universe—organic and inorganic. Engels makes this clear: "All nature, from the smallest thing to the biggest, from a grain of sand to the sun, from the protista [the primary living cell] to man, is in a constant state of coming into being and going out of being, in a constant flux, in a ceaseless state of movement and change."[15]

DIALECTICS OPPOSED TO METAPHYSICS

Dialectics is a means of understanding the processes of life. Marxism took this method and applied it to its philosophy, which is foundational for its entire worldview. In making this application, Marxists have hastened to point out that dialectics is a method directly opposed to metaphysics, claiming that metaphysics is an outdated mode of viewing the world.

In making this claim, however, Marxists define metaphysics in a peculiar way. As normally understood, metaphysics is "the branch of philosophy that deals with first principles and seeks to explain the nature of being or reality *(ontology)* and of the origin and structure of the world *(cosmology)*"[16]—and every philosophy must confront these questions sooner or later. Marxists, however, attempt to dodge this branch of philosophy by claiming that metaphysics assumes that nature and being are stagnant and unchanging while dialectics views life as a constant process, and that metaphysics views reality as unconnected parts while dialectics views reality as an interconnected whole.

If we grant the Marxists their definition of metaphysics, then we cannot argue with their conclusion that dialectics is directly opposed to it. However, in the strict sense of the word, Marxists most definitely do maintain a metaphysics, and they are not shy about articulating it. Since understanding a philosophy's beliefs about the nature of being and the origin and structure of the universe is crucial to understanding the philosophy as a whole, we will now examine Marxist metaphysics (in the traditional sense of the word), beginning with its cosmology and moving on to its ontology.

A Brief Look At: Frederick Engels (1820-1895)

1844: Befriends Karl Marx in Paris

1848: Co-authors the *Communist Manifesto* with Marx

1849: Fights in revolutionary uprising in Baden and Palatinate

1850: Hired by his father to help run the family business

1864: Becomes a partner in his father's firm

1869: Sells his share in the firm, supports Marx with proceeds

1878: Publishes *Anti-Duhring*

1882: Publishes *Socialism, Utopian and Scientific*

MARXIST METAPHYSICS

As previously noted, Marxist theology and philosophy have no room for the supernatural. The universe is all that exists and all that ever will exist. "Materialism gives a true picture of the world, without any irrelevant adjuncts in the shape of spirits, of god who created the world, and the like. The materialists do not await the help of supernatural powers, they believe in man, in his capacity to transform the world by his own hand."[17]

Whether Marxists choose to admit it or not, their philosophy includes a metaphysical cosmology. They are far from bashful about declaring the absence of a God or anything supernatural in the universe, just as they are more than willing to proclaim that the material universe is all that exists and that it has always existed and always will.

Marxist philosophy relies on a specific ontology, as well. For Marxists, the ultimate substance and the ultimate cause is ever-changing dialectical matter. Perhaps this is why they choose to avoid metaphysics—it is difficult, in the face of modern physics, to argue that matter is the ultimate substance. Nonetheless, Marxist philosophy holds tenaciously to the view that matter is all that exists, it is eternal, and it is the ultimate substance or reality.

Alexander Spirkin, a modern Marxist author, writes that "matter is the only existing objective reality: the cause, foundation, content and substance of all the diversity of the world."[18] Engels says we know from experience and theory "that both matter and its mode of existence, motion, are uncreatable."[19]

Marxist dialectics, then, is not opposed to metaphysics in the traditional sense of the word. In truth, Marxist philosophy relies on its metaphysics (ontology and cosmology), which it assumes in its entirety without rational defense, to provide a basis and explanation for being, the nature of the universe, and ultimately man himself.

THE MIND-BODY PROBLEM

Like every philosophy, dialectical materialism must face the mind-body problem. The key word Marxists rely on when addressing this problem is *reflect*. It is their contention that the human mind reflects matter in a way that makes perception accurate for us. For Marx, "the ideal is nothing else than the material world reflected by the human mind, and translated into forms of thought."[20] Lenin echoes him: "The existence of the mind is shown to be dependent upon that of the body, in that the mind is declared to be secondary, a function of the brain, or a reflection of the outer world."[21]

Marxism uses the notion that consciousness is just a subjective reflection of objective reality to avoid calling consciousness supernatural. The question still arises, however: from whence did this ideal arise?

For the dialectical materialist, everything must have proceeded from matter, even societal interrelationships and the mind. Maurice Cornforth writes, "Mental functions are functions of highly developed matter, namely, of the brain. Mental processes are brain processes, processes of a material, bodily organ."[22] It is convenient for the Marxist to refer to thought as the "reflection" of objective reality, but in the final estimation he must admit that the mind is simply a function of matter.

Philosophy At A Glance

Secular Humanist	Marxist/Leninist
Naturalism	*Dialectical Materialism*

CONCLUSION

Dialectical materialism, the philosophy of Marxism, contains an epistemology, a cosmology, an ontology, and an answer to the mind-body problem. For the Marxist, science and practice refine knowledge, the universe is infinite and all that will ever exist, matter is eternal and the ultimate substance, life is a product of this non-living matter, and mind is a reflection of this material reality. But the Marxist philosophy embraces an even broader view of the world than is generally meant by the term *philosophy*. In truth, dialectical materialism is an entire method for viewing the world— it colors the Marxist perception of everything from ethics to history.

Marxist philosophy as a worldview must be understood by anyone who claims to support the Marxist cause. "One cannot become a fully conscious, convinced Communist without studying Marxist philosophy. This is what Lenin taught."[23] Why? Because, according to Marxism, the dialectic can explain every process and change that occurs. Marxist philosophy is process philosophy. This process is written not only in the metaphysical make-up of the matter, but also, and equally large, in the evolution of man and the evolving social and historical context of man's existence. It is this materialist belief that affects the Marxist view of history and causes Marxists to view the bourgeoisie and the proletariat as thesis and antithesis, clashing to form a synthesis.

While evolutionists believe that animals evolved certain physical characteristics to aid in their survival, Marxists believe their philosophy of dialectical materialism evolved to meet the needs of the proletariat.

Every Marxist recognizes this and is prepared to act in accordance with dialectical materialism. While many philosophies are chiefly theoretical, Marxism is concerned with theory *and practice*. Dialectical materialism is a worldview and a philosophy of *evolution and revolution*—the call to action is implicit in its makeup. Every good Marxist understands his philosophy and is prepared to act upon it, because Marx himself requires it: "The philosophers have only interpreted the world in various ways; the point, however, is to change it."[24]

Unfortunately from a Marxist point of view, all such change is merely transitory, since each new synthesis (including the long-anticipated communist classless society) inevitably becomes a new thesis in the never-ending process of dialectical materialism. Even the victorious dictatorship of the proletariat will be but a brief moment in evolutionary history. Communist dialectics decrees that communism itself is transitory. The synthesis of communism today will become the new thesis of tomorrow, and new struggles will evolve. Thus is it written in the laws of dialectical materialism.

CHAPTER 9

Cosmic Humanist Philosophy

"The mystery of life is beyond all human conception. . . . We always think in terms of opposites. But God, the ultimate, is beyond the pairs of opposites, that is all there is to it."[1]

—Joseph Campbell

INTRODUCTION

The Cosmic Humanist rejects naturalistic and materialistic philosophies because such explanations ignore the all-pervasive supernatural. "From a very early age," says David Spangler, "I was aware of an extra dimension or presence to the world around me, which as I grew older I came to identify as a sacred or transcendental dimension."[2] If Spangler's perspective is correct, and if (as pantheism declares) every aspect of existence is sacred, then everything must have a spiritual nature. And since it is the spiritual side of life that leads us to higher consciousness and inner truth, we should view all reality from a supernatural perspective. Thus, the Cosmic Humanist arrives at a philosophy of non-naturalism (there is nothing natural; everything is supernatural), a philosophy that focuses on the spiritual nature of all things, because the spiritual dimension of everything is the ultimate reality.

The Cosmic Humanist believes that all reality is God—from a grain of sand to the Milky Way—and his philosophy reflects this attitude by focusing on such principles as the Gaia hypothesis. This principle (Gaia is sometimes referred to as "Mother Nature")

A Brief Look At: David Spangler (1945-)

1952: Exposed to what he describes as "first mystical experience"

1964: Learns about the concept of a New Age

1965: Drops out of college and begins work with the Fellowship of Universal Guidance

1967: Publishes *The Christ Experience and the New Age*

1973: Founds the Lorian Association in California

1984: Publishes *Emergence: The Rebirth of the Sacred*

views the planet earth—indeed, the whole universe—as an actual living organism. Fritjof Capra says, "The universe is no longer seen as a machine, made up of a multitude of objects, but has to be pictured as one indivisible, dynamic whole whose parts are essentially interrelated and can be understood only as patterns of a cosmic process."[3]

How Do We Know?

> **"What's the meaning of the universe? What's the meaning of a flea? It's just there. That's it."**
>
> *Joseph Campbell*

This non-naturalism affects both the epistemological and the ontological aspects of the Cosmic Humanist philosophy. In terms of their theory of knowledge, proponents of the New Age movement emphasize the importance of getting in touch with one's higher self. When one gets in touch with the God-force within, one can intuitively "know" accurately and without limits. Says Shakti Gawain, "When we consistently suppress and distrust our intuitive knowingness, looking instead for [external] authority, validation, and approval from others, we give our personal power away."[4]

When we look within, we will find truth. But this truth is not "truth" as it is commonly understood; New Age truth is emotive rather than descriptive. Joseph Campbell, in the most influential New Age book of the decade (*The Power of Myth*), says,

"What's the meaning of the universe? What's the meaning of a flea? It's just there. That's it. And your own meaning is that you're there. We're so engaged in doing things to achieve purposes of outer value that we forget that the inner value, the rapture that is associated with being alive, is what it's all about."[5] The truth—what Cosmic Humanists can know—is a feeling, an experience. Knowledge doesn't contain the meaning of life or, for that matter, the meaning of anything.

Each one creates his own truth according to the principle "if it feels like truth to you it is." That is, all knowledge exists in the God-force within each individual, and any individual who connects with that power can tap that knowledge. Indeed, Jack Underhill believes that when the whole world gets in touch with its godhood, "They can turn off the sun and turn it back on. They can freeze oceans into ice, turn the air into gold, talk as one with no movement or sound. They can fly without wings and love without pain, cure with no more than a thought or a smile. They can make the earth go backwards or bounce up and down, crack it in half or shift it around. . . . There is nothing they cannot do."[6] But there is much they cannot explain.

WHAT IS ULTIMATE REALITY?

Similarly, Cosmic Humanists' ontological beliefs stem from their non-naturalistic pantheism. Ultimate being or substance, for a New Ager, is the God-force, the Christ consciousness. God is "the essence of existence, the life force within all things."[7] Philosophically, Cosmic Humanism is monism: All reality is one. Robert Muller hints at this when he states, "Oh God, I know that I come from you, that I am part of you, that I will return to you, and that there will be no end to my rebirth in the eternal stream of your splendid creation."[8] However, this statement only implies that God is the ultimate essence of man. A more accurate description of New Age ontology is provided by Spangler when he admits that

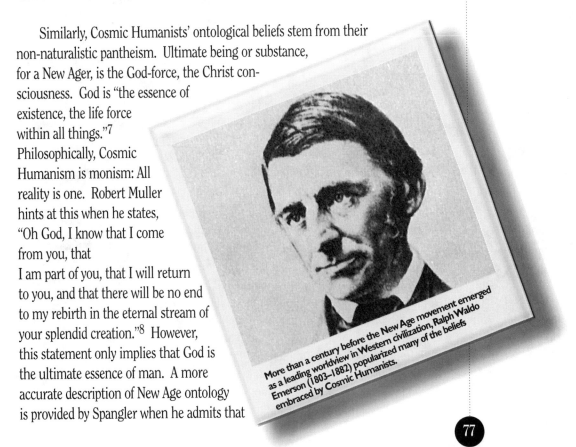

More than a century before the New Age movement emerged as a leading worldview in Western civilization, Ralph Waldo Emerson (1803–1882) popularized many of the beliefs embraced by Cosmic Humanists.

Snapshots In Time

Ralph Waldo Emerson, a famous 19th century lecturer and essayist, began his career as a Unitarian minister. As a Unitarian, Emerson disputed the reality of the Trinity, and questioned other doctrines essential to Christianity. After his wife died, he began to doubt even the few dogmas adhered to by the Unitarian church; in 1832, he denied the significance of Holy Communion in his farewell sermon.

From that time forward, Emerson championed many of the basic tenets of New Age belief. He is often described as a transcendentalist (a person who emphasizes the intuitive over the empirical), and in that capacity he encouraged others to "trust" their inner selves. Emerson believed in the innate nobility of man—a belief that led him to declare that every man can harmonize with his version of God: the Over–soul. This Over–soul is close kin to the New Age concept of Collective Consciousness—that is, Emerson was not far from pantheism.

"this worldview encourages us to treat all things not only as ourselves, as the holistic view would see it, but as honored and precious manifestations of God."[9]

Philosophically speaking, this ontological perspective might not be entirely satisfactory. What substance, if substance there be, makes up this God-force? Because every individual arrives at his own truth, New Age thinkers often differ in their interpretations. Gary Zukav believes that consciousness is ultimate reality:

> All that is can form itself into individual droplets of consciousness. Because you are part of all that is, you have literally always been, yet there was the instant when that individual energy current that is you was formed. Consider that the ocean is God. It has always been. Now reach in and grab a cup full of water. In that instant, the cup becomes individual, but it has always been, has it not? This is the case with your soul. There was the instant when you became a cup of energy, but it was of an immortal original Being. You have always been because what it is that you are is God, or Divine Intelligence, but God takes on individual forms, droplets, reducing its power to small particles of individual consciousness.[10]

Other Cosmic Humanists may have other answers, based on their personal "experience" of the truth. Cosmic Humanists prefer to acknowledge their godhood without insisting on dogmatic views of its final nature. Marilyn Ferguson states, "We need not postulate a purpose for this Ultimate Cause nor wonder who or what caused whatever Big Bang launched the visible universe. There is only the experience."[11]

Philosopy At A Glance

Secular Humanism	Marxist/Leninist	Cosmic Humanist
Naturalism	Dialectical Materialism	Non-naturalism

CONCLUSION

Since all is one, according to the Cosmic Humanist, only one type of ultimate reality can exist. This reality must be spiritual, because God—which is everything—is ultimately spiritual. Only one substance really exists: spiritual stuff. Matter is only a manifestation of spirit.

The purpose of knowing is not to explain or describe reality; rather, knowledge is useful only as experience—getting in touch with everything and its godhood. We may "experience different truth" because truth resides within each individual, manifested as we manifest our godhood.

Philosophy is useful to the Cosmic Humanist not as a systematic method for discovering reality, but as a means to learn to think thoughts that lead to feelings of unity. Marianne Williamson, a popular New Age feminist author, says that most people don't think this way, but they should: "To say, 'God, please help me,' means, 'God, correct my thinking.' 'Deliver me from hell,' means 'Deliver me from my insane thoughts.'"[12] The best thoughts are not necessarily logical, but they are "sane": they remind us to feel at one with God.

CHAPTER 10

Biblical Christian Philosopy

"A little philosophy inclineth man's mind to atheism, but depth in philosophy bringeth men's minds about to religion."[1]

—Sir Francis Bacon

INTRODUCTION

After an examination of Cosmic, Marxist and Humanist philosophies, one might assume that the Christian worldview cannot possibly have a philosophy of its own, since it requires faith in Biblical revelation. According to the secular worldviews, naturalism and materialism are grounded firmly in modern scientific methodology and enlightened human experience. How can the Christian, who is required to postulate existence or reality outside the material realm, ever hope to prove his beliefs true, reasonable, rational, and worth living and dying for?

Unfortunately, some Christians adopt just such an attitude—conceding that their faith is indefensible. They attempt to avoid the whole problem by stating that what they believe is "beyond reason." These Christians point to Colossians 2:8, where Paul writes, "See to it that no one takes you captive through hollow and deceptive philosophy . . . ," and from this they draw the conclusion that God does not want us to meddle in such a vain and deceitful discipline as philosophy. However, people who point to this verse as a warning against philosophy often omit the rest of the verse, in which Paul describes the kind of philosophy he is warning against, viz., philosophy "which

81

> **Faith is critical in every philosophy. The individual developing a philosophy must be extremely careful to base his case on the most truthful assumptions ...**

depends on human tradition and the basic principles of this world rather than on Christ."

The Bible does not ask the Christian to abandon reason in accepting its truth. "Come now," records Isaiah, "and let us reason together, saith the Lord: though your sins be as scarlet, they shall be white as snow" (Isaiah 1:18). 1 Peter 3:15 encourages Christians to understand and be able to present logical, compelling reasons for their hope in Christ. But is this possible? Is Christian faith and, more specifically, Christian philosophy defensible?

C.E.M. Joad, who lived most of his life believing that the concept of God was unacceptable, finally concluded, "It is because . . . the religious view of the universe seems to me to cover more of the facts of experience than any other that I have been gradually led to embrace it."[2] He concluded his long personal pilgrimage by admitting, "I now believe that the balance of reasonable considerations tells heavily in favor of the religious, even of the Christian view of the world."[3] This is the same Joad who appeared on BBC radio with Humanist Bertrand Russell attacking Christianity.

Many who finally begin to reflect on the deeper things of life—"How did I get here? Why am I here? Where am I going?"— simply discover that Christianity answers more questions more completely than any other worldview. Those who earnestly seek truth will ultimately find themselves face-to-face with the God of the Bible.

It is all well and good to debate whether God exists, but for the average person the debate is a moot point—people are aware of His existence in their very souls. Even today the vast majority of human beings in the world (some polls place the figure as high as 95 percent) believe in a God. Paul found this to be true also in Athens (Acts 17:23).

People tend to believe the most likely solution to a problem. That's why most people believe, "In the beginning God created the heavens and the earth" (Genesis 1:1) and "all things therein" (Acts 17:24). Jean Piaget, a child psychologist, has found that a seven year-old almost instinctively believes that everything in the universe has a purpose. It makes more (common) sense to believe Genesis 1:1 than to believe that a series of cosmic accidents brought about the orderly, beautiful, meaningful cosmos.

A Brief Look At: Alvin Plantinga (1932-)

1955: Marries Kathleen De Boer

1958: Receives his PhD from Yale University

1965: Hired as professor of philosophy by Calvin College

1967: Publishes *God and Other Minds*

1980: Publishes *Does God Have a Nature?*

1981: Serves as president of American Philosophical
Association (Western)

1982: Hired as professor of philosophy at
University of Notre Dame

1993: Publishes *Warrant and Proper Function*

FAITH AND EPISTEMOLOGY

The basic tenets of Christian philosophy can be demonstrated to be rational, for they are held by average, rational men and women. But surely, Christianity must still run into an epistemological problem—how does the Christian "know" without clashing with science and experience? How can the knowledge we gain through faith in Biblical revelation compare to knowledge gained by a scientific investigation of the universe?

The answer is not as difficult as one might imagine. When all is said and done, all knowing requires faith. Faith precedes reason or, as W. J. Neidhardt puts it, "Faith correctly viewed is that illumination by which true rationality begins."[4]

While Marxists and Humanists like to portray science as primary knowledge and faith in Biblical revelation as some blind second-class epistemology or even superstition, the fact remains that all methods of knowing ultimately rely on certain assumptions. Edward T. Ramsdell writes, "The natural man is no less certainly a man of faith than the spiritual, but his faith is in the ultimacy of something other than the Word of God. The spiritual man is no less certainly a man of reason than the natural, but his reason, like that of every man, functions within the perspective of his faith."[5]

The basic problem of philosophy is not the old problem of faith versus reason. "The crucial problem," says Warren C. Young, "is that some thinkers place their trust in a set of assumptions in their search for truth, while other thinkers place their trust in a quite different set of assumptions."[6] That is, Humanists and Marxists place their trust in certain findings of science and experience, neither of which can be rationally demonstrated to be the source of all truth. Christians also put some faith in science, history, and personal experience, but they know such avenues for discovering truth are not infallible. Christians know that men of science make mistakes and scientific journals can practice discrimination against views considered dangerous. Christians know that history can be perverted, distorted or twisted, and that some personal experiences are not a good source of fact or knowledge. On the other hand, Christians believe that Biblical revelation is true and that God would not fool or mislead His children.

Christian philosophy does not throw out reason or tests for truth. Christianity says the New Testament is true because its truths can be tested. Christians aren't asking the non-believer to believe a revelation of old wives' fables, but instead to consider certain historical evidences that reason itself can employ as an attorney building a case uses evidences "in the law to determine questions of fact." Christian epistemology is based on special revelation, which in turn is based on history, the law of evidence, and the science of archaeology.

Philosophical naturalists also make assumptions that they necessarily accept on faith. All naturalists agree that there is no supernatural. "This point," says Young, "is emphasized by the naturalists themselves without seeming to be at all troubled by the fact that it is an emotional rather than a logical conclusion."[7]

Faith is critical in every philosophy. The individual developing a philosophy must be extremely careful to base his case on the most truthful assumptions—otherwise, should one of the assumptions be demonstrated to be untrue (as it appears the assumptions of the theory of evolution will be), the whole philosophy will crumble. If evolution crumbles (which is quite possible—Dr. Karl Popper doesn't even believe evolution fits the definition of "a scientific theory"), Marxism and Humanism are intellectually dead.

Up to this point we have established two things regarding Christian philosophy: many hold it to be the most rational of all worldviews, and it requires virtually no more faith than any other philosophy. Indeed, one could argue that it takes a great deal more faith to believe in the spontaneous generation doctrine of Marxism and Humanism or the randomness of all nature (i.e., that the universe happened by accident) than it does to accept the Christian doctrine of Creator/Creation.

RECONCILING SCIENCE AND CHRISTIAN PHILOSOPHY

At the outset of this chapter, it appeared that reconciling supernaturalism with science would be difficult. However, in light of the previous discussion, little reconciliation, if any, is necessary.

In fact, the wise Christian philosopher recognizes the scientific method as a limited but valuable ally. In addition to lending support for the teleological argument, science also shores up the cosmological argument and raises serious questions about the materiality of the atom (which doesn't bode well for either naturalism or materialism).

Joad reinforces the idea that science does not threaten Christianity, stating, "It has often been represented that the conclusions of science are hostile to the tenets of religion. Whatever grounds there may have been for such a view in the past, it is hard to see with what good reason such a contention could be sustained today."[8] Stephen D. Schwarz cites four specific scientific discoveries that support the conclusion that God exists: the Second Law of Thermodynamics, the impossibility of spontaneous generation of life from non-life, genetic information theory (DNA), and the Anthropic Principle.

> **"The Supernatural is not remote and abstruse: it is a matter of daily and hourly experience, as intimate as breathing."**
>
> *C.S. Lewis*

For the Christian, then, science need not be an enemy—indeed, science should be accepted as a somewhat successful method of obtaining knowledge about God's design in the universe. As C.S. Lewis says, "In science we have been reading only the notes to a poem; in Christianity we find the poem itself."[9]

THE ORIGIN OF SCIENCE

An examination of the history of modern science reaffirms the supernaturalist's premise that science is not hostile to his position.

Modern science was founded by men who viewed the world from a Christian perspective. Neither the Marxist nor the Humanist worldview, with their corresponding beliefs that the universe was brought about by a series of accidents, could serve as a fitting base for modern science. Francis Schaeffer writes, "Since the world had been created by a reasonable God, [scientists] were not surprised to find a correlation between themselves as observers and the thing observed—that is, between subject and object.... Without this foundation, modern Western science would not have been born."[10]

Christianity was "the mother of modern science."[11] Norman L. Geisler and J. Kerby Anderson's *Origin Science* contains a chapter titled "The Supernatural Roots of

Modern Science." Both Alfred North Whitehead and J. Robert Oppenheimer defended this view. Philosopher and historian of science Stanley L. Jaki notes that historically the belief in creation and the Creator was the moment of truth for science: "This belief formed the bedrock on which science rose."[12] Jaki has powerfully defended this position in *The Origin of Science* and *The Savior of Science*.

Re-examine the statements by Schaeffer and Jaki for a moment. Notice that each claim is grounded on the fact that science assumed an orderly universe. If man believed the universe to be disorderly or chaotic, he never would have bothered with science, which relies on matter to behave in certain meaningful ways under controlled conditions. On earth, we always expect an apple to fall down rather than up, because we believe in a consistent law—the Law of Gravity. Lewis says men became scientific because they expected Law in Nature, and "they expected Law in Nature because they believed in a Legislator."[13] In other words, the origin of modern science itself provides grounds for the teleological argument—the argument from design to Designer.

METAPHYSICS: ONTOLOGY/COSMOLOGY

The Christian view of metaphysics—of ultimate reality (ontology and cosmology)—is part of what C. S. Lewis termed "Mere Christianity." There are certain things virtually all Christians believe, and one is that God is the supreme source of all being and reality. He is the ultimate reality and because He is, we are. The entire space-time creation, says Carl F.H. Henry, depends on the Creator-God "for its actuality, its meaning and its purpose."[14] This creation is intelligible because God is intelligent, and we can understand the creation and Creator because He made us in His image with the capacity to understand Him and His intelligent order.

"In the Beginning was the LOGOS…"

John 1:1

For the Christian, matter exists but it is not the ultimate substance. It is real, but it is not ultimate reality. It is not eternal. Rather, the material universe was created on purpose out of the mind of the living Logos (John 1:1-4), and all the cosmos, existing independently of God, relies on God for its very existence and explanation. In other words, the Christian explanation for the world of matter or nature is that the supernatural created the natural. And since the supernatural God of the Bible is a rational, purposeful, powerful God, the created universe itself contains such qualities. It is no accident that at every level of the cosmos—sub-atomic, atomic, organic, inorganic, sub-human, human, earth, moon, sun, stars, galaxies—all things manifest amazing order and rationality that can be reasonably explained only as the result of a deliberate, creative act of God. Christianity considers entirely irrational the notion that the orderly cosmos is the result of a series of accidents, chance, or random happenings. Such a position is tantamount to having a bridge, an airplane, an automobile, or a skyscraper, without an architect, plan, or engineer. It doesn't happen that way in the real world; only in the minds of those who lack faith in the supernatural and in the Bible.

The early verses of John 1 contain the Christian's metaphysics in a nutshell. "In the beginning [of the cosmos] was the Word [Logos, mind, reason, thought, wisdom, intelligence, idea, law, order, purpose, design], and the Word was with God, and the Word was God. The same [Word] was in the beginning with God. All things were made by him; and without him was not anything made that was made. In him was life; and the life was the light of men" (John 1:1-4).

The flow of this passage sets forth the parameters of Christian philosophy: mind before matter; God before man; plan and design before creation; life from life; and enlightenment from the Light. The orderly universe was conceived in the orderly and rational mind of God before it was created. Without the Logos there would be no cosmos. From the Christian perspective it is no surprise to see philosophers and scientists refer to the universe as a manifestation of mathematical law, order, design, beauty, etc. This is the way it was created "in the beginning."

Young says, "Christian realists are contingent dualists but not eternal dualists. They hold that there are two kinds of substance: Spirit (or God) and matter which was created by God ex nihilo as Augustine suggested. Matter is not spirit, nor is it reducible to spirit, but its existence is always dependent upon God Who created it out of nothing."[15] Young chooses to use the term *Christian realism* to represent the Christian philosophy. In an effort to stress the existence of something other than the material, we employ the term *supernaturalism*. Regardless of the name, true Christian philosophy requires a metaphysics consistent with Biblical teaching.

MIND-BODY PROBLEM AND THE MENTAL PROOF

The supernaturalist believes that the mind, or consciousness, exists as a separate entity from the purely physical. The Christian believes that his mind is a reflection of the Universal Mind that created the universe ex nihilo, and he sees the mind as an additional proof for the existence of the supernatural.

Most men perceive their thinking process as something different from the material world. Young says, "Man is so made that his spirit may operate upon and influence his body, and his body is so made that it may operate upon his mind or spirit."[16]

This distinction between brain and mind implies a distinction about the whole order of things: matter exists, and something other than matter exists. "We find in the created universe an important difference between beings which think, and beings which are spatially extended, or spiritual beings and material beings. . . . In the body and mind of man we see integrated interaction between the spiritual thinking being, and the material extended being."[17]

Many Christian thinkers believe this distinction between the brain and the mind is intuitively obvious, and this is the beginning of the mental proof for the existence of a Higher Mind responsible for our minds. Other Christian thinkers begin with the untenability of the materialist position that the mind is only a material phenomenon and draw the conclusion that since the materialist explanation is irrational, the supernatural explanation must be the acceptable position. Again, science aids the Christian philosopher in undermining the materialist worldview. Writes Buswell, "The mind is not the brain. The 'brain track' psychology has failed. . . . It is a known fact that if certain parts of the brain are destroyed, and the functions corresponding to those parts impaired, the functions may be taken up by other parts of the brain. There is no exact correspondence between mind and brain."[18]

Sir John Eccles has made a voluminous contribution to this discussion in recent years. His three works, *The Self and Its Brain* (with Karl Popper), *The Human Mystery* and *The Human Psyche* are considered classics in the field. Eccles maintains that having a mind means one is conscious, and that consciousness is a mental event, not a material event. He further contends that there are two distinct, different orders, i.e., the brain is in the material world and the mind is in the "world of subjective experience."

Lewis cuts to the heart of the materialist and naturalist dilemma when he writes, "The Naturalists have been engaged in thinking about Nature. They have not attended to the fact that they were thinking. The moment one attends to this it is obvious that one's own thinking cannot be merely a natural event, and that therefore something other than Nature exists. The Supernatural is not remote and abstruse: it is a matter of daily and hourly experience, as intimate as breathing."[19]

D. Elton Trueblood believes that supernaturalism is unavoidable: "How can nature include mind as an integral part unless it is grounded in mind? If mind were seen as something alien or accidental, the case would be different, but the further we go in modern science the clearer it becomes that mental experience is no strange offshoot. Rather it is something which is deeply rooted in the entire structure."[20] Implied, then, is the existence of a God that could create an entire structure with mind as an integral part. Once an individual grants the existence of an orderly mind separate from the physical universe, belief in the Ultimate Mind becomes the only rational option.

Christians must remember, however, that God is much more than an "Ultimate Mind." The mental proof may help to establish the existence of God, but the God of rational "proofs" alone is unworthy of worship—only the Christian God, in all His power and holiness, elicits awe and love in their proper proportion.

Secular Humanism	Marxist/Leninist	Cosmic Humanist	Christianity
Naturalism	**Dialectical Materialism**	**Non-naturalism**	**Super-naturalism**

CONCLUSION

Just like evolutionary naturalism and dialectical materialism, supernaturalism is more than a philosophy in the narrow sense. Christian philosophy represents an entire worldview, a view that is consistent with the Bible throughout. In the end, everyone must choose basically between a materialist/naturalist worldview and a supernaturalist worldview—and the choice will create repercussions throughout every aspect of the individual's life.

The Christian philosophy embraces the meaningful, purposeful life, a life in which each of us shapes his beliefs according to a coherent, reasonable, truthful worldview. A Christian with such a worldview will not be tossed to and fro by every secularist doctrine. "In the same way," says Dr. Young, "it can be said that the Christian philosopher and theologian must be acquainted with the contending world-views of his age. Philosophy after all is a way of life, and the Christian believes that he has the true way—the true pattern for living. It is the task of the Christian leader to understand the ideologies of his day so that he may be able to meet their challenge. The task is a never-ending one, for, although the Christian's worldview does not change, the world about him does. Thus the task of showing the relevance of the Christian realistic philosophy to a world in process is one which requires eternal vigilance. To such a task, to such an ideal, the Christian leader must dedicate himself."[21]

FOUR WESTERN WORLDVIEW MODELS

SOURCES	SECULAR HUMANISM HUMANIST MANIFESTOS I AND II	MARXISM/LENINISM WRITINGS OF MARX AND LENIN	COSMIC HUMANISM WRITINGS OF SPANGLER, FERGUSON, ETC.	BIBLICAL CHRISTIANITY BIBLE
THEOLOGY	Atheism	Atheism	Pantheism	Theism
PHILOSOPHY	Naturalism	Dialectical Materialism	Non-Naturalism	Supernaturalism
ETHICS	Relativism	Proletariat Morality	Relativism	Absolutes
BIOLOGY	Darwinian Evolution	Darwinian/Punctuated Evolution	Darwinian/Punctuated Evolution	Creation
PSYCHOLOGY	Self-Actualization	Behaviorism	Collective Consciousness	Mind/Body
SOCIOLOGY	Non-Traditional Family	Abolition of Home, Church and State	Non-Traditional Home, Church and State	Traditional Home, Church and State
LAW	Positive Law	Positive Law	Self-Law	Biblical and Natural Law
POLITICS	World Government (Globalism)	New World Order (New Civilization)	New Age Order	Justice, Freedom and Order
ECONOMICS	Socialism	Socialism	Universal Enlightened Production	Stewardship of Property
HISTORY	Historical Evolution	Historical Materialism	Evolutionary Godhood	Historical Resurrection

CHAPTER 11

Secular Humanist Ethics

"The fundamental question of ethics is, who makes the rules? God or men? The theistic answer is that God makes them. The humanistic answer is that men make them. This distinction between theism and humanism is the fundamental division in moral theory."[1]

—Max Hocutt

INTRODUCTION

The atheist theology of Humanism presents a special problem for Humanists; namely, what code of ethics should they embrace? Humanists reject the unchanging moral codes posited by the Christian religion—in fact, Paul Kurtz, author of *Humanist Manifesto II*, states, "The traditional supernaturalistic moral commandments are especially repressive of our human needs. They are immoral insofar as they foster illusions about human destiny [heaven] and suppress vital inclinations."[2] Humanists find religious ethical codes, such as the Ten Commandments, too restrictive to allow the human race to achieve fulfillment of the good life.

Humanists are working toward a "science of ethics" that is specifically in keeping with their beliefs in atheism, naturalism, and evolution. Kurtz, in *The Humanist Alternative*, calls for Secular Humanism to be "interpreted as a moral point of view."[3] Indeed, in the preface to the *Humanist Manifestoes I & II*, Kurtz defines Humanism "as a philosophical, religious, and moral point of view."[4]

Can morality be achieved without the foundation of religious beliefs? Humanists hope so. But they have difficulty agreeing about what morality apart from God means.

The need for a consistent Humanist stand on ethics to supplant supernaturalistic morality gave rise to a book edited by Morris B. Storer, entitled simply *Humanist Ethics*. Storer summed up the multitude of Humanist views regarding ethics in his preface: "Is personal advantage the measure of right and wrong, or the advantage of all affected: Humanists differ. Is there truth in ethics? We differ. Are 'right' and 'wrong' expressions of heart or head? Do people have free wills? Do you measure morality by results or by principles? Do people have duties as well as rights? We have our differences on all these and more."[5]

THE FOUNDATION OF HUMANIST ETHICS

This conflict of ethical concepts among Humanists results largely from their disagreement over the foundation of morality. Kurtz is quick to state that he believes in "a limited number of basic values and principles,"[6] but he does not point to a specific foundation for these principles, saying only that they are "naturalistic and empirical phenomena."[7]

Mihailo Markovic, another Humanist writing in Storer's collection of essays, takes exception to Kurtz's assumption about the origin of these principles, pointing out that Humanists have no unchanging standard that requires people to act in a certain way: "It remains quite unclear where this 'ought' comes from. It is one thing to describe a variety of actual historical patterns of conduct and moral habits. It is a completely different thing to make a choice among them and to say that we 'ought' to observe some of them. Why some and not others?"[8]

Markovic has cut to the heart of the problem Humanists face when discussing ethics. If man is going to decide what he "ought" to do, then he must refer to a moral code, or foundation, which dictates this "ought." Kurtz, when challenged by Markovic, admitted, "I can find no ultimate basis for 'ought.'"[9] If there is no ultimate basis for "ought," then there is no basis for determining right or wrong, which means the Hitlers, Stalins, and Maos of the world are innocent of any wrongdoing.

This difference over foundation causes Humanists to be divided regarding the "absolute" nature of ethics. The problem, according to Humanist Max Hocutt, is that "The nonexistence of God makes more difference to some of us than to others. To me, it means that there is no absolute morality, that moralities are sets of social conventions devised by humans to satisfy their need. To [Alastair] Hannay, it means that we must postulate an alternative basis for moral absolutism."[10]

This debate over the foundation of ethics is fundamental to the whole concept of Humanist ethics. Without a God who sets down an absolute moral code, Humanists must believe either that the code is subjective and should be applied differently to each changing situation, or that an absolute code exists, somehow outside of man, but within the whole evolutionary scheme of things.

Hocutt maintains that an absolute moral code cannot exist without God, and there is no God. "Furthermore, if there were a morality written up in the sky somewhere but no God to enforce it, I see no good reason why anybody should pay it any heed, no reason why we should obey it. Human beings may, and do, make up their own rules."[11] This view is more consistent with the Humanist view that life evolved by chance—otherwise, the Humanist has a difficult time explaining where an absolute code outside of man originated. If man is the highest being in nature and did not develop the absolute moral code himself, then what creature in nature did?

Some Humanists have gone so far, however, as to cast doubt on the idea that man can even perceive what is right or wrong. Kai Nielsen, who signed the *Humanist Manifesto II*, proposed a "no-truth thesis" that states that no question of the truth or falsity of moral values can sensibly arise. Nielsen's statement would appear to be the proper conclusion for Humanists, since most are unwilling to grant the existence of an absolute moral code. Without this code, what standard does mankind have for judging its actions right or wrong, or its moral beliefs true or false? Humanists, however, recognize the dilemma of being unable to determine the difference between right and wrong and have attempted to explain away the "no-truth thesis" in a number of ways.

Most Humanists dodge the "no-truth thesis" by claiming that reason can be used to determine right and wrong in the context of ethical relativism. A general statement of policy issued by the British Humanist Association states, "Humanists believe that man's conduct should be based on humanity, insight, and reason. He must face his problems with his own moral and intellectual resources, without looking for supernatural aid."[12]

Many other Humanists echo this call for the use of reason and experience as a guide for moral conduct. Lamont says that as long as man "pursues activities that are healthy, socially useful, and in accordance with reason, pleasure will generally accompany them; and happiness, the supreme good, will be the eventual result."[13]

Lamont's optimism, significantly, is based on the "hope" provided by evolutionary theory. Man can reason his way to the good, and to happiness, because evolution is constantly improving upon things, even man. This is the view most consistent with Humanism, since evolution is the best possible explanation as the source for ethics, assuming that morals do not arise from God or exist independently of nature.

A serious problem is created, however, by Humanism's desire to wed ethics to biology: this view allows Darwin's concept of the struggle for existence to become the absolute on which moral decisions are based. Such a morality allows men like Friedrich von Bernhardi, in his work *Germany and the Next War*, to insist, "War is a biological necessity; it is as necessary as the struggle of the elements of Nature; it gives a biologically just decision, since its decisions rest on the very nature of things."[14] Most Humanists would rather not open this can of worms, but it lurks in the background under the guise of social or ethical Darwinism.

ETHICAL RELATIVISM

By rejecting any kind of purpose behind the existence of a code of ethics, one necessarily finds himself rejecting any code that may exist outside of man. This done, all ethics are relative to man's interpretation of them in any given situation. Ethical relativism consists of little more than experimenting with ethics in every new scenario. Mason Olds describes it: "Of course, humanism has no single ethical theory, therefore ethical theory and moral subject must be chosen, examined, and even debated."[15]

It is important to note that these ideas about Humanist ethics are not just the radical ideas of a few Humanists on the fringe. Rather, *ethical relativism is the generally accepted morality for Humanists.* "The morality or immorality of any behavior," says Dr. Arthur E. Gravatt, "including sexual behavior, has been put in the context of 'situation ethics.' In this approach moral behavior may differ from situation to situation. Behavior might be moral for one person and not another or moral at one time and not another."[16]

Joseph Fletcher says that "rights and wrongs are determined by objective facts or circumstances, that is, by the situations in which moral agents have to decide for the most beneficial course open to choice."[17] Herbert W. Schneider calls morality "an experimental art," saying it is the "basic art of living well together. Moral right and wrong must therefore be conceived in terms of moral standards generated in a particular society."[18] Kurtz says "moral principles should be treated as hypotheses," tested by their practical worth and judged by what they cause to happen.[19]

PROBLEMS WITH ETHICAL RELATIVISM

The first problem Humanists recognize is the effect ethical relativism might have on average men and women. Humanists generally call for avoiding all dogma, since they believe it unnecessarily restricts man in his pursuit of happiness. But how will the common man react to a society without rules and corresponding penalties? Kurtz writes,

Nevertheless, the humanist is faced with a crucial ethical problem: Insofar as he has defended an ethic of freedom, can he develop a basis for moral responsibility? Regretfully, merely to liberate individuals from authoritarian social institutions, whether church or state, is no guarantee that they will be aware of their moral responsibility to others. The contrary is often the case. Any number of social institutions regulate conduct by some means of norms and rules, and sanctions are imposed for enforcing them. . . . Once these sanctions are ignored, we may end up with [a man] concerned with his own personal lust for pleasure, ambition, and power, and impervious to moral constraints.[20]

While Humanists refuse to give credence to the religious doctrine of original sin (because it is part of the religious myth), most recognize the folly of untempered optimism with regard to mankind.

In the end, however, the biggest problem with ethical relativism is still that basically anything can be construed as "good" or "bad" under the assumption that it is all relative to the situation in which a man finds himself. Even if individuals are striving to do the right thing, they may honestly disagree about what is the right thing, since there is no absolute standard. Baier writes, "Plainly, it is not easy to determine in an objective way what conduct is morally ideal. Hence even among people of good will, that is, among people perfectly willing to do what is morally ideal, there may be sincere disagreement."[21]

Lamont adds one final twist to ethical relativism which creates another problem. "For the Humanist," he says, "stupidity is just as great a sin as selfishness; and 'the moral obligation to be intelligent' ranks always among the highest of duties."[22]

Lamont seems to imply that only intelligent people are really capable of making the correct moral choices, which logically leads to the assumption that Lamont expects intelligent people to be the moral guides for the rest of society. Isn't this giving the power to a select few to create a dogma that others must follow? And isn't this precisely what Humanists have been trying to avoid all along by ignoring religious codes of ethics?

Three Humanists of the year— Margaret Sanger, Mary Calderone, and Faye Wattleton —have served in key positions in ... Planned Parenthood.

FROM THEORY TO PRACTICE

We have outlined the theoretical base of humanist ethics—now we will examine how their relativistic ethics translates into practice, specifically in human sexuality.

Earlier we acknowledged Kurtz's contention that supernatural ethics are immoral since they: (a) foster illusions about human destiny, and (b) "suppress vital inclinations." What are these vital inclinations?

Some are described by Kirkendall in *A New Bill of Sexual Rights and Responsibilities*. They include homosexuality, bisexuality, pre- and extra-marital sexual relations, and something called "genital association."

Legitimate alternative lifestyles include homosexuality, for the Humanist, because it has been "scientifically" proven that some men are born homosexual. Alfred Kinsey concluded that homosexuality was a biologically determined lifestyle from birth. The next two lifestyles that Humanists are studying to see if they are biologically determined are pedophilia (man/boy sex) and incest. Humanist Vern Bullough, historian of the homosexual movement, is involved in the move to declare pedophilia "biologically determined."

Humanists act in accordance with their desire to further the sexual revolution by becoming involved in agencies like Planned Parenthood. Three Humanists of the Year—Margaret Sanger, Mary Calderone, and Faye Wattleton—have served in key positions in that organization. Wattleton, a former president of Planned Parenthood, argues that the organization's focus is not to stop teenage sexual activity through education, but to stop "teenage pregnancy." She champions easier access to condoms for teens and more school-based health clinics "that provide contraceptives as part of general health care." The goal of Planned Parenthood, according to one staffer, is to help "young people obtain sex satisfaction before marriage. By sanctioning sex before marriage, we will prevent fear and guilt."[23]

Lamont also believes in sex without guilt. He concludes that an experimental period of living together "for at least six months," with strict birth control in effect, would be desirable for all who are formally engaged or seriously contemplating matrimony. The "science" that makes Lamont's scientific ethics possible is that of birth control and abortion. Says Lamont, "Historically, a primary reason for the enormous importance given to genital faithfulness and unfaithfulness was the lack of reliable birth-control techniques. Now that those techniques, including abortion, are generally available, this importance has more and more diminished."[24] The scientific approach has placed the matter of faithfulness/unfaithfulness into a new dimension.

Ethics

At A Glance

Secular Humanism

Ethical Relativism

CONCLUSION

With all the squabbling among Humanists, it is difficult to pin down their ethical ideals enough to present them as a body of facts. It is safe to say that most Humanists are ethical relativists, and in fact must be if they are to be consistent with their philosophy and theology. It is difficult, however, to standardize what ethical relativism entails. Humanists are aware of the logical inconsistencies and the dangers of ethical relativism; consequently, their ethical assertions are necessarily vague.

When one sorts through the haze of vague assertions, there emerges one foundational assumption that all Humanists hold dear: a system of ethics must allow more "freedom" than Judeo-Christian ethics. Absolutes must give way to suggestions and guidelines. Humanist ethical theories, however they are formulated, are all fundamentally justifications for denying God's moral order.

CHAPTER 12

Marxist/Leninist Ethics

"Is there such a thing as communist morality? Of course, there is. It is often suggested that we have no ethics of our own; very often the bourgeoisie accuse us Communists of rejecting all morality. This is a method of confusing the issue, of throwing dust in the eyes of the workers and peasants."[1]

—V.I. Lenin

INTRODUCTION

Marxist ethics proceeds out of Marxist theology, philosophy, biology, economics, and history. Whereas Humanists have a difficult time reaching a consensus regarding their ethical beliefs, Marxists do not face such a problem—mainly because of their single-minded approach to all five aforementioned disciplines. Their approach is rooted in dialectical materialism and the class struggle. While there is no absolute foundation for Marxism's ethical ideals, most Marxists believe the dialectical view of the class struggle is foundation enough.

According to the Marxist dialectic, everything in the universe, including society, is in a state of flux or constant change. This change in society is a move upward toward the elimination of all social and economic class distinctions. The next social advance in history will be the move from capitalism to socialism. This will inevitably result in a change in society's ideas about morals.

The dialectical view of history dictates the clash of thesis and antithesis—in this historical context, the relentless clash between the proletariat and the bourgeoisie. Marxist/Leninists believe that the morality of these two classes is totally different, and when the proletariat finally destroys the bourgeoisie, a new morality will reign—a new morality for the new man.

Marxists believe that "old morality"—the morality of the reigning capitalist class—exploits the workers. According to this view, the old religious moral codes must be abandoned. For Karl Marx and Frederick Engels, "Thou shalt not steal" establishes a society in which some have property and some don't; such an establishment is the root of the problem.

"It must be constantly borne in mind," says Howard Selsam, "that Marx and Engels denied that moral ideals, moral considerations, are central in human life and social evolution."[2] Rather, it is the biological and social evolution that dictates and determines morality. What is moral, what is right or wrong, is determined by what is best for this evolution. If the bourgeois class hinders either biological or social evolution, nature dictates the removal of that class.

A Brief Look At: Vladimir Ilich Lenin (1870-1924)

1887: Older brother Alexander executed
1891: Receives law degree from Kazan University
1897: Arrested and exiled to Siberia for three years
1903: Leads Bolsheviks in split with other Russian Marxists
1909: Publishes *Materialism and Empirio–criticism*
1917: Emerges from the October Revolution as the leader of the Soviet Republic
1918: Publishes *State and Revolution*
1921: Bolsheviks gain control after three years of civil war
1922: Suffers two strokes

THE EVOLUTION OF MORALITY

The inevitability of change is the cornerstone for the Marxist ethical code. Marx writes in the *Manifesto of the Communist Party*, "Does it require deep intuition to

comprehend that man's ideas, views and conceptions, in one word, man's consciousness, changes with every change in the conditions of his material existence, in his
social relations and in his social life?"[3] Because social and economic status are, by
Marx's definition, always changing according to the laws of the dialectic, mankind's
ideas about morality must also be in a state of change.

This inevitability of change, in both history and ethics, causes some to question
the existence of a moral code in Marxist philosophy. V.I. Lenin answers,

Is there such a thing as communist morality? Of course there is. It is often suggested that we have no ethics of our own; very often the bourgeoisie accuse us
Communists of rejecting all morality. This is a method of confusing the issue, of
throwing dust in the eyes of the workers and peasants.

In what sense do we reject ethics, reject morality?

In the sense given to it by the bourgeoisie, who based ethics on God's commandments. On this point we, of course, say that we do not believe in God, and that
we know perfectly well that the clergy, the landowners and the bourgeoisie invoked
the name of God so as to further their own interests as exploiters.[4]

Morality for the communists has evolved beyond what is
used by the "exploiting classes." God's commandments are considered an outdated myth
concocted by the exploiting
class to suppress the
exploited class.

When all class distinc-
tions are erased, however,
the Marxist moral view necessarily must change again—
because promoting class struggle will no longer be the immediate moral necessity. We say
"immediate" because the dialectic is
an eternal process that entails a continuing thesis/antithesis struggle. The
ever-changing nature of history will dictate a new moral view for the Marxists.
When Marxists say there is no system of
morality that fits all times, they include the
future in their philosophy, realizing that histo-

During his reign as General Secretary of the USSR from 1927–1953,
Joseph Stalin created a monolithic system of gulags (Soviet prison
camps) to ensure that his dictatorship could not be undermined.

ry will change man's perceptions of life again after their present aims are attained. Something can only be morally right in its context in history. Today the morally right is the action necessary to attain the victory of the proletariat over the bourgeoisie.

So how will the new morality of the future be determined? The new classless society will determine the new morality, just as this move toward a classless society is dictating the morality for today. For Marxists, morality is that conduct which is in harmony with history as it flows in the direction of a classless society, and beyond.

OLD MORALITY

Marxist/Leninists wholeheartedly reject moral codes with foundations in religious beliefs, including traditional universal moral ideals. They reject such ideals as "old morality," as the products of the bourgeoisie, codes invented and used by that propertied class to oppress the propertyless proletariat. G.L. Andreyev, in *What Kind of Morality Does Religion Teach?* states, "In the reigning morality under capitalism that act is considered moral which promotes the preservation and strengthening of the system of exploitation and the acquirement of profits. Religion merely justifies this unjust and oppressive, bloody, and inhuman system in the name of God."[5]

> Hatred can be moral, according to the Marxist, as long as it is directed toward the proper institution, class, or enemy.

It is important to understand that Marxists perceive what is generally regarded by society as moral to be in direct contradiction to the Marxist goal of a classless society. Nikita Khrushchev states, "So long as classes exist on the earth, there will be no such thing in life as something good in the absolute sense. What is good for the bourgeoisie, for the imperialists, is disastrous for the working class, and, on the contrary, what is good for the working people is not admitted by the imperialists, by the bourgeoisie."[6]

This, then, is the whole problem with the old morality as perceived by the Marxist. The old morality has simply been a tool for the oppressing classes to maintain their position in society. Christian ethics, for the Marxist, is just the means by which the rich control the working class poor.

Marx says that, for the proletariat, "Law, morality, religion, are . . . so many bourgeois prejudices, behind which lurk in ambush just as many bourgeois interests."[7] Lenin agrees with Marx: "The old society was based on the principle: rob or be robbed; work for others or make others work for you; be a slave-owner or a slave."[8]

CLASS MORALITY

For the present historical period, from the Marxist point of view, the proper morality to adopt is a class morality—specifically, the morality of the proletariat, the propertyless masses. According to *Scientific Communism: A Glossary,* "Devotion to the cause of the working class, collectivism, mutual aid, comradely solidarity, hatred toward the bourgeoisie and toward traitors to the common cause, internationalism, and stoicism in struggle are traits which not only define the content of proletarian ethics, but also characterize the moral image of the typical representatives of the working class."[9] This is precisely the code of ethics that all Marxists believe must be adopted.

It is interesting to note that included in this code is the call for hatred of the bourgeoisie. Robert Conquest's *The Harvest of Sorrow,* a documentation of the inhumanity of applied Marxist theory, contains illustration after illustration of "class hatred" or communist class morality in practice. Hatred can be moral, according to the Marxist, as long as it is directed toward the proper institution, class, or enemy.

Hatred becomes a necessary ingredient in the clash between the proletariat and the bourgeoisie. It follows, then, that society's generally accepted moral principles (which Marxists claim are bourgeois tools) are in direct opposition to the moral principles of the proletariat. If this is the case, could any member of the bourgeoisie do anything right in the Marxist's eyes? Apparently not. It would seem that unless a member of the propertied class could somehow become a proletarian, anything he does, no matter how moral by his standards, will be greeted with contempt by Marxists.

JUSTIFICATION OF THE MEANS

According to the Marxist, the acceptable form of conduct in class morality is whatever it takes to accomplish the ultimate goal—namely, a classless communist society. In other words, the end justifies the means. Regardless of what you do, it is moral if it brings the world closer to eradicating social classes. An action is moral when it helps overthrow the bourgeoisie.

Freedom can only be achieved when all class barriers are erased, and therefore anything that serves that end can be judged as moral. "Ethics, in short," says Selsam, "is good only as anything else is good, for what it can accomplish, for the direction in which it takes men."[10]

The problem, of course, is that man can justify mistreating his fellow man by claiming that it will serve in the long run a "higher good." Ivan Bahryany, a Ukrainian citizen who estimates that the Soviets killed 10 million of his countrymen between

1927 and 1939, states the problem this way: "The party clique which follows the slogan expressed by the saying 'the end justifies the means' is actually always ready to use any means."[11] In the case of the Ukrainians, the "means" included shooting, starvation, and slave labor in Siberia. Joseph Stalin referred to such action as the liquidation of the kulak class. Lenin admitted that the proletariat would be willing to work with the "petty bourgeois proprietors" as long as it furthered the Marxist cause, "But after that our roads part. Then we shall have to engage in the most decisive, ruthless struggle against them."[12]

MORAL REVOLUTION

What are the most efficient means for creating a society without class distinctions? According to Marxists, revolution is unavoidable—it is the only way to overthrow the bourgeoisie and lift up the proletariat.

Communist revolution is unquestionably moral. "From the point of view of communist morality the struggle against everything which hinders the cause of communist construction is moral and humane," says Andreyev, "and for this reason we consider the struggle against the enemies of communism to be of a moral nature."[13]

This class struggle is definitely not peaceful—but then the struggle for survival in nature is not peaceful. According to the Marxists, those who criticize the elimination of the bourgeoisie for social evolutionary reasons fail to remember the cost in death and suffering caused by biological evolution. Nature accumulates the good and disposes of the bad. The fit must survive both biologically and socially. The unfit, along with their social institutions, must perish.

Marx states, "The Communists disdain to conceal their views and aims. They openly declare that their ends can be attained only by the forcible overthrow of all existing social conditions."[14] This forcible overthrow is perceived as morally right. It is right because it destroys the hindrances to a communist society. Morally speaking, it is not just okay to work for the forcible overthrow of capitalism—it is the communist's ethical duty, and he is morally wrong if he shirks that duty.

Does this obligation to overthrow the bourgeoisie include killing? Khrushchev answers,

> Our cause is sacred. He whose hand will tremble, who will stop midway, whose knees will shake before he destroys tens and hundreds of enemies, he will lead the revolution into danger. Whoever will spare a few lives of enemies, will pay for it with hundreds and thousands of lives of the better sons of our fathers.[15]

How will an individual always know if his actions are the proper ones for accomplishing the Marxist goal? He won't. And he will make mistakes. Lenin says, "Even if for every hundred correct things we committed 10,000 mistakes, our revolution would still be—and it will be in the judgment of history—great and invincible. . . ."[16]

The Marxist revolution is morally right even if mistakes are made and even when it involves mass killings. Stalin took this philosophy to heart, stating, "To put it briefly: the dictatorship of the proletariat is the domination of the proletariat over the bourgeoisie, untrammelled by the law and based on violence and enjoying the sympathy and support of the toiling and exploited masses."[17] For this reason Stalin announced on December 27, 1929, "the liquidation of the kulaks as a class."[18] British journalist D.G. Stewart-Smith estimates that international communism has been responsible for 83 million deaths between 1917 and 1964. From a Marxist/Leninist perspective, if 83 million died to abolish social classes and private property, it was worth the price—even morally just. Marxists judge the result, not the methods; the consequences, not the act.

Stalin, therefore, acted always within the Marxist/Leninist ethical code. He used

Ethics
At A Glance

Secular Humanism	Marxist/Leninist
Ethical Relativism	**Proletariat Morality**

means that he assumed would serve his ends—the destruction of the class enemy—and should those ends ever be accomplished, Marxists would have to applaud Stalin as an individual with the proper ideas about morality.

CONCLUSION

Many uncertainties surround Marxist ethics. While virtually all Marxists agree on the dialectical materialist foundation for their morality and the inevitability of change involved in moral precepts, these same Marxists would have difficulty predicting the ethics of a classless society. They are quick to label Christian ethics "immoral" because these ethics theoretically maintain the dominion of the bourgeoisie over the proletariat, but they cannot conceive of a moral scheme of their own other than the vague idea of "creation of a new moral man."

This type of ethical ideology, including the belief about the inevitability of change and the evolutionary nature of morals, leaves Marxists free to abandon today's generally accepted moral standards in pursuit of a greater good—the creation of a communist society. This pursuit requires the Marxist to dedicate his life to the cause and to use whatever action he believes will eventually result in a classless society. Therefore, his course of action, no matter how immoral it appears to a world that believes in an absolute or at least a universal moral standard, is perceived as moral by the Marxist/Leninist.

CHAPTER 13

Cosmic Humanist Ethics

"It [is] not possible to judge another's truth."[1]

—Shirley MacLaine

INTRODUCTION

Cosmic Humanism's ethical perspective is based on its theological pantheism and philosophical monism. If each person is God, then all final authority resides within, and individuals must seek the freedom to act in harmony with their inner truth. "Free will," says Shirley MacLaine, "is simply the enactment of the realization you are God, a realization that you are divine: free will is making everything accessible to you."[2] Individual autonomy is the only ethical absolute promoted by the New Age movement.

This autonomy places the authority for judging values squarely within the soul of each human being. Marilyn Ferguson writes, "Most importantly, when people become autonomous, their values become *internal.*"[3] Internalized values are a must for every person seeking higher consciousness; any outside limit or external authority blocks his ability to get in touch with his inner truth. Thus, Vera Alder tells us, "We should search ourselves very carefully to see if we have any fixed ideas, any great shyness or self–consciousness. If we have, we *must* seek freedom."[4]

Shakti Gawain provides us with a practical application of this call for total freedom when she calls for total sexual freedom: "If you're setting limits on your sexual energy, it becomes distorted. If you believe it is something to be hidden, ignored, and controlled, then you learn to hold back completely or act sexually only at certain safe moments."[5] According to the Cosmic Humanist worldview, such limitations sap our personal power and deny our godhood. Man must not acknowledge outside boundaries, especially the boundaries of the Ten Commandments. The Commandments are external authority and, as such, hinder one's evolutionary growth.

ETHICAL RELATIVISM

Of course, when we choose to ignore all outside authority and rational boundaries, boundless ethical relativism must result. Ferguson admits as much: "Autonomous human beings can create and invent. And they can change their minds, repudiating values they once held."[6]

This relativism means that no one may decide whether another's actions are right or wrong. Ferguson believes that once we have achieved the higher consciousness of the New Age, "There is less certainty about what is right for others. With an awareness of multiple realities, we lose our dogmatic attachment to a single point of view."[7]

In other words, we must never judge people's beliefs or actions. Tolerance is the buzzword: Cosmic Humanists must tolerate all other views regarding morality because ethics is relative to the truth within each individual. "Adam and Eve," says Marianne Williamson "were happy until she 'ate of the knowledge of good and evil.' What that means is that everything was perfect until they began to judge—to keep their hearts open sometimes, but closed at others. . . . Closing our hearts destroys our peace. It's alien to our real nature."[8]

Randall Baer, a former Cosmic Humanist who converted to Christianity, translates:

> There's a basic credo that says "create your own reality according to what feels right for you." For example, whether a person chooses to be homosexual, bisexual, monogamous, polygamous or whatever is OK as long as "It's right for me" or "It's done with love and no one's hurt." This is a kind of relativistic, human–founded ethics (or design–your–own ethics). In effect, New Age persons pick and choose from the multitudes of options in each area of life according to their own personal preferences.[9]

> **"Christ is the same force as Lucifer . . . . Lucifer prepares man for the experience of Christhood."**
>
> *David Spangler*

A Brief Look At: Marilyn Ferguson (1938-)

1960: Begins studies at University of Colorado

1963: Marries Michael Ferguson

1973: Publishes *The Brain Revolution*

1979: Divorces husband

1980: Published *The Aquarian Conspiracy*

1983: Re–marries

THE UNITY OF GOOD AND EVIL

According to the Cosmic Humanist, we must simply assume that everyone acts morally by following inner truth. Gawain, in fact, absolves Adolf Hitler and every other human being of moral responsibility by claiming that everyone is following the shortest path to higher consciousness and therefore acting morally: "I believe that every being chooses the life path and relationships that will help him or her to grow the fastest."[10]

Ethical relativism, as one would expect, has led the Cosmic Humanist to a point where the distinction between good and evil has become hopelessly blurred. No absolute right or wrong exists; only what is right or wrong according to each individual's truth. If everything is one, it is difficult to distinguish between good and evil. What may appear evil in this life could be the reverse in a reincarnated existence.

Such a concept involves what New Agers refer to as *karma.* According to MacLaine, karma means,

> Whatever action one takes will ultimately return to that person—good and bad—maybe not in this life embodiment, but sometime in the future. And no one is exempt. . . . For every act, for every indifference, for every misuse of life, we are finally held accountable. And it is up to us to understand what those accounts might be.[11]

Unfortunately, since there is no standard by which to judge what may be "an indifference," or "a misuse of life" it is difficult to know if there is any difference between them or, for that matter, if there is any difference between cruelty and non–cruelty.

This is an alarming conclusion, but one the Cosmic Humanist is more than willing to accept. This willingness results from the New Age concept of unity. If all is one, then good and evil are one, and so are right and wrong.

Ferguson states, "This wholeness unites opposites. . . . In these spiritual traditions [that form the basis for New Age thought] there is neither good nor evil. There is only light and the absence of light . . . wholeness and brokenness . . . flow and struggle."[12] David Spangler echoes this view, in more startling language: "Christ is the same force as Lucifer. . . . Lucifer prepares man for the experience of Christhood. . . . Lucifer works within each of us to bring us to wholeness as we move into the New Age."[13] What the world considers evil—war, murder, etc.—is part of the evolutionary flow and struggle of reality as supraconsciousness strives to be born on a higher level.

Ethics At A Glance

Secular Humanism	Marxist/Leninist	Cosmic Humanism
Ethical Relativism	Proletariat Morality	Ethical Relativism

CONCLUSION

Morality, for the Cosmic Humanist, is a nebulous thing. Each person must listen to the "God within" to determine their own ethical system, but they may never hold others accountable to their system. Nothing is ever really *wrong*, ironically, except judging other people's moral beliefs and actions.

Of course, judging can't be completely bad, either, since it is part of the unity of reality. Since "all is one," then even horrible mistakes like judgmental actions are manifestations of God.

Difficulties multiply like dandelions for the Cosmic Humanist. Certain things, like murder, must be wrong—and yet we may not judge and call it "wrong"; in fact, we must believe that murders are carried out *by God on God*.

Such a skewed worldview leads to drastically skewed thinking. Perhaps the finest example of this, with regard to ethics, is provided by Kevin Ryerson as he discusses karma:

> Criminals and murderers sometimes come back around to be murdered themselves, or perhaps to become a saint. For instance, Moses was a murderer. . . . He beat the fellow to death out of rage, which was not exactly the most ethical decision. But he went on to become a great intellect, a great law–giver, and is considered a saint by many people. So basically, you get many chances. Your karma is your system of judgment. There is justice.[14]

Don't ask questions. Don't worry about making the "right" ethical decisions. What goes around comes around, and you can't help it. Neither could Hitler.

CHAPTER 14

Biblical Christian Ethics

"Let love be sincere and without hypocrisy. Abhor that which is evil; cleave to that which is good."

—Romans 12:9

INTRODUCTION

Christian ethics is inseparable from theology because Christian ethics is grounded in the character of God. "One of the distinctions of the Judeo-Christian God," says Francis Schaeffer, "is that not all things are the same to Him. That at first may sound rather trivial, but in reality it is one of the most profound things one can say about the Judeo–Christian God. He exists; He has a character; and not all things are the same to Him. Some things conform to His character, and some are opposed to His character."[1] *The task of Christian ethics is determining what conforms to God's character and what does not.*

While Marxists and Humanists rely almost exclusively on their economic or naturalistic philosophy to determine ethics, the Christian places ethics in a moral order revealed by the Divine Creator. Rather than believing in some passing fancy bound to society's ever-changing whims, the Christian answers to a specific moral order revealed to man both through general and special revelation.

The Christian knows this ethical order to be the only true source of morality. "The human mind," says C.S. Lewis, "has no more power of inventing a new value than of imagining a new primary colour, or, indeed, of creating a new sun and a new sky for it to move in."[2] Those talking about establishing a new moral order are talking nonsense. This is no more possible than establishing a new physical order. Both are givens. For the Christian, the moral order is as real as the physical order—some would say more real. The Apostle Paul says the physical order is temporary, but the order "not seen" is eternal (2 Corinthians 4:18). This eternal moral order is a reflection of the character of God.

A Brief Look At: Clive Staples Lewis (1898-1963)

1925: Begins teaching at Magdalen College in Oxford University

1931: Converts to Christianity

1933: "Inklings" (including J.R.R. Tolkien) begins meeting regularly

1941: Delivers first series of BBC lectures

1942: Publishes *The Screwtape Letters*

1950: Publishes first book in *Narnia* series; completed in 1956

1952: Publishes *Mere Christianity*

1956: Marries Joy Davidman Gresham

1960: Joy dies of cancer

REVELATION AND OUR COMMON MORAL HERITAGE

Christian ethics in one sense is simply an expansion on a moral order that is generally revealed to all men. Despite some disputes regarding the morality of certain specific actions, comments Calvin D. Linton, "there is a basic pattern of similarity among [ethical codes]. Such things as murder, lying, adultery, cowardice are, for example, almost always condemned. The universality of the ethical sense itself (the 'oughtness' of conduct), and the similarities within the codes of diverse cultures indicate a common moral heritage for all mankind which materialism or naturalism cannot explain."[3]

This common moral heritage could be defined as anything from an attitude to a conscience, but however one defines it, one is left with the impression that some moral absolutes exist outside of man. According to this concept, whenever man judges he is relying upon a yardstick that measures actions against an absolute set of standards. Without a standard, there could be no justice; without an ethical absolute, there could be no morality.

This absolute standard outside of man is apparent throughout all of mankind's attitudes toward morality. Secular man should, according to his own philosophy, lead a life that treats all morals as relative—but in practice, secular man treats some abstract values (such as justice or fairness, love, and courage) as consistently moral. What's more, secular man has cringed at Auschwitz and the gulags, at child abuse and lies. How can this phenomenon be explained unless we accept the notion that certain value judgments are universal and inherent to all mankind?

Christian morality is founded on this belief in an absolute moral order existing outside of, and yet somehow inscribed into, man's very being. It is a morality flowing from the nature of the Creator through the nature of created things, not a construction of the human mind. It is part of God's general revelation to man.

This rule of right, this moral light, is what the Apostle John refers to as having been lit in the hearts of all men and women—"That was the true Light, which lighteth every man that cometh into the world" (John 1:9). It is what St. Paul referred to as "the work of the law written in their hearts, their conscience" (Romans 2:15).

This morality is not arbitrarily handed down by God to create difficulties for mankind. God does not make up new values according to any whim. Rather, God's very character is holy and cannot tolerate evil or moral indifference—what the Bible calls sin. Therefore, if we wish to please God, we must act in accordance with His moral order so as to prevent sin from separating us from Him.

Christians are assured of these truths about God's nature and judgment as a result of special revelation. Whereas general

God gave Moses the Ten Commandments, one of the oldest codified sets of laws, on Mt. Sinai. Moses delivered God's law to the nation of Israel.

Snapshots In Time

The Ten Commandments

I. "You shall have no other gods before me."
II. "You shall not make for yourself an idol in the form of anything in heaven above or on the earth beneath or in the waters below...."
III. "You shall not misuse the name of the Lord your God, for the Lord will not hold anyone guiltless who misuses his name."
IV. "Remember the Sabbath day by keeping it holy...."
V. "Honor your father and your mother, so that you may live long in the land the Lord your God is giving you."
VI. "You shall not murder."
VII. "You shall not commit adultery."
VIII. "You shall not steal."
IX. "You shall not give false testimony against your neighbor."
X. "You shall not covet your neighbor's house. You shall not covet your neighbor's wife, or his manservant or maidservant, his ox or donkey, or anything that belongs to your neighbor."

—Exodus 20:3–17

revelation has informed all of mankind of the existence of a moral order, special revelation—the Bible—reveals specifics regarding such an order. Christian ethics, in the final analysis, relies on God and His Word for the full explanation of the moral order.

THE CHRISTIAN RESPONSE TO SECULAR ETHICS

It is important for the Christian to be able to recognize secular ideas regarding ethics and the flaws inherent in these ideas. For the Christian, morality is a lifestyle for glorifying God, and it is crucial for man's moral health to stay away from the hazy thinking that creates less-than–absolute moral values. The so-called "new morality" is nothing but an excuse to do as one pleases under the banner of morality. Mankind should have learned from its history that the consequences of such a morality is death. Instead, thousands today are dying as a direct consequence of their immoral behavior.

Secular moralities fall back on believing men's ideas about morality to be enough for an ethical code. This leaves man without a standard for judging actions with regard to his morality. Schaeffer insists that there must be an absolute if there is to be a moral order and real values. "If there is no absolute beyond man's ideas, then there is no final appeal to judge between individuals and groups whose moral judgments conflict. We are merely left with conflicting opinions."[4]

> **"The character of Jesus has not only been the highest pattern of virtue, but the strongest incentive to its practice … "**
>
> *W.E.H. Lecky*

This is the Achilles' heel of ethical relativism—it leaves mankind with no standards, only conflicting opinions or subjective value judgments that translate into no morality. This ethical vacuum created by relativism allows leaders to misuse their power without having to answer to a specific moral code. "Those who stand outside all judgments of value cannot have any ground for preferring one of their own impulses to another except the emotional strength of that impulse,"[5] wrote Lewis.

For the Christian, God is the ultimate source of morality, and it is nothing short of blasphemy when we place ourselves in His role. And yet, if one does not submit his nature entirely to the moral absolutes founded in God's character, logically the only ethical authority residing over mankind is our own impulses. It is important for the Christian to understand the fallacies of secular ethics, so that he can avoid the inconsistencies of unfounded ethical ideals. All secular ethical codes are an aberration of God's code and should be recognized as such.

CHRISTIAN ETHICS AND SPECIAL REVELATION

Christians emphatically embrace the concept of moral absolutes and believe they should be taught to our children. But what specific absolutes make up the moral order professed in Christian ethics? What ought we to do? How should we live?

Absolutes are revealed to man in the Bible. While it is impossible for every situation requiring moral decisions to be contained in the Bible, the Christian is given enough specific values and guidelines to have a sense of what is right and what is wrong in all situations. The most obvious absolutes, of course, are the Ten Commandments—the Decalogue. This acts as the "basic law" for mankind, but it is not the only law revealed in the Bible. Much of the Old Testament is dedicated to describing God's moral order.

After outlining the moral order, the Bible introduces us to God Incarnate, Jesus Christ, and describes His ministry and teachings so that Christians might better understand the implications of this order. The apex of Christ's ethical teaching is encapsulated in the Sermon on the Mount, found most comprehensively in Matthew 5-7.

For the Christian, the ethical exhortations in the Sermon on the Mount, coupled with the ethical pronouncements of the Old Testament, create a very specific ethical order. And, as if this code were not enough, Christians have the perfect role model to dictate the proper moral course of action: Jesus Christ, as revealed to mankind in the Bible. W.E.H. Lecky, who never claimed to be a Christian, admitted, "The character of Jesus has not only been the highest pattern of virtue, but the strongest incentive to its practice . . ."[6]

In fact, the call to follow Jesus is the simplest summation of Christian ethics, and at the same time, the most difficult thing for man to do. Dietrich Bonhoeffer, a Christian martyr, notes, "On two separate occasions Peter received the call, 'Follow me.' It was the first and last word Jesus spoke to his disciple (Mark 1:17, John 21:22)."[7] Christ really asks but one thing of Christians: follow Me!

As a result of the special revelation given to us in the Bible, man can never excuse himself for doing wrong because he has not been told what is morally correct. Throughout the Bible, the question of ethics is specifically addressed; in truth, it cannot be separated from the Christian faith.

RESPONSIBILITY IN CHRISTIAN ETHICS

Christians are called to "love the Lord your God with all your heart and with all your soul and with all your strength and with all your mind, and love your neighbor as yourself" (Luke 10:27). This command, like all of the other commands in the Bible, implies that Christians have responsibilities.

This responsibility to love others calls for an attitude not merely compassionate but servantlike. If we love God, we demonstrate it through serving our fellow man. It is our duty. "The Apostle John," says Carl F.H. Henry, "appeals to the explicit teaching of the Redeemer to show the inseparable connection between love of God and love of neighbor: 'If a man say, I love God, and hateth his brother, he is a liar: for he that loveth not his brother whom he hath seen, how can he love God whom he hath not seen? And this commandment have we from him, that he who loveth God love his brother also' (1 John 4:20f). 'God is love, and he that dwelleth in love dwelleth in God, and God in him' (4:16). The love of God is the service of man in love."[8]

This duty toward our fellow man requires more than serving his spiritual needs. "[M]an is more than a soul destined for another world;" says Norman Geisler, "he is also a body living in this world. And as a resident of this time-space continuum man has physical and social needs which cannot be isolated from spiritual needs. Hence, in order to love man as he is—the whole man—one must exercise a concern about his social needs as well as his spiritual needs."[9]

The Christian cannot claim that his faith in God and resulting perspective on life and ethics exempt him from concerns about worldly matters. Just the opposite is true (Matthew 25:31–46). Because a person is a Christian, he must be concerned with working to achieve God's will for the world. God commands it.

In examining the Christian's obligation to love his neighbor, one encounters an even more fundamental obligation: the Christian's duty to love God. "The moral end, or highest good, is the glory of God," writes William Young. "In declaring by word and deed the perfections, especially the moral perfections of the most High, man finds true happiness."[10] Our duty toward God is inextricably tied up with our other duties as Christians; it is accurate to state, as Henry does, "Hebrew-Christian ethics unequivocally defines moral obligation as man's duty to God."[11] This is the heart and soul of the Christian ethic.

THE INEVITABILITY OF SIN

The Bible does not concern itself only with outlining the moral order, however. It also speaks of a time when God will judge man for his character and conduct. Revelation 22:11-15 warns that at that time many will be left outside the city of God. This has staggering implications for humanity. "Christianity declares that God is more than the ground and goal of the moral order," explains Henry.

Unequivocally it lays stress on the reality of God's judgment of history. It affirms, that is, the stark fact of moral disorder and rebellion: "the whole world lieth in wickedness" (1 John 5:19). By emphasis on the fact of sin and the shattered moral law of God, on the dread significance of death, on the wiles of Satan and the hosts of darkness, Christian ethics sheds light on the treacherous realities of moral decision.[12]

The reality, of course, is that we "all have sinned and fall short of the glory of God" (Romans 3:23). This is a unique aspect of the Christian ethical system. "When a person makes up his own ethical code," D. James Kennedy says, "he always makes up an ethical system which he thinks he has kept. In the law of God, we find a law which smashes our self-righteousness, eliminates all trust in our own goodness, and convinces us that we are sinners. The law of God leaves us with our hands over our mouths and our faces in the dust. We are humbled before God and convinced that we are guilty transgressors of his law."[13]

This conviction of guilt is crucial for a Christian to understand the incredible sacrifice God made when He sent His Son to die for us. The Christian ethical code calls for perfection, and no man other than Christ has ever achieved that. Thus, it is the ethical code itself that points man first to his own sinful nature and then to the realization that the only One who can save him is the Man who has not stepped outside the moral code, Jesus Christ. The absolute moral code shows us our absolute dependence on Him. Put more simply, "The law is given to convince us that we fail to keep it."[14] And on realization of this truth, we are driven for salvation to the One who has not failed.

The Christian cannot, however, simply rely on Christ to save him, and then continue in his sinful ways. Rather, once the Christian understands the ultimate sacrifice God made for him, he cannot help but respond with a grateful desire to please God by adhering to His moral order. This does not mean it becomes easier for a Christian to do what is morally right—it simply means that he is willing to strive to do God's will. This willingness to choose the morally right action is crucial for the Christian truly concerned with pleasing God. As Lewis says, "There is nowhere this side of heaven where one can safely lay the reins on the horse's neck. It will never be lawful simply to 'be ourselves' until 'ourselves' have become sons of God."[15] Christian ethics requires a firm commitment to and an unflagging zeal for what is right and good in the Lord's sight. As Paul said, Christians must "abhor that which is evil; cleave to that which is good" (Romans 12:9).

Ethics At A Glance

Secular Humanism	Marxist/Leninist	Cosmic Humanism	Christianity
Ethical Relativism	Proletariat Morality	Ethical Relativism	Ethical Absolutes

CONCLUSION

The Christian ethical system is both like and unlike any other system ever postulated. Every ethical system contains some grain of the truth found in the Christian code, but no other system can claim to be the whole truth, handed down as an absolute from God to man.

Christians, the very people who recognize this truth, must be dedicated to not just espousing it, but also living it. This dedication has become far too rare in present-day society. "Who stands fast?" asks Bonhoeffer. "Only the man whose final standard is not his reason, his principles, his conscience, his freedom, or his virtue, but who is ready to sacrifice all this when he is called to obedient and responsible action in faith and in exclusive allegiance to God—the responsible man, who tries to make his whole life an answer to the question and call of God. Where are these responsible people?"[16]

Where are they? Wherever Christians are willing to treat God's moral order with the same respect they show His physical order; wherever God is loved with an individual's whole body, soul, spirit, mind, and strength. They may be found in the halls of government, standing firm against tyranny and slavery, or in the mission field, sacrificing everything for the sake of the gospel. More often, these people are quite ordinary Christian men and women living extraordinary lives, showing the world that Christ can be believed and His standards lived. It is our Christian duty to join the ranks of these morally responsible people.

FOUR WESTERN WORLDVIEW MODELS

SOURCES	SECULAR HUMANISM HUMANIST MANIFESTOS I AND II	MARXISM/ LENINISM WRITINGS OF MARX AND LENIN	COSMIC HUMANISM WRITINGS OF SPANGLER, FERGUSON, ETC.	BIBLICAL CHRISTIANITY BIBLE
THEOLOGY	Atheism	Atheism	Pantheism	Theism
PHILOSOPHY	Naturalism	Dialectical Materialism	Non-Naturalism	Supernaturalism
ETHICS	Relativism	Proletariat Morality	Relativism	Absolutes
BIOLOGY	Darwinian Evolution	Darwinian/Punctuated Evolution	Darwinian/Punctuated Evolution	Creation
PSYCHOLOGY	Self-Actualization	Behaviorism	Collective Consciousness	Mind/Body
SOCIOLOGY	Non-Traditional Family	Abolition of Home, Church and State	Non-Traditional Home, Church and State	Traditional Home, Church and State
LAW	Positive Law	Positive Law	Self-Law	Biblical and Natural Law
POLITICS	World Government (Globalism)	New World Order (New Civilization)	New Age Order	Justice, Freedom and Order
ECONOMICS	Socialism	Socialism	Universal Enlightened Production	Stewardship of Property
HISTORY	Historical Evolution	Historical Materialism	Evolutionary Godhood	Historical Resurrection

CHAPTER 15

Secular Humanist Biology

"Man is the result of a purposeless and natural process that did not have him in mind. He was not planned. He is a state of matter, a form of life, a sort of animal, and a species of the Order Primates, akin nearly or remotely to all of life and indeed to all that is material."[1]

—George Gaylord Simpson

INTRODUCTION

Belief in evolution is as crucial to Humanism's worldview as are its atheistic theology and naturalistic philosophy. In fact, the Humanist's ideas about the origin of life can be considered a special dimension of their theology and philosophy. Without the theory of evolution, the Humanist would have to rely on God as the explanation for life, which would necessarily destroy his atheism and hence his Humanism. Therefore, every Secular Humanist embraces the theory of evolution.

The *Humanist Manifesto I* states, "Humanism believes that man is a part of nature and that he has emerged as the result of a continuous process."[2] This belief is echoed in the *Humanist Manifesto II*, which claims that "science affirms that the human species is an emergence from natural evolutionary forces."[3]

For the Humanist, atheistic evolution is not one option among many, but rather the only option compatible with their worldview. Creationism is considered an enemy of science, despite the fact that the Christian worldview had far more to do with the founding of modern science than did Humanism.

125

THE ROLE OF SCIENCE

Humanism relies on science as its basic source of knowledge. Its interpretation of science excludes any supernatural explanation for any event occurring in nature, including the origin of life. For Humanists, the lesson of science is that whatever takes place in nature is "natural" not supernatural. Humanists believe that, for science, *supernatural* is a meaningless word.

Obviously, when one assumes that science is the best method of obtaining knowledge and that science must exclude the supernatural, one cannot accept the supernatural as a possible explanation for the origin of life. The only other possibility is evolution beginning with spontaneous generation. Julian Huxley sums it up: "Modern science must rule out special creation or divine guidance."[4]

> **The Humanist considers evolution the correct foundation for every individual's worldview and believes that the world can be properly understood only from this perspective.**

And why must "modern" science rule out creation? Because, as we have noted, science cannot observe or measure the supernatural and therefore is incapable of obtaining any knowledge about it. But by this definition science cannot render judgment on the theory of evolution, either. One-time-only historical events fall outside the parameters of the scientific method because such events cannot be repeated, observed, tested, or falsified. Accordingly, neither creationism nor evolution is strictly "scientific."

Still, Humanists insist that evolutionary theory is scientific and creation is not. Just how closed-minded the Humanists are toward creation is summed up by Isaac Asimov: "To those who are trained in science, creationism seems like a bad dream, a sudden reliving of a nightmare, a renewed march of an army of the night risen to challenge free thought and enlightenment."[5]

Carl Sagan states simply, "Evolution is a fact, not a theory."[6] Huxley claims, "The first point to make about Darwin's theory is that it is no longer a theory, but a fact. . . . Darwinianism has come of age so to speak. We are no longer having to bother about establishing the fact of evolution."[7] Antony Flew is scandalized by the notion that there was a time "unbelievably" when the Vatican questioned "the fact of the evolutionary origin of the species."[8]

These statements would not be quite so alarming if the Humanists were simply claiming that evolution within a species (microevolution) is a fact; unfortunately, each of these statements was made by an individual who believes that macroevolution, or the transmutation of species, is a scientific fact. Humanists are not just claiming that science has proved that dogs can change or "evolve" into faster or bigger breeds; rather, they are claiming that all dogs, indeed all mammals, evolved from reptiles, that reptiles evolved from amphibians, that amphibians evolved from fish, and so backward to the first speck of life. They wholeheartedly believe Darwin's conclusion that since microevolutionary changes occur among species (Darwin bred pigeons and saw such changes; dog and cattle breeders likewise see such changes), these changes can accumulate until macroevolution occurs.

However, macroevolution can only be embraced as a fact by those who have enough faith to deny all possibility of the supernatural. Science has never observed macroevolution, and there is no indication of such a series of "miracles" occurring in the fossil records. Therefore, the evolutionist must (just as the Christian does) "live by faith, not by sight" (1 Corinthians 5:7). In accord with this faith, Humanist biology clings dogmatically to a number of ideas that are not grounded in scientific fact. The following discussion will outline these ideas; the problems posed by them will be explained in the Christian Biology chapter and the Conclusion of this book.

SPONTANEOUS GENERATION

The first idea Humanist biology accepts is that life arose spontaneously from non-living matter by natural, random processes. Without this concept, Humanism would have to postulate a supernatural force to explain the existence of the first life form on earth. Any supernatural force would be in direct contradiction with Humanism's atheistic theology and naturalistic philosophy. Therefore, Humanists are left with the pre-scientific theory of spontaneous generation, a theory so fraught with difficulties that few scientists consider it science at all.

Faith in spontaneous generation is essential for the theory of evolution as described by the Humanist. Ironically, however, not even Charles Darwin was willing to postulate a theory that hinged on spontaneous generation. Rather, he wrote, "Probably all the organic beings which have ever lived on this earth have descended from some one primordial form, into which life was first breathed."[9] Darwin himself felt the need to rely on some supernatural force to explain the existence of life—but the Humanist cannot afford such a concession. The existence of the supernatural has disastrous consequences for the entire Secular Humanist worldview.

A Brief Look At: Charles Darwin (1809-1882)

1831: Receives theology degree from Cambridge University

1836: Completes five year stint as naturalist on the H.M.S. Beagle

1838: Reads Thomas Malthus's *Essay on the Principle of Population*

1855: Begins studying pigeon breeding and other forms of artificial selection

1858: Reads essay on *Theory of Natural Selection* by Alfred Russel Wallace

1859: Publishes *Origin of Species*

1872: Publishes *The Expression of the Emotions in Man and Animals*

1882: Allegedly experiences deathbed conversion to Christianity

NATURAL SELECTION

The second idea Humanists embrace in biology is natural selection. Natural selection is the mechanism proposed by Darwin that, through competition and other factors such as mutations, predators, geography, and time, naturally and randomly allows only those life forms best suited to survive to live and reproduce. By reproducing, slight variations emerge that ultimately make it possible for the molecule, cell, plant, or animal to literally self-create new molecules, cells, plants, and animals. Tied up in this theory are the notions of the "survival of the fittest" and the struggle for existence, which we will examine shortly. Carl Sagan insists that "Natural selection is a successful theory devised to explain the fact of evolution."[10]

Darwin relied on natural selection as the mechanism for his theory of evolution largely because he felt that it was something man had already observed artificially through breeding. When one breeds horses to create faster offspring, Darwin believed, one is artificially selecting a beneficial trait for that horse and therefore engaging in a microevolutionary process. Darwin was convinced that, given enough time, nature can use the process of selection to evolve all forms of life from the single original life form.

Indeed, Darwin believed that "natural selection is daily and hourly scrutinizing . . . every variation, even the slightest; rejecting that which is bad, preserving and adding up all that is good; silently and insensibly working. . . at the improvement of each organic being."[11] While a breeder purposely (i.e., not randomly) controls selection so that each generation of animal contains the best improvements, Darwin believed that random variations were responsible for such improvements in nature.

Since this is the most credible mechanism proposed to "drive" evolution, most Humanists accept it with the same blind faith exuded by Darwin.

STRUGGLE FOR EXISTENCE AND SURVIVAL

Inherent in the idea of natural selection is the notion that those life forms best equipped to survive will win the struggle for existence. This allegedly explains why life forms have become better equipped to survive as time passes.

Humanist biologists accept this concept, although they are usually careful about acknowledging it. Corliss Lamont, however, is not bashful: "The processes of natural selection and survival of the fittest, with the many mutations that occur over hundreds of millions of years, adequately account for the origin and development of the species."[12]

The reason most Humanists are more cautious than Lamont lies in the ethical implications of survival of the fittest: the only moral good becomes survival. The only value in the struggle is existence itself. Survival of the fittest is bloodthirsty; it cares not for the weak or the poor. As one would expect, both Hitler's Aryan policies and Engels' Marxism were based on this belief in survival of the fittest.

> **"Evolution is a fact, not a theory."**
>
> *Carl Sagan*

There is also another problem with survival of the fittest that the Humanists recognize. Asimov describes it this way: "In the first place, the phrase 'the survival of the fittest' is not an illuminating one. It implies that those who survive are the 'fittest,' but what is meant by 'fittest'? Why, those are 'fittest' who survive. This is an argument in a circle."[13] In other words, when you say "survival of the fittest," you really aren't saying anything of consequence. It is a tautology—an explanation that includes its own definition.

Obviously, the Humanist biologist would like to avoid discussing the struggle for existence whenever possible—but at the same time, he needs it to explain natural selection as a mechanism for evolution.

MUTATIONS AND ADAPTATIONS

Combining mutations with the theory of natural selection provides an explanation for adaptation, yet another theory that Humanists accept. Adaptation helps explain why life forms seem to have evolved specialized abilities that allow them to survive better in their particular niches in the environment.

Of course, in accepting adaptation as part of the mechanism of evolution, the Humanist must overlook (or explain away) all the apparently meaningless adaptations existing in our world. Darwin admits, "I did not formerly consider sufficiently the existence of structures which, as far as we can . . . judge, are neither beneficial nor injurious, and this I believe to be one of the greatest oversights as yet detected in my work."[14]

Huxley attempts to solve this problem for Darwin by explaining seemingly harmful or meaningless adaptations in such a way that they could rightly be labeled beneficial. His attempt becomes absurd, however, when he tries to describe schizophrenia as a useful adaptation. He claims that "genetic theory makes it plain that a clearly disadvantageous genetic character like this cannot persist in this frequency in a population unless it is balanced by some compensating advantage. In this case it appears that the advantage is that schizophrenic individuals are considerably less sensitive than normal persons to histamine, are much less prone to suffer from operative and wound shock, and do not suffer nearly so much from various allergies."[15] Huxley does not say whether he would rather be schizophrenic or suffer from allergies.

THE FOSSIL RECORD

The final plank on which the theory of evolution rests is the claim that the fossil record gives an accurate account of the process of transmutation of the species, or macroevolution. "Evolution is a fact," says Sagan, "amply demonstrated by the fossil record."[16] The fossil record is crucial for the evolutionist because it is the only means available to the scientist to observe steps in the evolutionary process. In Darwin's day, the actual evidence was missing. There was no fossil evidence that any of the major divisions of nature (fish, amphibians, reptiles, mammals) had been crossed gradually.

Without convincing evidence from fossils, the theory of evolution would have no basis for grounding itself in the scientific method and would be left in the realm of faith. Therefore, we find Julian Huxley stating, "Most of evolution is thus what we may call short-term diversification. But this kaleidoscopic change is shot through with a certain proportion of long-term diversification in the shape of the long-range trends revealed in fossils by the paleontologist . . ."[17] From this claim it would seem that the fossil record provides indisputable proof for macroevolution. This, however, is not the case—as will be demonstrated in the Christian Biology chapter.

PUNCTUATED EQUILIBRIUM

If the fossil record is the only means available for employing the scientific method to "observe" macroevolution, and if that record provides nothing observable that corresponds with the theory, then the evolutionist is left holding a groundless theory. This is intolerable for the Humanist—so a theory has been proposed that forces the fossil record to fit into the evolutionary mold. This theory is referred to as punctuated equilibrium. *Equilibrium* refers to the fact that species manifest a stubborn stability (stasis) in nature and *punctuated* refers to the dramatic changes deemed necessary to explain how the gaps are bridged in the fossil record between the major divisions in nature.

Chris McGowan, after admitting that the fossil record does not contain evidence of macroevolution, jumps to the conclusion that a theory that allows for evolution and gets around the dilemma presented by the fossil record must be the scientific solution: "New species probably evolve only when a segment of the population becomes isolated from the rest. Speciation occurs relatively rapidly, probably in a matter of only a few thousand years and possibly less."[18] That is, punctuated equilibrium claims that science cannot discover the links between species in the fossil record because the change from one species to another occurs too rapidly to leave accurate fossil documentation.

How does punctuated equilibrium mesh with the theory of evolution as presented by Darwin? Not as well as one might expect—in fact, it clashes directly with Darwin's ideas. He writes, "If it could be demonstrated that any complex organ existed, which could not possibly have been formed by numerous, successive, slight modifications, my theory would absolutely break down."[19] Apparently, some evolutionists are willing to "break down" Darwin's theory in an effort to make some form of evolution fit the facts.

CONCLUSION

Secular Humanist biology rests its case for evolution on six specific planks: spontaneous generation, natural selection, struggle for existence, beneficial mutations, adaptations, and the observable nature of evolution through the fossil record. In recent times, because the fossil record has only hindered their attempts to prove the "fact" that macroevolution occurs, some evolutionists have been forced to abandon the most important parts of Darwin's theory and postulate punctuated equilibrium. In the context of every idea, the Humanist is forced to rely on the extrapolation of the observable through enormously long periods of time to account for apparent contradictions and to create miraculously varied forms of life.

Humanism relies on evolution for much more than a theory about the origin of life. The Secular Humanist trusts evolution as a "fact" worthy of use as a foundation for many of his ideas about theology, philosophy, ethics, and even his social and political ideals for the future. In truth, the Humanist considers evolution the correct foundation for every individual's worldview and believes that the world can be properly understood only from this perspective. For this reason, Humanists encourage teaching evolution as "fact" throughout our educational system—thereby relegating the supernatural, especially God, to the world of literary mythology. The Humanist does not just expect evolution to be taught as a theory in the biology classroom, but

Biology
At A Glance

Secular Humanist

Darwinian Evolution

rather believes, in the words of Julian Huxley, that "it is essential for evolution to become the central core of any educational system, because it is evolution, in the broad sense, that links inorganic nature with life, and the stars with earth, and matter with mind, and animals with man. Human history is a continuation of biological evolution in a different form."[20]

CHAPTER 16

Marxist/Leninist Biology

"Darwin's [Origin of Species] is very important and provides me with the basis in natural science for the class struggle in history."[1]

—Karl Marx

INTRODUCTION

While Karl Marx and Frederick Engels were developing their communistic worldview, Charles Darwin was presenting his theory of evolution and creating quite a stir among the intellectuals of the nineteenth century. Many people perceived Darwin's theory as providing the foundation for an entirely materialistic perspective on life. Marx and Engels were among those who recognized the usefulness of Darwin's theory as just such a foundation.

In a letter to Engels, Marx writes, "During . . . the past four weeks I have read all sorts of things. Among others Darwin's work on Natural Selection. And though it is written in the crude English style, this is the book which contains the basis in natural science for our view."[2] John Hoffman tells us that Marx so admired Darwin's work that he "sent Darwin a complimentary copy of Volume I of *Capital* and tried unsuccessfully to dedicate Volume II to him."[3]

DARWIN, MARX, AND SOCIETY

Marx believed that Darwin's evolutionary theory could be extended naturally to answer questions about human society. He felt that society, like life itself, had gone through an evolutionary process and must continue to undergo such a process until a classless society evolved. Marx integrated this notion of evolution into his worldview, writing, "Darwin has interested us in the history of Nature's technology, i.e. in the formation of the organs of plants and animals, which organs serve as instruments of production for sustaining life. Does not the history of the productive organs of man, of organs that are the material basis of all social organization, deserve equal attention?"[4] Engels makes the claim even more straightforward: "Just as Darwin discovered the law of evolution in organic nature, so Marx discovered the law of evolution in human history."[5]

This claim has been reaffirmed throughout Marxism's development. V.I. Lenin echoes the founding fathers, stressing the scientific nature of their theory: "Just as Darwin put an end to the view of animal and plant species being unconnected, fortuitous, 'created by God' and immutable, and was the first to put biology on an absolutely scientific basis . . . so Marx . . . was the first to put sociology on a scientific basis . . ."[6]

Virtually all Marxists understand evolution to be an essential pillar in their worldview. This is due largely to the fact that it complements their social and historical theory so well; but of course, there is another, more important reason.

DARWIN AND TELEOLOGY

Just as the notion of God destroys the Humanist theology, the slightest hint of God is directly opposed to the Marxist theology. Atheism is the very core of Marxist theory—their worldview is only consistent and coherent without God in the picture. As soon as one acknowledges the existence of God, or even of the supernatural, Marxism crumbles. Therefore, Marx and his followers eagerly embraced a theory that makes God unnecessary for the origin of life.

Marx proclaims that *Origin of Species* dealt the "death-blow . . . to 'teleology.'"[7] F.V. Konstantinov, in *The Fundamentals of Marxist-Leninist Philosophy*, echoes him: "Darwin's theory of evolution is the third great scientific discovery that took place in the middle of the 19th century. Darwin put an end to the notion of the species of animals and plants as 'divine creations', not connected with anything else, providential and immutable, and thus laid the foundation of theoretical biology."[8]

This "great scientific discovery" is crucial. Without the theory of evolution, the design of the universe could be explained only by postulating a rational, purposeful, powerful God, and this is inconceivable for the Marxist. There is no room for miracles in a materialistic worldview, so Marxism must accept evolution unreservedly.

SPONTANEOUS GENERATION

The aspect of evolutionary theory that is most dear to Marxists, of course, is spontaneous generation. To completely abandon God, one must fervently believe in the doctrine that life, at some point, arose from non-life.

Marx uses spontaneous generation to back both his philosophy and his theology, stating, "the idea of the creation of the earth has received a severe blow . . . from the science which portrays the . . . development of the earth as a process of spontaneous generation;" then he adds, "*generatio aequivoca* [spontaneous generation] is the only practical refutation of the theory of creation."[9]

Marxists continue to embrace spontaneous generation long after Marx and Engels. A.I. Oparin, a Marxist scientist, "was the first to enunciate the theory of abiogenic origin of life."[10] Oparin claimed, "We have every reason to believe that sooner or later, we shall be able practically to demonstrate that life is nothing else but a special form of existence of matter."[11]

Even modern Marxist textbooks embrace the theory of spontaneous generation. M.V. Volkenshtein, author of *Biophysics,* declares that Oparin "presumed that the origin of life had been preceded by chemical evolution. . . . Today these ideas are widely accepted."[12]

It is interesting to note just what kind of proof it would take to convince the "scientific" Marxist that spontaneous generation is unscientific. Louis Pasteur (1822-1895) disproved the theory of spontaneous generation, but apparently not to Engels' satisfaction: "Pasteur's attempts in this direction are useless; for those who believe in this possibility [of spontaneous generation] he will never be able to prove their impossibility by these experiments alone. . . ."[13] In fact, the impossibility of spontaneous generation can never be proven to one like Engels, since proving the impossibility of an event in one situation does not preclude the possibility of that event under any given situation. The key phrase from Engels, of course, is "for those who believe;" Engels has faith in the possibility of spontaneous generation occurring sometime, somewhere, and his faith will always shield him from proofs of impossibility—scientific or not.

DARWIN AND DIALECTICS

Marxists' faith in spontaneous generation has not wavered for more than a century. But Marxist faith in Darwin's specific version of evolutionary theory has faltered considerably since Marx and Engels first embraced it.

Marx writes, "You will see from the conclusion of my third chapter . . . that in the text I regard the law Hegel discovered . . . as holding good both in history and natural science."[14] But if nature is dialectical and Darwin's notion about the mechanism employed by nature to create species is correct, then Darwin's theory must be dialectical. This, however, does not prove to be the case.

Darwin's theory of evolution appeared dialectical to early Marxists for the specific reason that it portrays development as a process. Engels believed that Darwin's "new outlook on nature was complete in its main features; all rigidity was dissolved, all fixity dissipated, all particularity that had been regarded as eternal became transient, the whole of nature was shown as moving in eternal flux and cyclical course."[15] This eternal flux is important for the Marxist worldview, for as Engels says, "The world is not to be comprehended as a complex of ready-made things, but as a complex of processes."[16]

> **Punctuated equilibrium ... speaks the language of dialectical materialism. It speaks the language of revolution within evolution.**

Another reason Darwin's theory seemed to reinforce dialectics was that it called for the evolution of the simple to the more complex. Marxist dialectics states that process is always spiraling upward—that the synthesis is always a more advanced stage than the previous thesis. Apparently, Darwin's theory of natural selection calls for the same thing—more advanced species better suited to live in their environment, nature accumulating the good and disposing of the bad.

At first glance, then, Darwin's theory appears to fit perfectly with Marx's notions about dialectics. Closer inspection, however, shows otherwise. Lenin hints at a problem when he places Marx's theories separate from and above Darwin's, claiming, "Still, this idea, as formulated by Marx and Engels on the basis of Hegel's philosophy, is far more comprehensive and far richer in content than the current idea of [Darwinian] evolution is."[17] Lenin feels that there is a difference between Darwinian evolution and the dialectic applied to nature.

PUNCTUATED EQUILIBRIUM

Lenin is right. When examined closely, Darwinian evolution actually works contrary to the dialectical method. According to dialectical materialism, whenever thesis and antithesis clash, the new synthesis created occurs rapidly, in the form of a jump, rather than in the form of a long, gradual process. Thus, according to this view, both evolution and revolution are necessary in the social sphere to move from a capitalist society to a classless society; the change must occur rapidly, as did the overthrow of the Russian government. When thesis (bourgeoisie) and antithesis (proletariat) clash (through revolution), the resulting synthesis is a necessary leap resulting from the nature and flow of the dialectic. Darwin's slow, gradual natural selection theory does not fit well with the Marxist requirements of progress—either natural or social.

Darwin's theory emphasized gradual progress *as opposed to* sudden "leaps in being." Early in the twentieth century, Marxists acknowledged this difference, and abandoned Darwin's theory. But they did not abandon evolution. Plekhanov espouses the new Marxist attitude toward Darwin when he says, "Many people confound dialectic with the theory of evolution. Dialectic is, in fact, a theory of evolution. But it differs profoundly from the vulgar [Darwinian] theory of evolution, which is based substantially upon the principle that neither in nature nor in history do sudden changes occur, and that all changes taking place in the world occur gradually."[18]

Marxists expect evolution to work according to the dialectic: when thesis (a species) and antithesis (some aspect of the environment) clash, the synthesis (a new species) occurs rapidly. In 1972, an evolutionary theory that better fit the dialectical process was postulated: punctuated equilibrium.

Punctuated equilibrium contains room for jumps and rapid change. It speaks the language of dialectical materialism. It speaks the language of revolution within evolution.

This evolutionary model sees evolution "as an episodic process occurring in fits and starts interspaced with long periods of stasis [i.e., lack of change]."[19] New species are said to rise rapidly "in small peripherally isolated populations." Instead of the Darwinian gradualist model of evolution in which new species occur slowly over long periods of time, punctuated equilibrium calls for long periods marked by little change, and then short, isolated periods of rapid change. Americans most closely associated with this theory are Stephen Jay Gould, Richard Levins, Richard Lewontin, Niles Eldredge, and Steven Stanley.

Both Gould and Eldredge admit that their theory of punctuated equilibrium coincides with the Marxist interpretation of biology:

Alternative conceptions of change have respectable pedigrees in philosophy. Hegel's dialectical laws, translated into a materialist context, have become the official "state philosophy" of many socialist nations. These laws of change are explicitly punctuational, as befits a theory of revolutionary transformation in human society.

In light of this official philosophy, it is not at all surprising that a punctuational view of speciation, much like our own, but devoid (so far as we can tell) of references to synthetic evolutionary theory and the allopatric model, has long been favored by many Russian paleontologists. It may also not be irrelevant to our personal preferences that one of us [Gould] learned his Marxism, literally, at his daddy's knee.[20]

Marxists are pleased with the theory of punctuated equilibrium and how it affirms their worldview. Volkenshtein actually uses the fossil record as proof for the veracity of Marxist biology, claiming, "Whereas it was believed earlier that evolution occurs slowly, by way of gradual accumulation of small changes, at present biology takes into account a multitude of facts indicating that macroevolution occurred in a jumpwise manner and was not reduced to microevolution. The absence of transient forms in the paleontological records points, in a number of cases, not to a deficiency but to the absence of such forms. Small changes are often not accumulated at all."[21] In other words, since evolution across species is not observable in the fossil record, and since the theory of evolution cannot be wrong, the theory of the mechanism of evolution must be revised to fit the facts. Volkenshtein cites other "proof" for punctuated equilibrium as well, pointing out that "No gradual transition can take place between feathers and hair, etc."[22] Creationists have cited these facts for years in criticizing evolutionary theory, but they take on new importance for Marxists when they can be used as "proof" for a new theory of evolution better designed to account for the lack of real evolutionary proof in the fossil record!

Marxists are delighted that punctuated equilibrium is now considered a viable scientific explanation for the origin of the species, since it is more closely aligned with Marxist dialectics. However, Marxists will embrace virtually any idea about evolution as long as it fits their worldview and disallows the existence of anything supernatural. This can be demonstrated by examining an episode from the era after Marxists became disappointed with the gradualism of Darwin, and before punctuated equilibrium theory was postulated.

LYSENKO AND MENDEL

During World War II, Darwin's notions about struggle for existence and survival of the fittest were unpopular with Marxists. So Marxists attempted to "customize" evolutionary theory so that it better fit the dialectic.

This effort was spearheaded by T.D. Lysenko, the leading Soviet biologist from the early 1930s into the 1950s, and President of the Academy of Sciences during the height of his prestige (1936-45). Lysenko claimed that Gregor Mendel's discoveries about genetics were inconclusive, declaring, "it is time to eliminate Mendelism in all its varieties from all courses and textbooks."[23] With full support from the Marxist government (indeed, most Soviet biologists who disagreed with Lysenko either repented or met untimely deaths), Lysenko began to preach a biology strictly denying Mendel's genetics: "[A]ny little particle, figuratively speaking, any granule, any droplet of a living body, once it is alive, necessarily possesses the property of heredity . . ."[24]

Naturally, Lysenko's notions about heredity eventually led him to embrace Lamarckism, a theory that states that acquired characteristics can be passed from one generation to the next through heredity. He did not publicly admit his Lamarckian views, however, until it came to light that Stalin, years earlier, had supported neo-Lamarckism. Once it became clear that both Stalin and Lysenko supported some form of Lamarckism, Marxist biology had no choice but to embrace this theory of acquired

Biology
At A Glance

Secular Humanist	Marxist/Lennist
Darwinian Evolution	**Darwinian/ Punctuated Evolution**

characteristics unreservedly. And on the surface, Lamarckism did seem to complement Marxist dialectics better, since it called for a more consistently progressive view of evolution than Darwin's theory.

Unfortunately for Lysenko and the Marxists, they could only hide their heads in the sand so long before they had to face two facts the rest of the world had accepted long ago: Mendel's ideas about genetics were correct, and Lamarck's idea of acquired characteristics was absurd.

Conclusion

The Marxist interpretation of evolution has undergone a number of changes since Marx first embraced Darwin's theory. These changes demonstrate the willingness of Marxists to revise and distort the theory of evolution in an effort to make it more compatible with their dialectic. Marxism will interpret the theory of evolution in any way that supports the dialectic and still allows them to retain the use of the theory as a "scientific" answer to anyone suggesting the existence of the supernatural.

Regardless of how scientific or unscientific the theory of evolution is, we can be certain of one thing: Marxist biology will consistently declare it as factual and grounded in science. As we have seen, evolution provides a basis for both Marxist theology and Marxist philosophy, and without this foundation, Marxists are unable to explain the teleology of our universe and the phenomena of the human mind. As Engels says, "in our evolutionary conception of the universe, there is absolutely no room for either a creator or a ruler."[25] But without evolution, there can be no avoiding a Creator. And the Marxist must avoid a Creator at all costs.

CHAPTER 17

Cosmic Humanist Biology

"Evolution is a light illuminating all facts, a curve that all lines must follow....
Man discovers that he is nothing else than evolution become conscious of itself."[1]
—Pierre Teilhard de Chardin

INTRODUCTION

It would seem that a worldview based on pantheism would embrace a creationist perspective of biology, viewing God as the power that brought all life forms into existence in a single, creative act. Surprisingly, the Cosmic Humanist instead believes that God acted as the Ultimate Cause of the universe and then allowed evolution to direct it to its present state.

Cosmic Humanists embrace evolutionary theory because evolution provides the best mechanism for ushering in a New Age. While a standard creationist view of biology seems to contradict the concept that man will eventually progress toward a heaven on earth (especially in light of the Laws of Thermodynamics), evolution provides just such a framework. Cosmic Humanists need reassurance that progress will occur because of their belief that mankind is moving upward toward an age of higher consciousness. The "science" of evolution provides the guarantee that all humanity will one day achieve this consciousness.

This union with the God-force will be collective—that is, man will achieve unity with his fellow man and everything else, because everything is God. Collective consciousness means that the "ultimate end of the individual is to expand into the universal oneness, which really means that the individual disappears as a separate person."[2] Because the Cosmic Humanist believes this, he postulates an evolutionary theory that allows for not only individual but also collective development. Marilyn Ferguson writes, "The proven plasticity of the human brain and human awareness offers the possibility that *individual evolution* may lead to *collective evolution*. When one person has unlocked a new capacity its existence is suddenly evident to others, who may then develop the same capacity."[3]

Not every individual in the world will evolve at an even rate toward higher consciousness; rather, when enough people have achieved higher consciousness, other unenlightened individuals will be naturally absorbed (or evolved) into the collective consciousness. Thus, not everyone in the world must embrace the New Age movement before it can become a reality—dedicated Cosmic Humanists can simply act as the catalyst for an evolutionary leap into utopia.

> "The final appearance of the Christ will not be a man in the air before whom all must kneel. The final appearance of the Christ will be an evolutionary event."
>
> John White

LEAPS IN BEING

Some New Age thinkers recognize that this view of evolution best fits the specific hypothesis known as *punctuated equilibrium*. When one speaks in terms of leaps or shifts, one is abandoning Darwinian theory and embracing the "hopeful monster" hypothesis. David Spangler, for example, uses the terminology of punctuated equilibrium when he states, "In this [evolutionary] context, civilizations, like individuals, go through profound changes from time to time which represent discontinuities; that is, a jump or shift is made from one evolutionary condition to another. The New Age is such a shift."[4] Cosmic Humanists believe an elite "enlightened" element of the human race will "jump" into this New Age as an evolutionary leap and drag the rest of humanity with it.

Ferguson agrees that the New Age "requires a mechanism for biological change more powerful than chance mutation." What is biologically necessary is the "possibility of rapid evolution in our own time, when the equilibrium of the species is punctuated by stress. Stress in modern society is experienced at the frontiers of our psychological rather than our geographical limits."[5] Instead of further human physical evolution determined by geography, environment, and natural selection, Cosmic Humanists advocate psychological evolution. This evolution guides mankind to a higher social order, "a New One-World Order, all to occur sometime before the year 2000."[6]

A Brief Look At: Pierre Teilhard de Chardin (1881-1955)

1911: Ordained Jesuit priest

1912: Assigned research position at Museum of Natural History in Paris

1915: Begins service as a priest and medic in World War I

1923: Travels to China to study geology and botany

1924: Returns to Paris to teach at Institut Catholique

1926: Removed from Jesuit Order because of his unorthodox beliefs

1947: Finishes writing *The Phenomenon of Man*

1951: Travels to South Africa to study *Australopithecines*

THE NEXT EVOLUTIONARY STEP

And what will man be like after the evolutionary leap into the New Age has occurred? Armand Biteaux explains, "Every man is an individual Christ; this is the teaching for the New Age. . . . Everyone will receive the benefit of this step in human evolution."[7] Every man will achieve the higher consciousness or godhood. "The final appearance of the Christ will not be a man in the air before whom all must kneel," says John White. "The final appearance of the Christ will be an evolutionary event. It will be the disappearance of egocentric, subhuman man and the ascension of God-centered Man. A new race, a new species, will inhabit the Earth—people who collectively have the stature of consciousness that Jesus had."[8] Once this collective higher consciousness is achieved, every human will be perfectly at one with every other human in collective godhood.

Much of the basis for this New Age belief rests on the writings of one man, Pierre Teilhard de Chardin. A paleontologist and a heretic, de Chardin worked to reconcile Christianity and evolution. He accomplished this reconciliation by substituting pantheism for Christianity. De Chardin believed that "A very real 'pantheism' if you like, but an absolutely legitimate pantheism."[9]

This leap into "a very real pantheism" may mean a leap into a unified God-consciousness, or it may mean something even better. Peter Russell believes,

> Evolutionary trends and patterns . . . suggest a further possibility: the emergence of something beyond a single planetary consciousness or Supermind: a completely new level of evolution, as different from consciousness as consciousness is from life, and life is from matter.[10]

Realistically, however, most Cosmic Humanists are willing to settle for achieving divinity.

Biology At A Glance

Secular Humanism	Marxist/Leninist	Cosmic Humanist
Darwinian Evolution	Darwinian/ Punctuated Evolution	Darwinian/ Punctuated Evolution

CONCLUSION

Biology provides a generous guarantee for the Cosmic Humanist. Man is guaranteed to make "leaps in being" that will ultimately lead the whole human race—and the universe—to godhood. The Garden of Eden is not a real place in the past where Adam and Eve committed the original sin; rather, the Garden is in our present and our future. Joseph Campbell teaches that we are living in Eden today, and evolution simply refers to our increasing awareness that we reside in paradise.

This provides a great comfort for the Cosmic Humanist, largely because it promises a shared future divinity. Further, it solves sin, by denying the reality of any Fall or the inherent sinfulness of man.

Unfortunately, it also paints a pretty shoddy picture of paradise. If we're actually in paradise right now, and evolving more awareness of it all the time, why has the 20th century been racked by so many wars and so much pain? How can the Garden of Eden be so barren? Campbell can only respond, "That is the way it feels, but this is it, this is Eden." Humans need, says Campbell, to "see not the world of solid things but a world of radiance."[11]

CHAPTER 18

Biblical Christian Biology

"And God created great whales, and every living creature that moveth, which the waters brought forth abundantly, after their kind, and every winged fowl after his kind."

—Genesis 1:21

INTRODUCTION

Perhaps no other aspect of Christianity has troubled believers more in the last century than the question of origins. Because many biologists treat evolution as a scientific fact, Christians have struggled to reconcile their faith in the Bible with the "fact" that man and all living things evolved from a single speck of life.

This reconciliation is impossible from a rational perspective. Christians who believe that God created the first glimmer of life on earth and then directed its evolution to generate man (the belief known as theistic evolution) must take substantial liberties in interpreting the Bible, and they face most of the same arguments Christians use against atheistic evolution.

Jesus Christ declares in Mark 10:6, "But at the beginning of creation God 'made them male and female.' " Theistic evolutionists have, through semantic acrobatics, managed to interpret this verse and others like it so that they appear to support the evolutionary position. Theistic evolutionists contend that the term creation simply means that God created the first spark of life and then directed His creation through the vehicle of evolution.

Thus, some Christians believe that the Bible does not necessarily deny evolutionary theory as an explanation for origins. This may appear to be a tenable position when discussing only verses concerned strictly with the question of origins; however, when one examines the entire message of the Bible, the doctrine of theistic evolution severely undermines the Christian understanding of God and man's place in His universe.

For example, while it is true that God is capable of anything that is logically

A Brief Look At: James Orr (1844-1913)

1870: Receives his M.A. from the University of Glasgow

1874: Serves as minister of East Bank United Presbyterian Church for 17 years

1874: Hired as professor of church history by the Theological College of the UPC

1891: Delivers *The Christian View of God and the World* as a series of Kerr lectures

1901: Hired as professor of apologetics and theology by Glasgow College

1905: Publishes *God's Image in Man*

1908: Publishes *The Resurrection of Jesus*

possible, so that He could have used evolution to generate all species, why would He employ such an inefficient (and often totally ineffective) mechanism? If God designed the world to operate according to specific natural laws requiring minimal routine interference, why would He use an evolutionary mechanism that would require His constant meddling with the development of life? Further, such a mechanism seems an especially cruel method for creating man. As Jacques Monod notes, natural selection is the "blindest and most cruel way of evolving new species."[1]

More important, if evolution is true, then the story of the Garden of Eden and original sin must be viewed as nothing more than allegory, a view that undermines the significance of Christ's sinless life and sacrificial death on the cross. Why? Because the Bible presents Jesus as analogous to Adam. The condemnation and corruption brought on us by Adam's sin are the counterparts of the justification and sanctification made possible for us by Christ's righteousness and death (Romans 5:12-19). If Adam was not a historical individual, and if his fall into sin was not historical, then the Biblical doctrines of sin and of Christ's atonement for it collapse.

Of course, this conclusion is unacceptable for the Christian. Thus, it is our contention that the proper Christian worldview requires a belief in the Creator as He is literally portrayed in Genesis.

For a Christian to have believed in creation forty, thirty, or even twenty years ago might have seemed radical because, until recently, evolution appeared to be unassailable scientifically. Understandably, many Christians turned to theistic evolution as the only means of reconciling their reason with their faith. Today, however, the scientific objections to evolution are so strong that Christians who wish to integrate faith and reason would do well to abandon evolution as a rational explanation for the origin of species.

CHRISTIANITY AND SCIENCE

Modern science's roots are grounded in a Christian view of the world. This is not surprising, since science is based on the assumption that the universe is orderly and can be expected to act according to specific, discoverable laws. An ordered, lawful universe would seem to be the effect of an intelligent Cause, which was precisely the belief of many early scientists.

Renowned philosopher and historian of science Stanley L. Jaki specifies that "from Copernicus to Newton it was not deism but Christian theism that served as a principal factor helping the scientific enterprise reach self-sustaining maturity."[2]

Inherent to this early scientific dependence on the orderliness of the world was the belief that the world was ordered by a Divine creator. As Langdon Gilkey points out, "The religious idea of a transcendent creator actually made possible rather than hindered the progress of the scientific understanding of the natural order."[3] Modern evolutionists have lost sight of this order. According to their perspective, all life is the result of chance processes.

This problem of perspective causes many evolutionists to lose sight of the marvels that abound in our universe. Whereas earlier scientists accepted Christianity and therefore were able to recognize the order of their world as a reflection of the Creator's omniscience, evolutionists must now view everything as fortunate accidents (with emphasis on chance instead of cosmos).

153

Creationists understand that the vast order and design in our world point unequivocally toward a Designer and Creator. Thus, creationists use teleology—design in nature—to support creationism.

TELEOLOGY SUPPORTS CREATIONISM

William Paley presented the most famous version of the teleological argument—that of the watch and the watchmaker. Since the nineteenth century, however, it has been widely believed that Paley's argument for a universal Designer was effectively answered by the philosopher David Hume. Hume claimed that Paley's analogy between living things and machines was unfounded and unrealistic and, therefore, that life does not need an intelligent designer, as machines do. Hume's reply to Paley caused many people to discredit the teleological argument in all its forms, which also contributed to science's willingness to ignore design in nature and suggest that all life arose by chance.

But science can no longer ignore teleology. Indeed, science has recently discovered that life really is analogous to the most complex of machines, thereby reinforcing Paley's argument. Michael Denton, a molecular biologist, states, "Paley was not only right in asserting the existence of an analogy between life and machines, but was also remarkably prophetic in guessing that the technological ingenuity realized in living systems is vastly in excess of anything yet accomplished by man."[4]

Science is re-learning an old lesson: the more one discovers about the universe, the more one discovers design. Many notable scientists inadvertently support Paley nowadays as they describe the design in nature revealed to them through science. Physicist Paul Davies, who does not profess to be a Christian, supports teleology—and ultimately creationism—when he says, "Every advance in fundamental physics seems to uncover yet another facet of order."[5]

At first, this seems to be an obvious conclusion of little significance. But strict evolution demands chance rather than a Law-maker as the guiding force. When a world-class non-Christian scientist like Davies declares that the universe cannot be viewed as a product of chance, it is a severe blow to materialistic evolutionary theory.

When one truly understands the ordered complexity of life, it is hard to imagine chance producing even bacterial cells, which are the simplest living systems. Denton explains: "Although the tiniest bacterial cells are incredibly small, weighing less than 10(-12) gms, each is in effect a veritable micro-miniaturized factory containing thousands of exquisitely designed pieces of intricate molecular machinery, made up altogether of one hundred thousand million atoms, far more complicated than any machine built by man and absolutely without parallel in the non-living world."[6]

As Paley pointed out almost two centuries ago, this type of design requires an intelligent mind—chance processes cannot produce such intricate order.

DNA: CREATED OR EVOLVED?

The existence and properties of deoxyribonucleic acid (DNA) support creationism both through the teleological argument and by demonstrating evolutionary theory's inability to explain crucial aspects of life. DNA contains the genetic information code and is a crucial part of all living matter, yet evolutionary theory is powerless to explain how it came into existence, let alone why DNA evinces such phenomenal design.

This teleological quality of DNA is overwhelming. Charles Thaxton believes DNA is the most powerful indicator of intelligent design: "Is there any basis in experience for an intelligent cause for the origin of life? Yes! It is the analogy between the base sequences in DNA and alphabetical letter sequences in a book. . . . there is a structural identity between the DNA code and a written language."[7] That is, we can assume DNA is the product of intelligence because it is analogous to human languages, which are, without exception, products of intelligent minds.

Even excluding the teleological nature of DNA, its very existence severely undermines evolutionary theory. Walter Brown points out, "DNA can only be produced with the help of at least 20 different types of proteins. But these proteins can only be produced at the direction of DNA. Since each requires the other, a satisfactory explanation for the origin of one must also explain the origin of the other. Apparently, this entire manufacturing system came into existence simultaneously. This implies Creation."[8]

DNA obviously presents one of the most pressing problems for evolutionists. It is an intensely complex substance, yet it must be present in the very earliest forms of

The peculiar "double helix" design of the deoxyribonucleic acid (DNA) molecule was discovered by two scientists, Francis Crick and James Watson, in 1953. This design explains how DNA molecules replicate themselves when cells divide.

Snapshots In Time

Man's understanding of genetics takes profound strides as scientists discover more about DNA. Each new discovery, it seems, makes it less and less likely that such a complex system could have evolved by chance.

In the 20th century, scientists discovered that, even though the chemical make–up of DNA is identical in every organism, the base sequences of DNA vary from organism to organism. The unique physical aspects of every living being are "coded" within the tiny molecules—and what a code it is! The genetic information in each cell of the human body is equivalent to a library of about 4,000 books. Such intricate design makes a weighty case for a Designer. Percival Davis and Dean H. Kenyon write, "Since both written language and DNA have that telltale property of information carried along by specific sequences of 'words,' and since intelligence is known to produce written language, why isn't it reasonable to identify the cause of the DNA's information as an intelligence too?"

living matter. How can evolutionists explain this?

They cannot. In fact, no one has shown how life itself could arise from non-living chemicals, let alone such a complex aspect of life as DNA. This inability to demonstrate spontaneous generation (the development of life from non-life) is another key weakness in evolutionary theory.

SPONTANEOUS GENERATION

For the atheistic evolutionist's belief to be rational, the major problem biology must overcome is the impossibility of spontaneous generation. In order for life to have arisen due to random processes, at some point in time non-living matter must have come alive.

Many evolutionists point to the work of Alexander Oparin in defense of spontaneous generation. Oparin described a theory that supposedly allowed for chance processes working in a prebiotic soup to give rise to life. Unfortunately for evolutionists, this theory is rapidly being refuted by science.

In fact, the further science progresses, the more unlikely spontaneous generation seems. Dean Kenyon, a biochemist and a former chemical evolutionist, now writes, "When all relevant lines of evidence are taken into account, and all the problems squarely faced, I think we must conclude that life owes its inception to a source outside of nature."[9] He bases this conclusion on four premises: (1) the impossibility of the spontaneous origin of genetic information, (2) the fact that most attempts to duplicate the conditions necessary for chemical evolution yield non-biological material, (3) the unfounded nature of the belief (necessary for the chemical evolutionist) that prebiotic conditions encouraged a trend toward the formation of L amino acids, and (4) the geochemical evidence that O2 existed in significant amounts in the Earth's early atmosphere (organic compounds decompose when O2 is present).

> **From Copernicus to Newton it was not deism but Christian theism that served as a principal factor helping the scientific enterprise reach self–sustaining maturity.**

Brown also believes the existence of O2 creates an insurmountable problem for chemical evolutionists: "If the earth, early in its alleged evolution, had oxygen in its atmosphere, the chemicals needed for life to begin would have been removed by oxidation. But if there had been no oxygen, then there would have been no ozone in the upper atmosphere. Without this ozone, life would be quickly destroyed by the sun's ultraviolet radiation."[10] Ozone and life, therefore, must have originated simultaneously—at the time of creation.

THE SECOND LAW OF THERMODYNAMICS

In order to understand the clash between evolution and the second law of thermodynamics, we must first understand a few of the implications of the second law. A.E. Wilder-Smith explains, "The second law of thermodynamics states that, although the total energy in the cosmos remains constant, the amount of energy available to do useful work is always getting smaller."[11]

This law has important implications regarding the effect of time on the orderliness of the universe. While the evolutionist calls for the universe to grow more orderly as evolution progresses, the second law of thermodynamics assures us that order tends to disintegrate into disorder. Wilder-Smith puts the contrast clearly: "The theory of evolution teaches, when all the frills are removed, just the opposite to this state of affairs demanded by the second law of thermodynamics."[12]

The second law of thermodynamics doesn't just contradict evolution, either—it also reinforces the creationist explanation of man's origins. First, it suggests that the universe had a beginning. "If the entire universe is an isolated system, then, according to the Second Law of Thermodynamics," says Brown, "the energy in the universe that is available for useful work has always been decreasing. However, as one goes back in time, the amount of energy available for useful work would eventually exceed the total energy in the universe that, according to the First Law of Thermodynamics, remains constant. This is an impossible condition. Therefore, it implies that the universe had a beginning."[13]

Second, it suggests that the universe began as a highly ordered system. Wilder-Smith says, "The second law of thermodynamics seems thus to describe the whole situation of our present material world perfectly and the Bible very clearly confirms this description. For example, Romans 8:22-23 teaches us that the whole creation is subjected to 'vanity' or to destruction. Everything tends to go downhill to chaos and destruction as things stand today."[14]

The creationist position, then, is more in sync with science than evolutionary theory. This becomes even more obvious when one considers genetics.

THE GENE POOL AND THE LIMITS TO CHANGE

Evolutionists believe that no breeding limits exist, since life-forms must ultimately break these "species barriers" to create new species. Indeed, evolutionists see beneficial mutations as breaking all barriers to change, since these mutations supposedly can produce a vast array of structures, even a human eye, given enough time.

Unfortunately for evolutionists, however, science simply has not been able to demonstrate that any mutations break these limits to change. Pierre Paul Grasse, after studying mutations in bacteria and viruses, concludes, "What is the use of their unceasing mutations if they do not change? In sum, the mutations of bacteria and viruses are merely hereditary fluctuations around a median position; a swing to the right, a swing to the left, but no final evolutionary effect."[15]

If indeed such limits exist, then evolution is a meaningless explanation. If a species can only evolve so far before it hits a barrier and is forced to remain the same species, then no macroevolution occurs. This notion of the gene pool limiting the possible variation of species has troubled a great number of evolutionists, including Alfred Russell Wallace, one of the founders of the theory of natural selection. Wallace grew to doubt his theory later in life, largely because he became aware of Gregor Mendel's genetic laws, and could not reconcile the apparent limits to change with evolution's need for boundless development.

Incredibly, Edward Deevey, Jr. also recognizes these limitations, and yet remains an evolutionist: "Some remarkable things have been done by crossbreeding and selection inside the species barrier, or within a larger circle of closely related species, such as the wheats. But wheat is still wheat, and not, for instance, grapefruit; and we can no more grow wings on pigs than hens can make cylindrical eggs."[16]

How can Deevey remain an evolutionist in the face of such evidence? How can one believe in virtually unlimited change when limits abound within species? Rationally, one cannot. The creationist believes the evolutionary position is opposed to reason, and therefore rejects it.

It would seem that the case against evolutionists and in favor of creationism is quite formidable—indeed, retreat appears to be the only option available to the evolutionist. Incredibly, this conclusion seems justifiable even without reference to what many consider the most powerful refutation of evolutionary theory: the gaps in the fossil record and the absence of transitional forms. A brief examination of this evidence should leave few doubts as to the bankruptcy of evolutionary theory.

FOSSIL GAPS AND INTERMEDIATE FORMS

So far each of our arguments has focused on whether evolution is theoretically possible. Now we turn to the question of whether the empirical evidence suggests that it happened.

Over one hundred years ago, Darwin wrote, "The geological record is extremely imperfect and this fact will to a large extent explain why we do not find intermediate varieties, connecting together all the extinct and existing forms of life by the finest graduated steps. He who rejects these views on the nature of the geological record, will rightly reject my whole theory."[17] When Darwin made this claim, he was correct in asserting that the geological record, as scientists knew it then, was imperfect. A century later, it is safe to say that the geological record has been thoroughly scrutinized. And rather than confirming Darwin's theories, the fossils condemn them.

One reason the fossil record condemns evolutionary theory is that many complex life forms appear in the very earliest rocks without any indication of forms from which they could have evolved. Creatures without ancestors cannot help but imply special creation. As Brown says, "The evolutionary tree has no trunk."[18]

This explosion of complex life is not the only way in which the fossil record condemns evolution. The lack of fossils supporting the transitional phases between species is perhaps the single most embarrassing topic for evolutionists. And yet, this absence of transitional fossils is undeniable.

> **The lack of fossils supporting the transitional phases between species is perhaps the single most embarrassing topic for evolutionists.**

This fact is grudgingly recognized by leading evolutionists. David Raup, a geologist, admits, "The record of evolution is still surprisingly jerky and, ironically, we have even fewer examples of evolutionary transition than we had in Darwin's time."[19]

The problem for evolutionists unable to produce transitional fossils is made clear by Brown: "If [Darwinian] evolution happened, the fossil record should show continuous and gradual changes from the bottom to the top layers and between all forms of life. Actually, many gaps and discontinuities appear throughout the fossil record."[20] An evolutionary tree with no trunk (no life forms earlier than the already very complex ones in Cambrian rocks) and no branches (no transitional forms) can hardly be called a tree at all.

This problem presented by the lack of transitional forms in the fossil record also extends to the lack of transitional forms observable in nature or even conceivable in the human mind. Evolutionists are unable not only to point to a specific form observed by science as an indisputable transitional form, but also to present a reasonable explanation for the survival of any hypothetical transitional forms in nature, since many forms would be useless until fully developed.

Evolution demands that mutations be beneficial to cause them to be reproduced and become dominant in nature, and yet half-developed transitional forms provide no clear advantage; on the contrary, they are more likely to be handicaps. Brown elaborates: "If a limb were to evolve into a wing, it would become a bad limb long before it became a good wing."[21] Again, underneath the whole current of debate, we find the teleological argument to be among the best answers to evolutionists and the strongest support for creationism. It is clear that God as Designer provides a much better explanation for the design evidenced by life than does a theory that requires transitional forms guided by natural selection.

The fossil record, the observation of living organisms, and the teleological nature of numerous forms testify to the impossibility of gradual change. Yet gradual change is absolutely critical to traditional evolutionary theory. Darwin himself admits, "If it could be demonstrated that any complex organ existed, which could not possibly have been formed by numerous, successive, slight modifications, my theory would absolutely break down."[22]

This is precisely what creationists have claimed for years—that Darwin's evolutionary theory is bankrupt. Reason requires the biologist to abandon evolution and embrace the more rational explanation: creation. Of course, creationism is untenable for all atheists; therefore, even if the atheist recognizes the irrationality of traditional evolutionary theory, he must postulate an equally indefensible theory to circumvent the notion of God.

PUNCTUATED EQUILIBRIUM

Thus, evolutionists recently have suggested the theory of punctuated equilibrium. This theory allows the materialistic evolutionist to escape some of the inconsistencies of neo-Darwinian evolution while ignoring the possibility of the existence of God.

Punctuated equilibrium basically claims that evolution occurs in spurts, in relatively short periods of time, which supposedly accounts for the absence of transitional forms. Stephen Jay Gould is the theory's leading proponent, largely because he recognizes the untenability of any evolutionary theory that requires gradual, intermediate change, but is still unwilling to abandon the theory of evolution. This forces him to postulate an alternate evolutionary theory custom-built to fit the facts.

The alternative, unfortunately for evolutionists, still faces severe problems. Punctuated equilibrium still relies on the Darwinian mechanisms of natural selection and survival of the fittest (albeit at a much faster pace and in isolated segments of a species' population). The problem with this reliance on Darwinian mechanisms, even if the mechanisms themselves were viable, is that Darwin explicitly declared that they must work gradually, imperceptibly.

The biggest problem with punctuated equilibrium, however, is that it is not based on evidence. Instead, it is assumed to be the correct explanation because it fits the lack of empirical evidence. But this is an illogical assumption—the lack of evidence for one proposed method of evolution does not necessarily prove the veracity of another proposed method. It might, instead, be interpreted as evidence that evolution itself did not occur.

An origins theory that cannot postulate a satisfactory mechanism but rather is based on the absence of evidence is no better than its parent theory, neo-Darwinism. Further, the speculations of punctuated equilibrium may avoid the problem of transitional forms, but they still are faced with the insurmountable problems presented by spontaneous generation, the lack of observed beneficial mutations, and evolution's contradiction of the second law of thermodynamics.

Punctuated equilibrium, then, is every bit as faulty as traditional evolutionary theory. Creationism proves to be a much better explanation of man's origin, when one takes into account evidences of intelligent design throughout the universe, the complexity and ingenuity of DNA, the fossil record showing no transitional forms but rather "kind begetting kind," the extinction of species rather than new species evolving through natural selection or punctuated equilibrium, the law of biogenesis, and the second law of thermodynamics.

Secular Humanism	Marxist/Leninist	Cosmic Humanist	Christianity
Darwinian Evolution	Darwinian/ Punctuated Evolution	Darwinian/ Punctuated Evolution	Special Creationism

CONCLUSION

Evolutionary theory has come full circle—from an assumption of the gradual appearance of all species to an assumption of the virtually instantaneous (geologically speaking) appearance of all species. From the Christian biologist's perspective, this is an interesting turn of events. It suggests that the evolutionists' faith in evolution is so unshakable they are willing to believe any theory that they can twist to fit the "facts" (or absence of facts).

The belief that God created all things, including man in His own image, requires faith. But evolutionary theory requires more faith, since evolution runs contrary to reason, science and history. Still, many evolutionists hold desperately to their theory, simply because it is the only explanation of origins that excludes God. The scientist who believes that everything can be explained in natural terms cannot tolerate the concept of a supernatural Being. But for the Christian biologist, the world is only comprehensible in light of God's existence.

Ironically, it was Darwin's wife who eloquently verbalized the creationists' remonstrance to evolutionists. In a letter to her husband, she wrote, "May not the habit in scientific pursuits of believing nothing till it is proved, influence your mind too much in other things which cannot be proved in the same way, and which if true, are likely to be above our comprehension?"[23]

FOUR WESTERN WORLDVIEW MODELS

SOURCES	SECULAR HUMANISM HUMANIST MANIFESTOS I AND II	MARXISM/LENINISM WRITINGS OF MARX AND LENIN	COSMIC HUMANISM WRITINGS OF SPANGLER, FERGUSON, ETC.	BIBLICAL CHRISTIANITY BIBLE
THEOLOGY	Atheism	Atheism	Pantheism	Theism
PHILOSOPHY	Naturalism	Dialectical Materialism	Non-Naturalism	Supernaturalism
ETHICS	Relativism	Proletariat Morality	Relativism	Absolutes
BIOLOGY	Darwinian Evolution	Darwinian/Punctuated Evolution	Darwinian/Punctuated Evolution	Creation
PSYCHOLOGY	Self-Actualization	Behaviorism	Collective Consciousness	Mind/Body
SOCIOLOGY	Non-Traditional Family	Abolition of Home, Church and State	Non-Traditional Home, Church and State	Traditional Home, Church and State
LAW	Positive Law	Positive Law	Self-Law	Biblical and Natural Law
POLITICS	World Government (Globalism)	New World Order (New Civilization)	New Age Order	Justice, Freedom and Order
ECONOMICS	Socialism	Socialism	Universal Enlightened Production	Stewardship of Property
HISTORY	Historical Evolution	Historical Materialism	Evolutionary Godhood	Historical Resurrection

CHAPTER 19

Secular Humanist Psychology

"For myself, though I am very well aware of the incredible amount of destructive, cruel, malevolent behavior in today's world—from the threats of war to the senseless violence in the streets—I do not find that this evil is inherent in human nature."[1]
—Carl Rogers

INTRODUCTION

Humanist psychology, like all aspects of the Humanist worldview, is strongly influenced by Humanist assumptions about theology, philosophy, and biology. Leading Humanist psychologists begin with the assumption that a personal God is a myth, and then assume that man is simply a product of spontaneous generation and billions of years of evolution. A naturalistic philosophy fits hand-in-hand with these first two assumptions.

Because Secular Humanists deny the existence of the supernatural—including the mind, soul, and personality in any meaningful sense—they are left with very little for the "science" of psychology to study. Humanist psychology, when consistent, should focus on strictly material things: the brain, environmental stimuli, and tangible human responses to that stimuli. The branch of psychology that concerns itself solely with such material data is called behaviorism. Behaviorists believe all human "thoughts" and "personality" are merely by-products of physical interactions of the brain. For them, psychology is a science of behavior—understanding how physical stimuli encourage our physical brains and bodies to behave.

The Humanist consistent with his worldview must embrace behaviorism. If the supernatural does not exist, then one must practice a psychology that only admits the natural. Logically, Humanists should be behaviorists.

In practice, few Humanists accept behaviorism. The reason for their inconsistency is simple: behaviorism is a stultifying theory that reduces men to mere automatons. Behaviorist theory does not allow for human freedom, because ultimately personal freedom must be grounded in the will, soul, or mind. According to the behaviorist model, men and women are merely physical, and so their behavior is dictated by their physical environment. This is not an attractive theory; nor does it seem to match our day-to-day experience. Thus, Humanist psychologists abandon logic and the consequences of their atheistic evolutionary naturalism.

Most Humanists call their psychology "third force" psychology because they are unwilling to embrace behaviorism or the other popular model, Freudianism. On the one hand, Humanists reject behaviorism because it destroys their necessary concept of freedom. On the other hand, they reject Freudianism because it focuses too much on the individual apart from society. The Humanist, unsatisfied with the two popular branches of psychology, creates a third branch.

A Brief Look At: Erich Fromm (1900-1980)

1922: Receives PhD in philosophy from the University of Heidelberg

1924: Completes his training in psychoanalysis at the University of Munich

1926: Abandons the Judaism of his father

1934: Leaves Nazi Germany and becomes United States citizen

1941: Publishes *Escape from Freedom*

1951: Hired as professor of psychoanalysis by the National University of Mexico

1966: Publishes *You Shall Be as Gods*

1966: Elected Humanist of the Year

IS MAN GOOD OR EVIL?

Whereas Christianity believes man to be a fallen creation, Secular Humanist psychology emphatically proclaims the innate goodness of man. Abraham Maslow writes, "As far as I know we just don't have any intrinsic instincts for evil."[2] Carl Rogers says much the same thing: "I see members of the human species, like members of other species, as essentially constructive in their fundamental nature, but damaged by their experience."[3] Paul Kurtz views man as "perfectible."[4]

This portrayal of man is so incompatible with the Christian view that Humanists feel compelled to attack the doctrine of original sin. Some go so far as to reinterpret the Bible to distort the concept of man's fall. Erich Fromm claims, "The Christian interpretation of the story of man's act of disobedience as his 'fall' has obscured the clear meaning of the story. The biblical text does not even mention the word 'sin'; man challenges the supreme power of God, and he is able to challenge it because he is potentially God."[5]

Still other Humanistic psychologists choose to attack the whole Christian view in an effort to avoid the concept of original sin. Wendell W. Watters writes, "The Christian is brainwashed to believe that he or she was born wicked, should suffer as Christ suffered, and should aspire to a humanly impossible level of perfection nonetheless."[6] According to Watters, all this confusion and guilt heaped on the Christian helps promote mental illness: "A true Christian must always be in a state of torment, since he or she can never really be certain that God has forgiven him or her . . ."[7]

Clearly, Humanistic psychologists are uneasy with the whole Christian concept of original sin. This is largely because this doctrine provides an explanation for the existence of man-caused evil in the world, whereas Humanist psychology (on the surface) does not. However, Humanism has devised a theory to go hand-in-hand with the idea of man's innate goodness; a theory designed to explain the existence of wars, crime, etc. This theory is also crucial to the Humanistic psychological framework.

WHY DO GOOD PEOPLE DO BAD THINGS?

The good impulses within people, says Maslow, "are easily warped by cultures—you never find them in their pure state."[8] Virtually every Humanistic psychologist shares this view of culture as the force responsible for the evil in mankind. It is the only means available for explaining the odd fact that man can be inherently good and still show such a tendency to commit evil acts.

167

Thus, Rogers notes that "experience leads me to believe that it is cultural influences which are the major factor in our evil behaviors."[9] Humanism must explain evil in the world as the result of societal influences thwarting men's natural tendencies for good.

Humanist psychologist Rollo May, however, is unwilling to accept this premise. In response to claims by Rogers, May cuts to the heart of the matter when he writes, "But you say that you 'believe that it is cultural influences which are the major factor in our evil behaviors.' This makes culture the enemy. But who makes up the culture except persons like you and me?"[10] Indeed, how could culture or society ever have become evil if there were no tendency within man toward evil?

Humanist psychologists offer no solution to this dilemma. They seem to acknowledge the dilemma, however, when they focus on healing individuals rather than society.

A SELF-CENTERED WORLDVIEW

Every Humanist psychologist believes the secret to better mental health lies in getting in touch with the unspoiled, inner self. When man strips himself of all the evil forced on him by society, he will become a positive agent with virtually unlimited potential. Just how much potential man is assumed to have is reflected by the title of one of Fromm's most important works, *You Shall Be as Gods*.

The Humanist emphasis, then, is on self-reliance, even self-centeredness. Harold P. Marley states, "To know Humanism, first know the self in its relation to other selves. Trust thyself to stand alone; learn of others, but lean not upon a single saviour."[11] This call to trust yourself and your natural inclinations is voiced powerfully by Maslow: "Since this inner nature is good or neutral rather than bad, it is best to bring it out and to encourage it rather than to suppress it. If it is permitted to guide our life, we grow healthy, fruitful, and happy."[12] We must focus on our own self, our own will and desires, for only then can we become good.

In fact, self-centeredness is believed by Humanists to be the wave of the future—an entirely new philosophy of life. Rogers, when considering what the philosophy of the future will be like, guesses, "It will stress the value of the individual. It will, I think, center itself in the individual as the evaluating agent."[13]

Humanist psychologists perceive this self-centered attitude as crucial for the mental health of the individual as well as for the eventual restructuring of society. Only when mankind accepts the need for the individual to be completely in control can we tap the unlimited potential of being human.

SELF-ACTUALIZED MAN

Maslow refers to the person in touch with his inherent goodness as "self-actualized." He categorizes this drive to get in touch with our inherent goodness as a need that can be attended to only after the individual has satisfied his lower needs—namely, physiological, safety, social, and ego needs. The individual must satisfy these needs as well as the need for self-actualization before he can truly be declared mentally healthy.

> ## "As far as I know we just don't have any intrinsic instincts for evil."
>
> *Abraham Maslow*

According to Maslow, few people in modern society are self-actualized. Thus, when attempting to study self-actualized individuals, he relied to some extent on historical figures as models. Maslow feels "fairly sure" that Abraham Lincoln "in his last days" and Thomas Jefferson were self-actualized. He also singles out Albert Einstein, Eleanor Roosevelt, Jane Addams, William James, Albert Schweitzer, Aldous Huxley, and Benedict de Spinoza as "highly probable" examples of self-actualization.[14]

What character traits mark these historical figures as more in tune with their real, creative selves? What are the characteristics of the self-actualized individual? Maslow says that self-actualization "stresses 'full-humanness,' the development of the biologically based nature of man."[15] This emphasis relies, as does all Humanist psychology, on the assumption of man's innate, evolved goodness.

MAN-CENTERED VALUES

This inherent goodness should not be understood as "good" in the traditional, biblical sense. It is an evolving, relative goodness. Maslow says self-actualized people's "notions of right and wrong and of good and evil are often not the conventional ones."[16] Ellis G. Olim agrees: "[M]an is constantly becoming. . . . What we want, then, is not to encourage a static type of personality based on traditional notions of right and wrong, but the kind of person who is able to go forward into the uncertain future."[17]

For the Humanist, ethics is inseparable from psychology. Fromm believes that "values are rooted in the very conditions of human existence; hence that our knowledge of these conditions—that is, of the 'human situation'—leads us to establishing values which have objective validity; this validity exists only with regard to the existence of man; outside of him there are no values."[18]

Therefore, man must turn his eyes inward to determine what is right. He needn't worry about helping others; rather, he should simply concentrate on creating a good self. Maslow describes this view succinctly: "In general, it looks as if the best way to help other people grow toward self-actualization is to become a good person yourself."[19] The Humanist embraces self-centeredness in an effort to create a better world.

This call for the individual to be true to his feelings and innermost nature obviously allows for a great deal of experimentation. If an individual feels like his innermost nature is calling for him to act in a specific way, who has the authority to tell him he is misinterpreting his feelings? Humanism affirms man's freedom to experiment with values, to test which aspects of morality truly mesh with his inner nature.

Humanist psychologists perceive self-actualized man as the final authority for ethics, regardless of how much scientific experimentation it requires to discover "the good." Unfortunately, "the good" discovered is only "the good" for that individual. Others may decide something else is "good." Some may decide there is no "good," and there are no rules.

Humanist psychologists try to put a halt to this line of thinking, however, by arguing that few people are self-actualized, and the non-self-actualized must look to the self-actualized for guidance. According to Maslow, people not yet self-actualized can learn what is right by watching those who already are in touch with their true selves. Thus, the Humanists must look to mentally healthy (self-actualized) people to determine "scientifically," for example, if pedophilia (man/boy sex) is moral. Maslow says, "I propose that we explore the consequences of observing whatever our best specimens choose, and then assuming that these are the highest values for all mankind."[20]

Is Humanist Psychology Scientific?

Humanists would have us adhere to Maslow's suggestions because they are based on a "realistic" worldview grounded in science. The problem, as we have noted, is that Humanist psychology is far from scientific.

Humanists therefore attempt to redefine science to make it broad enough to include Humanist psychology. They justify their new definitions by pointing to the failure of existing psychological models to help the individual understand his nature. May complains, "Today we know a great deal about bodily chemistry and the control of physical diseases; but we know very little about why people hate, why they cannot love, why they suffer anxiety and guilt, and why they destroy each other."[21]

Humanists believe their psychology better explains why people act the way they do, and is therefore "scientific." Rogers believes true science "will explore the private worlds of inner personal meanings, in an effort to discover lawful and orderly relationships there. In this world of inner meanings it can investigate all the issues which are meaningless for the behaviorist—purposes, goals, values, choice, perceptions of self, perceptions of others, the personal constructs with which we build our world, the responsibilities we accept or reject, the whole phenomenal world of the individual with its connective tissue of meaning."[22] Unfortunately for the Humanists, definitions of "scientific" studies such as these allow not only Humanist psychology to be termed scientific, but also every major religion, including Christianity. After all, isn't every major religion an attempt to explore "inner personal meanings"?

Humanists, of course, will not stand for the treatment of Christianity as a viable option, so they continue to restructure their definition of the new science in an effort to include Humanist psychology and exclude religion. It is unlikely they will ever succeed, since their psychology requires more leaps of faith than most religions.

Psychology
At A Glance

Secular Humanism

Monistic Self-
actualization

CONCLUSION

The Secular Humanists admit that they begin their study of the self, mind, and mental processes with certain assumptions. The three major assumptions of Humanist psychology are: man is good by nature and therefore perfectible; society and its social institutions are responsible for man's evil acts; and mental health can be restored to everyone who gets in touch with his inner "good" self. Marxists agree with the first two, Christians deny all three. Christians insist that individuals should face up to their own sinful nature and take responsibility for their immoral actions instead of blaming someone or something else. Humanists merely give intellectual ammunition to those who never can accept moral responsibility.

Humanists need to keep May's observation in mind: If man is so good, why is society so evil? Perhaps this is what Rogers was thinking about when he wrote, "I should like to make a final confession. When I am speaking to outsiders I present Humanistic psychology as a glowing hope for the future. But . . . we have no reason whatsoever for feeling complacent as we look toward the future."[23]

CHAPTER 20

Marxist/Leninist Psychology

"Only science, exact science about human nature itself, and the most sincere approach to it by the aid of the omnipotent scientific method, will deliver man from his present gloom, and will purge him from his contemporary shame in the sphere of interhuman relations."[1]

—Ivan P. Pavlov

INTRODUCTION

Marxist psychologists seem to be tied even more inextricably than Humanists to the behaviorist view of man, since Marxism describes man's development as an inevitable march toward communism. This notion of a determined development of man seems to exclude free will, which approximates the behaviorist view that man's decisions and actions are simply the result of his brain's response to environmental stimuli.

Further, Marxism accepts evolution as fact and perceives materialism to be the only proper means of understanding the world. These beliefs, in turn, affect the Marxist view of the mind/body relationship. The Marxist, like the Humanist, believes the mind is no more than the purely physical activity of the brain.

Since psychology is the study of the mind and its processes, a philosophy that denies the mind as a supernatural phenomenon logically confines one to the behaviorist school of thought. When V.I. Lenin declares the mind to be strictly organized matter, he forces Marxism to accept behaviorism in order to be consistent with Marxist theology and philosophy.

The type of behaviorism embraced by Marxists, however, differs significantly from traditional behaviorism; their theories are based on the work of Ivan P. Pavlov, an early twentieth century Russian physiologist. Although he rejected Marxist theory for most of his life, Pavlov served as the adopted father of Marxist psychology—largely because his attempts to reconcile materialism with psychology seem to fit the dialectic.

Before we examine this special brand of behaviorism, we must understand what traditional behaviorism generally entails. This can be accomplished best by studying the thought of behaviorism's most popular proponent, B.F. Skinner.

BEHAVIORISM DEFINED

Behaviorism perceives man as simply a stimulus receptor, a creature capable of responding only one predetermined way to any given set of circumstances in his environment. Skinner believes this is the only truly scientific means of approaching psychology: "A scientific analysis of behavior dispossesses autonomous man and turns the control he has been said to exert over to the environment. The individual . . . is henceforth to be controlled by the world around him, and in large part by other men."[2]

Skinner roots this behaviorist view of man in an evolutionary perspective of the world: "The environment not only prods or lashes, it selects. Its role is similar to that in natural selection, though on a very different time scale . . ."[3] Obviously, when the environment does the selecting, man can no longer be perceived as a free agent. So Skinner declares, "The hypothesis that man is not free is essential to the application of scientific method to the study of human behavior."[4]

The essence of traditional behaviorism is the belief that man is controlled by stimuli from the environment and never makes a decision in which he exercises free will. This view of man as a receptor for outside stimuli is consistent with the materialist belief that man's brain is no more than a bundle of nerves and synapses ready to respond in a determined way to the environment.

PAVLOV'S ROLE IN MARXIST PSYCHOLOGY

Pavlov's theories sound a lot like Skinner's theories. Like Skinner, Pavlov believes that much of mankind's mental processes are the result of purely physical causes, and that behavior can be regulated.

Pavlov concentrated his studies, for the most part, in animal psychology. He is perhaps most famous for experiments in which he induced salivation in dogs simply by ringing a bell. These experiments are significant, of course, because they led Pavlov to propose a theory of conditioned reflexes that claimed that animals can learn to respond in a specific, predetermined way when exposed to certain stimuli. Pavlov's dogs originally salivated when a bell was ringing because they were eating food at the same time, but soon they "learned" the conditioned reflex that caused them to salivate simply because they were exposed to the stimulus of a ringing bell.

Pavlov believes that all of an animal's activities can be accounted for in purely behavioristic terms. He declares that "the whole complicated behaviour of animals" is based on "nervous activity."[5] As an avowed evolutionist, he does not hesitate to apply his conclusion to the highest animal, man: "I trust that I shall not be thought rash if I express a belief that experiments on the higher nervous activities of animals will yield not a few directional indications for education and self-education in man."[6]

Indeed, Pavlov believed (just as Skinner and other behaviorists believe today) that man can be educated and controlled so that he only does good. Shortly before his death, he told his laboratory assistants, "Now we can and must go forward. . . . [W]e may use all of the experimental material for the investigation of the human being, striving to perfect the human race of the future."[7]

Clearly, Pavlov's theories mesh well with the Marxist worldview. They also seem

A Brief Look At: Ivan Petrovich Pavlov (1849-1936)

1864: Studies religion and philosophy at the Theological Seminary of Ryazan

1883: Receives M.D. from the Military Medical Academy

1888: Discovers the secretory nerves of the pancreas

1896: Assumes chair of physiology at the Academy

1901: Coins the phrase "conditioned reflex" to describe learned response to stimuli

1904: Receives the Nobel Prize in physiology

1917: Expresses distrust of Bolsheviks after October Revolution

1923: Publishes *Conditioned Reflexes*

1935: Allegedly reconciles himself with communism

to mesh perfectly with traditional behaviorism—but they do not. Pavlov's theories "improve" upon behaviorism in a way that is convenient for Marxists. Thus, where Pavlov parts company with traditional behaviorism, so does Marxism.

MARXISM'S REJECTION OF TRADITIONAL BEHAVIORISM

Marxism rejects some of the logical conclusions that flow from traditional behaviorism. Joseph Nahem writes, "From this dialectical viewpoint, behaviorism in psychology, such as the theories of J.B. Watson or B.F. Skinner, must be criticized as mechanical, as the reduction of the psychological process of human functioning to the physiological process of behavior alone."[8]

Why can't Marxism accept traditional behaviorism as a coherent psychological view? Nahem hints at the reason: "Marxism maintains that there are laws of social development which will lead, through conscious struggle, to a better society, socialism. Skinner believes that his 'Behavioral Engineering' will make for a better society. What kind of society will Skinner produce?"[9]

> **Behaviorism perceives man as ... a creature capable of responding only one predetermined way to any given set of circumstances in his environment.**

This is the bottom line. The Marxists fear that a behaviorist psychology might not encourage the development of a *communist* society, since it denies the possibility of man's making a "conscious struggle" to achieve such a society. Free will is, after all, crucial for Marxist psychology. Marxism faces the same dichotomy it created for itself in economics: it declares communism to be inevitable, but it requires the willed revolt of the people to bring about its occurrence. Therefore, the Marxist must avoid a traditional behaviorism that denies the free will of the proletariat to revolt and overthrow the oppressive upper classes.

Karl Marx, who lived prior to the development of behaviorist theory, recognized the incompatibility of a materialist philosophy and the notion of free will. He attempted to resolve the problem by claiming, "The materialist doctrine that men are the product of circumstances and education—forgets that circumstances are changed precisely by men."[10] More than one hundred years later, Marx's followers are still trying to resolve the conflict, which has been made more obvious since the inception of behaviorist theory.

Perhaps once a communist world is achieved, Marxist psychologists will be willing to accept traditional behaviorism. However, while revolution is still required to bring about the perfect society, free will is a more important psychological concept than deterministic behaviorism.

SPEECH AND STIMULI

How can the Marxist embrace so many aspects of behaviorism and still deny the final conclusion—the non-existence of free will? How can Marxist psychologists ground themselves in Pavlovian thought and ignore his behavioristic conclusions? As previously noted, the answer for the Marxists comes from Pavlov himself.

Nahem tells us that "Pavlov identified the qualitative difference between humans and animals in the possession by humans of a second signal system, i.e., speech, which was 'the latest acquisition in the process of evolution.'"[11] That is, man differs from the rest of the animal world because he is capable of responding to word stimuli as well as to common environmental stimuli.

Marxist psychologists view this concept of speech as a "second signal system" as the key to synthesizing behaviorism with free will. Nahem says simply, "A . . . devastating refutation of Skinner is Pavlov's profound contribution to psychology by his analysis of speech and language as a second signal system."[12] This concept of speech as another stimulus allows the Marxist to perceive man as shaped by environmental stimuli but also shaped by (and able to shape) his society. That is, speech is instrumental in defining and maintaining society, and it is a tool for man to shape the stimuli acting upon him, to a large extent, by shaping his own environment.

SOCIETY AND HUMAN BEHAVIOR

For the Marxist psychologist, speech—and therefore society—affect the individual's behavior. "Most decisive in its influence on our thoughts, feelings, and behavior" says Nahem, "is society and social relations. . . . Human beings are distinguished from animals by their social labor, their social communication, their social groupings, by their social acquisition and use of language, and by their involvement in the ideas, attitudes, morality and behavior of their society."[13] Indeed, according to A.R. Luria, the individual longs for this type of societal influence, actually creating society so as to produce more external stimuli.

The next logical step is obvious. Marxists declare socialist society to be far superior to capitalist society in terms of encouraging desirable behavior. Accordingly, capitalism has failed dramatically; only socialism can provide the proper setting for psychologically healthy individuals.

Capitalism's Failure and Socialism's Success

The major problem with capitalist society, according to the Marxist, is the divisive nature of classes. The oppression of one or more classes by a ruling class (the bourgeois) is deviant, and creates more deviant behavior. This behavior will always become manifest in capitalist society, and can only be eradicated by restructuring society.

Religious faith, for example, is one of the intolerable results of a capitalist society. "The essence of man is presented in a mystical way," says L.P. Bueva of bourgeois psychology; "the idea of the primacy of the spirit and of a full non-acceptance of objectivity, a rejection of the real world in favour of God, the idea of 'a revolution within man' through his spiritual renaissance based on religious faith—these are all ideological expressions of the crisis of capitalism's social system and of the contemporary bourgeois world's values."[14] The "crisis," of course, occurs when man turns to God.

What will save mankind from psychologically unsound societies? Only socialism as presented by Marxists! In fact, Marxist society will encourage only mentally healthy individuals. Bueva declares, "Socialist social relations develop an ability of the individual for self-regulation, control over his social behaviour and for developing an active attitude in relation to life."[15] For the Marxist, society can only shape an individual's behavior positively when it is socialist.

Dialectics and Marxist Psychology

This Marxist perception of the individual as determined by both society and typical environmental stimuli meshes well with Marxism's dialectical view. According to Marxist psychology, man's freedom to create whatever society he chooses clashes with societal forces and other environmental factors that determine behavior. The individual's freedom (thesis) attracts to itself and struggles with man's behavioristic tendencies (antithesis).

This concept is built on the foundation set down by Marx in the declaration that "men make their own history, but they do not make it under circumstances chosen by themselves, but under circumstances directly encountered, given and transmitted from the past."[16]

In the final estimation, the Marxist psychologist uses dialectics as his support for rejecting traditional behaviorism. Nahem states, "Skinner abandons freedom and dignity and espouses a rigidly determinist view, a view that Marxism calls mechanical materialism. It was only with the development of Marxism that the full relationship between freedom and determinism could be explained. Materialism needed dialectics to delineate the true meaning of freedom."[17]

For the Marxist psychologist, the dialectical view of behavior and freedom is the only truly scientific view. It can be worded so that it appears to be consistent with Marxism's over-all worldview, and it seems to explain the urgency and inevitability of establishing world communism while still allowing for some concept of freedom.

Psychology At A Glance

Secular Humanism	Marxist/Leninist
Monistic Self-actualization	Monistic Pavlovian Behaviorism

CONCLUSION

Unfortunately, the term *freedom* does not mean the same thing to Marxist psychologists as it does to the rest of mankind. For the Marxist, freedom is simply the opportunity for the individual to choose what type of society will determine his behavior; it does not mean choosing his behavior himself. Consequently, whenever the individual is not exercising his freedom in selecting a society, he is controlled by his particular situation. This is at best a stunted concept of freedom—man is free to select the society that will determine his every action.

Marxists cloak this notion of a controlling society in vague descriptions of society's responsibility to "regulate" man. In reality, this "regulation" involves exposing individuals to the proper stimuli to elicit the proper behavior. Marxists believe the necessary stimuli can only be found in a communist society. This society would "regulate" men and women so that they would be faithful always to the collective and to "internationalism."

In such a context, freedom means virtually nothing. When the Marxist speaks of a society scientifically "regulating" human development, he envisions a society much like the one described by George Orwell in *1984*. According to Marxist psychologists, man is merely an animal in need of some chemical fine-tuning before heading on to perfection in the coming world order—an order in which all mankind will be stimulated to perfection. Unfortunately, this new order will deprive human beings of the same two things Skinner and all other materialists ultimately eradicate: freedom, and dignity.

CHAPTER 21

Cosmic Humanist Psychology

*"Everyone anywhere who tunes into the Higher Self becomes part of the
transformation. Their lives then become orchestrated from other realms."[1]*

—Ken Carey

INTRODUCTION

The belief that an individual can hasten the work of evolution by achieving a
higher consciousness is tied closely to Cosmic Humanist psychology. Achieving
higher consciousness is the central goal for any member of the New Age movement—
and only psychology provides the means for unlocking the secrets of this higher
mindset.

Cosmic Humanists sometimes refer to their approach to psychology, with its
emphasis on higher consciousness, as "fourth force" psychology. John White explains,
"Fourth force psychology covers a wide range of human affairs. All of them, however,
are aimed at man's ultimate development—not simply a return from unhealthiness to
normality—as individuals and as a species."[2]

This ultimate development, according to the New Age movement, represents the
only truly healthy mindset. Marilyn Ferguson writes, "Well-being cannot be infused
intravenously or ladled in by prescription. It comes from a matrix: the bodymind. It
reflects psychological and somatic harmony."[3] One's consciousness affects both body
and soul, and only a constant state of higher consciousness can ensure mental and

185

physical well-being. Thus, psychology plays a crucial role in Cosmic Humanism's worldview not only because it can hasten the evolution of all mankind to a collective God-consciousness, but also because it works to ensure perfect health for every individual.

A Brief Look At: Marianne Williamson (1952-)

1965: Travels to Saigon with her father to learn about war

1969: Decides God is "a crutch I didn't need"

1975: Moves to San Francisco; toys with Buddhism and Ouija board

1977: Begins studying *A Course in Miracles*

1983: Moves to Los Angeles; begins sharing her insights about the *Course*

1992: Publishes *A Return to Love*

1993: Publishes *A Woman's Worth*

MIND OVER MATTER

The message from Cosmic Humanist psychologists to people suffering health problems is simple: mindset is responsible for health. People suffering through painful sickness or disease are doing so because they have not yet achieved higher consciousness. "Every time you don't trust yourself and don't follow your inner truth," says Shakti Gawain, "you decrease your aliveness and your body will reflect this with a loss of vitality, numbness, pain, and eventually, physical disease."[4]

This same general failing to contact the "God within" creates criminal tendencies. Vera Alder explains that in the New Age, "A criminal or an idler will be recognized as a sick individual offering a splendid chance for wise help. Instead of being incarcerated with fellow unfortunates in the awful atmosphere of a prison, the future 'criminal' will be in much demand."[5] Criminals can be put in touch with their higher consciousness, thus becoming capable of leading healthy lives—spiritually, physically, and *ethically*.

By attaining higher consciousness, we guarantee ourselves excellent all-around health. "Health and disease don't just happen to us," says Ferguson. "They are active processes issuing from inner harmony or disharmony, profoundly affected by our states of consciousness, our ability or inability to flow with experience."[6] Further, those enlightened individuals who maintain higher consciousness can solve more than their own personal problems. Shirley MacLaine found that "Somewhere way underneath *me* were the answers to everything that caused anxiety and confusion in the *world.*"[7] If this is true, of course, then the most important thing any individual can do is attain higher consciousness. Indeed, the salvation of the world depends upon it.

METHODS FOR ACHIEVING HIGHER CONSCIOUSNESS

What methods does "fourth force" psychology employ to induce states of higher consciousness in willing individuals? Most often it relies on meditation (often aided by crystals or mantras). An author in *Life Times Magazine* states emphatically, "My message to everyone now is to learn to meditate. It was through meditation that many other blessings came about."[8]

According to the Cosmic Humanist, higher consciousness will naturally flow from meditation as one of its many "blessings." But other "blessings" may manifest themselves as well. For example, meditation often creates in an individual the ability to channel spirits, according to Kathleen Vande Kieft:

> *Almost without exception, those who channel effectively meditate regularly.* The process of channeling itself is an extension of the state of meditation . . . the best way to prepare, then, for channeling is by *meditation.*[9]

Channeling refers to the Cosmic Humanist belief that spirits will sometimes speak to and through a particularly gifted individual engaged in meditation. Elena, a spirit allegedly channeled by John Randolph Price, describes beings like herself as "angels of light—whether from earth or other worlds. They search, select and guide those men and women who may be suitable subjects."[10]

Not every member of the New Age movement would see much significance in channeling, but every New Ager embraces meditation as an important psychological tool for attaining higher consciousness. Channeling and other practices (including astrology, firewalking, ouija boards, and aura readings) are often suggested by New Age psychologists strictly as means of enhancing the higher consciousness achieved through meditation.

> **"Health and disease don't just happen to us. They are active processes issuing from inner harmony or disharmony . . ."**
>
> *Marilyn Ferguson*

Regardless of the specific psychological package prescribed by various individual Cosmic Humanists, New Age psychology is based on a simple rule: commune with the God within. This is the fundamental difference between New Age and Christian meditation. New Age meditation focuses on the "God within," while Christian meditation focuses on the God outside us—our Maker and Judge and Savior—and on His objective, external revelation of truth to us in the Bible. This distinction is spelled out most dramatically in the New Age children's book *What is God?*—a book that teaches Cosmic Humanist meditation couched in more traditional terms:

> And if you really want to pray to God, you can just close your eyes anywhere, and think about that feeling of God, that makes you part of everything and everybody. If you can feel that feeling of God, and everybody else can feel that feeling of God, then we can all become friends together, and we can really understand, 'What is God?' So, if you really want to feel God, you can close your eyes now, and listen to your breath go slowly in and out, and think how you are connected to everything, even if you are not touching everything.[11]

Psychology At A Glance

Secular Humanism	Marxist/Leninist	Cosmic Humanist
Monistic Self-actualization	Monistic Pavlovian Behaviorism	Collective Consciousness

CONCLUSION

New Age psychology provides the jargon and the tools for the Cosmic Humanist's relentless pursuit of higher consciousness. Before utopia (the New Age) can be achieved, many people must evolve past their present pain and into an awareness of their godhood. Psychology is man's effort to direct this evolution.

Each individual must choose the psychological tools that most help him achieve his godhood. For some, firewalking may be profoundly useful; others may need seances or hypnosis. Most everyone must rely regularly on meditation.

The value of the tools for each individual can be measured by how much pain they cure. Higher consciousness implies "wellness," so that anything that leads to higher consciousness will necessarily reduce physical, mental, and spiritual pain.

Cosmic Humanists, when consistent, apply this theory to even the most drastic scenarios. Even life-threatening cancer, according to Marianne Williamson, is just a sign that our psyche is not healthy. "Healing results," she says "from a transformed perception of our relationship to illness, one in which we respond to the problem with love instead of fear."[12] If we find the right tools, we can cure the cancer by curing the mind.

The tool Williamson recommends is visualization—that is, imagining events happening in the future and then willing these events to come true. Williamson suggests, "Imagine the AIDS virus as Darth Vader, and then unzip his suit to allow an angel to emerge. See the cancer cell or AIDS virus in all its wounded horror, and then see a golden light, or angel, or Jesus, enveloping the cell and transforming it from darkness into light."[13]

If the cancer patient works hard enough, and chooses the right psychological tools, he might save himself. Redemption, according to Cosmic Humanism, is in our own hands. We can save ourselves, if we are God enough.

CHAPTER 22

Biblical Christian Psychology

"He breathed into his nostrils the breath of life and man became a living soul."
—Genesis 2:7

INTRODUCTION

Christian psychology appears, at first glance, to be a contradiction in terms. After examining both Marxist and Humanist psychology and touching on still other theories of "secular" psychology, the Christian is tempted to conclude that psychology is a discipline unworthy of his attention. William Kirk Kilpatrick boldly declares, "if you're talking about Christianity, it is much truer to say that psychology and religion are competing faiths. If you seriously hold to one set of values, you will logically have to reject the other."[1]

What Kilpatrick says is true. But when he uses the term *psychology,* he is referring specifically to secular psychology. He can make this generalization, of course, because the secular schools of psychology (based on the work of men like Sigmund Freud, B.F. Skinner, I.P. Pavlov, Carl Rogers, Abraham Maslow, and Erich Fromm) comprise virtually all of modern psychology.

Just because so many lies flourish in the realm of psychology, however, does not mean Christians should abandon it. Instead, Christians must bring God's truth to a deceived discipline. Psychology is the study of the mind—and no worldview other than Christianity has true insight into the spiritual and mental realm. As Kilpatrick says, "In short, although Christianity is more than a psychology, it happens to be better psychology than psychology is."[2]

Christianity and psychology are compatible for the simple reason that the worldview of Biblical Christianity contains a psychology. As Charles L. Allen aptly points out, "the very essence of religion is to adjust the mind and *soul* of man. . . . Healing means bringing the person into a right relationship with the physical, mental and spiritual laws of God."[3] Man created "in the image of God" (Genesis 1:27) requires a worldview that recognizes the significance of the spiritual.

THE SUPERNATURAL MIND

Christianity acknowledges the existence of the supernatural, including a consciousness within man that is more than an epiphenomenon of the brain. The Bible's statements regarding body, breath of life, soul, spirit, and mind suggest a dualist ontology; that is, the view that human nature consists of two fundamental kinds of reality: physical (material or natural) and spiritual (supernatural). Christ's statement about fearing the one who could put "both soul and body" in hell (Matthew 10:28), and Paul's statement regarding body, soul, and spirit (1 Thessalonians 5:23) enforce the distinction between man's material and spiritual qualities. The Bible does not deny body; it simply says man is more than body.

Sir John Eccles, one of the world's most respected neuro-physiologists, believes dualism is the only explanation for many of the phenomena of consciousness. One of the reasons Eccles reaches this conclusion is the individual's "unity of identity." Paul Weiss explains: "[E]ven though I know I am constantly changing—all molecules are changing, everything in me is being turned over substantially—there is nevertheless my identity, my consciousness of being essentially the same that I was 20 years ago. However much I may have changed, the continuity of my identity has remained undisrupted."[4] The point, of course, is that since the physical substance of the brain is constantly changing, no unity of identity could exist if consciousness were a condition wholly dependent on the physical brain. Something more than the physical brain, something supernatural, must exist.

Human memory is another facet of the unity-of-identity argument that supports the existence of a supernatural mind. Arthur Custance writes, "What research has shown thus far is that there is no precise one-to-one relationship between any fragment of memory and the nerve cells in which it is supposed to be encoded."[5]

Without any concept of a supernatural mind, the Humanist and the Marxist have difficulty explaining unity of identity and memory. Still another problem arose in both the Humanist and Marxist psychology chapters: how can the materialist position account for free will? Only a worldview that postulates something other than the environment manipulating the human physical machine can account for free will. Christian dualism provides a better foundation for psychology because it defends the integrity of the mind and human free will.

A Brief Look At: Jonathan Edwards (1703-1758)

1722: Completes his theological studies at Yale College

1724: Begins teaching at Yale

1729: Grandfather dies; Edwards assumes his position as pastor of Northampton church

1734: Begins first revival

1740: The Great Awakening begins

1741: Preaches "Sinners in the Hands of an Angry God"

1750: Preaches farewell sermon at Northampton

1751: Serves as a missionary to Indians

1754: Publishes *Freedom of the Will*

1758: Begins service as president of the College of New Jersey (now Princeton)

HUMAN NATURE AND SIN

A proper understanding of man's nature does not, however, end with affirming the existence of a spirit within man. The Christian position goes on to define man's nature as inherently evil because of man's decision to disobey God in the Garden of Eden. This understanding of man's sinful bent is critical for understanding man's nature and mental processes.

This revolt by man against God caused a dramatic, reality-shattering change in the relationship of man to the rest of existence and even to himself. This change has severe ramifications for all aspects of reality, including psychology. In fact, man's sinful nature, his desire to rebel against God and his fellow man, is the source of all psychological problems, according to the Christian view. Francis A. Schaeffer sums up: "The basic psychological problem is trying to be what we are not, and trying to carry what we cannot carry. Most of all, the basic problem is not being willing to be the creatures we are before the Creator."[6]

This view is crucial for Christian theology because it allows us to understand our tremendous need for Christ's saving power. It is crucial on a lesser level, as well, for Christian psychology. In order to properly understand human nature, the psychologist must understand that man has a natural tendency to revolt against God and His laws.

If the Christian view of man's nature is correct, then only Christianity can develop a true, meaningful, and workable psychology, since only Christianity recognizes the problem of the will in relation to God. Further, only Christianity provides a framework in which man is truly held responsible for his thoughts and actions. "The great benefit of the doctrine of sin," says Paul Vitz, "is that it reintroduces responsibility for our own behavior, responsibility for changing as well as giving meaning to our condition."[7]

Only the Christian psychologist perceives man's nature in a way that is consistent with reality and capable of speaking to man's most difficult problems. The Christian psychologist sees man as not only physical but also spiritual, as morally responsible before God, as created in God's image, and as having rebelliously turned away from his Creator. Only Christianity is prepared to face the problem that necessarily arises out of man's nature: the existence of guilt.

GUILT: PSYCHOLOGICAL OR REAL?

Both Humanists and Marxists speak only of "psychological guilt" because, for them, only society is evil—people do nothing individually that would incur actual guilt. For the Christian, however, each time a man rebels against God he is committing a sin, and the feeling of guilt that results from this rebellion is entirely justified. "Psychological guilt is actual and cruel," writes Schaeffer. "But Christians know that there is also real guilt, moral guilt before a holy God. It is not a matter only of psychological guilt; that is the distinction."[8]

Because only Christian psychology acknowledges the existence of real, objective guilt, only it can speak to a person who is experiencing such guilt. As Schaeffer says,

> "Psychological guilt is actual and cruel. But Christians know that there is also real guilt, moral guilt before a holy God."
>
> Francis A. Schaeffer

"When a man is broken in these [moral and psychological] areas, he is confused, because he has the feelings of real guilt within himself, and yet he is told by modern thinkers that these are only guilt-'feelings.' But he can never resolve these feelings, because . . . [he] has true moral awareness and the feeling of true guilt. You can tell him a million times that there is no true guilt, but he still knows there is true guilt."[9]

Christianity understands man's nature, including why this guilt arises and how to deal with it. While other schools of psychology must invent fancy terms to explain away the existence of real guilt as a result of real sin, Christian psychology deals with the problem at its roots.

MENTAL ILLNESS

Modern secular psychologists often speak of "mental illness." Yet many Christian psychologists deny the existence of a large proportion of mental illnesses. Jay Adams writes, "Organic malfunctions affecting the brain that are caused by brain damage, tumors, gene inheritance, glandular or chemical disorders, validly may be termed mental illnesses. But at the same time a vast number of other human problems have been classified as mental illnesses for which there is no evidence that they have been engendered by disease or illness at all."[10]

Why is Adams so suspicious of problems that cannot be directly linked to organic causes being termed "mental illness"? "The fundamental bent of fallen human nature is away from God. . . . Apart from organically generated difficulties, the 'mentally ill' are really *people with unsolved personal problems.*"[11]

This view follows logically from the Christian perception of human nature: man has rebelled against God, he has real guilt feelings about this rebellion, and so he must reconcile himself with God or face unsolved personal problems. Lawrence Crabb, Jr. writes, "An appreciation of the reality of sin is a critically necessary beginning point for an understanding of the Christian view of anything. A psychology worthy of the adjective 'Christian' must not set the problem of sin in parallel line with other problems or redefine it into a neurosis or psychological kink."[12]

THE REALISTIC APPROACH TO SIN AND GUILT

If the Christian psychologist denies the existence of most mental illnesses, what good is his psychology? That is, how can the Christian psychologist propose to help people if he views their mental problems as spiritual problems caused by alienation from God? Doesn't this view just place too much guilt on people and avoid any real therapy?

If by the word *therapy* one means consciousness-raising seminars or primal scream workshops, then it is true the Christian psychologist does away with therapy. However, the Christian psychologist still offers solutions for the troubled person.

Because man has a conscience, and because he rebelled and continues to rebel against God, he is bound to experience real guilt. This guilt is acknowledged by the Christian psychologist, who points the hurting person toward Christ's sacrificial death and resurrection, so that the guilty can know deliverance from his guilt. Our sins will dog us daily—unceasingly—until they are washed away by Christ's shed blood.

The Christian psychologist, then, must stress personal moral responsibility. Without this responsibility, the individual may deny any real guilt caused by his sins and thereby avoid the heart of his problem—his alienation from God. Only through recognizing one's sinful nature and guilt before God can anyone reconcile his guilt feelings with reality.

This may seem like a rather insensitive approach to helping people with very sensitive problems. But what could be more cruel than treating just a symptom of the problem and ignoring the actual sickness? Who would fault a doctor for giving his patient a shot to fight a disease rather than a cough drop to mask a symptom? As Adams puts it, "It is important for counselors to remember that whenever clients camouflage, . . . sick treatment only makes them worse. To act as if they may be excused for their condition is the most unkind thing one can do. Such an approach only compounds the problem."[13]

The first step for the Christian psychologist in dealing with many mental and spiritual problems is to hold each client personally responsible for the sin in his life. Crabb writes, "Hold your client responsible: for what? For confessing his sin, for wilfully and firmly turning from it, and then for practicing the new behavior, believing that the indwelling Spirit will provide all the needed strength."[14]

This is the key for all Christian healing of "mental illnesses" that are not organically caused: confession of sin, forgiveness of sin through Christ (1 John 1:9), reconciliation with God (2 Corinthians 5:17-21), and sanctification through the disciplining work of God's Spirit (1 Thessalonians 5:23; Hebrews 12:1-11). Christian psychology, for all its fascination with human nature and the existence of guilt, leads to one simple method, summarized in James 5:16: "Therefore confess your sins to each other and pray for each other so that you may be healed. The prayer of a righteous man is powerful and effective."

THE PROBLEM OF SUFFERING

Most secular psychologies attempt to alleviate all suffering for the individual. Psychologists speak of methods of "successful living" that are supposed to eradicate most pain and anguish. Vitz says this "self-ist" psychology "trivializes life by claiming that suffering (and by implication even death) is without intrinsic meaning. Suffering is seen as some sort of absurdity, usually a man-made mistake which could have been avoided by the use of knowledge to gain control of the environment."[15]

In contrast, Christian psychology believes that God can use suffering to bring about positive changes in the individual. This difference between "secular" and Christian psychology has serious implications. For the non-Christian, suffering is a harsh reality that must be avoided at all cost; for the Christian, suffering may be used by God to discipline and lead us (Hebrews 12:7-11)—indeed, Christians are sometimes called to plunge joyously into suffering in obedience to God (Acts 6:8-7:60).

Meaning in suffering is a feature unique to Christian psychology. Thus we find Kilpatrick concluding, "The real test of a theory or way of life, however, is not whether it can relieve pain but what it says about the pain it cannot relieve. And this is where, I believe, psychology lets us down and Christianity supports us, for in psychology suffering has no meaning, while in Christianity it has great meaning."[16]

> "The real test of a theory or way of life, however, is not whether it can relieve pain but what it says about the pain it cannot relieve. And this is where, I believe, psychology lets us down and Christianity supports us ..."
>
> *William Kilpatrick*

SOCIETY AND THE INDIVIDUAL

Christian psychology's view of human nature grants the individual moral responsibility, works to reconcile the individual with God, and gives meaning to suffering. An offshoot of this perspective is that the Christian views society as the result of individuals' actions—that is, individuals are understood to be responsible for the evils in society. This view is in direct contradiction to the Marxist and Humanist view that man is corrupted by evil societies.

As always, these opposing views have logical consequences. For Marxists and Humanists, society must be changed, and then man can "learn" to do right. For the Christian, however, the individual must change for the better before society can. For the Christian, blaming individual sins on society is a cop-out. As Karl Menninger says,

"If a group of people can be made to share the responsibility for what would be a sin if an individual did it, the load of guilt rapidly lifts from the shoulders of all concerned. Others may accuse, but the guilt shared by the many evaporates for the individual. Time passes. Memories fade. Perhaps there is a record, somewhere; but who reads it?"[17]

The Christian, of course, knows there is a record somewhere, and is uncomfortably aware that Someone reads it. A day will come when no one can blame his sins on society. It is the Christian psychologist's duty, then, to realize the importance of personal responsibility and to impart this realization to anyone he counsels.

Secular Humanism	Marxist/Leninist	Cosmic Humanist	Christianity
Monistic Self-actualization	Monistic Pavlovian Behaviorism	Collective Consciousness	Dualism

CONCLUSION

The Christian view of human nature is complex; ironically, it logically leads to a simple method for counseling people. Further, Christians who properly understand human nature may never need to seek professional counseling—they may maintain spiritual well-being by remaining in submission to Christ. Schaeffer outlines a simple approach to "positive psychological hygiene": "As a Christian, instead of putting myself in practice at the center of the universe, I must do something else. This is not only right, and the failure to do so is not only sin, but it is important for me personally in this life. I must think after God, and I must will after God."[18]

198

The choice between Christian psychology and all other psychological schools is clear-cut. As Kilpatrick says, "Our choice . . . is really the same choice offered to Adam and Eve: either we trust God or we take the serpent's word that we can make ourselves into gods."[19]

FOUR WESTERN WORLDVIEW MODELS

SOURCES	SECULAR HUMANISM HUMANIST MANIFESTOS I AND II	MARXISM/LENINISM WRITINGS OF MARX AND LENIN	COSMIC HUMANISM WRITINGS OF SPANGLER, FERGUSON, ETC.	BIBLICAL CHRISTIANITY BIBLE
THEOLOGY	Atheism	Atheism	Pantheism	Theism
PHILOSOPHY	Naturalism	Dialectical Materialism	Non-Naturalism	Supernaturalism
ETHICS	Relativism	Proletariat Morality	Relativism	Absolutes
BIOLOGY	Darwinian Evolution	Darwinian/Punctuated Evolution	Darwinian/Punctuated Evolution	Creation
PSYCHOLOGY	Self-Actualization	Behaviorism	Collective Consciousness	Mind/Body
SOCIOLOGY	Non-Traditional Family	Abolition of Home, Church and State	Non-Traditional Home, Church and State	Traditional Home, Church and State
LAW	Positive Law	Positive Law	Self-Law	Biblical and Natural Law
POLITICS	World Government (Globalism)	New World Order (New Civilization)	New Age Order	Justice, Freedom and Order
ECONOMICS	Socialism	Socialism	Universal Enlightened Production	Stewardship of Property
HISTORY	Historical Evolution	Historical Materialism	Evolutionary Godhood	Historical Resurrection

CHAPTER 23

Secular Humanist Sociology

"Essentially man is internally motivated toward positive personal and social ends; the extent to which he is not motivated results from a process of demotivation generated by his relationships and/or environment."[1]

—Robert Tannenbaum and Sheldon A. Davis

INTRODUCTION

Humanist sociology and psychology are basically two sides of the same coin. Both disciplines act on the same premises; the former concentrates on society, the latter on the individual.

Because of this similarity, Humanist sociologists face the same basic problem as their psychologist brothers: the unscientific nature of their approach. Just as Humanist psychologists struggle to redefine science in a way that included their approach while excluding a religious approach, Humanist sociology struggles to fit the "scientific" label.

"Supernaturalism in all its forms is dying out," says Read Bain. "Science has been slowly destroying it for over three hundred years, with rapid acceleration during the last century. Its final stronghold is in the psychosocial realm. During the last fifty years the social sciences have made great strides toward becoming natural sciences and most of the former psychosocial mysteries have become matters of rapidly developing scientific knowledge."[2]

Regardless of Bain's unbridled optimism, even a superficial examination of Humanist sociology reveals that it is less than on par with the natural sciences. Most leading Humanist sociologists recognize this and struggle to infuse value into their discipline through other than purely scientific means.

HUMANIST SOCIOLOGY AS A CATALYST

Many Humanist sociologists attempt to give meaning to their work by viewing it as an instrument for actively bettering the world. They believe they must work not only as observers but also as catalysts. In this way, Humanists believe they can ascribe value to their sociology despite its unscientific nature.

Patricia Hill Collins declares that "the discipline of sociology thus is highly political."[3] This attitude differs from the attitude of scientists, who concern themselves more with adding to human knowledge than with politics. However, since the Humanist sociologist is unsure of the scientific nature of his methods for attaining knowledge, he relies on activism to enforce the meaning and validity of his work. A perfect example of this is Humanist historian Vern Bullough's observation that "Politics and science go hand in hand. In the end it is Gay activism which determines what researchers say about gay people."[4]

This raises a question. How can the Humanist be certain that such activism is called for? Why does the Humanist sociologist feel so strongly that society must be changed for the better?

SOCIETY AS EVIL

As was pointed out in the Humanist Psychology chapter, the Humanist views man as inherently good; therefore he must pin the blame for man's evil actions elsewhere. This blame falls on society—especially traditional institutions. Erich Fromm, who speaks of "the social process which creates man,"[5] believes, "Just as primitive man was helpless before natural forces, modern man is helpless before the social and economic forces created by himself."[6] Fromm wrote *The Sane Society*, which is based on the premise that today's society is insane and therefore corrupting the individual.

The focus of the Humanist sociologist's studies and activism, then, must be the restructuring of society in an effort to do away with the old social order and create a new social order based on Humanist values. The "old culture"—that is, the culture we are a part of right now, is assumed to inhibit man's natural tendency to grow and become a better human being.

The Humanist's antagonism toward modern society and his desire for change naturally manifest themselves in an outspoken distrust of tradition. This distrust is seldom supported with any more evidence than the assumption that all of society inhibits the individual's moral nature, and therefore all the tradition behind society must be flawed.

Naturally, this Humanist disdain for tradition carries over to traditional religions. Walda Katz Fishman and C. George Benello declare that Humanist sociology "seeks the concrete betterment of humankind and is opposed to theories that seek either to glorify the status quo or to march human beings lockstep into history in the interests of a vision imposed from above."[7] Since the Humanist denies the existence of God and embraces the evolutionary perspective, any traditions still a part of our society are simply traditions created by men less advanced than modern man, and are therefore in need of revision.

A Brief Look At: Isaac Asimov (1920-1992)

1923: Moved to United States from Soviet Union

1948: Receives his PhD from Columbia University

1949: Begins teaching at Boston University

1950: Publishes first two science fiction books

1973: Signs *Humanist Manifesto II*

1982: Publishes *How Did We Find Out About the Beginning of Life?*

1984: Elected Humanist of the Year

1989: Serves as the director of the American Humanist Association (AHA)

THE FAILURE OF TRADITIONAL MARRIAGE

Humanist sociologists are especially intolerant of the traditional, biblical family. In fact, Humanists often cite the institution of marriage as a prime example of the failure of Christian culture to provide freedom for the individual to grow. Marriage is considered too restrictive, inhibiting "vital inclinations." Heterosexual monogamy, for the Humanist, epitomizes social slavery.

Thus, Lawrence Casler declares that "marriage and family life have been largely responsible, I suggest, for today's prevailing neurotic climate, with its pervasive insecurity, and it is precisely this climate that makes so difficult the acceptance of a different, healthier way of life."[8]

This notion of marriage having outlived its usefulness arises from the concept of biological and cultural evolution. As the human species and culture progress, old traditions must be traded for new concepts that speed our evolutionary journey. In the overall evolutionary scheme of things, the western family system is even now losing its struggle for existence.

> "Just as primitive man was helpless before natural forces, modern man is helpless before the social and economic forces created by himself."
>
> Erich Fromm

Why are marriage and the family relics of the past? Largely because they have been used by men to dominate women, according to Humanist sociologists. Sol Gordon believes that "The traditional family, with all its supposed attributes, enslaved woman; it reduced her to a breeder and caretaker of children, a servant to her spouse, a cleaning lady, and at times a victim of the labor market as well."[9]

Gordon, of course, is talking the language of feminism—a movement that emerged from the Secular Humanist worldview. "The feminist movement was begun and has been nourished by leading humanist women,"[10] says Paul Kurtz. He specifically mentions Elizabeth Cady Stanton, Betty Friedan, Gloria Steinem, and Simone deBeauvoir. "Humanism and feminism are inextricably interwoven,"[11] according to Kurtz.

THE FAMILY ACCORDING TO HUMANIST SOCIOLOGY

Humanist sociologists are willing to propose a number of alternatives to traditional marriage. Robert N. Whitehurst's suggestions include modified open marriage (open to adultery), triads, cooperatives, collectives, urban communes, extended intimates, swinging and group marriage, and part-time marriage. Lester Kirkendall, in *A New Bill of Sexual Rights and Responsibilities*, a declaration signed by a number of Humanists including Kurtz and Albert Ellis, advocates a similar list of alternative lifestyles, including homosexuality, bisexuality, pre- and extra-marital sexual relationships, and something called "genital associations."

Humanist sociologists go so far as to suggest that the new family in the new world order will no longer have to concern itself with childrearing. Casler proposes a society in which "there would be no compulsory responsibility for child-rearing . . ."[12] He believes that this is a better alternative for all involved and that future generations will be more likely to stay in touch with their inherent goodness when raised in institutions. He writes, "It is supposed that the principles of ethical, productive, and happy living will be learned more readily when children are free of the insecurities, engendered chiefly by parents, that ordinarily obstruct the internalization of these modes of thought."[13]

The Humanist sociologist's disdain for Christian culture and its traditions causes him to suggest radical changes for the brave new world. But suggestions are not enough; most Humanist sociologists believe that they must actively strive to see these suggestions implemented. Sometimes this means using the classroom as a means for swaying student opinion in favor of creating an entirely new social order.

THE POWER OF THE CLASSROOM

Most Humanist sociologists are not at all bashful about acknowledging the usefulness of the public school classroom in promoting activism. Collins believes that teachers automatically become activists when they walk into the classroom: "To me, teaching is much more than the passive transfer of technical skills from teacher to learner. Rather, teaching has political implications that reach far beyond the classroom."[14] Obviously, if this is the case, the classroom is the ideal place for the Humanist to further the "new" faith of Humanism.

John J. Dunphy, in an article in The Humanist titled "*A Religion for a New Age,*" insists that teachers in the classroom "will be ministers of another sort." Utilizing the classroom, they will "convey humanist values in whatever subject they teach."[15] John Dewey also recognized the value of the classroom for achieving these purposes.

Of course, Humanists are only willing to allow the classroom to be a place of activism for Humanist teachers. Any *Christian* activism, even hanging the Ten Commandments on the wall, is violently opposed by the Humanist under the pretense of enforcing the separation of church and state. Thus, the *Humanist Manifesto II* declares, "The separation of church and state and the separation of ideology and state are imperatives."[16]

THE SELF-ACTUALIZING SOCIETY

We have seen that the Humanist sociologist is dissatisfied with Christian culture and is attempting to create a new society through remodeling the family and activism in the classroom. What type of new world order does the Humanist sociologist envision?

Humanists are necessarily vague about their new society. Fromm defines his "sane society" as "that which corresponds to the needs of man—not necessarily to what he feels to be his needs, because even the most pathological aims can be felt subjectively as that which the person wants most; but to what his needs are *objectively,* as they can be ascertained by the study of man."[17]

Man's highest need, according to Abraham Maslow's hierarchy of needs, is self-actualization. For the Humanist, a society that creates self-actualized individuals is the ideal society. Maurice R. Stein puts the ideal society in evolutionary perspective, declaring that "humanist sociology views society as an historically evolving enterprise that can only be understood through the struggle to liberate human potentialities."[18]

This call for human growth and liberating our potential is exactly what Humanist psychologists such as Maslow and Carl Rogers have emphasized. Humanist sociologists simply focus on creating a society that encourages self-actualized behavior—that is, a society in which everyone can get in touch with his true self, his innate goodness. John F. Glass and John R. Staude sum up: "Just as the humanistic psychologist is concerned with individual change in a growthful direction, the humanistic sociologist is concerned with a society which would encourage and sustain such growth—a self-actualizing society, as it were."[19]

Economics and the New Society

It should be noted that Humanist sociologists, perhaps because they view society as needing radical changes, hold slightly more radical views than the average Humanist. Thus, virtually all Humanist sociologists favor socialism as the economic order for a self-actualized society, and many endorse a Marxist approach to economics. For various reasons, the Humanist sociologist believes that socialism is more conducive than capitalism to the individual's self-actualization.

We have already noted that since the Humanist views society as responsible for man's evils, he perceives Christian culture, with all the evil individual actions it causes, as hopelessly flawed. Therefore, all aspects of Western civilization, including capitalism, have serious flaws as well. Fromm describes capitalism as tending to alienate men from each other: "What is modern man's relationship to his fellow man? It is one between two abstractions, two living machines, who use each other."[20]

According to most Humanist sociologists, socialism is much more humane than capitalism. "The only constructive solution is that of Socialism," says Fromm, "which aims at a fundamental reorganization of our economic and social system in the direction of freeing man from being used as a means for purposes outside of himself, of creating a social order in which human solidarity, reason and productiveness are furthered rather than hobbled."[21]

Humanist sociology expects radical changes in our society, especially in our economic system. It is important to remember that the Humanist sociologist does not stop at looking for these changes; he also works as an activist to cause them.

Sociology At A Glance

Secular Humanism

Non-traditional Family
World State
Ethical Society

CONCLUSION

Humanist sociologists believe in social activism partly because it gives more meaning to their discipline, and partly because they genuinely believe that our culture could evolve so that it encourages universal self-actualization. This optimism is best summed up by Reese, who states, "Informed and active people can make of society what they want it to become."[22]

Such optimism in turn causes the Humanist sociologist to feel particularly antagonistic toward our present society, because today's social institutions are inferior to the utopian society the Humanist believes is possible. His disdain for modern society manifests itself in an open distrust for any and all traditions and a desire to abandon or rework all existing social institutions. The Christian institution of the family must be radically remodeled or eliminated altogether. The institution of the church must be kept under wraps by insisting on the separation of church and state (but such separation must not apply to the religion of Secular Humanism). The institution of the state (and especially the judiciary) must be used to establish the Humanist agenda, including child care centers, gay rights, abortion, and animal rights. Humanists call for the eradication of all Christian institutions, traditions, and symbols, and a complete overhaul of American society. Only then will America be prepared to merge slowly with other like-minded Humanist states to forge a new world order.

CHAPTER 24

Marxist/Leninist Sociology

"With the transfer of the means of production into common ownership [commu-nism], the single family ceases to be the economic unit of society ... The care and education of the children becomes a public affair; society looks after all children alike, whether they are legitimate or not."[1]

—Frederick Engels

INTRODUCTION

Marxist sociologists, like all Marxists, claim that their approach to their discipline is more scientific than any other approach. While Humanist sociologists will some-times confess the unscientific nature of sociology (some refer to it as an art instead of a science), Marxists compare their sociology with the natural sciences.

On what scientific foundation do the Marxists base their sociological approach? G. V. Plekhanov claims that Marxism is "Darwinism in its application to social science."[2] That is, the Marxist sociologist perceives his social theory as rooted in the scientific "fact" of Darwinism. This Marxist reliance on evolution as a basis for its social theory greatly influences Marxists' perception of the mechanisms of society. Just as man is evolving biologically, so also man is evolving sociologically. As man improves through the evolutionary chain of being, so also does society. The scientific fact of biological evolution guarantees both the truth of Marxist social theory and the outcome of the process: a communist world.

Society as an Evolving Entity

Whereas Charles Darwin outlined the concept of the evolution of the *species,* Marxism describes the evolution of *society* as a whole. Thus, Marxist sociologists constantly discuss the "development of society."

Karl Marx and V.I. Lenin both believe that man can truly understand society only in the context of this concept of development. At a certain stage of social development, says Marx, "the material productive forces of society come into conflict with the existing relations of production. . . . From forms of development of the productive forces these relations turn into their fetters. Then begins an era of social revolution. The changes in the economic foundation lead sooner or later to the transformation of the whole immense superstructure."[3]

Development, for the Marxist, is initiated by changes in the economic system of a society. Man's economic system determines how men must relate to each other in order to operate efficiently within the system. These forms of relation, in turn, dictate the societal norms in general, including the political and legal aspects of society.

For the Marxist, the stages in the development of society must parallel the economic stages in mankind's history. Marx divides the history of society into four stages: "In broad outline, the Asiatic, ancient, feudal and modern bourgeois modes of production may be designated as epochs marking progress in the economic development of society."[4] Society, however, does not stop developing at the bourgeois stage. Rather, society will develop eventually into a communist stage. This evolution will occur due to specific economic forces.

Society as Predetermined

On the surface, it appears that the Marxist allows these economic forces to supplant free will. Society appears to be determined by the type of economic system upon which it is founded. "It is not the consciousness of men that determines their existence," writes Marx, "but their social existence that determines their consciousness."[5] That is, man's very consciousness is determined by a society predetermined by its economic system.

Apparently, man could no more choose to change society than the earth could choose to change its orbit. Both men and planets behave according to merciless scientific laws.

The individual is insignificant in the face of the powerful forces of society. Joseph Stalin believes that to understand the historical process one must rely "on the concrete conditions of the material life of society, as the determining force of social development; not on the good wishes of great men."[6] Indeed, Marxists view the changes in society as often contrary to the efforts of even the best of individuals.

A Brief Look At: Mao Tse-tung (1893-1976)

1918: Works under a Marxist "pioneer" at Peking University

1921: Helps found the Chinese Communist Party (CCP)

1934: Begins the Long March, a retreat from persecution

1935: Elected chairman of the Politburo

1949: Rises to power as leader of the CCP

1958: Experiments with the Great Leap Forward

1969: Wins the cultural revolution, solidifies power

MAN'S ONE CHANCE TO CREATE HIS OWN SOCIETY

Why, then, should men work for the advent of communism? If man is a pawn in the hands of economic forces driven by the dialectic, why should he act as though he has free will?

Supposedly, Marxist sociologists have solved this problem as well. Now that Marx and Engels have made men conscious of the forces that cause society to evolve, certain men may—to a limited extent—exercise some free will.

One class of men, according to the Marxist, has not been tainted by the capitalistic economic system. This class—the proletariat—can consciously work toward the next phase of societal development.

It is interesting to note how closely Marxist sociology parallels Marxist psychology at this point. As demonstrated in the chapter on psychology, the Marxist grants the individual virtually no free will until this will is necessary for the revolution to overthrow capitalism. The same phenomenon occurs in the sociological arena of Marxist thought.   Society determines the individual, until the free will of the individual is required to create a socialistic society. Then the Marxist sociologist finds himself willing to ignore the previously postulated impotency of man, claiming instead that some men now have the opportunity to finally rise up and be "free."

Of course, for the Marxist, the advent of communism is viewed as inevitable regardless of the number of individuals who ignore Marx's "sociological laws" or strive against them. Thus, in Marxist theory, the proletarian is only free to create the next society if he is willing to go along with the evolutionary process and create a communist society.

THE ULTIMATE SOCIETY

Communism marches on, then, regardless of the number of men who oppose it. Those who choose to support this march will be "free," while all others will remain slaves to present-day capitalist society. This inevitable spread of communism will occur largely because this is the script of social evolution, an evolution based on biological conflict and the survival of the fittest economic system.

Socialism is seen as the first step toward a communist society because the Marxist sociologist emphasizes economics as the very foundation of society. A socialistic economic system can initiate all the other necessary changes to create a perfect society: communism.

When world-wide communism occurs, utopia will be established. This perfect society will differ significantly from modern bourgeois societies: the evils of competition will vanish, and all classes will be abolished.

Further, the communist utopia will no longer need a government to keep it running smoothly. "Only in Communist society," declares Lenin, "when the resistance of the capitalists has been completely broken, when the capitalists have disappeared, when there are no classes . . . only then the State ceases to exist."[7] We will examine the Marxist view of the state more closely in the chapter on Marxist politics. For the remainder of this chapter, we will concern ourselves with the Marxist sociologist's view of the church, the family, and education—their role in modern society, and the changes they will undergo in the transition to the ultimate society.

> "It is not the consciousness of men that determines their existence, but their social existence that determines their consciousness."
>
> *Karl Marx*

THE CHURCH IN MARXIST SOCIOLOGY

As demonstrated in the chapter on Marxist theology, Marxists have little patience with religion or any notion of God. The Marxist sees religion as a stumbling block, slowing the development of the ultimate society:

The influence of the church promotes the schism of the workers movement. Reactionary churchmen everywhere try to isolate religious workers from their class brothers by attracting them into separate organizations of a clerical nature . . . and thus diverting them from the struggle against capitalism.[8]

In the former Soviet Union, Marxists used many different methods in their effort to abolish religion. In the early days following the October Revolution, the Marxists simply discriminated against priests in an effort to discourage anyone who wanted to be in the clergy. When discrimination failed to wipe out religion, the Marxists tried to further restrict the church through state controls. On April 8, 1929, for example, the USSR enacted a law that forbade religious organizations from creating mutual assistance funds or providing any aid to their members, and from meeting at any time other than for religious services.

Marxist sociologists, in effect, declare war on the church.

EDUCATION IN MARXIST SOCIOLOGY

> "The family deprives the worker of revolutionary consciousness."
>
> *Aleksandra M. Kollontai*

According to the Marxist, a society's educational system follows directly from the means of production extant in that society. Thus, education in modern bourgeois society reflects all the evils of that mode of production. Madan Sarup believes, "The [modern] educational system thus meshes with capital to ensure the maintenance of women's oppression."[9]

What type of education would the Marxist sociologist provide? Prior to the proletarian revolt and the institution of socialism as the new means of production, the proletariat—the only class that will survive the transition to Marxism—can only be educated in terms of the dialectical struggle.

Once the struggle is over, however, and the proletariat has ushered in a socialistic economic system, the Marxist sociologist perceives education as playing a different role in creating the ultimate society. This role is delineated in the text *People's Education:*

The basic task of communist education and overcoming the survivals of religiousness in our present condition is to prove to the pupils the complete contrast and complete irreconcilability between science, the real and correct reflection of the objectively existing world in the consciousness of people—and religion as a fantastic, distorted and, consequently, harmful reflection of the world in the consciousness of the people.[10]

For the Marxist sociologist, education is a valuable tool for shaping the ideology of individuals. This tool must be used to create citizens more likely to cooperate with and fit into the Marxist notion of the ultimate society. Accordingly, the individual must be educated to detest religion and embrace the Marxist materialistic view of the world.

THE FAMILY IN MARXIST SOCIOLOGY

Obviously, the family type extant in bourgeois society is not the advanced family necessary for communism. Like religion and bourgeois education, the modern family is viewed by Marxist sociology as a great failure.

Only the proletariat has remained untainted by this bourgeois institution. According to the Marxist sociologist, proletarians will never enter into family relations as they exist in present society, because the proletariat is destined to usher in a new, utopian society, complete with a higher form of "family." Until this occurs, the proletariat must shun the bourgeois society family type, because, as Aleksandra M. Kollontai says, "The family deprives the worker of revolutionary consciousness."[11]

What type of "family" will evolve when the proletariat seizes the means of production and ushers in communist society? Engels predicts,

> With the transfer of the means of production into common ownership, the single family ceases to be the economic unit of society. Private housekeeping is transformed into a social industry. The care and education of the children becomes a public affair; society looks after all children alike, whether they are legitimate or not. This removes all the anxiety about the consequences which today is the most essential social-moral as well as economic-factor that prevents a girl from giving herself completely to the man she loves. Will not that suffice to bring about the gradual growth of unconstrained sexual intercourse and with it a more tolerant public opinion in regard to a maiden's honor and a woman's shame?[12]

That is, the new social order will accept, and even encourage, premarital sex and adultery, as long as it is done in a spirit of freedom and responsibility. Indeed, within the context of community where there is no private property and everyone belongs to everyone, premarital sex and adultery cease to have any meaning.

It is important to note, too, that Marxists believe the care of children should become "a public affair." In the family in the ultimate society, children play an insignificant role, since they are the entire community's responsibility. In fact, children are basically disengaged from the family in socialist society—"school becomes literally a home."[13]

This alienation of children from their parents helps ensure that children formulate their worldviews according to education provided by the Marxist state. This aspect of the new "family" prevents the child from learning the outdated views held by his parents, especially about religion.

Sociology At A Glance

Secular Humanism	Marxist/Leninist
Non-traditional Family World State Ethical Society	Abolition of Home, Church and State

CONCLUSION

Marxist sociology perceives all social institutions as determined by the economic system on which the society is based. The economic system is in a process of constant development, and therefore the resultant societies are perceived as constantly evolving as well. This social evolution occurs regardless of the actions of individuals—in fact, it often occurs in spite of their actions.

Marxists believe that the next step in this social and cultural evolutionary process will be a world socialist system and that a new world order will emerge as a result of the changed means of production. This society will move toward abolishing religion, the nuclear family, and government, and will develop a proletarian system of public education and "family." The Marxist sociologist is confident in this prediction, because he believes that Marx's approach to sociology is based on science—the scientific fact of evolution.

CHAPTER 25

Cosmic Humanist Sociology

"Communities, nations and cultures—all of our collective creations . . . reflect the decisions of our species to learn through fear and doubt."[1]

—Gary Zukav

INTRODUCTION

Once every individual makes the evolutionary leap to collective godhood, Cosmic Humanist psychology and sociology will merge—both will study a society unified into one mind (the mind of God). Until that happens, New Age sociology must concentrate on exploding the limits of our current societies, because modern societies inhibit man's ability to achieve higher consciousness. Marilyn Ferguson complains, "Every society, by offering its automatic judgments, limits the vision of its members. From our earliest years we are seduced into a system of beliefs that becomes so inextricably braided into our experience that we cannot tell culture from nature."[2]

According to the Cosmic Humanist, all of our institutions should encourage individuals to seek the inner truth of their perfectible human nature. Specifically, societies must adopt a pantheistic perspective. David Spangler says that the New Age approach

is to look at the objects, people, and events in our lives and to say "You are sacred. In you and with you I can find the sacramental passages that reconnect me to the wholeness of creation." It is then to ask ourselves what kind of culture, what kind of institutions—be they political, economic, artistic, educational, or scientific—we need that can honor that universal sacredness.[3]

A Brief Look At: Aldous Huxley (1894-1963)

1887: Oldest brother Julian is born

1895: Grandfather T.H. Huxley dies

1910: Almost blinded by an eye infection

1914: Older brother Trev commits suicide

1926: Begins friendship with D.H. Lawrence

1932: Publishes *Brave New World*

1945: Publishes *The Perennial Philosophy*

1953: Begins experimenting with psychedelic drugs

1963: Takes two doses of LSD on the day he dies

BEYOND MARRIAGE AND FAMILY

Most Cosmic Humanists point to marriage and family as examples of outdated, unenlightened institutions. Both marriage and family, in their traditional Judeo-Christian forms, are regarded as too limiting and too hopelessly blind to universal sacredness to be useful in achieving full enlightenment. Thus, Vera Alder claims that in the New Age the concept of family will have so evolved that "the idea that an unmarried person of either sex should have to remain childless will seem far-fetched."[4]

Shakti Gawain believes we need to re-work our attitude about divorce to create a society more conducive to mankind's evolution to godhood: "People who divorce almost inevitably feel that they have failed, because they assume all marriages should last forever. In most such cases, however, the marriage has actually been a total success—it's helped each person to grow to the point where they no longer need its old form."[5]

According to this sociological view, it is counter-evolutionary to attempt to maintain the institutions of marriage and family in the traditional sense. Writes Gawain,

> Relationships and families as we've known them seem to be falling apart at a rapid
> rate. Many people are panicky about this; some try to re-establish the old traditions
> and value systems in order to cling to a feeling of order and stability in their lives. It's
> useless to try to go backward, however, because our consciousness has already
> evolved beyond the level where we were willing to make the sacrifices necessary to
> live that way.[6]

Going forward requires accepting total sexual freedom. This includes embracing homosexuality, according to Kevin Ryerson: "Sexuality, whether homosexual or heterosexual, is the exploring of the personalities of yourselves as incarnate beings, or as a spirit inhabiting the flesh. An individual's sexual preference should be viewed as neither good nor evil—such preferences are but the functioning of the body's dialogue to and with another."[7] If every individual is to achieve higher consciousness, society must not hinder our evolution by limiting our options.

EDUCATING FOR THE NEW AGE

Cosmic Humanists hope to encourage a "limit-less" society by working within an already existing institution: our educational system. By teaching children the proper attitudes toward themselves and their consciousness, New Age educators believe that they can create a generation capable of ushering in the New Age. For this reason, many Cosmic Humanists choose careers in education. In fact, Ferguson admits that out of all the New Age professionals she surveyed for *The Aquarian Conspiracy*, "more were involved in education than in any other single category of work."[8]

> "An individual's sexual preference should be viewed as neither good nor evil ..."
>
> *Kevin Ryerson*

Many of these Cosmic Humanists use their positions to promote their worldview. John Dunphy, in an article entitled "A Religion for the New Age," says the battle for the future will be fought in the classroom:

I am convinced that the battle for humankind's future must be waged and won in the public school classrooms by teachers who correctly perceive their role as prose-lytizers of a new faith: a religion of humanity that recognizes and respects the spark of what theologians call the Divinity in every human being. These teachers must embody the same selfless dedication as the most rabid fundamentalist preachers.[9]

With the implementation of Values Clarification, sex clinics, moral relativism, biological evolution, *Cosmos,* and globalism in most public schools, Dunphy's "proselytizers" have already established the foundation for their new faith.

CONCLUSION

Modern society, as seen by the Cosmic Humanist, hinders mankind's evolution in a number of ways. Traditional views of the family, church, and state often prevent peo-

Sociology
At A Glance

Secular Humanism	Marxist/Leninist	Cosmic Humanist
Non-traditional Family World State Ethical Society	**Abolition of Home, Church and State**	**Non-traditional Home, Church and State**

ple from travelling their path to godhood. In an effort to change this, many Cosmic Humanists choose to work as educators, so that the next generation will learn to over-step traditional limits and achieve higher consciousness.

Significantly, Cosmic Humanists rarely champion specific changes to societal institutions. New Agers tend to be suspicious of institutions in general, because institutions imply form and limits. Cosmic Humanism ultimately declares that meaningful change in society will occur only when enough meaningful changes in individuals occur. "Your decision to evolve consciously through responsible choice," says Gary Zukav, "contributes not only to your own evolution, but also to the evolution of all of those aspects of humanity in which you participate. It is not just you that is evolving through your decisions, but the entirety of humanity."[10]

Thus, Cosmic Humanist sociology is tied closely to Cosmic Humanist psychology. Since each individual has a God within, individuals have all the power necessary to change society. Societal change is secondary; individual change is primary. Society must simply refrain from inhibiting each individual's transition to higher consciousness.

CHAPTER 26

Biblical Christian Sociology

"For this reason a man will leave his father and mother and be united to his wife, and the two will become one flesh."

—Ephesians 5:31

INTRODUCTION

Every sociologist acknowledges the existence of certain social institutions such as family, church, and government. Sociologists differ, however, when describing the origin of these institutions and their relationship to the individual. This difference results from the assumptions inherent to the sociologist's worldview.

The Christian views mankind as specially created in God's image, while atheistic worldviews see man as simply an emerging animal. Unfortunately, this latter view is the predominant perspective among modern sociologists. God, Adam and Eve, the Garden of Eden, and the sacred character of the family are considered pre-scientific myths. Christians believe that this erroneous view is largely responsible for the many failures in modern sociology (e.g., its inability to suggest proper solutions to drug abuse, crime, and poverty).

A Brief Look At: Dietrich Bonhoeffer (1906-1945)

1927: Receives his doctorate from Berlin University

1931: Lectures in theology at Berlin University

1933: Helps organize the Pastors' Emergency League in response to Hitler

1935: Founds an underground seminary in Germany to train anti–Nazi pastors

1937: Publishes *The Cost of Discipleship*

1943: Arrested and imprisoned for his anti–Nazi activities

1945: Hanged after spending two years in prison camp

FREE WILL AND SOCIETY

One of the fundamental ways in which Christian sociology differs from the Humanist and Marxist approaches is Christianity's affirmation of individual free will and responsibility. While atheistic approaches, when consistent, believe that society determines man's consciousness and actions, Christianity describes man as a creature with the freedom to choose between right and wrong and to shape society.

The Christian view grants individual man much more control over his society, but it also burdens him with much more responsibility. Man, in the Christian perspective, must face the consequences of his decisions. This point is made painfully clear in the opening chapters of Genesis, when Adam and Eve bring a curse on the whole human race and are exiled from the Garden of Eden, all because they choose to disobey God. "If man's behavior were somehow conditioned by genetic code or social externals," says William Stanmeyer, "then no just judge could blame him for the evil he commits. But the scripture teaches unequivocally that God blamed Adam and Eve for succumbing to the temptation to disobedience and punished them accordingly."[1]

The Genesis account of Adam and Eve not only demonstrates that man is responsible for his actions, but also describes another key belief for Christians: every human is guilty before God. "The fact of guilt," according to one Christian author, "is one of the major realities of man's existence."[2]

Christian sociology attempts to understand society in light of man's free will and the consequences of his freely choosing to turn from God. The Fall caused every society created by man to be marked by alienation. To put it bluntly, ever since God gave man free will and the ability to create his own societies, man's record has been one of degeneration, not evolution. The alienation caused by man pervades all relationships.

Man's alienation from God, the rest of mankind, and himself plays a crucial role in the Christian approach to sociology. A sociologist who believes that man is alienated will interpret data differently from one who believes that man is inherently good but corrupted by society.

THE INHERENT WORTH OF THE INDIVIDUAL

It would seem, at this point, that the Christian sociologist is the most pessimistic of all sociologists, since he perceives man as constantly making the wrong decisions. In reality, however, God's saving grace makes the Christian position the most optimistic. Free will and responsibility before God grant mankind far more significance than man is granted by views based on atheism or pantheism. Man "is not a cog in a machine," says Francis A. Schaeffer, "he is not a piece of theater; he really can influence history. From the biblical viewpoint, *man is lost, but great*."[3]

The Christian perspective sees every individual as valuable and capable of making an important contribution to society. While other sociologists view the individual as basically helpless in the face of societal pressures, the Christian sees every individual as free and therefore capable of influencing society. To the Christian, the individual is more important than any institution or society.

C.S. Lewis drives this point home by observing that atheists think "nations, classes, civilizations must be more important than individuals," because "the individuals live only seventy odd years each and the group may last for centuries. But to the Christian, individuals are more important, for they live eternally; and races, civilizations and the like, are in comparison the creatures of a day."[4]

> **"[Man] is not a cog in a machine, he is not a piece of theater; he really can influence history."**
>
> *Francis A. Schaeffer*

MAN AS A SOCIAL BEING

The fact that Christians value the individual over the social order, however, does not diminish the importance of sociology in a Christian worldview. The Christian understands that society plays a key role in history and in the individual's relationship with God. Above all, he recognizes that man was created a social being (Genesis 2:20).

S.D. Gaede stresses the inherent social nature of man, stating, "God designed the human being to be a relational creature. Note this point well. Humankind was created to relate to other beings. It was not an accident. It was not the result of sin. It was an intentional, creational given."[5]

Of course, mankind's relations in this life will always be hindered by feelings of alienation. Gaede refers to this problem as the "relational dilemma" and views it as truth that must be recognized by all sociologists who wish to understand society in the proper perspective. In this context, Christians recognize the true cause of alienation in society and can competently study the results and offer a solution to the world.

CHRISTIAN PLURALISM

Christian sociologists maintain that the individual is more important than any institution in society, and society is important because man was created a social being. This sociological perspective is referred to as a pluralist view, because the sociologist does not perceive society or the individual as the only true reality. The view that society exclusively shapes reality is called collectivism; the view that only individuals can change reality is called individualism.

Both the Humanist and the Marxist approach sociology from the collectivist perspective. That is, because these worldviews hold that man is inherently good but is caused by society to either deny or embrace his goodness, they perceive society as creating reality and the individual as helpless and insignificant.

The proper perspective is a pluralist view of man and society. This perspective ensures that man "can never be reduced to either a mere atomistic individual or a mere integer in some social whole."[6] It also holds both man and society accountable to God (2 Kings 17:7f; Acts 17:31).

By making every member and aspect of society responsible, the Christian sociologist naturally expects each institution in society to focus on governing its own realm of interests properly and to allow other institutions the same freedom.

BIBLICALLY PRESCRIBED INSTITUTIONS

Every Christian sociologist believes that family, church, and state are institutions ordained by God. Some Christians, such as Dietrich Bonhoeffer, would add labor to this list of God-ordained institutions. For the Christian, it is extremely significant that God ordained certain societal institutions, because this indicates the relevance of Christianity to every aspect of reality. As Bonhoeffer says, "It is God's will that there shall be labour, marriage, government, and church in the world; and it is His will that all these, each in its own way, shall be through Christ, directed towards Christ, and in Christ. . . . This means that there can be no retreating from a 'secular' into a 'spiritual' sphere."[7]

This concept is an important one for the Christian sociologist (indeed, for all Christians) to grasp. After examining a list of the social institutions Christians perceive as ordained by God, one might get the impression that some aspects of society are outside the realm of Christianity. This, however, is not the case. All of society, indeed, all of life, is bound up inextricably with God and His plan for mankind—as Bonhoeffer says, "the world is relative to Christ."[8]

In the remainder of this chapter, we will focus on the Christian view of two social institutions: the family and the church. The state is examined in the Christian Politics chapter, labor in the Christian Economics chapter.

MARRIAGE AND THE FAMILY

For the Christian, marriage and the family are ordained by God (Genesis 2:23-25) and will always be the fundamental institution of society. The Christian believes that the family and its role are strictly defined in the Bible; as James Dobson and Gary Bauer say, the family exists when "husband and wife are lawfully married, are committed to each other for life, and [the family] adheres to the traditional values on which the family is based."[9]

George Gilder believes, as do many Christian sociologists, that the condition of marriage and family in any given society describes the condition of the entire society. If the family is troubled, so is society. It is to society's advantage to build and encourage the God-ordained social institution of marriage and the family.

Unfortunately, modern American society does more to discourage marriage and fam-

The research of Dr. Louis Pasteur (1822–1895) in bacteriology was the single-most important enhancement of hospital safety. Dr. Pasteur laid the foundation for pasteurization, sterilization, and the development of numerous vaccines.

ily than to build it up. This disdain for marriage and the family stems largely from the popularity of the Secular Humanist perspective and its brainchild, the sexual revolution. Even as you read this, public school children in sex-education courses are being subjected to some of the most bizarre concepts and practices imaginable. Not only is homosexuality being taught as a normal lifestyle, and not only are students given condoms and advised to practice their usage, but also teenage girls are being instructed about obtaining abortions without parental knowledge or consent. As Dobson and Bauer note, such sex-ed programs are "a crash course in relativism, in immorality, and in anti-Christian philosophy."[10]

It is not coincidental that these attacks on the traditional family come largely from proponents of relativistic, materialistic worldviews. The Humanist and the Marxist disregard the existence of the spirit and the soul and thereby devalue the family's importance for mankind; the Christian, however, recognizes marriage and the family as the institution that nurtures the whole individual. The family should provide an environment that encourages both mental and spiritual growth.

THE CHURCH IN SOCIETY

God ordained the church to serve specific functions. One of the principal roles of the church (a role that would disappear if Christ were shut out) is the proclamation of sin and salvation. By making society aware of sin, the church can effect great positive changes. If society does not repent of its sin, it will be judged. But the church can play a critical role in turning a society toward God by explaining that both the individual and society have sinned and are responsible for their actions.

The church also can cause a society to face God by providing an example of true community. If the Christian church could show the rest of society that it is possible to live according to the command "Love your neighbor as yourself," then individuals and society might be more willing to turn to God and acknowledge Him as the initiator of all relations. Schaeffer is adamant about the need for community in the Christian church: "I am convinced that in the 20th century people all over the world will not listen if we have the right doctrine, the right polity, but are not exhibiting community."[11] This sentiment is grounded in Ephesians 4:11-16.

CONCLUSION

Christian sociology values both the individual and society. The individual is seen as capable of free choice, though alienated because of man's decision to turn from God. Society is also seen as fallen and imperfect, as well as responsible for its decisions and attitudes. It is in this perspective that both society and the individual gain value: only people and institutions capable of choosing are truly significant—any man or society whose actions are determined by uncontrollable forces has no more value than a tree or a stone.

In this context of responsibility, the Christian recognizes that man must face the consequences for the choices he makes in creating his society. Man is charged with the duty of protecting and directing the growth of societal institutions ordained by God, including family, state and church. The family is charged with the generational or reproductive responsibilities; the state is charged with justice issues, which primarily involve maintaining law and order; the church is charged with making sure Christian love is the cement of the social institutions. Mankind is answerable to God for the direction in which society is led by these institutions. The same burden of responsibility points mankind to our blessing: we are the free creatures of a loving and just God.

Sociology At A Glance

Secular Humanism	Marxist/Leninist	Cosmic Humanist	Christianity
Non-traditional Family World State Ethical Society	Abolition of Home, Church and State	Non-traditional Home, Church and State	Home, Church and State

FOUR WESTERN WORLDVIEW MODELS

SOURCES	SECULAR HUMANISM HUMANIST MANIFESTOS I AND II	MARXISM/LENINISM WRITINGS OF MARX AND LENIN	COSMIC HUMANISM WRITINGS OF SPANGLER, FERGUSON, ETC.	BIBLICAL CHRISTIANITY BIBLE
THEOLOGY	Atheism	Atheism	Pantheism	Theism
PHILOSOPHY	Naturalism	Dialectical Materialism	Non-Naturalism	Supernaturalism
ETHICS	Relativism	Proletariat Morality	Relativism	Absolutes
BIOLOGY	Darwinian Evolution	Darwinian/Punctuated Evolution	Darwinian/Punctuated Evolution	Creation
PSYCHOLOGY	Self-Actualization	Behaviorism	Collective Consciousness	Mind/Body
SOCIOLOGY	Non-Traditional Family	Abolition of Home, Church and State	Non-Traditional Home, Church and State	Traditional Home, Church and State
LAW	Positive Law	Positive Law	Self-Law	Biblical and Natural Law
POLITICS	World Government (Globalism)	New World Order (New Civilization)	New Age Order	Justice, Freedom and Order
ECONOMICS	Socialism	Socialism	Universal Enlightened Production	Stewardship of Property
HISTORY	Historical Evolution	Historical Materialism	Evolutionary Godhood	Historical Resurrection

CHAPTER 27

Secular Humanist Law

"As with laws, so with morals: human beings seem quite capable of making, on their own, sensible and sensitive decisions affecting conduct.."[1]

—Frederick Edwords

INTRODUCTION

No Humanist leader has ever written a book specifically addressing the Humanist attitude toward law. This does not mean, however, that the Humanist worldview does not contain a legal theory. On closer examination, we find that basic assumptions of that theory are revealed throughout the works of a number of Humanists.

As with all other aspects of the Humanist worldview, their legal theory is founded on the basic assumptions that God does not exist and that man, as an evolving animal, is perfectible. Any doubts about the Humanist's belief that evolution is enormously significant for his worldview are erased by a single statement by Julian Huxley: "Our present knowledge indeed forces us to the view that the world of reality is evolution—a single process of self transformation."[2]

Mankind's focus, according to this view, must be on creating an environment that encourages further evolutionary progress. As already demonstrated in the Humanist sociology chapter, Humanists believe that any evil manifested in man is really caused by a less-than-perfect environment. If the environment could be perfected, then mankind could learn consistently to choose what is morally correct. This attitude greatly influences Humanism's approach to law. Law is seen as a tool manipulating society so that it influences men to get in touch with their evolving inner goodness.

IF GOD DOES NOT EXIST

Humanists deny not only God but also the existence of an absolute moral code to which they might owe obedience. Indeed, many Humanists see God's commands (which are traditionally viewed as the absolute moral code) as a potentially malignant fiction. Paul Kurtz declares, "The traditional supernaturalistic moral commandments are especially repressive of our human needs. They are immoral insofar as they foster illusions about human destiny and suppress vital inclinations."[3]

Humanists have no qualms about rejecting an absolute moral code because they believe man is capable of devising his own code, with regard to both morals and law. Frederick Edwords declares, "It should be obvious from the most casual observation that human beings are quite capable of setting up systems and then operating within them."[4]

The Humanist method of governing oneself requires a system of man-centered ethics. If ethics are not grounded in God's nature, then they must be discovered in man's relations with man. This man-centered morality evolves right along with the development of man. "Moral behavior of a rudimentary type," says V.M. Tarkunde, "is found in the higher animals and can be traced even to lower forms of life. This fact is enough to establish that the source of morality is biological and not theological."[5]

DO RIGHTS EVOLVE?

Clearly, Charles Darwin's evolutionary theory profoundly impacts the Humanist's conception of law. "There proceeded during the 19th Century," says Huxley, "under the influence of the evolutionary concept, a thoroughgoing transformation of older studies like . . . Law."[6] This transformation of the attitude toward law shines forth in a comment by Oliver Wendell Holmes, Jr.: "I see no reason for attributing to man a significance different in kind from that which belongs to a baboon or a grain of sand."[7]

This belief that man is an evolving animal on par with the baboon immediately creates a moral and legal dilemma for the Humanist: why should man enjoy rights not enjoyed by other animals? Morris B. Storer puts the question this way: "What is there that's different about a human being that dictates the right to life for all humans (unarguably in most circumstances) where most people acknowledge no such right in other animals? That justifies equal right to liberty where we fence the others in, equal justice under law where the other animals are not granted any trial at all."[8] Further, if laws and morality evolve, why don't rights evolve? Could certain rights evolve out of existence tomorrow?

Such questions and issues seem unanswerable when God is removed from the equation. Still, the Humanist makes many bold claims about, and even champions, "human rights." Kurtz declares, "There are common human rights that must be respected by everyone."[9] The Humanist accepts the existence of certain rights as indisputable. But how can the Humanist be so certain of rights worthy of protection by law, and indeed law itself, when their source is man the evolving animal?

A Brief Look At: Roscoe Pound (1870-1964)

1889: Receives M.A. from University of Nebraska

1890: Passes bar exam; begins teaching at the Nebraska Law School

1901: Begins service as commissioner of appeals of the Supreme Court of Nebraska

1909: Teaches law at the University of Chicago until 1910

1916: Begins 20–year career as dean of Harvard Law School

1947: Retires from Harvard

1959: Publishes five–volume *Jurisprudence*

NATURAL LAW

Some Humanists attempt to use the concepts of natural law and natural rights to provide a standard that transcends specific men and governments. The concept of natural law assumes that there is one true morality—one proper way for man to behave—and it is discoverable by man. Laws arise from this natural law to enforce adherence to its code. Likewise, natural rights exist independent of man, much like the law of gravity, but mankind may discover them and enact laws in conformity to them.

A belief in natural law and natural rights lets the Humanist off the hook in one sense, because it provides a more stable source for law than does any human interpretation of legal principles. However, the Humanist is faced with the problem of explaining the origins of this natural law. Whereas the Christian believes God implanted law in the universe and inscribed natural law on the hearts of men, the Humanist cannot tolerate such an explanation. Thus, Humanism falls back on evolutionary theory as the source for natural law, which is in turn the source of all rights and laws.

Julian Wadleigh asserts that evolution is just as viable an explanation for the existence of natural law as a Creator, thereby claiming natural law for the Humanist worldview and solving many of Humanism's dilemmas in the realm of ethics and law.

> **How does one convince citizens to obey laws that have no other foundation than the state? The question seems unanswerable.**

He writes, "The Declaration [of Independence] speaks of natural law as an endowment by a creator, whereas I speak of it as the result of humankind's evolution as a social animal. There is a difference, but that difference concerns the questions of how and why we have natural law—not whether or not natural law exists. Regardless of its origin, it is the same natural law."[10]

Unfortunately for the Humanist, this explanation ignores the fact that, according to Humanist biology, evolution is a continuous process. Therefore, while natural law may appear concrete today, it is undergoing constant change, just as man's genetic behaviors and understanding of natural law evolve. If this is true, rights or laws recognized by man today may evolve right out of existence. Thus, the Humanist once again is left with an uncertain and unstable source of law.

Wadleigh tries to integrate this uncertainty caused by evolution, stating, "Natural law is not a set of precise rules but a guide that must be followed using plain common sense."[11] As soon as the Humanist concedes this point, however, he nullifies the central precept of natural law theory—natural law becomes simply a relative guide, not a stable foundation for morality.

Humanism is incompatible with the theory of natural law and natural rights. Delos McKown makes this clear when he asks the pointed question, "When, one wonders, in evolutionary history did hominids first acquire natural rights?"[12] Obviously, the Humanist must abandon natural law to develop a legal theory consistent with the basic assumptions of his worldview.

NATURAL LAW DENIED

This denial of natural law begins with a denial of natural rights deserving protection under law. "Am I not bringing in a doctrine of natural rights that are prior to political policy?" asks Kurtz. "No, I reject any such fiction."[13] Indeed, Kurtz sees rights as recently evolved through human systems: "Most . . . rights have evolved out of the cultural, economic, political, and social structures that have prevailed."[14]

The Humanist consistent with his worldview will deny natural rights. This, in turn, leads to a denial of natural law. John Herman Randall, Jr., proclaims, "The Humanist temper has always protested against any subserviences to an external law, whether religious or mechanical, imposed upon man from without."[15] Interestingly, Randall bases his denial of natural law on the concept of freedom—like Erich Fromm, many other Humanists believe man must not be "subservient" to any force other than his own human understanding.

Kurtz also denies the existence of natural law: "How are these principles [of equality, freedom, etc.] to be justified? They are not derived from a divine or natural law, nor do they have any special metaphysical status. They are rules offered to govern how we shall behave. They can be justified only by reference to their results."[16] Here, then, is a statement attempting to create a coherent Humanist approach to law. Kurtz believes that laws are derived not from natural law but from a relative criterion judged by the reason of men. This approach to legal theory leads to a view known as legal positivism.

HUMANIST POSITIVE LAW

In its strict sense, legal positivism claims that the state is the ultimate authority for creating law. That is, since God is a mythical being and natural law is simply legal fiction, man must rely on his reason to discern what is legal—and the men

Snapshots In Time

From "The Declaration of Independence"

"When in the course of human events, it becomes necessary for one people to dissolve the political bands which have connected them with another, and to assume among the powers of the earth, the separate and equal station to which the laws of nature and of nature's God entitle them, a decent respect to the opinions of mankind requires that they should declare the causes which impel them to the separation. "We hold these truths to be self–evident, that all men are created equal; that they are endowed by their Creator with certain unalienable rights; that among these are life, liberty, and the pursuit of happiness. That to secure these rights, governments are instituted among men, deriving their just powers from the consent of the governed; that whenever any form of government becomes destructive of these ends, it is the right of the people to alter or to abolish it, and to institute new government . . ."

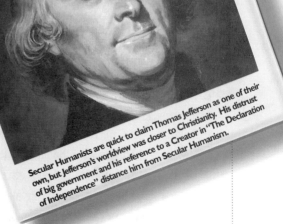

Secular Humanists are quick to claim Thomas Jefferson as one of their own, but Jefferson's worldview was closer to Christianity. His distrust of big government and his reference to a Creator in "The Declaration of Independence" distance him from Secular Humanism.

237

who decide the law are the men in power, in government. At first glance, it seems like an unqualified leap to call the Humanist legal position positivist solely on the basis of Kurtz's statement that rules "can be justified only by reference to their results."[17] However, when one follows the basic assumptions of the Humanist worldview to their logical conclusion, positivism clearly shows itself to be the only legal theory consistent with Humanism. Humanists willing to draw the necessary conclusions will make this point obvious.

Max Hocutt is one such Humanist. He understands that Humanism must abandon natural law, thereby causing mankind to be responsible for the creation of all laws: "Human beings may, and do, make up their own rules. All existing moralities and all existing laws are human artifacts, products of human society, social conventions."[18] If this is true, then government must be the final source of legal truths—since it is the state, not the individual, that enacts laws.

Thus, the consistent Humanist legal position denies natural law and embraces a positivist view, which grants the state the role of ultimate source of legal truth. This positivism spills over into the realm of rights as well. The state becomes the source of all human rights, which no longer are referred to as natural—only constitutional. McKown says, "Natural human rights exist only among human beings; that is, one holds natural rights only against other natural rights holders. Maintaining this point, however, begs the question of natural rights and leaves us wondering how such rights differ from constitutional or legal rights."[19] McKown draws the conclusion that if the concept of natural rights is simply question-begging, then legal rights are all that exist: "Our eyes and our idealism ought to be focused, rather, on the only kind of rights that can be realized: legal rights . . ."[20]

The consistent Humanist position is legal positivism. This position (based on the state as the final source of law) results in an arbitrary legal code. Indeed, when one combines this positivism with the Humanist position that mankind and his laws are in a constant state of evolution, the Humanist legal theory grows capricious. Just how capricious is made clear by Kurtz, who declares, "Laws, however, provide us only with general guides for behavior; how they work out depends upon the context."[21]

Arbitrary law is a disastrous house of cards. Says Roscoe Pound, "From the time when lawgivers gave over the attempt to maintain the general security by belief that particular bodies of human law had been divinely dictated or divinely revealed or divinely sanctioned, they have had to wrestle with the problem of proving to mankind that the law was something fixed and settled, whose authority was beyond question, while at the same time enabling it to make constant readjustments and occasional radical changes under the pressure of infinite and variable human desires."[22] How does one convince citizens to obey laws that have no other foundation than the state? The question seems unanswerable.

The real problem created by Humanist legal theory, however, is not the potential disobedience of citizens; rather, it is the government's potential to take advantage of its position as ultimate source of legal truth. Some Humanists recognize this danger: "If there were no moral, humanistic foundations for the legal rights we ought to have," says Tibor Machan, "we would face the prospect of governments that exist without any limits, without any standards by which to ascertain whether or not they are just and morally legitimate."[23] This is the heart of the problem created by Humanist legal theory: the state is given the authority of a god. "Big Brother" wields all power; the individual is merely a cog in the machinery of the state.

Law At A Glance

Secular Humanism

Positive Law

CONCLUSION

Law, while discussed infrequently by Humanists, is nevertheless a very real aspect of Humanism's worldview. The Humanist, to be consistent with his basic assumptions that God does not exist and that man is an evolving, perfectible animal, must embrace specific legal theories. For example, the consistent Humanist frowns on legal systems that punish lawbreakers, since, according to Humanism, the guilty party cannot, ultimately, be held responsible for his actions. Also, the Humanist must deny any source of ethics, rights, or laws that exists outside of man, including natural law. While many Humanists recognize the problems created by denying natural law and attempt to escape them by redefining natural law to fit their worldview, the consistent Humanist understands that he must abandon natural law and embrace legal positivism.

Legal positivism, however, creates a number of dilemmas of its own. Because it is based on evolutionary theory and the whims of the state, it produces an arbitrary legal system that discourages obedience and grants the state virtually unlimited authority. Humanist law faces a bitter choice: an inconsistent legal theory that embraces natural law, or a consistent legal positivism. Alastair Hannay sums up the dilemma faced by a theory of law that rejects the Lawgiver: "Humanists naturally want to believe that we have moral obligations, duties in some virtually legalistic sense but not the product of arbitrary legislation, to one another. But on what can the belief be based?"[24]

CHAPTER 28

Marxist/Leninist Law

"Law, morality, religion, are to [the proletariat] so many bourgeois prejudices, behind which lurk in ambush just as many bourgeois interests."[1]

—Karl Marx

INTRODUCTION

As with Humanist law, Marxist law is based on the assumptions that God does not exist and that man is an evolving animal. And just as these assumptions cause the Humanist to abandon the concept of an absolute moral code or natural law, they force the Marxist to deny the existence of any law grounded in an authority outside of man.

V.I. Lenin asks, "In what sense do we repudiate ethics and morality?" He answers, "In the sense in which it was preached by the bourgeoisie, who derived ethics from God's commandments. We, of course, say that we do not believe in God."[2] This attitude is echoed by modern-day Marxists. L.S. Jawitsch, a Marxist law theorist, writes, "There are no eternal, immutable principles of law."[3] Since the supernatural does not exist, the Marxist must find another basis for law and ethics.

Naturally, this basis is the same as the Humanist foundation: mankind. Without the supernatural, only the highest animal in nature can be responsible for determining law. Lenin states, "We repudiate all morality taken apart from human society and classes."[4]

The Marxist perceives rights and law as arising from mankind and society, rather than from the moral order of a supernatural Being. This implies that law arose at a specific point in history, sometime after the emergence of man on the evolutionary scene. Thus, the Marxist must address the question: When and how did law originate?

A Brief Look At: Yuri Andropov (1914-1984)

1930: Joins the Young Communist League

1936: Graduates from Rybinsk Water Transportation Technicum, a vocational school

1951: Travels to Moscow for "further training"

1954: Begins serving as the Soviet ambassador to Hungary

1957: Returns to Moscow as party secretary for the Central Committee

1967: Begins ten–year stint as chairman of the KGB

1973: Achieves full membership in the Politburo

1982: Assumes leadership of USSR as Communist party general secretary

THE ORIGIN OF LAW

According to the Marxist, as soon as man formed a society and the most rudimentary economic structure involving class distinctions, two things came into existence simultaneously: law and the state. Such regulation must exist in societies divided into classes because class distinctions will always create conflict and disorder and must be kept in check as much as possible. Frederick Engels writes, "In order that these . . . classes with conflicting economic interests, may not annihilate themselves and society in a useless struggle, a power becomes necessary that stands apparently above society and has the function of keeping down the conflicts and maintaining 'order.' And this power, the outgrowth of society, but assuming supremacy over it and becoming more and more divorced from it, is the State."5

Unfortunately, this state that arises to subdue class conflict actually winds up perpetuating the conflict, since the dominant class always wields the power of the state. Lenin declares, "The State is an organ of class domination, an organ of oppression of one class by another; its aim is the creation of 'order' which legalises and perpetuates this oppression by moderating the collisions between the classes."[6] Laws are the rules imposed by the state to moderate these collisions.

BOURGEOIS LAW AND THE PROLETARIAT

Today, according to the Marxist, there are only two basic classes that can be in control of the government and creating laws: the bourgeoisie and the proletariat. The Marxist believes that all societies that allow the bourgeoisie to make moral decisions and formulate laws are unjust.

Karl Marx clearly denounces bourgeois law as nothing more than a reflection of the desires of that class. In the *Communist Manifesto,* he tells the bourgeois: "[Y]our jurisprudence is but the will of your class made into a law for all, a will, whose essential character and direction are determined by the economic conditions of existence of your class."[7] This law, according to the Marxist, invariably discriminates against the propertyless working class. The main reason for the oppressive nature of bourgeois law, of course, is that it is based on the concept of private property. This basis causes the law to promote unequal rights. There can never be equal rights in a capitalistic society, according to the Marxist, since the very nature of the system creates haves and have-nots. Maurice Cornforth sums up: "There cannot be equality between exploiters and exploited."[8]

Bourgeois law contains another inherent flaw. According to Marxism, laws promoting unequal rights breed protest in the form of lawlessness. Says Engels, "The contempt for the existing social order is most conspicuous in its extreme form—that of offences against the law."[9] Accordingly, society is more responsible for lawlessness than the individual. Indeed, the criminal need feel no remorse for his actions, since the unjust bourgeois society leaves no alternative but to lash out against it.

Marxism proposes a clear-cut solution to injustice and crime: overthrow the bourgeoisie, thereby allowing the proletariat to make the laws. Jawitsch believes, "Complete success in the masses' struggle for their democratic rights and liberties can

> **"The revolutionary dictatorship of the proletariat is rule won and maintained by the use of violence by the proletariat against the bourgeoisie, rule that is unrestricted by any laws."**
>
> *V. I. Lenin*

only be achieved by overcoming monopoly capital's economic and political domination and establishing a state authority that expresses the interests of the working people."[10]

The need for a society in which the proletariat make the laws is so pressing, and the laws of bourgeois society are so unjust, that the Marxist believes the working class is justified in ignoring modern capitalistic laws in their pursuit of equality. Indeed, this need to create a dictatorship of the proletariat is so strong that every hint of bourgeois law may be ignored by the revolutionary in the pursuit of his goal. Lenin proclaims, "The revolutionary dictatorship of the proletariat is rule won and maintained by the use of violence by the proletariat against the bourgeoisie, rule that is unrestricted by any laws."[11]

Judging from the Marxist's disdain for bourgeois law, it would seem that Marxism would also largely ignore law once the dictatorship of the proletariat is established. This, however, is not the case. The Marxist has specific ideas about law in a socialist society.

LAW AND SOCIALIST ECONOMICS

Socialist law will reflect the desires of the working people rather than of the bourgeois. By basing law on the will of the proletariat, the Marxist believes he will be creating a less exploitative society. Jawitsch states, "An anti-exploiter tendency is what characterises the special features of all the principles of the law of socialist society in most concentrated form."[12]

The basis in Marxist society for all judgments regarding exploitation, rights, and the law is the will of the proletariat. God, an absolute moral code, and natural law have no bearing on these judgments. "Marxism, which has been so often accused of seeking to eliminate moral considerations from human life and history," writes Howard Selsam, "emphasizes rather the moral issues involved in every situation. It does so, however, not by standing on a false platform of absolute right, but by identifying itself with the real needs and interests of the workers and farmers."[13]

> **Individuals who act in a way deemed unacceptable by the Marxist/Leninist party will quickly find themselves without any rights.**

Obviously, law based on such an unstable foundation will not be consistent. Rather than calling law based on the whims of the proletariat inconsistent, however, Marxism calls it flexible. The Marxist claims that law requires elasticity—even to the point of abandoning any comprehensive legal system. E.B. Pashukanis writes, "We require that our legislation possess maximum elasticity. We cannot fetter ourselves by any sort of system."[14]

This view is quite consistent with the Marxist evolutionary perspective. Since

246

man is in a constant state of evolution and law is founded on man, law must also be constantly changing. Socialist laws and rights are completely arbitrary, since they are based on the will of the ruling class—which in socialist society is the proletariat. As demonstrated in the Humanist Law chapter, a system basing laws on the decisions of those in power is nothing more than legal positivism.

LEGAL POSITIVISM

Legal positivism is a theory that bases all legal truth on the decisions of the state. While the Marxist is unwilling to admit that his theory of law is based on positivism, the conclusion becomes inescapable when one combines the Marxist assumptions that no absolutes exist and that law is the will of the ruling class. Indeed, many statements by Marxists betray the positivist nature of their legal theory.

For example, Lenin proclaims, "A court is an organ of state power. Liberals sometimes forget that. It is a sin for a Marxist to forget it."[15] Courts are created to dispense justice—and from whence do they derive this justice? From the state, according to the Marxist.

The Marxist betrays his positivist approach to law in other ways, as well. Jawitsch believes, "As a component of the legal superstructure law is closely linked with the political superstructure and with the state."[16] This seems a reasonably clear admission that justice in socialist society is created by the state, under the guidance of the proletariat.

As with the Humanist, the Marxist must embrace legal positivism to be consistent with his worldview. However, because Marxism bases much of its legal theory on economics, the Marxist version of legal positivism differs in one sense from the Humanist approach.

LAW AS AN EXTENSION OF PARTY POLITICS

Since the Marxist believes that the proletariat must gain control of the state and formulate new laws to create a truly just society, the Marxist brand of legal positivism takes on a distinctive class character. While the Humanist simply believes that the state is responsible for establishing rights and promoting justice, the Marxist believes that the proletarian state is the only government capable of promoting justice. Thus, Marxist law requires a state led by the proletariat.

As explained in the Marxist Politics chapter, however, the Marxist believes his political party must act as the guiding force for the workers once they achieve power— so the actual source for determining all justice becomes not a class, but a political party: the Marxist/Leninist party. Thus, Andrei Y. Vyshinsky states, "There might be collisions and discrepancies between the formal commands of laws and those of the proletarian revolution. . . . This collision must be solved only by the subordination of the formal commands of law to those of party policy."[17] In the end, Marxist/Leninist party policy becomes the ultimate criterion for determining law.

Marxist law adds a new twist to legal positivism. Marxism declares the proletariat to be the only true source of justice and requires the proletariat to gain power to begin to correct old, unjust bourgeois laws. Thus, the state is seen by the Marxist to be the ultimate source of justice only when the dictatorship of the proletariat has been established. This dictatorship, in turn, requires the guidance of the Marxist/Leninist party—thereby making the party the final source for all legal and moral truth.

MARXIST LAW AND THE ENEMIES OF THE PROLETARIAT

As one might imagine, if the Marxist/Leninist party is the ultimate source of justice, then anyone in Marxist society who disagrees with this view is guilty of lawlessness. Since the party gets to decide what is legal, it can easily condemn any displeasing actions as illegal.

Thus, the 1936 Soviet Constitution affirmed that all citizens are granted certain rights "In conformity with the interests of the working people, and in order to strengthen the socialist system."[18] Citizens in a Marxist society are guaranteed certain rights as long as they never exercise those rights in a way that hinders the advance of communism. Individuals who act in a way deemed unacceptable by the Marxist/Leninist party will quickly find themselves without any rights. This has been documented in such works as Alexander Solzhenitsyn's *The Gulag Archipelago*.

This legal discrimination by the Marxist/Leninist party against any individual who disagrees with their political agenda should be relentless, according to Vyshinsky: "The task of justice . . . is to assure the precise and unswerving fulfillment of . . . laws by all the institutions, organizations, officials, and citizens of the [state]. This the court accomplishes by destroying without pity all the foes of the people in whatsoever form they manifest their criminal encroachments upon socialism."[19] A law that is created and enforced by a specific ideology will not tolerate actions opposed to its belief system.

Marxism's approach to legal positivism is unique in another way. As demonstrated in the Marxist Politics chapter, Marxism expects the state to wither away as socialist society moves toward communism. But if the state is to wither away, then the source of all justice will disappear as well. A positivist view of law that calls for the disappearance of the state must also call for the disappearance of law.

Law Withers Away

The Marxist is willing to accept the conclusion that law will wither away in communist society, since he views law as arising from class conflicts caused by property. Since communism will abolish all classes, the need to promote order between classes will no longer exist; therefore law will become unnecessary.

Secular Humanism	Marxist/Leninist
Positive Law	**Positive Law**

It would seem that the disappearance of law in communist society creates a grave problem for the Marxist. How will order be maintained without law? No action, no matter how irresponsible, could be deemed unlawful by society. Would not chaos result?

The Marxist is untroubled by these possibilities. According to his view, when classes are abolished man will live in an environment that promotes harmony. Criminal actions will almost never occur, since injustice and inequality (catalysts for such anti-social activity) will not exist. J. Plamenatz says that in a communist society crime will be "virtually unknown," because "motives will be less urgent and frequent, and the offender will be more easily brought to his senses by the need to regain the good opinion of his neighbours."[20]

CONCLUSION

Marxist law is very similar to Humanist law in that both views assume that God does not exist and man and his social institutions are evolving. Because of these assumptions, both Marxism and Humanism must rely on some version of legal positivism. However, the Marxist version of legal positivism is unique in that it assigns a class character to the state's role as ultimate source of justice. Since the Marxist believes that law is always the will of the ruling class and that only the proletariat is capable of creating justice, he must call for rule by the proletariat to create a just system of law. Further, since the proletariat must rule under the guidance of the Marxist/Leninist party, the party becomes the final authority on morality and law.

But a system of law determined by individuals adhering to a specific ideology will consistently create laws prejudiced against people with opposing worldviews. In such a society, freedom disappears. Each citizen is held hostage by the arbitrary laws of the state.

CHAPTER 29

Cosmic Humanist Law

"As extensions of God, we are ourselves the spirit of compassion, and in our right minds, we don't seek to judge but to heal."[1]

—Marianne Williamson

INTRODUCTION

According to the Cosmic Humanist, all authority resides within each individual. Since every person is God, and God is every person, man can only decide the legality of an action by getting in touch with this God within. Thus, every individual must act as his own legal authority, because any manifestation of outside authority hinders communion with one's godhood. "The real problem with commitment to an external form," explains Shakti Gawain, "is that it doesn't allow room for the inevitable changes and growth of people and relationships. If you promise to feel or behave by a certain set of rules, eventually you are going to have to choose between being true to yourself and being true to those rules."[2]

Should one choose to honor a certain set of rules rather than inner truth, one sacrifices his godhood. As we noted earlier, "When we consistently suppress and distrust our intuitive knowingness," writes Gawain, "looking instead for [external] authority, validation, and approval from others, we give our personal power away."[3] Personal power can only be perfectly exercised in societies that have abandoned law.

253

A Brief Look At: Robert Muller (1923-)

1948: Receives doctorate from University of Strasbourg

1959: Hired as special assistant to an under–secretary–general at the United Nations

1964: Serves as political advisor to U.N. forces in Cyprus

1969: Serves as director of the budget for the U.N.

1970: Begins service as director of the office of secretary–general for the U.N.

1978: Publishes *Most of All They Taught Me Happiness*

1982: Publishes *New Genesis: Shaping a Global Spirituality*

LEGAL ABSOLUTES OR "FREEDOM"?

Cosmic Humanists who have achieved higher consciousness act under proper authority (the God within). Their actions will be proper because they will conform with the reality that the Cosmic Humanists, as part of God, are creating. "As each of us connects with our inner spiritual awareness," says Gawain, "we learn that the creative power of the universe is within us. We also learn that we can create our own reality and take responsibility for doing so."[4] Thus, under the New Age legal perspective, any action man might choose will be perceived as lawful, as long as it is an action true to the God within. Once mankind has achieved collective consciousness, we will all be co-creators of reality; therefore we will all work according to our own authority.

This attitude causes the Cosmic Humanist to view Biblical Christianity with distaste, since the Christian worldview describes both an outside Authority and a specific moral order based on the transcendent nature of God. These concepts are far too restrictive for members of the New Age movement. David Spangler (more specifically, a spirit channeled by Spangler) disdains Christians and all others opposed to the New Age worldview, declaring, "Their world (of darkness) is under the law and shall disappear."[5] In stark contrast, Cosmic Humanists are under no outside authority. They create their own reality and their own rules; they are a law unto themselves.

Put simply, Christians think we need laws because man is inherently sinful and is capable of doing the wrong thing. Cosmic Humanists, as Kevin Ryerson told Shirley MacLaine, believe "mankind, and all life, is basically good."[6] If man is basically good, who needs law? Law just keeps us from being totally free to achieve godhood.

In an effort to deceive Christians, many Cosmic Humanists claim that the Bible really teaches individual autonomy—in other words, that the Bible calls for total personal freedom to allow us to "tune in" to our godhood. Ryerson says that the Bible has been twisted through the centuries by the Church, and that the "real truth" contained in the real Bible is that each soul has "responsibility for its own behavior in the realization of its own divinity."[7] Christians, therefore, should also abandon law and focus on achieving higher consciousness.

> **Cosmic Humanists are under no outside authority. They create their own reality and their own rules; they are a law unto themselves.**

Secular Humanism	Marxist/Leninist	Cosmic Humanist
Positive Law	Positive Law	Self-law

CONCLUSION

Law, for the Cosmic Humanist, is unnecessary. In fact, laws and authorities are counter-evolutionary: they can prevent people from achieving godhood. If anything hinders us—even law—it must be abandoned. As Mark Satin says, "Getting in touch with our selves would appear to be, not just fun (though it can be that), and not self-indulgence at all, but an imperative for survival that's built right in to the structure of the universe. (Maybe even an evolutionary imperative.)"[8]

Christianity and the New Age worldview clash dramatically here. Christians believe legal systems are a necessity, because men "getting in touch with themselves" often act badly, even violently. Cosmic Humanists believe Christian morality and absolute law are the very reasons people have trouble growing to godhood.

"I always tell my students," says Joseph Campbell, "go where your body and soul want to go. When you have the feeling, then stay with it, and don't let anyone throw you off."[9] The problem, as Christians know, is that sinful man occasionally feels like killing or stealing or cheating; legal systems must "throw him off" in order to protect the innocent. The Cosmic Humanist faces a dilemma: either legal systems must exist, or I may "follow my bliss" right into his living room and steal his VCR.

CHAPTER 30

Biblical Christian Law

"To cut off Law from its ethical sources is to strike a terrible blow at the rule of law."[1]
—Russell Kirk

INTRODUCTION

The Christian believes that God has provided laws (and a means of discovering those laws) for mankind. "God is the only Legislator," says Carl F.H. Henry. "Earthly rulers and legislative bodies are alike accountable to Him from whom stems all obligation—religious, ethical and civil."[2]

If this is true, it presents serious implications for all of mankind, and not only in the realm of law. This becomes obvious when one examines the assumptions and consequent failings implicit to every man-centered system of law. Systems which deny God as Law-giver ultimately fail and will always adversely affect every individual mired in them. They fail because they recognize neither the dignity of man created in the image of God nor the fallen nature of man.

SYSTEMS OF MAN-CENTERED LAW

If God does exist and does create law, then any society that ignores His laws will be out of step with reality. Further, a society or state that forgets God will promote arbitrary laws, consequently causing its subjects to lose respect for the legal system. John

259

Whitehead believes that when fundamental principles of law are undermined, "public confidence in law and public willingness to abide by law are also sapped."[3] The reason public trust disappears is simple: when law is not considered sacred, neither is it considered binding. If fallen man is in charge of creating law, one can rest assured that he will constantly recreate the law to better suit his selfish needs or the selfish needs of his constituents.

Man's disregard for man-made law causes the individual to adopt an arbitrary attitude toward other areas in his life, most notably ethics. Without a law that is both unchanging and worthy of obedience, where can the individual discover a moral code (apart from mankind)? Man quickly realizes that if God does not exist, all things are permissible.

Unfortunately, many modern states and the United Nations are based on positive law. As predicted, this absence of a proper legal foundation is creating breakdowns throughout societies. Indeed, the bankruptcy of the modern world's legal and ethical codes powerfully demonstrates the need for a legal basis outside of man. "The horrors of our recent history," writes John Warwick Montgomery, "[have] forced us to recognize the puerile inadequacy of tying ultimate legal standards to the mores of a particular society, even if that society is our own."[4]

AN ABSOLUTE STANDARD

Clearly, the weakest aspect of the entire theory of legal positivism is its founding of law on an everchanging basis: governmental authority. Legal positivists believe a "flexible" system of law is desirable, since man and his laws are caught up in the process of evolution. But the failings of such a system are obvious, as A.E. Wilder-Smith points out: "Since humans are allegedly accidents, so are their laws."[5]

The legal positivist would not put it quite that way. Positivists believe laws are logically formulated by the state to best suit mankind's evolutionary needs (for example, homosexuality might be legalized to avoid the hypothetical danger of over-population). However, this does not erase the fact that laws become arbitrary in such a system. Indeed, legal positivism creates a profound danger: the all-powerful state.

Society is faced with a choice: "[I]f there is no fixity in law and no reference point," writes Whitehead, "then law can be what a judge says it is. If, however, there is a fixity to law, there is some absolute basis upon which judgment can be made."[6] Society must decide whether an absolute legal standard exists. It does not matter whether society would prefer fixed or flexible laws; what matters is whether an absolute code is *real*. If such a code does exist, we, as mortals, must discover and obey it, for it points to a Law-giver worthy of our obedience and worship.

The Christian, of course, believes such law and such a Law-giver exist. For the Christian, law is grounded on the firmest foundation and therefore does not flex or evolve. Whitehead insists that law in the Christian sense has something more than mere form. "Law has content in the eternal sense. It has a reference point. Like a ship that is anchored, law cannot stray far from its mooring."[7] The Christian legal perspective creates a legal system that does not fluctuate according to the whims of man and, therefore, is more just.

The Christian approach to law not only provides law with an absolute foundation in God as the ultimate Law-giver but also clears up the confusion over law's nature. Whereas legal positivists can explain neither why laws must exist nor why man can never develop a just system of law, the Christian legal theorist provides a simple, logical answer: man is in rebellion against God and His law; earthly laws are required to curb that rebellion; but the implementation of these laws will always be imperfect, since man's fallen nature keeps him from formulating and enforcing a just legal system.

But if man is truly corrupted by sin, how can he discover any of God's laws? If human nature is fallen, and man is no longer in touch with God's will, how can mankind know what God commands him to do? The answer lies in both general and special revelation.

A Brief Look At: John Jay (1745-1829)

1768: Passes the bar exam

1777: Appointed chief justice of New York

1783: Helps negotiate the peace treaty between Britain and the U.S.

1784: Serves as Secretary of Foreign Affairs under the Articles of Confederation

1788: Writes five essays for *The Federalist Papers*

1789: Appointed first chief justice of the U.S. Supreme Court

1795: Begins six–year stint as governor of New York

Natural and Biblical Law

God revealed his law to mankind, generally, through natural law. Every person has a conscience—some inherent sense of right and wrong. The Apostle Paul says, "Indeed, when Gentiles, who do not have the law, do by nature things required by the law, they are a law for themselves, even though they do not have the law . . ." (Romans 2:14). Christianity teaches that mankind can, to some extent, perceive the will of God, and that this perceived will is the law of nature. William Blackstone, a Christian and one of the most influential figures in the history of law, describes natural law this way: "Man, considered as a creature, must necessarily be subject to the laws of his creator, for he is an entirely dependent being. . . . And consequently as man depends absolutely upon his maker for every thing, it is necessary that he should in all points conform to his maker's will. This will of his maker is called the law of nature."[8]

> "Law has content in the eternal sense. It has a reference point. Like a ship that is anchored, law cannot stray far from its mooring."
>
> *John Whitehead*

This view is consistent with the Biblical account of Creator, creation, moral order, and law. The Apostle Paul specifically discusses the concept of natural law in Romans 1-2, claiming that every man has a fundamental knowledge that there is a transcendental law by which he should abide, and yet which he fails to obey. Man's fallen nature does not destroy his awareness of this general revelation. Though man sees "through a glass, darkly," he still sees.

The theory that natural law is grounded in God as general revelation is crucial for the Christian's entire legal perspective. Understood properly, natural law explains why all men are considered accountable to God for their actions: because all men are aware of the existence of a transcendent law and still consciously disobey it. If the Christian legal theorist wishes to remain consistent with his worldview, he must incorporate this truth into his legal theory.

Further, the Christian legal theorist must reckon with God's special revelation. God has made His law known to man through the Bible. Natural law provides man with a general concept of right and wrong, and then the Bible fleshes out this skeletal framework so that man may know what God considers lawful. A classic example of this is found in Leviticus 18. God warns Moses about the legal structures of Egypt and Canaan—"neither shall ye walk in their ordinances"—and insists that Israel not legally permit incest, adultery, infanticide (abortion), homosexuality, and bestiality. These practices still intrigue the natural, fallen man, but God considers them an abomination because they are contrary to nature (Romans 1:26-27) and undermine the dignity and sanctity of the God-ordained home.

Together, general and special revelation give man enough information to implement a legal system that need not depend on the wisdom of sinful men. Indeed, this revelation is made available to all men, regardless of their intellectual capacities. General and specific revelation provide all men with the guidance necessary to create a reasonably just system of law. Says Blackstone, "Upon these two foundations, the law of nature and the law of revelation [the Bible], depend all human laws . . ."[9] These two foundations may be called Christian or divine law.

This divine law provides mankind with a definite means of judging laws enacted by men. While legal positivists have no criterion for judging the appropriateness of a law other than man's perceived needs, the Christian can (and must) refer to the divine law as his basis for declaring a law just or unjust. This creates certain implications for Christian legal theory.

DIVINE LAW

If God has given man a means of discovering and implementing divine law, then the true and just legal system must be based on this revealed law. Without divine law, the individual has no standard for judging any legal system imposed upon him.

Thus, government exists not so much to create laws as to secure laws, to apply God's laws to general and specific situations, and to act as the impartial enforcer of such laws. Whitehead argues that the very term "legislator" means not one who makes laws but one who moves them—moves them "from the divine law written in nature or in the Bible into the statutes and law codes of a particular society."[10]

As demonstrated in the Christian Politics chapter, government, according to God's plan, should concern itself with encouraging people to obey God's will and with punishing evildoers (Romans 13:3-4). Legal systems should consist of laws conforming to divine law such that wrongdoers are punished by the system and those who walk according to God's will are protected. Paul says in 1 Timothy 1 that the righteous do not fear state law because they already obey nature's law, which is God's eternal law, internally and externally. The unrighteous need the law to keep them within certain boundaries of acceptable behavior, thereby protecting the innocent citizen from lawlessness.

The courts should reflect this attitude. Rather than concerning themselves with creating laws, courts must simply apply laws so that God's justice is served. In the past, this attitude was implicit to legal theory. The Christian calls for a return to this approach. The "fact that courts were once seen as institutions of justice (not legislating bodies) cannot be underscored enough,"[11] says Whitehead.

False law-making—such as "concessions to the majority" as a basis for the legalization of abortion, homosexuality, pedophilia, or incest will not be tolerated by God. A society that consciously turns away from divine law will suffer the consequences. "The clear pattern throughout Scripture," says Montgomery, "is that those who do God's will live and those who flaunt His commands perish."[12]

It is in man's best interests to ground a society's legal system in divine law. Indeed, it is doubly in man's interest, because obedience to divine law is the only true freedom—all disobedience results in personal and/or political enslavement. This is consistent with Paul's assertion, "But now that you have been set free from sin and have become slaves to God, the benefit you reap leads to holiness, and the result is eternal life" (Romans 6:22).

Christian law consists of five basic precepts: (1) The source of all divine law is the character or nature of God. Says Francis A. Schaeffer, "God has a character, and His character is the law of the universe."[13] Not all things are the same to Him. Some things conform to His character, and some do not. (2) Out of the character of God proceeds the moral order. This order is as real as the physical order and reflects God's character—His holiness, justice, truth, love, and mercy. (3) Man is created in the image of God and therefore has significance. Life is not an afterthought. God established human government to protect human life, rights and dignity (Genesis 9:6). (4) When Jesus Christ took human form (John 1:14), human life took on even greater significance. God the Creator was now God the Redeemer. (5) Christian law is also based on the fact that some day God through Christ will judge the whole human race (Acts 17:31; Romans 2:16) according to a standard of good and evil (2 Corinthians 5:10). Christians, realizing that they stand guilty before such an awesome God, flee to Jesus Christ for safety.

The extent to which society and the individual acknowledge and obey divine law powerfully affects the entire fabric of their existence. Nowhere is the truth of this assertion more obvious than in the realm of human rights. As Gary Amos points out, "The Biblical model of rights cannot be separated from the Biblical teaching about justice."[14] A people's response to divine law creates a specific attitude about human rights.

DUTIES AND RIGHTS

The Christian calls for man to discover human rights in God's revealed Word, the Bible. Indeed, the Christian believes that the Bible is the only true source of rights, since it is the only special revelation of God's truth. Under this system man is more certainly guaranteed specific rights than under any other system proposed in any other worldview.

The reason is simple. If, as the Bible claims, man is created in the image of God, then each human life becomes inestimably precious and meaningful. This, in turn, creates a firm foundation on which a system of human rights can be built.

These rights are tied to the concept of Christian law much more closely than in other legal systems. According to the Christian perspective, God commands men to obey divine law, and this obedience is what guarantees the protection of rights for all humans. God causes man to be responsible for upholding human rights by binding man's duties to human rights. If man lives biblically, each person will possess the whole range of rights granted by God. But if man disobeys God, then the system of rights revealed in the Bible will suffer.

> **"Do not show partiality in judging; hear both small and great alike."**
>
> *Deuteronomy 1:17*

Notice that this concept also places specific limitations on man's rights. Man may not trumpet, "I've got my rights!" and then act in any way that he pleases. Divine law constantly commands mankind to act according to the true order of the universe, to walk in God's will. Amos provides a fine example: "Men have rights, such as the right to life. But because a man has a duty to live his life for God, the right is inalienable. He can defend his life against all others, but not destroy it himself. No man has the right to do harm to himself, to commit suicide, or to waste his life. He has a property interest—dominion—in his own life, but not total control."[15]

America's Declaration of Independence was built on just such an unchanging basis for rights. Thomas Jefferson, author of the Declaration, proclaimed the need for such a basis when he asked rhetorically, "Can the liberties of a nation be thought secure when we have removed their only firm basis, a conviction in the minds of the people that these liberties are the gift of God?"[16]

BIBLICAL APPLICATIONS

The Bible contains God's guidelines for an earthly system of law. God expects man to devise an ordered legal system, providing him with an example of such a system in Exodus. In this system, judges were instituted (Exodus 18:13-16; cf. Deuteronomy 1:16-17; 19:15-21), along with a multi-tiered judicial system. "The judges were commanded to be honest and not to take bribes or favor the rich (Exodus 23:1-8),"[17] says John Eidsmoe.

From this we can conclude that God's ideal legal system is not only orderly but also equitable. Every man is granted the right to be judged according to the same standard of justice. Deuteronomy 1:17 clearly states, "Do not show partiality in judging; hear both small and great alike."

The Bible has a relevant message for legal theory in the realm of assigning guilt, as well. Simon Greenleaf says, "the importance of extreme care in ascertaining the truth of every criminal charge, especially where life is involved, may be regarded as a rule of law. It is found in various places in the Mosaic Code, particularly in the law respecting idolatry; which does not inflict the penalty of death until the crime 'be told thee,' (viz. in a formal accusation), 'and thou hast heard of it,' (upon a legal trial), 'and inquire diligently, and behold to be true,' (satisfactorily proved), 'and the thing certain,' (beyond all reasonable doubt)."[18]

Christian legal theory recognizes that an earthly judge should not be hasty in condemning any man. Because man is fallen and his reason exists in a less-than-perfect state, it is quite possible for man to err in meting out justice. According to the Christian position, it is better for the earthly judge to err in favor of the defendant than to punish an innocent man, because ultimately all lawbreakers will be judged by God. Where justice might not be served by earthly courts, it will most certainly be served on the final Judgment Day.

Unfortunately, modern man has lost his faith in an ultimate Judge and Judgment Day, and many of his evil tendencies go unchecked. The Bible clearly indicates how a system of law should respond to such criminal actions: not only with punishment, but with a sincere effort to restore God's order, which is disordered by the criminal act. Biblical law not only requires restitution to the offended person, but also demands the restoration of God's order.

The Christian believes it is proper to attempt to restore God's order in the world. This belief, however, should not cause the Christian to conclude that every sin should be made explicitly illegal.

Is it Possible to Legislate Morality?

In one sense, law and morality are inseparable. When one declares theft illegal, one is making a moral judgment—theft is condemned as immoral, because it violates divine law.

This does not mean that all morals must be enforced by specific laws. A system making all sin illegal would, among other things, cause government to become even more bloated in an effort to enact and enforce a vast array of new laws. Man must concentrate on formulating a legal system that legislates morality only to the extent that order is maintained and human rights are protected.

The task of earthly law, according to the Christian, is not to cause man always to

act morally. No law could ever hope to accomplish this. And yet, if law is tied so closely to morals, it must affect man's moral nature on a deeper level than simply causing
him to behave orderly and respect human rights. How, then, does law serve to bring
man to a right understanding of God's universe?

The answer is that no man is capable of living a completely lawful life. This inability on man's part always to act morally is made obvious to him by his violations of
God's divine law as stated in Scripture or enforced by earthly legal systems.

Thus, a Christian system of law, while stabilizing society and promoting justice
(by protecting the weak and innocent and punishing the guilty), also leads man to the
knowledge that he is a fallen creature desperately in need of a Savior. In a way similar
to the general revelation of natural law, earthly legal systems help the nonbeliever to
recognize the corrupt nature of man and seek the reasons behind this corruption and
the remedy for it. God in His wisdom uses law not only to ensure justice, but also to
demonstrate to man that, in his fallen state, it would be folly to demand his just
desserts. Rather, man should beg for mercy and turn to Christ for salvation, thereby
becoming a child of God (see Ephesians 2).

Secular Humanism	Marxist/Leninist	Cosmic Humanist	Christianity
Positive Law	Positive Law	Self-law	Biblical/ Natural Law

CONCLUSION

Christian law is based on God's unchanging character. This basis creates an absolute foundation for law, which in turn demonstrates Christianity to be better equipped to offer a system of law than all the worldviews that call for an evolutionary legal system. Christian law ensures specific, absolute human rights that cannot be ensured by worldviews that deny God's existence. Christian human rights are based on specific duties prescribed in the Bible—thus, God assigns specific rights to all humans, but man becomes responsible for obeying God and protecting those rights for himself and his fellow man.

God makes specific provisions in the Bible for earthly legal systems. He expects them to be both orderly and equitable. God further expects man's legal systems to hold man responsible for his actions and to restore God's order whenever and wherever possible. God does not expect, however, every sin to be declared illegal in human government. Rather, He expects a system of law that maintains both order and liberty by promoting justice as much as humanly possible.

The Bible tells what is good and what God requires of mankind: "to do justly, and to love mercy, and to walk humbly with thy God" (Micah 6:8). The Christian's motivation to "do justly" is knowing that "the Lord is slow to anger, and great in power, and will not at all acquit the wicked" (Nahum 1:3). His motivation to "love mercy" and "walk humbly" is the supreme example of the Law-giver himself—Jesus Christ— who showed mercy and walked humbly and told the woman taken in adultery, "Neither do I condemn thee: go, and sin no more" (John 8:11). As Christians we know we cannot live the perfect life exemplified by Christ, but we may also be assured that, because of God's grace, Christ will speak these same words to His followers on the Day of Judgment.

FOUR WESTERN WORLDVIEW MODELS

SOURCES	SECULAR HUMANISM — HUMANIST MANIFESTOS I AND II	MARXISM/LENINISM — WRITINGS OF MARX AND LENIN	COSMIC HUMANISM — WRITINGS OF SPANGLER, FERGUSON, ETC.	BIBLICAL CHRISTIANITY — BIBLE
THEOLOGY	Atheism	Atheism	Pantheism	Theism
PHILOSOPHY	Naturalism	Dialectical Materialism	Non-Naturalism	Supernaturalism
ETHICS	Relativism	Proletariat Morality	Relativism	Absolutes
BIOLOGY	Darwinian Evolution	Darwinian/Punctuated Evolution	Darwinian/Punctuated Evolution	Creation
PSYCHOLOGY	Self-Actualization	Behaviorism	Collective Consciousness	Mind/Body
SOCIOLOGY	Non-Traditional Family	Abolition of Home, Church and State	Non-Traditional Home, Church and State	Traditional Home, Church and State
LAW	Positive Law	Positive Law	Self-Law	Biblical and Natural Law
POLITICS	World Government (Globalism)	New World Order (New Civilization)	New Age Order	Justice, Freedom and Order
ECONOMICS	Socialism	Socialism	Universal Enlightened Production	Stewardship of Property
HISTORY	Historical Evolution	Historical Materialism	Evolutionary Godhood	Historical Resurrection

CHAPTER 31

Secular Humanist Politics

"All those who share the vision of the human community as part of one world should be willing to take any measures that will awaken world opinion to bring it about."[1]

—Lucile W. Green

INTRODUCTION

Virtually every Secular Humanist embraces democracy as the most acceptable form of government. Paul Kurtz declares, "The Humanist is also committed to democracy, particularly in the present epoch, as an ideal and a method for maximizing happiness and achieving the good society."[2] Rudolf Dreikurs says simply, "We believe sincerely in democracy."[3]

The Humanist conception of democracy differs significantly, however, from the more common attitude toward democracy; for the Humanist, democracy extends far beyond the realm of government. In fact, the Humanist believes democracy should color every aspect of man's life. Corliss Lamont states, "Humanist principles demand the widest possible extension of democracy to all relevant aspects of human living."[4]

The Humanist believes that applying democracy to most aspects of life will drastically change human relationships. Dreikurs says, "In an autocratic order all relations between individuals and between groups are those of superiors and inferiors. One is dominant, the other submissive. In contrast, the process of democratization entails a process of equalization."[5] This call for equalization greatly influences much of the Humanist's political theory.

MAN'S ROLE IN EVOLUTION

The Humanist perceives man as still evolving, always progressing toward perfection. Julian Huxley believes that "all reality is a single process of evolution."[6] Obviously, with this kind of attitude toward reality, the Humanist sees man's continued evolution as one of his most pressing concerns.

> "Humanism, we believe, can play a significant role in helping to foster the development of a genuine world community."
>
> *Paul Kurtz*

This becomes even more evident when one realizes that the Humanist believes man is capable of controlling his own evolutionary development. Huxley writes, "Today, in twentieth-century man, the evolutionary process is at last becoming conscious of itself and is beginning to study itself with a view to directing its future course."[7]

If man is truly capable of controlling his own evolution, and the possibilities of this evolution seem virtually limitless, then certainly this is the most important task with which the human race is faced. For the Humanist, then, the political arena becomes very significant, because government is one of mankind's most powerful agents for effecting the type of change necessary to further mankind's evolution. Indeed, Walt Anderson believes the evolutionary perspective "urges us to see political development *itself* as an advanced form of biological evolution, to look at humanity not as a cog in a vast social machine but rather as (in Julian Huxley's phrase) evolution become conscious of itself."[8]

Just what type of community should evolve through political action? The answer again lies in the Humanist's evolutionary perspective. Because man is seen as the highest of all evolved animals and simply one among many parts of the world's single ecosystem, he is viewed as violating his place in nature when he attempts to divide that ecosystem into states and nations. Timothy J. Madigan sums up, "Humanism holds that the planet Earth must be considered a single ecosystem, which is to say it is no longer feasible to arbitrarily divide it into separate states and hope that each one can satisfactorily manage itself."[9]

This notion of mankind as one part of a single ecosystem has concrete ramifications for the Humanist concept of community. According to Humanism, mankind should live in one community, without national borders and differing state policies.

GLOBALISM

Humanism believes that a world community necessitates a world government. Indeed, the Humanist believes that systems of national government are destined to fail and that world government is a virtually inevitable step up the evolutionary staircase. Kurtz is certain that "today there are powerful forces moving us toward a new ethical global consciousness."[10] To no one's surprise, the worldview that will most encourage the creation of this world community (according to the Humanist) is Humanism. Kurtz says, "Humanism, we believe, can play a significant role in helping to foster the development of a genuine world community."[11]

Why will Humanism be able to bring about this peaceful world community? Because man is perfectible and inherently good, and Humanism provides a framework for channeling that inherent goodness. The *Humanist Manifesto II* proclaims, "What more daring a goal for humankind than for each person to become, in ideal as well as practice, a citizen of a world community. It is a classical vision; we can now give it new vitality. Humanism thus interpreted is a moral force that has time on its side. We believe that humankind has the potential intelligence, good will, and cooperative skill to implement this commitment in the decades ahead."[12] Thus, peaceful world government appears to be inevitable, and it will occur because man is constantly evolving to a higher state and is now capable of controlling his own evolution (by following the guidelines set up by the Humanist worldview).

DISARMAMENT AND THE UNITED NATIONS

Humanists usually make only two rather vague suggestions when attempting to specify the steps necessary for the implementation of a democratic world community. Most Humanists call for universal disarmament and expanded power for the United Nations.

Although the United Nations was originally intended to be a coalition of the countries that had declared war on Germany or Japan by March 1, 1945, its membership was never that exclusive. The first conference (San Francisco, 1945) saw the inclusion of Argentina and Denmark, among others, and membership was almost immediately extended to countries like Afghanistan, Iceland, Israel, and Sweden. Today, Germany and Japan are also members of the United Nations.

The unwillingness of the United Nations to exclude any nations is a reflection of its basic purpose, which is very similar to the purpose of its predecessor, the failed League of Nations: "the maintenance of peace, arbitration of international disputes, and the promotion of international cooperation."

Most adherents to worldviews that champion world government are attracted to the United Nations, because they view it as a stepping-stone to the "global community." The most notable anti-Christian to influence United Nations policy is Alger Hiss, a Marxist who worked in the U.S. State Department from 1936 to 1947. Hiss helped organize the Dumbarton Oaks Conference (which produced proposals for the United Nations Charter) and the first conference in San Francisco (which ratified the United Nations Charter).

The name "United Nations" was coined by President Franklin D. Roosevelt in 1941. He used the term to describe the countries waging war against the Axis powers in World War II.

"The first steps in avoiding a nuclear cataclysm and preserving democracy," writes Erich Fromm, "are to agree on universal disarmament."[13] Linus Pauling believes, "The only hope for the world lies in achieving control of the methods of waging war and ultimately to reach the goal of total and universal disarmament."[14] Once disarmed, nations will be more willing to cooperate, and less ready to enforce nationalistic boundaries. Nations can more easily merge into a global community.

A Brief Look At: Julian Huxley (1887-1975)

1894: Younger brother Aldous is born

1909: Graduates from Balliol College of Oxford University

1914: Younger brother Trev commits suicide

1927: Publishes *Religion Without Revelation*

1946: Begins two–year stint as director–general of the United Nations Educational and Scientific Organization (UNESCO)

1957: Awarded the Darwin Medal by the Royal Society

1959: Delivers keynote address to the International Planned Parenthood conference

1961: Publishes *The Humanist Frame*

1962: Elected Humanist of the Year

At present, the only organization that is truly global in its scope is the United Nations, so much of Humanism's hope is pinned on increased power for this institution. William Carleton says simply, "Our hopes for political internationalism may have to center around the United Nations."[15]

With this hope in mind, Humanists have consistently worked in conjunction with the United Nations to bring the world closer to globalism. Julian Huxley served as the first Director General of the United Nations Educational, Scientific, and Cultural Organization (UNESCO). Lamont proclaims, "Ever since I was an undergraduate at Harvard, I have been active in endeavors to establish enduring world peace. I backed the League of Nations, and since World War II, I have vigorously supported the United Nations."[16]

Humanists point to both universal disarmament and increased power for the United Nations as two steps necessary for developing globalism. Before Humanism can move beyond these somewhat general recommendations, however, both nations and individuals will have to make ideological and ethical compromises.

IDEOLOGIES AND ETHICS

The *Humanist Manifesto II* plainly demands ideological compromise: "We thus call for international cooperation in culture, science, the arts, and technology *across ideological borders*. We must learn to live openly together or we shall perish together."[17] This Humanist belief in the need for compromise between ideologies is rooted in Humanism's definition of democracy. As noted earlier, democracy (for Humanists) implies not only a form of government but also an overall means of equalization. Proponents of specific ideologies do not perceive other ideologies as equal to their own, and Humanists believe this denial of equality creates tensions that cannot exist in a democratic world government. For the Humanist, the mere fact that some ideologies perceive themselves as more right than others is contrary to democracy.

This belief can best be understood by exploring Humanists' attitude toward the role of ethics in establishing the world community. Dreikurs believes, "It is the task of our generation to explore the means by which we can reach agreement, the basis for co-operation between equals. No pressure nor 'being right' will accomplish this."[18] That is, we must stop worrying about which ideology or worldview might be ethically correct and simply agree to begin agreeing.

According to Humanism, no ethical system holds all the answers, and no system is totally sinister—instead, we are asked to take a more "democratic" view of ideologies and their ethical systems. This does not mean, however, that Humanists would have us abandon every ideology. They believe that ideologies evolve continually and that we must simply embrace the newest, most highly-developed ideology. Huxley puts it this way: "[M]ajor steps in the human phase of evolution are achieved by breakthroughs to new dominant patterns of mental organization, of knowledge, ideas and beliefs—ideological instead of physiological or biological organi-

> "A world organization can not be based on one of the competing theologies of the world, but must, it seems, be based on some form of humanism . . ."
>
> *Julian Huxley*

275

zation."[19]

So which ideology is most highly evolved and capable of promoting tolerance in a world community? "A world organization can not be based on one of the competing theologies of the world," Huxley believes, "but must, it seems, be based on some form of humanism . . . a world humanism . . . a scientific humanism . . . an evolutionary humanism."[20]

How can the Humanist justify defending his ideology while viewing other ideologies as opposed to "democracy"? By claiming that Humanism is open-minded, whereas all other ideologies are dogmatic and far too dependent on absolutes. Francis Williams calls for mankind "to stop thinking politically as Capitalists, or Communists, Christians, Muslims, Hindus or Buddhists, and think as Humanists. . . . A world in which men have both hydrogen bombs and closed minds is altogether too dangerous."[21] World democracy can only truly flourish when every man abandons whatever backward ideology he is embracing and becomes a Humanist.

Morals and Politics

Humanists recognize that politics cannot be separated from ethical considerations. Sidney Hook believes the proper means of developing moral codes and re-examining standards lies in the practical application of political theory. Thus, once the democratic world society is established, mankind can go about the business of discovering what is morally acceptable. This business should be totally separated from religious notions about morality. Hook states, "The democratic open society must be neutral to all religious overbeliefs; but no matter how secular it conceives itself to be, it cannot be neutral to moral issues. It seeks to draw these issues into the area of public discussion in the hope that a reasonable consensus may be achieved."[22]

However, developing this universal moral awareness through the Humanist political system may not be easy. Mark Reader tells us that "In the end politics is the place of public happiness."[23] But when one accepts this premise, one necessarily runs into a dilemma with regard to developing morals or standards. As James R. Simpson points out, "The 'good life' or 'quality of life' is relative to each individual's preferences, desires, and needs."[24] Yet if politics is intrinsically tied to happiness, and happiness is relative to each individual, how can a government develop a proper moral awareness that encourages personal happiness? How can people democratically arrive at standards satisfactory to every world citizen if all morality is relative?

The Humanist political framework, which would do away with all other ideologies and their ethical systems, is unable to offer a satisfactory alternate means of establishing standards. Indeed, all that Humanism seems to be able to offer to a new democratic world community is its open-minded attitude, which is theoretically more conducive to cooperation and equalization.

HUMANISM AND "ECONOMIC DEMOCRACY"

The Humanist belief in equalization extends to the economic sphere as well. V.M. Tarkunde believes, "A genuine political democracy is not possible in the absence of economic democracy."[25] As we explore precisely what the Humanist means by *economic democracy,* it will become evident why many Humanists are socialists and favor the redistribution of wealth, as was demonstrated in the Humanist Economics chapter.

Many Humanists believe that man's evolution is being hindered by the unequal distribution of material goods in our world. Anderson claims that "when people are deprived of the fundamental necessities, as are millions of Americans and even more millions of human beings in other countries, their capacity for development is frustrated at the most basic level."[26] Logically, then, the redistribution of wealth is a necessary intermediate step in man's struggle to further his evolutionary development.

Lamont agrees with this conclusion, defining *economic democracy* as "the right of every adult to a useful job at a decent wage or salary, to general economic security and opportunity, to an equitable share in the material goods of this life, and to a proportionate voice in the conduct of economic affairs."[27]

How does the Humanist propose to initiate this economic democracy? Wealth could be redistributed through taxation. "We believe, however," says Kurtz, "that the more affluent nations have a moral obligation to increase technological and economic assistance so that their less developed neighbors may become more self-sufficient. We need to work out some equitable forms of taxation on a worldwide basis to help make this a reality."[28] And what type of system would best promote continued economic democracy? Tarkunde's solution sounds a lot like socialism: "A cooperative economy in which the workers in an undertaking will be the owners of the means of production employed in that undertaking is undoubtedly the most democratic economic institution conceived so far."[29]

CONCLUSION

Humanist politics is tied closely to Humanist biology, economics, ethics, and law. Because the Humanist perceives man as the highest rung on the evolutionary ladder, he concludes that man can use world politics to further his evolution. This evolutionary perspective views man as part of one ecosystem—the world—and consequently supports a one-world government. The Humanist sees universal disarmament and increased power for the United Nations as two crucial intermediate steps that must be taken before world government can be achieved.

What would a Humanist world government be like? Judging from the Secular Humanist movement in the United States, it would work to eradicate the Christian worldview and its symbols from the public square—removing the Ten Commandments from public schools, replacing Christian ethics with "values clarification" and replacing divine law with legal positivism.

Because the Humanist believes in the "equalization" of all aspects of living, he cannot support any ideology or worldview that claims to describe the only proper view of man and his place in the world. Rather, Humanism calls for a democracy that abandons absolute standards and encourages moral relativism. The Humanist recognizes this ethical dilemma as the most pressing problem facing a Humanist world order: "The essential ingredient in this new world of planetary humanism depends on the cultivation of ethical wisdom."[30] The question remains: can a Humanist political view that compromises traditional morals create its own ethical wisdom?

Politics
At A Glance

Secular Humanism

World Government

CHAPTER 32

Marxist/Leninist Politics

"In reality, however, the State is nothing more than a machine for the oppression of one class by another."[1]

—Frederick Engels

INTRODUCTION

As demonstrated in the Marxist Economics chapter, Marxism views the struggle to control the forces of production as the dynamic force behind man's development. The economic system in a society determines the other features of that society, including its political structure. Karl Marx believes that the *"economic structure* of society [is] the real foundation on which rise legal and political superstructure and to which definite forms of social consciousness correspond."[2]

According to Marxism, a socialist economy lays the foundation for genuine democracy, although an impure form of democracy can exist in capitalist nations. But is genuine democracy the supreme aim of Marxist politics? Not at all. In fact, the Marxist views democracy as little more than a necessary evil. "Democracy is a *state,"* explains V.I. Lenin, "which recognises the subordination of the minority to the majority, i.e., an organisation for the systematic use of *force* by one class against another, by one section of the population against another."[3] This definition of democracy is consistent with Marxism's emphasis on the class struggle.

CLASS ANTAGONISM

Because the Marxist sees our present world as a battle between the owners of the means of production (the bourgeoisie) and the workers (the proletariat), and because he views economics as the foundation on which the rest of society is built, he perceives the state as simply another arena in which the "haves" and the "have-nots" struggle. Thus, forms of government that the Western world would describe as desirable, such as a democracy or a republic, are still perceived by the Marxist as bad, especially if they co-exist with a capitalist economic system.

Since the government is founded (theoretically) on the existing economic system, and since capitalism is always undesirable, the government overseeing a capitalist economy is undesirable as well. "The modern state, no matter what its form," says Frederick Engels, "is essentially a capitalist machine . . ."[4] For the Marxist, a state so clearly based on exploiting its citizens is unacceptable.

However, as previously noted, the Marxist perceives not only a capitalist democracy, but also a socialist "genuine" democracy as unacceptable. What, then, causes the Marxist to describe the socialist democracy as genuine?

The reason, according to the Marxist, is that in a socialist society, the mode of production does not exploit any of the citizens, thereby encouraging a less-exploitative political system. Marxism believes a socialist government will tend to discourage class antagonism, since it will be founded on an economic system that is a step closer to abolishing classes. This less-exploitative nature of the government makes the democracy more "genuine." It makes socialism more appealing than capitalism, but still less appealing than communism. That is, a socialist democracy is more appealing than a capitalist democracy, but it is not the ideal (which can only be realized in world communism).

The ideal state, for the Marxist, is no state at all. Marxism perceives the state, whether a democracy or a dictatorship, as a vehicle for maintaining class antagonism. "Political power," writes Marx, "is merely the organised power of one class for oppressing another."[5] From this perspective, the state exists because class antagonism exists; however, once this antagonism is eradicated, the state will no longer be necessary. Lenin sums up this point: "According to Marx, the State could neither arise nor maintain itself if a reconciliation of classes were possible."[6]

THE DICTATORSHIP OF THE PROLETARIAT

The state is a necessary evil, however, in the transition between capitalism and communism. The concentration of all the means of production in the hands of the state is the first step in the Marxist formula to abolish all classes. Marx writes, "Between capitalist and communist society lies the period of the revolutionary transformation of the one into the other. Corresponding to this is also a political transition period in which the state can be nothing but *the revolutionary dictatorship of the proletariat.*"[7]

A Brief Look At: Mikhail Gorbachev (1931-)

1955: Receives law degree from Moscow State University

1970: Becomes one of the youngest provincial party chiefs

1978: Appointed agriculture secretary for Central Committee of the Communist party

1980: Attains full membership in the Politburo

1985: Begins term as general secretary of the USSR

1989: Berlin Wall crumbles

1991: Marxist hard–liners attempt to take over; coup fails

1991: Resigns as general secretary; Soviet Union disbands

Marxist/Leninists believe the proletariat must seize political power to instigate socialism and set the stage for the abolition of classes (and eventually the state). The puzzle is that Marxists continually speak of a "dictatorship" of the proletariat. Doesn't a "genuine democracy" arise in socialist states? How can Marxism reconcile this call for a dictatorship with their claim that a socialist society encourages true democracy?

Marxists reconcile this apparent contradiction simply by pointing to their definition of democracy. As noted earlier, Marxism perceives democracy as simply the oppression of the minority by the majority. Thus, democracy is similar to a dictatorship in that the majority dictates government policy and laws to the minority. In capitalist society, this means the bourgeoisie uses the state to oppress the proletariat. In socialist society, it means precisely the opposite—the proletariat will operate as the authoritarian majority.

Democracy, for the Marxist, is not the noble cause that much of the Western world perceives it to be. Rather, it is simply a means to an end—a necessary tool for maintaining the early stages of socialism. Democracy is useful in establishing the dictatorship of the proletariat; but it is this dictatorship, in the guise of a democracy, that is a crucial facet of Marxist political development.

This dictatorship of the proletariat is crucial for a number of reasons. Obviously, it is needed to consolidate the means of production in the hands of the state, which in turn takes society on the first step toward the abolition of classes. But on a more fundamental level, a dictatorship is necessary because the proletariat will have seized power through a revolution and will need a dictatorial state to thwart bourgeois efforts to reclaim power. Lenin bluntly declares, "Whoever expects that socialism will be achieved *without* social revolution and a dictatorship of the proletariat is not a socialist. Dictatorship is state power, based directly upon force."[8]

THE FATE OF THE BOURGEOISIE

The Marxist/Leninist is quite explicit about the need for suppression of the bourgeoisie by the proletariat. "The state is a special organisation of force," writes Lenin, "it is an organisation of violence for the suppression of some class. What class must the proletariat suppress? Naturally only the exploiting class, i.e., the bourgeoisie."[9]

Remarkably, Marxism is also brash in its admission that the bourgeoisie must be *actively oppressed*. Consider the words of Lenin: "We must crush [the bourgeoisie] in order to free humanity from wage-slavery; their resistance must be broken by force."[10] This breaking of the bourgeoisie requires the proletariat not only to confiscate all property, but also to hound the capitalists at every turn. This is one of the most crucial tasks faced by the dictatorship of the proletariat.

Such a task will not be easy. It is difficult to imagine workers organizing so efficiently that they can accomplish this while at the same time initiating socialism. Fortunately for the proletariat, the Marxist/Leninist party has vowed to guide them in establishing and governing their socialist society.

> "The state is a special organisation of force, it is an organisation of violence for the suppression of some class."
>
> *V.I. Lenin*

THE ROLE OF THE MARXIST/LENINIST PARTY

The Marxist recognizes the difficulties the workers will face as they attempt to create a dictatorship of the proletariat. The authors of *Socialism as a Social System* admit, "Marxist/Leninist theory and the experience of history show conclusively that the working class can carry out its historic mission only if led by a strong, well-organised party."[11]

Of course, these authors have only one "well-organised party" in mind: the Marxist/Leninist party. "Our Party guides the government," writes Joseph Stalin. "The Party supervises the work of the administration . . . and tries to secure for them the support of the masses, since there is not any important decision taken by them without the direction of the Party."[12]

According to the Marxist, the dictatorship of the Marxist/ Leninist Party is synonymous with the dictatorship of the proletariat. The state in the early stages of socialist society will be the rule of the majority—the proletariat—as guided by the principles of Marxism/Leninism. People opposed to the principles of the Party will be considered bourgeois or reactionary.

Eventually, those opposed to Marxism will disappear, and the dictatorship of the proletariat will be rendered unnecessary. When classes cease to exist, and the entire population is of like mind, no state will be needed to enforce one class's oppression of another.

THE STATE WITHERS AWAY

Marxists view the state as a transitory phenomenon. According to their perception of man's social development, the state arose at a point in history when it was necessary and will cease to exist when it is no longer an important facet of society. Engels says, "The State is . . . simply a product of society at a certain stage of evolution."[13]

Marxists believe this to be the case because they perceive capitalism as responsible for maintaining class antagonisms, and they believe the state is necessary only when class antagonisms exist. Thus, as soon as society begins to embrace a socialistic means of production, class antagonisms begin to vanish, and the state begins to be outdated.

Lenin adamantly supports this position, stressing the need to erase the bourgeois class from existence: "Only in communist society, when the resistance of the capitalists has been completely crushed, when the capitalists have disappeared, when there are no classes . . . only then 'the state . . . ceases to exist,' and *it becomes possible to speak of freedom.*' "[14] Before these events occur, however, the Marxist believes freedom is only an illusion. Freedom by Marxist definition means no government. "So long as the state exists," insists Lenin, "there is no freedom. When there is freedom, there will be no state."[15]

Thus, according to the Marxist, the only way for mankind to achieve freedom is to embrace a system that causes the state to wither away. And the Marxist believes "only communism makes the state absolutely unnecessary, for there is *nobody* to be suppressed . . ."[16] So humanity's only hope for freedom lies in abolishing the state through communism.

This withering away of the state must, for Marxism to consider its political ends achieved, occur throughout the world. If the state still exists somewhere in the world, then that means classes still exist and threaten the societies that are well on their way to being classless.

NEW WORLD ORDER

Marxists believe that the establishment of a new world order—world communism—and the withering away of the state are inevitable steps in mankind's biological and social evolutionary development. Just as man is evolving biologically, so society is evolving socially, economically, and politically. The new world order is an evolutionary advance over nations, states, tribes and other race and class distinctions.

Georgi Shakhnazarov, a top aide to former Soviet President Mikhail Gorbachev, writes, "Our epoch is the epoch of the revolutionary transformation of capitalist society into communist."[17] Elsewhere he says, "the building of a new world order . . . was begun in October 1917 by revolutionary Russia, proclaiming socialist principles."[18]

Only communism puts the means of production in the hands of the people, abolishes classes, abolishes the state, and so leads man into a world of cooperation. Thus, the ultimate political aim of the Marxist is the establishment of world communism.

Politics
At A Glance

Secular Humanism	Marxist/Leninist
World Government	**New World Order**

CONCLUSION

When Marxists envision their ideal society, they do not picture democracies, republics, or dictatorships governing the people. For the Marxist, all forms of government are ugly reflections of the fact that class antagonism exists. Marxists do call for a "democracy" known as the "dictatorship of the proletariat" (guided by the Marxist/Leninist Party), but this "democracy" is a necessary evil that exists in the early stages of socialism.

Eventually, when the socialist society evolves into communism, all class distinctions will have been abolished and therefore the state will no longer be necessary. When communist society exists throughout the world, and governments everywhere are outdated, then the ultimate Marxist political aim will have been achieved.

Until that end is achieved, the Marxists warn that there necessarily will be conflict between socialist societies (with states in the process of withering away) and capitalist nations. This conflict—which will include wars—will arise as an extension of class antagonism. Just as the bourgeoisie and the proletariat clash, so will nations controlled by capitalists clash with nations controlled by workers.

The Marxists are not bashful about admitting their political aims. World communism and the abolition of all government are their ultimate goals, and they are willing to suppress, persecute, and wage war against the enemy to achieve these ends. The political/military history of Marxism/Leninism, from the October Revolution of 1917 to Tiananmen Square, is the history of the most ruthless, efficient killing machine mankind has ever witnessed. The death toll of this seventy-year "scientific" experiment, according to University of Hawaii professor R. J. Rummel, author of *Death by Government*, is between 170 to 360 million human beings. Says Rummel, "It is as though our species has been devastated by a modern Balck Plague."[19]

CHAPTER 33

Cosmic Humanist Politics

"[T]he New Age solution does not call for top-down bureaucratic government, but for much more local autonomy than we have at the present, and much more planetary cooperation."[1]

—Mark Satin

INTRODUCTION

Cosmic Humanists perceive mankind as evolving toward a collective consciousness, one that will transcend all material and individual boundaries—including national and political boundaries. World government is a natural evolutionary step in this dissolution of boundaries. Thus, Donald Keys declares that humanity is "on the verge of something entirely new, a further evolutionary step unlike any other: the emergence of the first global civilization."[2]

This New Age call for world government is based less on political theory than on the New Age concepts that all is one and that evolution plus other scientific principles are leading mankind into this unity. World government is important to Cosmic Humanists because it removes barriers and limits, not because of specific mundane political considerations. "Unlike many historical expressions of the one-world idea," says David Spangler, "which focus in particular upon the establishment of a world government, the vision of the New Age qua planetary civilization arises less out of politics than out of what is called the holistic vision. This is the awareness that all life is interrelated and interdependent, that the formative elements of creation are not bits of matter but relationships, and that evolution is the emergence of ever more complex patterns and syntheses of relationships."[3]

The next pattern to emerge, if the Cosmic Humanist has his way, is the global civilization. This fits perfectly with the New Age belief that "Instead of understanding the world in parts, we need to think about the whole." Unity demands a one-world government.

A Brief Look At: Barbara Marx Hubbard (1929-)

1951: Graduates from Bryn Mawr College

1969: Publishes *The Search is On* (co-authored with her husband)

1970: Founds the Committee for the Future

1976: Publishes her autobiography, *The Hunger of Eve*

1984: Publishes *Happy Birth Day Planet Earth*

EVOLUTION'S GUARANTEE

The breakdown of political boundaries and the advent of a global civilization is guaranteed (just as the merging of humanity into the mind of God is guaranteed) by evolution. Evolution, for the Cosmic Humanist, is not just a physical process—it is a total spiritual development. We evolve into higher species; we also evolve into a higher consciousness. Part of this move toward higher consciousness will be a dissolution of political and national boundaries.

Evolution assures this. Randall Baer describes how Cosmic Humanism uses science to support the claim that we will soon have a global civilization:

> I read that startling advances in such diverse scientific fields as genetic engineering, telecommunications, supercomputers, nuclear fusion technology, artificial intelligence, solid state physics, quantum physics, advanced holography, laser optics, astrophysics, and others were to be combined with New Age spiritual philosophy in creating a utopian New World Order.[4]

Whether this New World Order is achieved in the near or distant future depends on mankind. Evolution will certainly lead us into this promised land, but mankind may either cooperate with or hinder this development. As Mark Satin says, "New Age politics is uncompromisingly evolutionary . . . though it does believe that evolution can be speeded up . . ."[5] The Cosmic Humanist, by achieving higher consciousness, may speed mankind's evolutionary ascent to the New World Order.

AUTONOMY OR ANARCHY?

The specific political nature of the global civilization is rarely discussed by Cosmic Humanists. Neither democracy nor totalitarianism is offered as a potential system of world government, for the simple reason that New Age thinkers believe that each person is rapidly evolving the capacity for self-government.

When mankind achieves a collective consciousness, world government will be synonymous with self-government. "The new political awareness has little to do with parties or ideologies," says Marilyn Ferguson. "Its constituents don't come in blocs. Power that is never surrendered by the individual cannot be brokered. Not by revolution or protest but by autonomy, the old slogan becomes a surprising fact: *Power to the people*. One by one by one."[6]

Thanks to the higher consciousness presently evolving in all mankind, centralized government will wither away. Autonomy—that is, every individual deciding what is right for that individual, without reference to institutional limits—will be the ruling order of the New Age. If such a system sounds like anarchy, it should. It is.

Cosmic Humanists, of course, make efforts to dodge the problem of anarchy. Satin, for example, says that "In New Age society we would learn to make our own decisions and not to hang on others. But that wouldn't isolate us from others; . . . it would make us more attractive to others and more confident about being in community with them."[7] By stressing the concept of community, Satin and other Cosmic Humanists attempt to distinguish their political theory from anarchy. Such a distinction cannot be made, however, because every community suggested by Cosmic Humanists is without political or legal form (basically, without limits)—which implies anarchy.

> "New Age politics is uncompromisingly evolutionary . . . though it does believe that evolution can be speeded up . . ."
>
> *Mark Satin*

CONCLUSION

The New World Order will be a place where every person "follows his bliss" uninhibited by government or laws. The world is evolving toward this ideal every day; it will reach it when enough people have achieved higher consciousness. The rest of mankind—those people not as highly evolved—will then find it much easier to attain higher consciousness, because they will be autonomous (i.e., in a state of anarchy).

At least, the New Age global civilization will be autonomous in most respects. There is, however, one significant aspect of personal freedom that will not be tolerated in the New Age. "Religions," says former U.N. assistant secretary-general Robert Muller, "must actively cooperate to bring to unprecedented heights a better understanding of the mysteries of life and of our place in the universe. 'My religion, right or wrong,' . . . must be abandoned forever in the Planetary Age."[8] This attitude is based on the knowledge that some religions, such as Christianity, are always incompatible with a Cosmic Humanist perspective. Christianity will always threaten the New Age evolution to godhood and hence must be stifled. You may follow your bliss, as long as your bliss is not found in obedience to Jesus Christ.

Politics At A Glance

Secular Humanism	Marxist/Leninist	Cosmic Humanist
World Government	New World Order	New Age Order

CHAPTER 34

Biblical Christian Politics

"Everyone must submit himself to the governing authorities, for there is no authority except that which God has established."

—Romans 13:1

INTRODUCTION

Throughout history, mankind has accepted the existence of the state, believing it to be as unavoidable as death and taxes. The Christian believes this certainty arises because government is an institution established by God (Genesis 9:6).

Christians recognize that government as an institution is sacred, and that its rulers are ministers of God (Romans 13). It is the Christian's duty to obey the state. "Submit yourselves for the Lord's sake to every authority instituted among men," says Peter, "whether to the king, as the supreme authority, or to governors, who are sent by him to punish those who do wrong and to commend those who do right" (1 Peter 2:13-14). Since government is appointed by God, as long as it is serving the purpose for which God created it, the Christian shows his allegiance to God by submitting himself to human government.

The Christian expects the state to accomplish limited, God-ordained tasks. Government should adhere to the principle, "Let all things be done decently and in order" (1 Corinthians 14:40; Exodus 18:19f) since this is a reflection of God's character, and it should be participatory, so that Christian citizens can better influence the state to conform to God's will as a social institution (Proverbs 11:11). Also, the Christian understands that power tends to corrupt, so that a government that disperses power is better than one that gathers power into the hands of a few. Christianity, however, does not single out any particular form of government as the only acceptable one. Rather, it expects any type of government to conform to Biblical principles, understanding that this is more likely to occur in a representative form of government than in a dictatorship.

The aspects of American government that most closely conform to the Christian ideal are, not surprisingly, the most valuable part of America's political heritage. These include America's division of governmental power into three branches—legislative, executive, and judicial—and the concordant system of checks and balances.

CREATION AND ORIGINAL SIN

Perhaps the Christian concept America's founders best understood was the Christian view of human nature. The United States was born in an environment in which men held a Christian view of man's fallen nature; but they did not forget that man was created in the image of God. These two beliefs about man have profound implications for a Christian view of politics, which is reflected in America's founding fathers' attempts to tailor a government suited to man's place in God's creative order.

Human government became necessary because of the Fall. Since every man is inherently sinful, our evil inclinations must be kept in check by laws and a government capable of enforcing such laws. Thus, government protects mankind from its own sinful nature. But who protects the society from the sinful inclinations of the men who make up the government? This was the problem with which America's early leaders grappled in attempting to create a just political system.

They solved the dilemma by creating a system of checks and balances within the government. America was designed in such a way that each of the three branches of government have unique powers that prevent the focus of governmental authority from falling into the hands of a select few. By broadly distributing power and responsibility, the American system removes much of the temptation of man's sinful nature to misuse political clout.

As James Madison says, "If men were angels, no government would be necessary. If angels were to govern men, neither external nor internal controls on government would be necessary."[1] This Christian understanding of man's nature helped form a more practical government than governments built on a faulty view of human nature.

Further, a Christian worldview is indispensable for guaranteeing basic human rights for individuals. Because the Christian believes man is *created in the image of God*, he believes that each individual has value (This becomes doubly clear when we remember that Christ took upon Himself human flesh and died for mankind). Each individual is granted by God certain rights founded on an absolute moral standard. This is the second facet of Christian belief that greatly affects Christian political theory.

This aspect of the Christian view of man was also taken into account by America's forefathers. Thus, in the Declaration of Independence, we find the proclamation that "all men are created equal; that they are endowed by their Creator with certain unalienable rights." Two assumptions are inherent to this declaration: first, man was created by a supernatural Being; second, this Being is the foundation for all human rights.

The fact that these unalienable rights have an unchanging Source is crucial for Christian politics. If man's rights were not tied inextricably to the character of God, then human rights would be arbitrarily assigned according to the whims of each passing generation. Rights are "unalienable" only because they are based on God's unchanging character. God established government to secure these rights. This protection of human rights is God's basic purpose for government.

A Brief Look At: Charles Colson (1931-)

1959: Receives law degree from George Washington University

1969: Begins serving as special counsel to President Richard Nixon

1973: Converts to Christianity

1974: Convicted for his role in Watergate scandal

1975: Released from prison

1976: Founds Prison Fellowship, a ministry to inmates

1983: Publishes *Loving God*

1987: Publishes *Kingdoms in Conflict*

THE PURPOSE OF GOVERNMENT

According to the Biblical Christian worldview, human government was instituted by God to protect man's unalienable rights from mankind's sinful tendencies (Genesis 9:6; Romans 13:1-7). Human nature being what it is, man will attempt to infringe on his fellow man's rights in an effort to improve his own life; therefore a political system must exist to protect rights and keep these evil tendencies at bay.

> **"If men were angels, no government would be necessary."**
>
> *James Madison*

Protecting human rights from evil tendencies, of course, simply means promoting justice. What is justice? E. Calvin Beisner says justice and truth are interrelated, for justice is the practice of truth in human relationships; he concludes that "justice is rendering to each his due according to a right standard."[2]

Most everyone believes that furthering justice is an important task of the state, but the Christian sees justice as the principal reason for the state's existence. Such a view of justice can follow only from a view grounded on an absolute guarantor of unalienable rights. Because the Christian view is based on such a foundation, promoting justice becomes more important than any other aspect of government. Rousas Rushdoony is correct to assert that whether a man "can vote or not is not nearly as important as the question of justice: does the law leave him secure in his governmental spheres, as an individual, a family, church, school, or business?"[3]

Government, according to this view, has limited responsibility. The state should concentrate on enforcing justice and avoid meddling in other institutions' business. It must never assume the responsibilities of other institutions, including church and family. Generally speaking, the church's responsibility is to manifest God's grace on the earth, and the family's responsibility is to manifest God's community and creativity (including procreativity).

Each of these institutions is limited by its own definition and by the other two. Because government is an institution of justice, not of grace or community or creativity, it should not interfere with freedom of religion, attempt to dispense grace through tax-funded handouts, control family size, interfere in raising children (including education), or control the economy. Government has a role; it should allow other God-ordained institutions the freedom to perform their roles.

SOVEREIGNTY APART FROM GOD

Unfortunately, human government almost always winds up overstepping its God-ordained role. Today, many leaders (both in politics and in other disciplines) do not understand mankind's true place in the universe; this incorrect perspective results in the usurpation of God's sovereignty. Whatever is placed in God's rightful position is granted authority that is not its own to wield (Psalm 103:19).

Abandoning God and placing one's trust in an individual or the state will always result in a power-mad and abusive state. Charles Colson explains, "Excise belief in God and you are left with only two principals: the individual and the state. In this situation, however, there is no mediating structure to generate moral values and, therefore, no counterbalance to the inevitable ambitions of the state."[4] "If we are not governed by God," says William Penn, "then we will be ruled by tyrants."[5]

Many today, including both Secular Humanists and Marxist/Leninists, are calling for a world state to serve as the ultimate political and economic authority and to assist mankind on its evolutionary journey. If the Marxists and Humanists get their way (and there is plenty of movement toward "a new world order"), it will be not only the Kingdom of Man but also the Kingdom of the Anti-Christ.

UTOPIANISM

Utopianism is a prime example of man's denial of God, placing absolute sovereignty in the hands of the state. This mistake results not only from willing disregard of God's ultimate authority but also from a misconception about man's nature. As stressed throughout this text, Marxists and Humanists believe in the perfectibility of human nature, and this belief leads them to conclude that once the correct environment is manufactured for mankind and man's mind is programmed correctly, everyone will live properly. The state (with proper input from the Humanists or Marxists, of course) becomes the manufacturer of the correct environment. The state quickly takes on the role of God.

This belief in man's perfectibility (called by Colson "the most subtle and dangerous delusion of our times")[6] is seen in our present society's denial of individual responsibility. Denying individual responsibility separates man from his only possible salvation—a knowledge and acceptance of Christ's sacrifice for the individual's sins—and condemns secular man to an endless search for the "proper utopian environment."

> **The state should concentrate on enforcing justice and avoid meddling in other institutions' business.**

Indeed, utopianism offers no salvation except through the hope that the state will someday create the perfect environment and the perfect man. Colson says, "While Christian teaching emphasizes that each person has worth and responsibility before God, utopianism argues that salvation can only be achieved collectively."[7] This reliance on the state results in the individual being trampled underfoot. History provides many chilling examples; most notably, Joseph Stalin's slaughter of millions of innocent "bourgeois."

The lack of legitimate authority caused by the denial of God reinforces the Christian's belief that God must be recognized as Ruler in every sphere, including politics. Infringements on human rights by various governments based on the sovereignty or whim of the state speaks eloquently of the need for a transcendent law.

A QUESTION OF OBEDIENCE

The Christian expects a lot from government. The state must recognize man's place in the universe and understand God as the ultimate source of authority and human rights. Conversely, God expects the Christian to respect, obey, and participate in governments that serve His will (Romans 13:1-2).

The reason God demands this is simple: government was instituted to promote justice. Obedience to just government is necessary to keep the need for governmental power at a minimum. Thus, the Christian is called to obey government, to honor justice, and to preserve order. However, this does not mean that Christians must obey government blindly. The political leader has a responsibility to God, and the Christian must hold him accountable.

When a political leader or government strays from obedience, the Christian must attempt to correct the deviance so that he or she will not be forced to disobey the state. This may involve registering to vote and voting; it may involve passing out petitions. Some Christians will be called to run for political office, and others will be called to serve in non-elected offices. Such involvement is a more effective way than civil disobedience to peacefully persuade government to be obedient to God. If the people rejoice when the righteous rule (Proverbs 29:2), the righteous need to rule.

But what if a Christian becomes as politically involved as possible and still finds himself faced with certain governmental policies that are unjust and therefore displeasing to God? As noted earlier, the Bible clearly instructs man to obey God even when His commands conflict with those of the state. Acts 4:19 says that when the Sanhedrin commanded Peter and John to stop teaching about Jesus, they replied, "Judge for yourselves whether it is right in God's sight to obey man rather than God."

This obedience to God is required even after the Christian has worked for reform through all possible political channels. If the system remains unjust, it becomes necessary for the Christian to engage in acts of civil disobedience in order to remain obedient to God. Francis Schaeffer sums up: "The bottom line is that at a certain point there is not only the right, but the duty, to disobey the state."[8] This disobedience may even result in being put to death by the state. In such instances it is better to die than to live. Daniel understood this truth and chose death over worshiping a king (Daniel 6:1-10). God honors such commitment.

Secular Humanism	Marxist/Leninist	Cosmic Humanist	Christianity
World Government	New World Order	New Age Order	Justice, Freedom and Order

CONCLUSION

The state was established to administer God's justice. When government rules within the proper boundaries of its role in God's plan, the Christian submits to the state because God has placed it in authority over him. However, when the state abuses that authority, or claims to be sovereign, the Christian acknowledges the transcendent law of God rather than the state. This loyalty to God motivates the Christian to become politically involved in an effort to create good and just government. The involvement of righteous people can significantly influence government for the better.

This constant battle by the Christian to create or maintain a just state may or may not have an effect on government policy. That's not the important issue. What is important is that the Christian remains obedient to God under all circumstances. Colson writes, "Christians are to do their duty as best they can. But even when they feel that they are making no difference, that they are failing to bring Christian values to the public arena, success is not the criteria. Faithfulness is."[9]

FOUR WESTERN WORLDVIEW MODELS

SOURCES	SECULAR HUMANISM — HUMANIST MANIFESTOS I AND II	MARXISM/ LENINISM — WRITINGS OF MARX AND LENIN	COSMIC HUMANISM — WRITINGS OF SPANGLER, FERGUSON, ETC.	BIBLICAL CHRISTIANITY — BIBLE
THEOLOGY	Atheism	Atheism	Pantheism	Theism
PHILOSOPHY	Naturalism	Dialectical Materialism	Non-Naturalism	Supernaturalism
ETHICS	Relativism	Proletariat Morality	Relativism	Absolutes
BIOLOGY	Darwinian Evolution	Darwinian/Punctuated Evolution	Darwinian/Punctuated Evolution	Creation
PSYCHOLOGY	Self-Actualization	Behaviorism	Collective Consciousness	Mind/Body
SOCIOLOGY	Non-Traditional Family	Abolition of Home, Church and State	Non-Traditional Home, Church and State	Traditional Home, Church and State
LAW	Positive Law	Positive Law	Self-Law	Biblical and Natural Law
POLITICS	World Government (Globalism)	New World Order (New Civilization)	New Age Order	Justice, Freedom and Order
ECONOMICS	Socialism	Socialism	Universal Enlightened Production	Stewardship of Property
HISTORY	Historical Evolution	Historical Materialism	Evolutionary Godhood	Historical Resurrection

CHAPTER 35

Secular Humanist Economics

"We socialists are not ashamed to confess that we have a deep faith in man and in a vision of a new, human form of society."[1]

—Erich Fromm

INTRODUCTION

While Secular Humanism requires agreement in the areas of theology, philosophy, and biology, it allows for varied opinions in the field of economics. Because Humanism has dogmatic foundational assumptions, however, it tends to encourage a particular economic approach: socialism. "Many humanists see socialism," writes Robert Sheaffer, "as a vital element of humanism; indeed, at one time, most humanists believed this."[2]

Today, some Humanists attack socialism. Marvin Zimmerman writes, "I contend that the evidence supports the view that democratic capitalism is more productive of human good than democratic socialism."[3] Sheaffer says, "[N]o intellectually honest person today can deny that the history of socialism is a sorry tale of economic failure and crimes against humanity."[4]

Also, some Humanists who were formerly socialists have recently recognized the impracticality of such a position. Paul Kurtz has turned from socialism to free enterprise. Sidney Hook, a lifetime socialist, finally acknowledges, "I no longer believe that the central problem of our time is the choice between capitalism and socialism but the defense and enrichment of a free and open society against totalitarianism."[5] Still, Hook cannot bring himself to completely abandon socialism.

The reason Hook (and many other Humanists) still cling to socialism lies in their misconceptions about human nature. Any view that does not accept man's fallen nature and the reality of original sin expects man to be able to overcome evil—and evil is, theoretically, the only thing preventing a socialist economy from working. If there were no such thing as greed, envy, or sloth, then socialism might bring about a more productive society.

A Brief Look At: Sidney Hook (1902-1989)

1927: Receives PhD from Columbia University

1939: Begins service as philosophy professor at New York University

1959: Serves as president of the American Philosophical Association (Eastern)

1968: Publishes *The Place of Religion in a Free Society*

1973: Signs *Humanist Manifesto II*

1983: Publishes *Marxism and Beyond*

1985: Awarded the Presidential Medal of Freedom

HUMANISTS IN FAVOR OF SOCIALISM

Both the *Humanist Manifesto I* and the *Humanist Manifesto II* contain passages calling for a more equitable distribution of wealth. Many individual Humanists openly proclaim the need for socialism.

Corliss Lamont championed socialism for more than half a century: "I became a convinced believer in socialism as the best way out for America and the world . . . about 1931 or 1932."[6] John Dewey, a former leader of the socialistic League for Industrial Democracy, also believed socialism was the best economic system. He claims that "social control of economic forces is . . . necessary if anything approaching economic equality and liberty is to be realized."[7] Dewey's worldview coincides with Karl Marx in this respect: both men believe mankind must embrace socialism to begin to be truly free.

Erich Fromm also supports socialism: "We are not forced to choose between a managerial free-enterprise system and a managerial communist system. There is a third solution, that of democratic, humanistic socialism which, based on the original principles of socialism, offers the vision of a new, truly human society."[8] In a more limited sense, John Kenneth Galbraith, a former Humanist of the Year, also supports socialism. "In an intelligently plural economy," says Galbraith, "a certain number of industries should be publicly owned."[9]

Clearly, most leading Humanists embrace socialism in one form or another. Some Humanists oppose socialism, but the leaders—the men who have played a role in shaping the whole Humanist worldview—generally regard socialism as the more humanistic economic system. This is true of Lamont, Dewey, Hook, Fromm, and Roy Wood Sellars, and has only recently become untrue of Kurtz.

> **"[S]ocial control of economic forces is … necessary if anything approaching economic equality and liberty is to be realized."**
>
> *John Dewey*

SOCIALISM AND ETHICS

Most Humanists who embrace socialism claim to do so for moral reasons. Hook says, "In my case, as in so many others, allegiance to socialism at first appeared to be primarily the articulation of a feeling of moral protest against remediable evils that surrounded us."[10]

Both Lamont and Dewey also chose socialism on ethical grounds. Lamont writes, "My own path to socialism, therefore, was that of analysis through reason, combined with belief in a humanist ethics and a deep attachment to democracy in its broadest sense."[11] Dewey's concept of liberty implies a moral ground for choosing socialism: "But the cause of liberalism will be lost for a considerable period if it is not prepared to go further and socialize the forces of production, now at hand, so that the liberty of individuals will be supported by the very structure of economic organization."[12] Dewey even goes so far as to adopt an "ends justify the means" approach to economics, stating that "socialized economy is the means of free individual development as the end."[13]

Why do many Humanists believe socialism is the most ethical economic system? Partly because they perceive it to allow more freedom, but also because they view it as more concerned with the common good. Fromm believes, "The aim of socialism is an association in which the full development of each is the condition for the full development of all."[14] When man, and not God, is used as the yardstick for measuring morality, then the common good becomes basically another name for utilitarianism—the greatest amount of happiness for the greatest number of people. And this, so the argument goes, can best be achieved through the equal distribution of wealth and work. More people will be able to concentrate on becoming self-actualized.

Socialism, for the Humanist, ties in closely with his ethical beliefs. The Humanist who embraces utilitarianism (or any version of the common good) finds socialism to be most compatible with his worldview.

THE FAILURE OF CAPITALISM

The second major reason Humanists cite for choosing socialism is the failure of capitalism. Humanists point to perceived evils extant under the capitalist system and assume that these evils will disappear in a socialist economy.

"The giant corporations which control the economic, and to a large degree the political, destiny of the country," writes Fromm, "constitute the very opposite of the democratic process; they represent power without control by those submitted to it."[15] Therefore, Fromm believes socialism is a more democratic economic system. Furthermore, he claims that capitalism has reduced man to a being concerned almost entirely with consumption. Capitalism, for Fromm, strips man of his humanity. Only socialism can restore it.

Lamont cites the "tremendous waste inherent in the capitalist system and its wanton exploitation of men and natural resources"[16] as one of his reasons for embracing socialism. His distrust of capitalism runs so deep that he believes, "Since fascism is simply capitalism stripped of all democratic pretenses and other unessentials—capitalism in the nude, as it were—the danger of fascism remains as long as the capitalist system is with us."[17]

Dewey believes that capitalism must create artificial scarcity to operate successfully, and he views this contrived scarcity as responsible for poverty and hunger. "There is an undoubted objective clash of interests between finance-capitalism that controls the means of production and whose profit is served by maintaining relative scarcity, and idle workers and hungry consumers."[18] He views this as a blatant infringement of liberty.

Humanists supporting socialism tend to stress the failures of capitalism and downplay any possible disadvantages of socialism. We are told that capitalism promotes materialism, strips man of his humanity, and creates artificial scarcity. The implied belief of many Humanists is: How can socialism be any worse than capitalism?

SPECIFICS FOR THE TRANSITION TO SOCIALISM

According to most of Humanism's leaders, many intermediate steps must be taken before the United States can achieve full-fledged socialism. Hook, for example, realizes that each job must be designed in a way that grants it inherent value: "But until some way can be found to organize a society in which everyone's way of earning a living is at the same time a satisfactory way of living his or her life, there will always be a problem of incentive."[19]

Lamont believes that the United States Constitution must still be honored, so he recommends that the American government purchase the means of production from their rightful owners. He does not specify whether the government or the capitalists will dictate the price, or where the government will get the money to pay for everything it buys.

Once the intermediate steps toward socialism in the United States are taken, the socialistic Humanists are largely in agreement regarding the means of assuring a more "equal" society. Lamont, Dewey, Fromm, and Sellars all call for a redistribution of wealth in the form of a "guaranteed income" for every person in the country.

Socialistic Humanists may not agree on all the intermediate steps necessary for the transition to socialism in the United States, but they do generally agree on the need for a redistribution of wealth. The idea of guaranteed income ties in with Dewey's notion of liberty, because it would (in theory) grant more economic freedom for all. It also ties in with Fromm's notion of the loss of man's humanity, because (presumably) man would gain his humanity back once he escaped the coercion of the capitalists.

CONCLUSION

Socialism is not an inescapable tenet for anyone claiming to be a Humanist. In fact, some Humanists, especially in the United States, avidly support the free enterprise system. However, socialism is more consistent with the Humanist worldview, and most of the men who have played a major role in shaping Humanist thought in the last century have been socialists.

If one denies the inherent fallen nature of man, socialism becomes the most attractive economic system for creating a heaven on earth. For the Humanist, there is no original sin to stand in the way of creating a helping, sharing, co-operative community on earth. Therefore, the economic system best suited to promote the ethics of Humanism and amend the evils of capitalism is socialism.

Economics
At A Glance

Socialism

Holding to the evolutionary perspective, some Humanists are convinced that socialism is the next, proper step in man's evolution to a better social being. Indeed, some Humanists view socialism in the United States as inevitable. "We are in for some kind of socialism," predicts Dewey, "call it by whatever name we please, and no matter what it will be called [managed competition?] when it is realized."[20]

CHAPTER 36

Marxist/Leninist Economics

"Communist society means that everything—the land, the factories—is owned in common. Communism means working in common."[1]

—V.I. Lenin

INTRODUCTION

Economics plays a much larger role in the Marxist worldview than in either Christianity or Secular Humanism. For the Marxist, a society's economic system determines the laws enacted, the type of government, and the whole role of society in day-to-day life and throughout history. While everyone would grant that economics affects these realms to some extent, the Marxist claims that economics dictates their precise character.

Working with this premise, Marxists naturally draw the conclusion that undesirable economic systems will create backward, undesirable societies. They point to the evils in capitalist society and conclude that capitalism is a bad economic system. For the Marxist, capitalism must be replaced with a more humane economic system.

According to Karl Marx, *the key problem with capitalism is that it breeds exploitation.* He says that in capitalist society the bourgeoisie (property-owners) equate personal worth with exchange value, and this leads to "naked, shameless, direct, brutal exploitation."[2]

THE EVILS OF CAPITALISM

For Marx, two flaws necessarily cause capitalism to be a system of exploitation. The first flaw Marx describes as the problem of surplus labor. According to this concept, the bourgeoisie make their profits not by selling their product at a price above the cost of materials plus labor, but rather by paying the worker less than the fair amount for his labor value.

This ability of the bourgeoisie to manipulate the workers allows them to devalue labor, thereby creating a profit for themselves by lowering the price they must pay for labor power. For the Marxist, capitalism creates a vicious circle, causing the workers to be exploited more and more. Within the capitalist system, says Marx, "Accumulation of wealth at one pole is, therefore, at the same time accumulation of misery, agony of toil, slavery, ignorance, brutality, mental degradation, at the opposite pole . . ."[3]

The second flaw in capitalism, according to Marx, is its chaotic nature. Whereas the state can control every aspect of socialism (from production to distribution), capitalism is controlled by the free market. Technically, capitalism is known as a market-directed economy, and socialism is referred to as a centrally planned economy, although in practice most economies are a mixture of both. At the very least, we may say that capitalism tends to be market-directed and socialism tends to be centrally planned. In a socialistic system, economic decisions regarding price, production, consumption, etc. are made by central planners affiliated with the government; whereas in capitalism, economic decisions are made by every producer and every consumer—a housewife with a shopping list, for example, is an economic planner in a capitalistic system.

> **Communism occurs when the government has withered away because classes have ceased to exist, and no one (and everyone) owns the means of production.**

Marxism stresses this difference, claiming that only a planned economy can truly discover the best methods of production and distribution. The capitalist economy not only flourishes in but also relies on crises to stimulate the economy, according to the Marxist. Marx believed this reliance on crises will create economic havoc in the long run. The spontaneous, erratic, free-wheeling system, therefore, must be replaced by a planned economy.

This move to socialism will occur because capitalism is doomed to fail. The Marxist believes all capitalist societies contain within themselves the seeds of their own destruction.

CAPITALISM'S SELF-DESTRUCTION

The capitalist system, according to the Marxist, will simply exploit more and more people until virtually everyone is a member of the proletariat. "Whilst the capitalist mode of production more and more completely transforms the great majority of the population into proletarians," says Frederick Engels, "it creates the power which, under penalty of its own destruction, is forced to accomplish this revolution. [Eventually] The proletariat seizes political power and turns the means of production into state property."[4]

A Brief Look At: Nikita Khrushchev (1894-1971)

1918: Joins the Communist party; enrolls in the Red Army

1925: Graduates from the Donets Industrial Institute

1938: Appointed first secretary of the Ukrainian Communist party

1949: Serves in the Communist party's Secretariat

1953: Joseph Stalin dies; Khrushchev becomes one of eight most powerful men in USSR

1955: Emerges as next leader of the Soviet Union

1962: President John F. Kennedy forces Khrushchev to remove missiles from Cuba

1964: Forced to retire by party leaders

This revolt by the proletariat is crucial for assisting the downfall of capitalism. The proletariat must act as the catalyst for the creation of the new system. Moscow's *Political Dictionary* (1940) states, "The extremely sharp class conflict between the exploiters and the exploited constitutes the basic trait of the capitalist system. The development of capitalism inevitably leads to its downfall. However, the system of exploitations does not disappear of itself. It is destroyed only as the result of the revolutionary struggle and the victory of the proletariat."[5]

This destruction of capitalism and victory of the proletariat is ultimately guaranteed by the dialectic. For the Marxist, it is historically inevitable: the thesis (bourgeoisie) and the antithesis (proletariat) must clash and create a synthesis—socialism—and socialism guarantees the advent of communism.

DIFFERENCES BETWEEN SOCIALISM AND COMMUNISM

But socialism and communism are not the same thing. Socialism, according to the Marxist, is the first phase of communism—it is a step in the transition to communism. Socialism will precede communism in the transition to the perfect economic system.

The basic difference between the two systems is best summed up by the *Political Dictionary:* "Socialism is the first phase of communism. The principle of socialism is: from each according to his abilities, to each according to his work. . . . Under communism the basic principle of society will be: from each according to his abilities, to each according to his needs."[6]

Socialism, as explained in the Marxist Politics chapter, is that historical phase during which the proletariat have seized both the means of production and the government. Communism occurs when the government has withered away because classes have ceased to exist, and no one (and everyone) owns the means of production. "Communism," as V.I. Lenin says, "means working in common."[7] Every man will be free to work doing whatever he wants for as long as he likes, and this free society will create fulfilled workers and an abundance of the necessary goods and services.

THE TRANSITION TO PURE COMMUNISM

Why must a transitional phase necessarily exist between capitalism and communism? Engels addresses this question by asking, "Will it be possible to abolish private property at one stroke?" and then answering: "No, . . . the proletarian revolution, which in all probability is impending, will transform existing society only gradually, and be able to abolish private property only when the necessary quantity of the means of production has been created."[8] Because both the abolition of private property and the refining of the means of production must happen gradually, the move to communism requires a transitional phase.

Marx tells us, "Between capitalist and communist society lies a period of revolutionary transformation from one to the other."[9] This transitional stage of socialism will be a blend between capitalism and communism. "Theoretically," says Lenin, "there can be no doubt that between capitalism and communism there lies a definite transition period which must combine the features and properties of both these forms of social economy."[10]

314

Pure communism, the final phase of society's development, will only result from society's constant maturation in the socialist phase. Engels describes the specifics for the new society's emergence: "Finally, when all capital, all production, and all exchange are concentrated in the hands of the nation, private ownership will automatically have ceased to exist, money will have become superfluous, and production will have so increased and men will be so much changed that the last forms of the old social relations will also be able to fall away."[11]

THE TRANSITION IN PRACTICE

In 1918, the Marxist effort to rapidly install socialism in Russia resulted in a Soviet Constitution that proclaimed that "all private property in land is abolished, and the entire land is declared to be national property and is to be apportioned among agriculturists without any compensation to the former owners, in the measure of each one's ability to till it."[12] The first phase in the transition to socialism requires taking property from its rightful owners.

Lenin quickly realized, however, that the Russian economy would never survive such a rapid move to socialism. In 1921 he declared, "We are no longer attempting to break up the old social economic order, with its trade, its small-scale economy and private initiative, its capitalism, but we are now trying to revive trade, private enterprise, and capitalism, at the same time gradually and cautiously subjecting them to state regulation just as far as they revive."[13]

Does it seem odd that such a dedicated Marxist would find himself forced to revert to capitalism? Lenin recognizes the danger of his position and is careful to justify his stance: "Capitalism is an evil in comparison with socialism, but capitalism is a blessing in comparison with medievalism, with small industry, with fettered small producers thrown to the mercy of bureaucracy."[14] Lenin claimed that Russia had not even progressed to an advanced stage of capitalism, and therefore must first undergo such a phase before the move to socialism.

During this move through advanced capitalism to beginning socialism, Lenin was willing to experiment with a number of other social methods to hasten the transition. He suggested experimentation to discover the best means of dealing with people not doing their share of the work, including imprisonment, forced labor, "one out of every ten idlers will be shot on the spot," etc.[15]

THE COMMUNIST UTOPIA

When communism is finally achieved world-wide, citizens will reap a number of benefits. For one thing, Marxists claim that communism provides more freedom than any other system. Man will finally achieve perfection, and therefore will no longer need government or laws to keep him in check.

Another theoretical benefit of communism lies in the Marxist belief that the redistribution of wealth will solve a great many problems. Redistribution of wealth is presented as a cure-all in the text *Political Economy: Socialism:* "Once the exploiting classes with their parasitic consumption have been abolished, the national income becomes wholly at the disposal of the people. Working conditions are radically altered, housing conditions in town and country substantially improved and all the achievements of modern culture made accessible to the working people."[16]

Still another Marxist-perceived advantage of communism lies in its ability to motivate workers. "Can capitalist society with its chronic unemployment ensure each citizen the opportunity to work, let alone to choose the work he likes? Clearly, it cannot. But the socialist system makes the right to work a constitutional right of a citizen, delivering him from the oppressive anxiety and uncertainty over the morrow."[17]

In short, communism is the ideal economic system—the foundation for utopia. The Marxist economic system, according to the Marxists, will have a positive impact on all aspects of our world, from ethics to politics.

Economics At A Glance

Secular Humanism	Marxist/Leninist
Socialism	Socialism/ Communism

CONCLUSION

Marxists see the world inevitably moving toward a socialistic system, which will eventually make the transition to communism. This move is inevitable because the dialectic ensures it—indeed, capitalism contains its own fatal flaw. Capitalism is advancing toward socialism every day, and socialist countries such as the People's Republic of China are advancing toward communism.

When communism becomes the world's economic system, the dialectical march toward utopia will have reached its destination. Kenneth Neill Cameron writes, "Marx and Engels expected that communist society would be the last form of human society, for once the world's productive forces were communally owned no other form could arise."[18]

Nothing could be more ideal, from the Marxist point of view. Indeed, nothing else will even allow the human race to survive, according to Lenin. "Outside of socialism," says Lenin, "there is no salvation for mankind from war, hunger and the further destruction of millions and millions of human beings."[19]

CHAPTER 37

Cosmic Humanist Economics

"Like everything else, money is either holy or unholy, depending on the purposes ascribed to it by the mind. We tend to do with money what we do with sex: we desire it but we judge the desire. It is the judgment that then distorts the desire, turning it into an ugly expression."[1]

—Marianne Williamson

INTRODUCTION

New Age beliefs about the need for a world system of self-government necessarily shape New Age economic theory. Predictably, some Cosmic Humanists have begun calling for one universal system of exchange. Vera Alder describes the system of the future: "As . . . individual needs would largely be supplied on the ration-card system, the need for handling of money would dwindle. There would, of course, be a universal currency the world over. There would be a central bank."[2]

However, most Cosmic Humanists don't discuss the specifics of a world economic system for the same reason they avoid concrete political declarations or definitive legal systems: the degree of autonomy the individual will experience in the New Age cannot be bound by the limitations of any present-day economic system. "Both capitalism and socialism," says Marilyn Ferguson, "as we know them, pivot on material values. They are inadequate philosophies for a transformed society."[3] A transformed society will enjoy so much personal freedom that all concern with the marketplace will be swept away. Future world citizens will not ask themselves, What goods can I produce or services can I perform to meet the needs (or demands) of my neighbors? Rather, they will ask, What is my inner voice calling me to do? Since the inner voice is the voice of God, the call will lead to the proper vocation.

A Brief Look At: Shakti Gawain (1948-)

1966: Begins studying psychology at Reed College

1971: Graduates from University of California, Irvine

1973: Enrolls in Silva Mind Control course

1974: Begins worldwide travels, studying meditation, yoga, etc.

1986: Publishes *Living in the Light*

1989: Publishes *Return to the Garden*

HIGHER CONSCIOUSNESS = HIGHER INCOME

Incredibly, everyone's inner voice will lead him or her in such a way that no member of society will want for anything. Shakti Gawain proclaims,

> We make a contribution to the world just by being ourselves in every moment. There are no more rigid categories in our lives—this is work, this is play. It all blends into the flow of following the universe and money flows in as a result of the open channel that's created. You no longer work in order to make money. Work is no longer something you have to do in order to sustain life. Instead, the delight that comes from expressing yourself becomes the greatest reward.[4]

Elsewhere she claims, "The more you are willing to trust yourself, and take the risks to follow your inner guidance, the more money you will have. The universe will pay you to be yourself and do what you really love!"[5] This concept was also accepted by Randall Baer. In New Age success philosophy, says Baer, "the more attuned a person is to the 'Universal Mind' the more the universe will demonstrate this level of enlightenment by mirroring more 'god-money in action.' The more enlightened a person is, the more money and success will naturally occur in life."[6]

In other words, says Marianne Williamson, "God does not demand sacrifice."[7] Far from it. God wants us to prosper materially. By getting in touch with our higher consciousness, we can ensure a higher income.

Do you want a brown Mercedes? Well, says Williamson, if you focus on that goal you will probably get it. But God may want you to have something even better than a brown Mercedes—so you really should just focus on attaining higher consciousness, trusting the God within to shower you with material blessings.

We can trust the world to grant us material blessings, according to Williamson, because "Our purpose on this earth is to be happy,"[8] and because we, as part of God, ultimately control reality. "God does not work *for* you," says Kevin Ryerson; "God works *through* you."[9]

CONCLUSION

Economic theory means very little to the Cosmic Humanist. Economic systems are for unenlightened societies. When most people have achieved higher consciousness, there will be no need for an economic system at all, because people will be led by the God within to always make wise economic decisions. In the New Age, men and women will "follow their bliss," and their bliss will cause them to provide whatever product or service will be best for the global civilization. Presumably, some people's bliss will be found in street-sweeping, sewage treatment, etc.

Likewise, no one really needs to worry about which economic system encourages the best standard of living, because people in touch with their higher consciousness will always achieve material success. Poverty gradually will slip away, as every person allows the God within to shower him with money and possessions.

In other words, man is basically good, and all we have to do is get in touch with our

Many Cosmic Humanists, including Shirley MacLaine, offer seminars to teach neophytes the path to godhood. The success of these conferences is something of an economic phenomenon.

Snapshots In Time

Cosmic Humanists believe in a peculiar form of economics: whatever the worker supplies (as long as he follows his bliss) will be in great demand. This belief is especially popular in modern America because some New Age leaders have reaped spectacular profits by doing what they like to do: writing books and sponsoring conferences.

Since 1980, Cosmic Humanists have had the opportunity to attend AIDS workshops led by Marianne Williamson, spirit channeling sessions by J.Z. Knight, a "World Peace Event" inspired by John Randolph Price, lectures by M. Scott Peck, or a host of other New Age seminars. Jach Pursel channels a spirit named Lazaris, who conducts four–day intensive meetings that cost $600 per person.

Such conferences provide significant income for the speakers and organizers, thus perpetuating the New Age deception: "We are poor because we do not work with love" (Marianne Williamson). As more and more New Age leaders get in touch with their godhood and make money doing it, their followers become more convinced that doing what feels right is the path to riches.

goodness to solve our economic dilemmas. Christians are wrong when they say that man is inherently sinful. Greed is not a problem. Shirley MacLaine theorizes that greed is only "a manifestation of the need for human love . . ."[10] In the New Age, there will be no greed or poverty—only people working harmoniously to increase shared wealth. "God does not require sacrifice;"[11] It just wants us to be happy.

Cosmic Humanists would rather not talk about the logical conclusion that follows from this, but they cannot avoid it. If higher income and prosperity flow naturally from higher consciousness, then everyone today who is poor or sick must have a "lower consciousness." In other words, your misery is your fault. If you were more in touch with your godhood, you would be healthy and rich beyond your wildest expectations—but alas, you are not. Here, then, is the cruelest aspect of the New Age worldview: suffering is always self-inflicted.

Economics
At A Glance

Secular Humanism	Marxist/Leninist	Cosmic Humanist
Socialism	Socialism/ Communism	Universal Enlightened Production

CHAPTER 38

Biblical Christian Economics

"Better a little with righteousness than much gain with injustice."

—Proverbs 16:8

INTRODUCTION

Christians are divided on the issue of economics. While many Christians believe the Bible encourages a system of private property and individual responsibilities and initiatives (citing Isaiah 65:21-2; Jeremiah 32:43-4; Acts 5:1-4; Ephesians 4:28), many others are adamant in their support for a socialist economy (citing Acts 2:44-45). In fact, some Christians proclaim that the Bible teaches a form of Marxism. These people—"liberation theologians"—expect some form of socialism to usher in the kingdom of heaven.

Such thinking is a trap every Christian must beware, because no economic system—whether communist, socialist or capitalist—is capable of saving mankind. No economic system is perfect. This does not mean, however, that all economic systems are equal. One system, in fact, is quite compatible with God's Word and our imperfect world.

A Brief Look At: Francis Schaeffer (1912-1984)

1935: Marries Edith Seville

1938: Ordained as a Presbyterian minister

1948: Begins serving as a missionary in Switzerland

1955: Establishes L'Abri Fellowship, a Christian community

1976: Publishes *How Should We Then Live?*

1981: Publishes *A Christian Manifesto*

1982: Daughter Susan publishes *How to be Your Own Selfish Pig*

SOCIALISM OR FREE ENTERPRISE?

On the most basic level, the Christian is faced with supporting either socialism or free enterprise. In the real world, neither socialism nor capitalism exists in "pure" form—that is, all capitalist systems contain certain elements of socialism, and vice versa. But for our purposes, we will discuss these opposing systems in terms of their least diluted states.

The simplest distinction between socialism and the free market system is outlined by Ronald Nash: "One dominant feature of capitalism is economic freedom, the right of people to exchange things voluntarily, free from force, fraud, and theft. Capitalism is more than this, of course, but its concern with free exchange is obvious. Socialism, on the other hand, seeks to replace the freedom of the market with a group of central planners who exercise control over essential market functions."[1] Christians who believe socialism (or communism) is the more desirable system trust that this centralized control will create a more just means of sharing scarce resources. They believe the Bible supports their call for socialism, often pointing to Acts 2:44-45 as evidence that God's Word calls for such an economic arrangement.

When one studies the Bible as a whole, however, it becomes obvious that God's Word is much more supportive of an economic system respecting private property and the work ethic (see especially Isaiah 65:21-2 and Jeremiah 32:43-44).

PRIVATE PROPERTY

Christians who adhere to socialism claim that private property encourages greed and envy and that public ownership would remove much temptation to sin. Is this compatible with Scripture? Irving E. Howard doesn't think so: "The commandment 'Thou shalt not steal' is the clearest declaration of the right to private property in the Old Testament."[2]

In fact, private ownership and stewardship of property is assumed to be the proper state of affairs throughout the Bible (Deuteronomy 8; Ruth 2; Isaiah 65:21-22; Jeremiah 32:42-44; Micah 4:1-4; Luke 12:13-15; Acts 5:1-4; Ephesians 4:28). E. Calvin Beisner demonstrates this by asking, "Why does Scripture require restitution, including multiple restitution, in cases of theft, even if paying the restitution requires selling oneself into slavery (Exodus 22:1ff)?"[3] Clearly, Scripture requires this because God has bestowed on mankind a right to property.

This right to property stems from our duty to work. After casting man out of Eden, God decreed that mankind must face a life of toil (Genesis 3:17-19). But God, in His mercy, allowed that men who conscientiously adhere to this duty may be rewarded with private property. Proverbs 10:4 states, "Lazy hands make a man poor, but diligent hands bring wealth." God has designed a world in which the existence of private property encourages men to be fruitful.

Further, since God grants man private ownership of certain aspects of His creation, man becomes accountable to God for the way in which he uses his property. In God's wonderfully intricate plan, the duty to work gives rise to the right to property, which in turn creates the duty to use the property wisely. Beisner states, "Biblical stewardship views God as Owner of all things (Psalm 24:1) and man—individually and collectively—as His steward. Every person is accountable to God for the use of whatever he has (Genesis 1:26-30; 2:15). Every person's responsibility as a steward is to maximize the Owner's return on His investment by using it to serve others (Matthew 25:14-30)."[4]

This use of property to serve others can only occur in a society in which property is privately owned. Publicly owned property destroys man's sense of responsibility to use his possessions wisely, because there is no incentive for selfish men to treat the property wisely.

Private property, from the Christian perspective, actually discourages greed and envy by causing man to focus on the need to work and serve others rather than accumulate more for himself. When one understands property in the context of stewardship, it becomes obvious that private property encourages a more careful attitude toward scarce resources than does public property.

At this point, however, the socialist may argue that we live in an imperfect world and that one cannot expect every man always to have an attitude of stewardship. This, unfortunately, is true. But is the socialist's conclusion—that allowing selfish men to compete in a free market system for limited property leads to counterproductive actions—also necessarily true? Is economic competition inherently evil?

ECONOMIC COMPETITION

Judging from aforementioned verses such as Proverbs 10:4, 14:23, and Luke 10:7, it would seem that the Bible calls for men to compete with each other in the work place to encourage fruitfulness. When this biblical principle is applied, it turns out to be very practical: economic competition tends to stifle man's sinful tendencies.

Competition encourages cooperation in a capitalist society, because men in such a system act in accordance with the principle of comparative advantage. This principle basically states that every member of a free market society can produce a valuable good or service by specializing in the area in which he enjoys the least absolute disadvantage. Thus, individuals find that they can be more successful operating in a free market by focusing their energies on production that is more beneficial to society as a whole—that is, by cooperating. This in turn creates more goods and services, making them available to poorer members of society.

When viewed from the perspective of comparative advantage, competition also creates another benefit: it promotes the worth of each individual. The free market preserves each man's dignity by granting the individual the opportunity to contribute to the welfare of the society. Comparative advantage allows everyone to be the "best" producer of some service or product. This meshes perfectly with the Biblical perspective, which describes each individual as intrinsically valuable because he is made in the image of God.

Competition, when it leads to cooperation and a recognition of individual worth, fits the Christian worldview. Indeed, when one understands that the only alternative to competition is contrary to Biblical revelation, one must admit the value of a capitalist system.

Or so it seems. However, Christians who view socialism as the proper economic system have an ace in the hole. They claim that social justice demands that each individual possess an equal share of scarce resources and that this primary principle overrules all other considerations.

> **In God's wonderfully intricate plan, the duty to work gives rise to the right to property, which in turn creates the duty to use the property wisely.**

328

THE PRINCIPLE OF SOCIAL JUSTICE

On the surface, demanding economic equality seems a noble ideal. What could be more fair than every man sharing equally the scarce resources available? But we have already demonstrated that God's Word calls for private property, and further, we are faced with the disturbing words of the Apostle Paul in 2 Thessalonians 3:10: "For even when we were with you, we gave you this rule: 'If a man will not work, he shall not eat.'" How does one reconcile the seemingly noble notion of economic equality with Biblical truth?

The answer, of course, is that one cannot. Beisner quotes Leviticus 19:15 and concludes, "God is not 'on the side of the poor,' despite protests to the contrary. Any law, therefore, that gives an advantage in the economic sphere to anyone, *rich or poor,* violates Biblical justice."[5] Why is this the case? Because justice requires equality before the law, not equality of incomes or abilities.

Indeed, justice will necessarily lead to economic inequality. As Beisner says, "the Bible demands impartiality, which—because people differ in interests, gifts, capacities, and stations in life—must invariably result in conditional inequality."[6]

> **"The only way to arrive at equal fruits is to equalize behavior; and that requires robbing men of liberty, making them slaves."**
>
> *E. Calvin Beisner*

Justice is based not on equal income but on opportunity equally unhindered by coercive shackles. "Given the diversity and liberty of human life," says Michael Novak, "no fair and free system can possibly guarantee equal outcomes. A democratic system depends for its legitimacy, therefore, not upon equal results but upon a sense of equal opportunity."[7] And equal opportunity means not that everyone must start with the same skills and social contacts, but that no one must be prohibited by law from attempting something morally legitimate in the marketplace. This conforms to the Biblical view.

THE RICH AND THE POOR

Much of the reason the Christian socialist insists upon the need for economic equality lies in his mistaken assumption that the rich take their wealth from the poor. If this view were correct, the socialist call for economic equality might be justified. However, this view is out of touch with reality.

First, the Bible makes it clear that poverty does not always result from exploitation by the rich. "It is certainly true," says Nash, "that Scripture recognizes that poverty sometimes results from oppression and exploitation. But Scripture also teaches that there are times when poverty results from misfortunes that have nothing to do with exploitation. These misfortunes include such things as accidents, injuries, and illness. And of course the Bible also makes it plain that poverty can result from indigence and sloth (Proverbs 6:6-11; 13:4; 24:30-34; 28:19)."[8]

Second, in market economies, the wealthy ordinarily create wealth. Socialists would have us view rich individuals as hoarding already scarce resources—but in truth, the wealthy often use the free market effectively to multiply the goods and services available. This in turn creates more opportunity for rich and poor alike. "Under capitalism," explains George Gilder, "when it is working, the rich have the anti-Midas touch . . . turning gold into goods and jobs and art."[9]

In this way, the rich aid the poor by constantly expanding the pool of wealth and opportunity. Gilder elsewhere explains that "most real wealth originates in individual minds in unpredictable and uncontrollable ways. A successful economy depends on the proliferation of the rich, on creating a large class of risk-taking men who are willing to shun the easy channels of a comfortable life in order to create new enterprise, win huge profits, and invest them again."[10] The free market encourages the wealthy to invest their wealth in productive enterprises, thus making jobs, goods, and services available to others. But a socialist economy encourages the wealthy to hide their wealth from taxation by hoarding it in the form of foreign bank accounts, superfluous luxuries, and other nonproductive uses.

This is a fundamental truth that socialists ignore: wealth comes more from the creativity and hard work fostered by free enterprise than from resources themselves. Indeed, resources are not strictly natural at all; they are all made by the application of human thought and energy to the raw materials around us. Land in and of itself produces only weeds and an occasional berry; land under the guidance of man's creativity and hard work can yield fruit and vegetables for an entire community.

FREEDOM AND ECONOMICS

We began our analysis of capitalism and socialism by noting that capitalism trusts the free market while socialism requires centralized control. From this most fundamental difference between the two systems springs a number of ramifications, including the counterproductive bureaucracies created by the welfare system in the United States. Because socialism requires a planned economy, including control over wealth distribution, pricing, and production, it also requires a powerful central government to initiate the plans. As P.T. Bauer points out, "Attempts to minimize economic differences in an open and free society necessarily involve the use of coercive power."[11]

Thus, the socialist must rely upon increased political power to achieve his goals of economic equality and a planned economy.

In a capitalist system, in contrast, far less political power is necessary, because the government need not worry about controlling incomes, prices, or production. Citizens are free to determine how they will spend their money and how they will use their resources.

Clearly, there is a relationship between the type of economy a society chooses and the amount of freedom the individual must sacrifice. In a socialist society, the individual must relinquish to the government much of the control over his life. "The only way to arrive at equal fruits is to equalize behavior," says Beisner; "and that requires robbing men of liberty, making them slaves."[12] Economic freedom and the right to private property are crucial for political freedom.

Economics At A Glance

Secular Humanism	Marxist/Leninist	Cosmic Humanist	Christianity
Socialism	Socialism/ Communism	Universal Enlightened Production	Stewardship of Property

CONCLUSION

The Christian worldview embraces democratic capitalism for a number of reasons. The Bible not only grants man the right to private property but also calls for man to be a good steward of his property—and the free enterprise system affords man the most opportunity to act as a responsible steward by creating wealth and opportunity. Further, the competition in a free market works according to the principle of comparative advantage, which affirms the inherent worth of every individual.

Capitalism is also more socially just than socialism. While the socialist calls for economic equality, capitalism respects the biblical requirement of equality before the law. This does not, as the socialist contends, cause the rich to get richer and the poor poorer. Rather, it encourages the rich to create more wealth, thereby aiding all of society. The policies of redistribution, including welfare systems, only multiply the problems for the poor—creating needless bureaucracies and concentrating too much power in the hands of the government. Conversely, capitalism encourages freedom in the political sphere. This removes the danger of granting sovereignty to the state instead of to God.

The Christian who accepts the Bible must also accept democratic capitalism or free enterprise as the system most compatible with his worldview. This truth was even apparent to Frederick Engels: "[I]f some few passages of the Bible may be favourable to Communism, the general spirit of its doctrines is, nevertheless, totally opposed to it."[13]

FOUR WESTERN WORLDVIEW MODELS

SOURCES	SECULAR HUMANISM HUMANIST MANIFESTOS I AND II	MARXISM/LENINISM WRITINGS OF MARX AND LENIN	COSMIC HUMANISM WRITINGS OF SPANGLER, FERGUSON, ETC.	BIBLICAL CHRISTIANITY BIBLE
THEOLOGY	Atheism	Atheism	Pantheism	Theism
PHILOSOPHY	Naturalism	Dialectical Materialism	Non-Naturalism	Supernaturalism
ETHICS	Relativism	Proletariat Morality	Relativism	Absolutes
BIOLOGY	Darwinian Evolution	Darwinian/Punctuated Evolution	Darwinian/Punctuated Evolution	Creation
PSYCHOLOGY	Self-Actualization	Behaviorism	Collective Consciousness	Mind/Body
SOCIOLOGY	Non-Traditional Family	Abolition of Home, Church and State	Non-Traditional Home, Church and State	Traditional Home, Church and State
LAW	Positive Law	Positive Law	Self-Law	Biblical and Natural Law
POLITICS	World Government (Globalism)	New World Order (New Civilization)	New Age Order	Justice, Freedom and Order
ECONOMICS	Socialism	Socialism	Universal Enlightened Production	Stewardship of Property
HISTORY	Historical Evolution	Historical Materialism	Evolutionary Godhood	Historical Resurrection

CHAPTER 39

Secular Humanist History

"Man's destiny is to be the sole agent for the future evolution of this planet."[1]
—Julian Huxley

INTRODUCTION

In 1933, Secular Humanists were positively giddy about mankind's potential. The *Humanist Manifesto I*, released that year, described history as one long story of humanity's progress to paradise.

Then came World War II, followed by the discovery of the atrocities of Joseph Stalin. Suddenly the unbounded optimism of the Humanists seemed farcical. The *Humanist Manifesto II* (published in 1973) was forced to admit, "Nazism has shown the depths of brutality of which humanity is capable. Other totalitarian regimes have suppressed human rights without ending poverty. Science has sometimes brought evil as well as good."[2]

Today, it seems impossible for the Humanist to view history with optimism. Assuming an atheistic stance, the Humanist must view mankind's history as a bumbling, chancy, often immoral enterprise, with little hope for improvement in the future. *The Humanist Manifesto II* apparently describes the modern Humanist's rejection of historical optimism.

Or does it? On the very next page of the second *Manifesto*, we find a statement of incomparable historical optimism: "Using technology wisely, we can control our environment, conquer poverty, markedly reduce disease, extend our life-span, significantly modify our behavior, alter the course of human evolution and cultural development, unlock vast new powers, and provide humankind with unparalleled opportunity for achieving an abundant and meaningful life."[3]

The Humanist claims to have adopted a realistic view of mankind's history, but time and time again he makes statements that betray his unlimited faith in evolving mankind. Why does the Humanist insist that mankind's future will always outshine his past?

A Brief Look At: Paul Kurtz (1925-)

1952: Receives PhD from Columbia University

1965: Begins serving as philosophy professor at
 SUNY—Buffalo

1970: Begins serving as editor-in-chief of Prometheus Books

1973: Publishes *Humanist Manifesto II*

1980: Founds *Free Inquiry* magazine

1983: Publishes *In Defense of Secular Humanism*

Two Reasons Humanists Must Be Optimistic

Despite the Humanist's desire to assume a realistic view of history, he must remain unrealistically optimistic for two reasons. The first and most telling is his belief that all life evolved from non-life. This evolutionary perspective colors the Humanist's attitude toward all reality.

If, as Humanists believe, all reality is an evolutionary pattern that has moved upward step by step to create rational thought and morality in the highest species, then mankind's history must also be a progressive march toward a better world. As the evolutionary process continues, so must progress continue. For the Humanist, all of history is a development from simple to more complex, from mindless to mind, from amoral to moral. Civilization constantly improves and ultimately carries the human race (or whatever race evolution dictates) into some type of world community.

John Dietrich sums up this view: "There never has been any Garden of Eden, or perfect condition in the past, there never has been any fall, there has been a constant rise. Man has been climbing slowly up the ages from the most primitive condition to the present civilization."[4]

The whole process of history is perceived by the Humanist as the evolution of cultures and civilizations into more desirable cultures and civilizations. Julian Huxley insists that the "rise and fall of empires and cultures is a natural phenomenon, just as much as the succession of dominant groups in biological evolution."[5] The Humanist feels confident that the future will improve on the past and the present because evolution demands progress.

The second reason Humanists adhere to an optimistic view is best summarized by Huxley: "In the evolutionary pattern of thought there is no longer either need or room for the supernatural."[6] Humanism denies the existence of God. This greatly reduces the importance of men's actions, since in this view, as Bertrand Russell notes, "The universe is vast and men are but tiny specks on an insignificant planet."[7] Oddly enough, this denial of a source of meaning in history pushes the Humanist toward historical optimism. While it seems that such a denial would generate pessimism, it instead spurs the Humanist to pin all his hopes on history and the future, because the progress of mankind becomes the only meaningful goal. The Humanist's atheism, instead of leading him into the trap of nihilism, make him dependent on the progress of human history to provide meaning for mankind. If the Humanist is to believe anything at all, he must believe that evolutionary progress is inevitable.

HUMANISM AND THE BIBLE

Ironically, Humanists use the discipline of history to support their atheism. They claim that historians have proven that the Bible consists chiefly of legends and that a scientific approach to history has exposed the mythological nature of the Bible and especially Christ's miracles.

Paul Kurtz declares, "There is no evidence that Yahweh spoke to Abraham, Moses, Joseph, or any of the Old Testament prophets."[8] Harry Elmer Barnes feels equally distrustful of the accuracy of the Bible: "Biblical criticism, applied to the New Testament, has removed the element of supernaturalism from the biographies of its founders as thoroughly as Old Testament criticism has from those of its heroes."[9]

The Humanist regards the Bible, and especially its historical account of Christ's resurrection and ascension, as historically inaccurate. Indeed, Humanists believe every account of the supernatural to be historically inaccurate, because Humanism's atheistic theology and naturalistic philosophy disallow the existence of the supernatural. But this leaves the Humanist with a major problem: who or what guarantees and directs progress in history?

WHO SHAPES HISTORY?

Some Humanists believe that man's environment plays the largest role in shaping history. Barnes writes, "History is a record of man's development as conditioned by his social environment."[10]

This attitude, at least at first glance, seems to be the most consistent with the Humanist worldview. After all, Humanist psychology describes man as an inherently good animal driven to evil by environmental stimuli. Isn't history just the story of man reacting to the influences of his environment?

Theoretically. In practice, however, the Humanist cannot accept this conclusion. As soon as the Humanist declares the environment the dynamic force behind history, man is stripped of purpose. The Humanist could not encourage the individual to act nobly or work to change the world, because man, according to this view, is nothing but a leaf swept along by the stream of environmental change. Thus, in order to grant man the power to control his own destiny and maintain an optimistic attitude toward history, the Humanist must abandon his belief in environmental influence and stress man's role in shaping history.

Humanism holds the carrot of personal freedom in front of mankind's nose in an effort to keep the individual motivated to improve his world. Corliss Lamont waves the carrot boldly, stating, "Within certain limits prescribed by our earthly circumstances and by scientific law, individual human beings, entire nations, and mankind in general are free to choose the paths that they truly wish to follow. To a significant degree they are the moulders of their own fate and hold in their own hands the shape of things to come."[11] The *Humanist Manifesto II* also singles out mankind as the dynamic force in history: "While there is much that we do not know, humans are responsible for what we are or will become. No deity will save us; we must save ourselves."[12]

By declaring man's actions to be the key force in history, the Humanist maintains both his optimism and his belief in purpose for mankind. However, this concession creates two new problems for Humanism. First, as we have seen, it is inconsistent with the Humanist assertion that man is a product of his environment. Second, by

> **"[The] rise and fall of empires and cultures is a natural phenomenon, just as much as the succession of dominant groups in biological evolution."**
>
> *Julian Huxley*

338

allowing that man shapes history, the Humanist opens the door for any individual to change the course of history—whether Humanist or Christian. This seriously hinders the cause of Humanism, because it suggests that any view may bring about valuable changes in history. The Humanist, however, believes that only his ideology is capable of ushering mankind into a future paradise. How can he convince the rest of humanity to adopt a Humanistic view of history?

IDEOLOGIES SHAPE HISTORY

The Humanist solves this dilemma in two steps. First, he clarifies his assertion: men in and of themselves do not shape history; rather, men's *ideologies* are the dynamic force in history. Second, he declares that ideologies evolve, and therefore some ideologies are better suited for effecting change in different periods of history. Huxley claims that "major steps in the human phase of evolution are achieved by breakthroughs to new dominant patterns of mental organization, of knowledge, ideas and beliefs—ideological instead of physiological or biological organization."[13]

> **The Humanist strives to redeem mankind by creating paradise on earth.**

The implications of this theory are clear: if man's systems of thought evolve, then some ideologies are hopelessly outdated and unsuited to modern problems, and other ideologies are precisely the solution for a certain era. It takes little imagination to guess which ideologies the Humanist considers outdated; any worldview that accepts the existence of the supernatural is scoffed at by Humanism. Thus, Humanists portray Christianity as a primitive ideology that may have been relevant in ancient history but is useless today.

So which ideology is most relevant for advancing the evolution of mankind? You guessed it. Humanists believe Humanism is the dominant ideology—which allows them to claim that man's ideologies influence history while they restrict Christianity and other worldviews from positively affecting the present or the future. Humanism becomes the single causal agent for effecting change in mankind's destiny.

MAN'S ROLE IN CREATING THE FUTURE

The Humanist believes that individuals embracing Humanism can affect history almost limitlessly. Lamont bluntly declares, "Humanism assigns to man nothing less than the task of being his own savior and redeemer."[14]

If anyone doubts that Humanism deifies man, this attitude toward history should bury such lingering uncertainty. The Humanist view of history portrays man as capable of both creating and redeeming humanity, given ample time. Man is described as Creator by Erich Fromm when he states, "Man creates himself in the historical process."[15] Later Fromm blatantly portrays man as redeemer: "The messianic time is the next step in history, not its abolition. The messianic time is the time when man will have been fully born. When man was expelled from Paradise he lost his home; in the messianic time he will be at home again—in the world."[16]

The Humanist strives to redeem mankind by creating paradise on earth. That paradise, however, might be populated by a species more highly evolved than humans. Lamont admits this when he says that "men can find plenty of scope and meaning in their lives through . . . helping to evolve a new species surpassing Man."[17]

What sort of species could be higher than man? Victor J. Stenger has an idea. He believes man is in the process of creating a greatly improved version of himself, "not by the painfully slow and largely random process of biological evolution," but by rapid and guided advances of technology. "This new form of 'life' I will call, for historical reasons, the *computer*."[18] Stenger is convinced that computers will eventually prove to be more capable than humans in every meaningful realm of life: "If there is anything we do that computers cannot, be patient. In time they will do it better, if it is worth doing at all."[19]

Of course, not every Humanist believes that mankind must focus all his energies on redeeming mankind by speeding up the evolution of the computer. But why shouldn't this be a possible future reality for the Humanist? It fits nicely with his optimism about the future, his belief that mankind can redeem itself through history, and his conviction that man can control future evolution.

History

At A Glance

Secular Humanism

Historical Evolution

CONCLUSION

For the Secular Humanist, history is not only about the past, it is also about an inevitable future paradise. While Humanism does not go so far as to predict when the new world order will be achieved, it does declare that man will at some future date redeem himself by creating the ultimate social order. Once this order is perfect, mankind (or computerkind) will be perfect also. This optimism is a natural offshoot of Humanism's evolutionary perspective and deification of man.

By dethroning God, however, the Humanist removes the most reliable guide for history and must grant this power to some other force. To be consistent with his philosophy, the Humanist should grant it to the environment—but this creates inescapable problems, so the Humanist falls back upon man as guide. More accurately, Humanists declare man's dominant emerging ideology to be the real dynamic force in history, and the elite few who embrace it the proper lords of the path to the future. Thus, man working within a Humanistic framework becomes the savior of the world.

The Humanist historian adheres to a *religious* creed: one holy god (mankind) offers a plan for salvation (Humanism) that ensures a future paradise (the global community).

CHAPTER 40

Marxist/Leninist History

"Whatever is the mode of production of a society, such in the main is the society itself, its ideas and theories, its political views and institutions. Or, to put it more crudely, whatever is man's manner of life, such is his manner of thought."[1]

—Joseph Stalin

INTRODUCTION

Marxists believe their historical perspective is based strictly on a scientific view of the world, and that this approach makes their view better suited than any other to interpret history. Naturally, Marxists eagerly integrate the "science" of evolution into their theory of history.

This belief in evolution shapes the Marxist view of history in much the same way it shaped Secular Humanism's view. The Marxist sees evolution as continuously encouraging development and progress in living things; therefore he assumes that man has been constantly improving himself and will continue to progress in the future.

Marxism's "scientific" approach to biology leaves no room in its worldview for God, especially a God who might influence history. For this reason, the Marxist view of history is termed *historical materialism*. In an effort to be consistent with their philosophy, Marxists cling to the "scientific" assumption that only matter exists and therefore history is merely the account of matter in motion.

This is the crucial proposition for the Marxist view of history and, indeed, for the Marxist worldview. Neither God, nor angels, nor men's souls act as the actual basis for the workings of history; rather, matter obeying specific laws drives the progress of the world. The questions arise, then: What specific material things form the foundation on which man's societies are based? And, Can people play any role in charting the course of history?

A Brief Look At: Joseph Stalin (1879-1953)

1899: Expelled from the Tpilsi theological seminary

1902: Arrested for revolutionary Marxist activities; banished to Siberia

1904: Helps support the Bolsheviks by organizing bank robberies

1922: Appointed secretary general of the Secretariat

1927: Wins power struggle with other Soviet leaders; effectively takes control of USSR

1927: Begins systematic "liquidation" of Ukrainians (more than 10 million killed)

1932: Second wife, Nadezhda, commits suicide

1935: Signs pact with Adolf Hitler, aligning USSR with Nazi Germany

1945: Creates Yalta agreement with F.D. Roosevelt and Winston Churchill

MATTER AS THE BASIS FOR THE SOCIAL SUPERSTRUCTURE

Karl Marx says simply, "It is not the consciousness of men that determines their existence, but, on the contrary, their social existence determines their consciousness."[2]

If one wants to get at the real driving force behind history, he must look beyond the ideas of men to the true reality: the material world. Specifically, the historian must examine mankind's means of production and exchange to understand the basis for all historical progress. Economics is the driving force of history—as Marx says, "With the change of the economic foundation the entire immense superstructure is more or less rapidly transformed."[3]

The Marxist believes that economics acts as the foundation for man's whole social superstructure, including the thoughts of individuals. Frederick Engels declares that "in every historical epoch, the prevailing mode of economic production and exchange, and the social organization necessarily following from it, form the basis upon which is built up, and from which alone can be explained, the political and intellectual history of that epoch."[4]

For the Marxist, governments, courts, philosophies, and religions are based on a society's economic system and therefore affect history only to the extent that economics shapes their ability to guide man's development. Economics is the only dynamic force in history, and all other aspects of mankind and his society are determined by it.

ECONOMIC DETERMINISM

Marx believes that man can still possess free will within this framework, but he carefully distinguishes between being totally free and being free within the constraints placed on man by all outside, material influences. He writes, "Men make their own history, but they do not make it just as they please; they do not make it under circumstances chosen by themselves, but under circumstances directly encountered, given and transmitted from the past."[5] Marx tries to have his cake and eat it, too: naming economics as the driving force of history, but still granting man a measure of freedom.

Such a view of history is self-contradictory. Marx seems to admit as much when he says, "Are men free to choose this or that form of society for themselves? By no means. . . . Assume particular stages of development in production, commerce and consumption and you will have a corresponding social structure, a corresponding organization of the family, of orders or of classes, in a word, a corresponding civil society. . . . It is superfluous to add that men are not free to choose their *productive forces*—which are the basis of all their history . . ."[6] But if man may not choose his society, his society's superstructure, or its mode of production, and if these things in turn determine his mode of thought, then what on earth can man choose? It would seem that man could choose only to go along with the flow of history as determined by the economic structure. Should he choose otherwise, history will sweep him aside.

This conclusion seems even more inescapable in light of the Marxist's belief that history is governed by certain scientifically discoverable laws. V.I. Lenin believes Marx drew attention "to a scientific study of history as a single process which, with all its immense variety and contradictoriness, is governed by definite laws."[7]

The sinister implications of belief in such laws appear when we realize that they allow the Marxist to abandon both morality and reason, since whatever he does he can justify as predetermined by the "hidden laws" that always govern historical events. Joseph Stalin claims, "Hence the practical activity of the party of the proletariat must not be based on the good wishes of 'outstanding individuals,' not on the dictates of 'reason,' 'universal morals,' etc., but on the laws of development of society and on the study of these laws."[8]

COMMUNISM AS INEVITABLE

Such laws will guide history through a series of economic systems to a system on which the perfect society can be built. This redemption is guaranteed, regardless of the action or inaction of individuals.

> "Are men free to choose this or that form of society for themselves? By no means."
>
> *Karl Marx*

The paradise to which all of history is leading, Marx discovered, is a socialist/communist society. Salvation, for the Marxist, lies in the consummation of the historical process in a one-world utopia. Lenin proclaims, "Communists should know that the future belongs to them . . . [I]n all cases and in all countries communism is becoming steeled and is spreading, its roots are so deep that persecution does not weaken it, does not debilitate it, but strengthens it."[9]

The laws leading the world toward communism are inexorable, and no amount of human will can stop the collapse of capitalism, the rise of socialism, and the steady transition from socialism to communism. Maurice Cornforth declares, "From the point of view of the capitalist class, Marx's theory is certainly 'fatalistic.' It says: You cannot contrive a managed capitalism, you cannot do away with the class struggle, you cannot keep the system going indefinitely."[10]

The Marxist believes that there are scientific laws that direct the evolution of economic systems toward a paradisiacal end. Marxism perceives men's efforts toward any other end as useless and insignificant, declaring that mankind will achieve utopia (a communist society) despite all efforts and desires to the contrary. Surely, this is the ultimate proof that Marxism's economic determinism leaves no room for men's ideas or societies as historical forces.

346

THE DIALECTIC APPLIED TO HISTORY

Free will, for the Marxist, becomes drastically truncated: man is free in the sense that he may influence history by striving to achieve communism, but he is determined in the sense that he can affect history in no other way and is headed toward communism whether he likes it or not. Communism is inevitable, as dictated by the laws of history. These laws, in turn, are governed by the dialectic.

Marxists believe that the dialectic (as explained in the Marxist philosophy chapter) has guided society through certain phases (all based on economic structures) in a constant upward spiral. They believe that human society began with primitive communism, but thesis and antithesis collided and gave birth to societies based on slavery, which in turn developed into feudalism. This phase progressed into capitalism, which is now moving toward socialism. The continued clash of the bourgeoisie (the present thesis) with the proletariat (the present antithesis) will lead society into a transitional phase—socialism—and when the clash is resolved due to the abolition of classes, society will have achieved communism. Thus, history must obey the laws of the dialectic, and these laws declare that economic structures will eventually evolve into communism, on which the perfect societal superstructure will arise.

> "Historical development is not determined by the personal decisions of public men, but by the movement of classes."
>
> *Maurice Cornforth*

The part of the dialectic that Marxists choose to emphasize when discussing man's free will is the clash. Because the dialectic requires a clash (read: revolution) to instigate progress, the activity of classes becomes important. The individual is still insignificant in the Marxist view of history, but classes of mankind (in modern times, the bourgeoisie and the proletariat) can play a role in the development of mankind. Cornforth states, "Historical development is not determined by the personal decisions of public men, but by the movement of classes."[11]

Thus, the dialectic appears to salvage an iota of free will for mankind. Men's actions matter, but only with regard to their movements as a class, and even then only if they are working in accord with the laws of history. In other words, in modern times, only the proletarian can work as a progressive force, and even then only under the guidance of the Marxist party (because only the party truly understands the historical process). Man's ability to shape history according to this view is, to say the least, limited. But the Marxist stresses this ability as much as possible.

In fact, Marxism so desperately requires the participation of the masses (from a practical standpoint) that it often describes the revolutionary's role as the most critical in history. Lenin went so far as to proclaim, "According to the theory of socialism, i.e., of Marxism . . . the real driving force of history is the revolutionary class struggle."[12]

In theory, however, the Marxist should not feel such a desperate need for the classes to act. According to Marxism's interpretation of history, a revolutionary class can only (at most) hasten the inevitable progress of history—indeed, historical laws guarantee the eventual achievement of paradise, whether the proletarian stage a revolution today or one hundred years from now. That the proletarian will eventually "choose" such a course of action is, for the Marxist, inevitable.

THE FUTURE ACCORDING TO MARX

Even supposing this view of the dialectic and classes fits reality, two more problems arise. If classes act as the catalyst for the dialectic, then what becomes of the dialectic when classes cease to exist? Under communism, the Marxist believes, all class distinctions will be abolished. But without classes, what will act as the thesis and the antithesis to drive the dialectic toward a clash and ultimately to a new synthesis? What will keep the wheels of history turning?

Further, the dialectic has (theoretically) improved mankind's economic structures (and consequently, mankind's societies and ideas) throughout history, but as soon as the dialectic leads the whole world to communism, the ultimate mode of production and exchange will have been achieved, and the need for the dialectic will have been erased. How can the dialectic lead mankind beyond communism? No better economic structure (and therefore, no better basis for society and men's ideas) exists. What is better than the perfect society?

CONCLUSION

Both Marxists and Humanists view history from an evolutionary perspective, and therefore both believe mankind's history will always progress, just as the development of life constantly progresses. Consequently, both worldviews perceive the historical process as guaranteeing the redemption of mankind through the future establishment of some kind of heaven on earth.

Marxism differs from Humanism, however, in that the Marxist establishes a much stronger basis for his faith in the historical process. He believes that history operates according to specific, discoverable laws of the dialectic, changing man's economic structures and thereby revolutionizing men's societies and ideas.

History

At A Glance

Secular Humanism   Marxist/Leninist

Historical Evolution

Historical Materialism

Marxists try to re-establish man as a driving force in history by declaring the revolution of the oppressed classes to be the catalyst for the dialectical process. According to this view, only people who act in accordance with the laws of history and the course of development have any impact. Thus the individual, in the Marxist view of history, is much like the fan at a fixed boxing match. No matter how long and loud the fan cheers, no matter how hard he claps and stomps his feet, the boxer "taking a dive" will undoubtedly lose; one might as well clap and cheer for the predetermined winner, perhaps encouraging him to win the bout more decisively.

Put in Marxist terms, whether mankind takes the direct route or zigzags, the final outcome of history is always the same. The Marxist believes his worldview alone adheres to the scientific conception of history and that natural laws guarantee inevitable progress. Marxism grants all power to the historical/dialectical process and calls for the individual only to work in submission to this omnipotent force. Says Marx, "History is the judge—its executioner, the proletarian."[13]

CHAPTER 41

Cosmic Humanist History

"For the first time in history, humankind has come upon the control panel of change—an understanding of how transformation occurs. We are living in the change of change, the time in which we can intentionally align ourselves with nature for rapid remaking of ourselves and our collapsing institutions."[1]

—Marilyn Ferguson

INTRODUCTION

Like the Secular Humanist and the Marxist/Leninist, the Cosmic Humanist trusts evolution to guide mankind unswervingly toward perfection. In a very real sense, members of the New Age movement place their faith in evolution as humanity's savior.

This faith in evolution causes the Cosmic Humanist to view human history as an ascent—a development from lower to higher levels of consciousness. Each jump of punctuated equilibrium is a jump upward. It is a jump upward because the God-force within the universe pulls it upward. Benjamin Ferencz and Ken Keyes state, "We have seen that humankind is not simply moving in a vicious killing circle; it is on *an upward climb* toward completing the governmental structure of the world. We are inspired by our great progress toward planethood."[2] Elsewhere they declare that this *"optimism is justified by the facts."*[3]

History, according to the Cosmic Humanist, is progressive—thanks to the redemptive force of evolution. Even the Second Law of Thermodynamics does not discourage their optimistic view of history. Indeed, learned physicist Paul Davies writes, "Far from sliding towards a featureless state, the Universe is progressing from feature-lessness to states of greater organization and complexity. This cosmic progress defines a global arrow of time that points in the opposite way to the thermodynamic arrow."[4]

A Brief Look At: Shirley MacLaine (1934-)

1954: Lands first major part in a Broadway musical

1968: Serves as delegate at Democratic Convention

1973: Travels to China as leader of first American women's delegation

1977: Divorces husband

1983: Wins Academy Award; publishes *Out on a Limb*

1987: Releases movie version of *Out on a Limb*

1989: Releases home video *Shirley MacLaine's Inner Workout*

THE IRRELEVANCE OF CHRISTIANITY

Part of "cosmic progress" is the evolution from religion to religion. Certain religions, according to the Cosmic Humanist, were beneficial for the evolution of mankind at certain times in history—until mankind "outgrew" them.

In other words, the Christian worldview might have helped man in his quest for godhood 1,000 years ago, but today it is hopelessly outdated. "The old-time religion," says Joseph Campbell, "belongs to another age, another people, another set of human values, another universe. By going back you throw yourself out of sync with history."[5] Modern man, in order to continue evolving, must (and will) abandon Biblical Christianity.

The New Age movement is quick to ascribe a number of faults to Christianity. Its most serious failing, of course, is its dogma—the Christian insistence that Christ is the only Savior (John 14:6). Further, various Cosmic Humanists attack Christianity on the grounds that it is nationalistic, or racist, or promotes feelings of guilt. These failings, and others, "disqualify [Christianity] for the future,"[6] according to Campbell. Christianity is no longer relevant, let alone true. Cosmic Humanism is the only appropriate religion for the age. Only Cosmic Humanism can foster an evolutionary leap into higher consciousness.

THE FUTURE OF MANKIND

Evolution guarantees that mankind will eventually embrace Cosmic Humanism and usher in the New Age. Faith in this sustained progress into the New Age has been demonstrated by a number of Cosmic Humanists, but it is defended especially by M. Scott Peck:

> God wants us to become Himself (or Herself or Itself). We are growing toward godhood. God is the goal of evolution. It is God who is the source of the evolutionary force and God who is the destination. This is what we mean when we say that He is the Alpha and the Omega, the beginning and the end.[7]

Human history began because of the actions of an Ultimate Cause, and it has been marked by a reliable, though bloody, evolution toward the New Age. During the New Age all mankind will achieve a unity of consciousness with God. Marianne Williamson believes that "When love reaches a critical mass, when enough people become miracle-minded, the world will experience a radical shift."[8]

What this entails has been revealed through the channeled work *A Course in Miracles*. Every person will be absorbed into a "Divine Abstract," where there are "no distinctions, where no words are communicated, and where there are no events—only a static, eternal now."[9] The jumps of evolutionary history, for some reason, cease. Everything becomes stasis.

Some members of the New Age movement, unsatisfied with the concept of evolution as the redemptive force in history, have postulated the appearance of a spiritual Savior who will guide mankind to higher consciousness and utopia. Thus, Donald H. Yott suggests that a "Savior appears every two thousand years (more or less) for the different ages. Each Savior brings the tone or key-note for the age."[10] A spirit channeled by Levi proclaims, "But in the ages to come, man will attain to greater heights. And then, at last, a mighty Master Soul will come to earth to light the

> "The old-time religion belongs to another age, another people, another set of human values, another universe. By going back you throw yourself out of sync with history."
>
> *Joseph Campbell*

way up to the throne of perfect man."[11]

These predictions are not intended to deny the evolutionary force's influence upon man's development. Rather, they simply add a "supernatural" dimension to human progress. While not every Cosmic Humanist would agree with the idea that a new Savior will appear in the future, all would agree with the assertion that man throughout history evolves from lower to higher consciousness.

History At A Glance

Secular Humanism	Marxist/Leninist	Cosmic Humanist
Historical Evolution	Historical Materialism	Evolutionary Godhead

Conclusion

A historical perspective that embraces evolution as the vehicle for change—that expects that it is only a matter of time until mankind achieves perfection—can be expected to tend toward complacency. If one believes that the evolutionary process will determine how and when man achieves godhood, then why bother working toward godhood in this lifetime?

Cosmic Humanists circumvent this apathetic attitude by stressing that man has already achieved a level of consciousness that allows him to work in harmony with evolution to hasten the advent of the New Age. This view not only encourages the Cosmic Humanist to act on his beliefs but also allows those with a higher consciousness to catapult the "backward" part of humanity into godhood.

"Every individual's consciousness is connected to, and is a part of, the mass consciousness," explains Shakti Gawain. "When a small but significant number of individuals have moved into a new level of awareness and significantly changed their behavior, that change is felt in the entire mass consciousness."[12] This is the goal that all Cosmic Humanists work toward in an effort to hasten the full-blown evolution of all things. David Spangler describes this as the "individual's sense of being a co-creator with history, of being involved in a process of conscious and participatory evolution."[13]

FOUR WESTERN WORLDVIEW MODELS

SOURCES	SECULAR HUMANISM HUMANIST MANIFESTOS I AND II	MARXISM/LENINISM WRITINGS OF MARX AND LENIN	COSMIC HUMANISM WRITINGS OF SPANGLER, FERGUSON, ETC.	BIBLICAL CHRISTIANITY BIBLE
THEOLOGY	Atheism	Atheism	Pantheism	Theism
PHILOSOPHY	Naturalism	Dialectical Materialism	Non-Naturalism	Supernaturalism
ETHICS	Relativism	Proletariat Morality	Relativism	Absolutes
BIOLOGY	Darwinian Evolution	Darwinian/Punctuated Evolution	Darwinian/Punctuated Evolution	Creation
PSYCHOLOGY	Self-Actualization	Behaviorism	Collective Consciousness	Mind/Body
SOCIOLOGY	Non-Traditional Family	Abolition of Home, Church and State	Non-Traditional Home, Church and State	Traditional Home, Church and State
LAW	Positive Law	Positive Law	Self-Law	Biblical and Natural Law
POLITICS	World Government (Globalism)	New World Order (New Civilization)	New Age Order	Justice, Freedom and Order
ECONOMICS	Socialism	Socialism	Universal Enlightened Production	Stewardship of Property
HISTORY	Historical Evolution	Historical Materialism	Evolutionary Godhood	Historical Resurrection

CHAPTER 42

Biblical Christian History

"Paul regarded the resurrection as an event in history supported by the strongest possible eyewitness testimony, including his own (1 Corinthians 15:5-8). For Paul, the historicity of the resurrection was a necessary condition for the truth of Christianity and the validity of Christian belief."[1]

—Ronald H. Nash

INTRODUCTION

Christians believe the basis for their entire worldview appeared in human history in the form of Jesus Christ about two thousand years ago. While "Christ died for our sins" is solid orthodox Christian *theology,* "Christ died" is *history.* To shatter Christian doctrine and the Christian worldview, one need only shatter its historical underpinnings.

The Christian also believes that the Bible is God's revealed Word in the form of a trustworthy book grounded in history. Thus, for the Christian, history is supremely important. Either Christ is a historical figure and the Bible is a historical document that describes God's communications with man and records events in the life of Christ, or the Christian faith is bankrupt (1 Corinthians 15:14).

History is as important for the Christian worldview as it is for the Marxist/Leninist and the Secular Humanist worldviews. And if the Christian perspective is correct, history has already revealed the worldview that fits the facts of reality. While the Humanist and the Marxist see mankind's salvation in the distant future, the Christian sees redemption offered to mankind two thousand years ago and working as powerfully today as it did then. If this is true, then the wise will discover all they can about Jesus Christ.

A Brief Look At: Martin Luther (1483-1546)

1502: Receives B.A. from the University of Erfurt

1505: Joins the Order of St. Augustine (i.e., becomes a monk)

1507: Ordained as a priest

1512: Receives his doctorate in theology from the University of Wittenberg

1516: Begins publishing lectures on Galatians and Hebrews

1517: Nails his 95 Theses to the door of a Wittenberg church; sparks Reformation

1521: Refuses to repudiate his writings at the Diet at Worms

1525: Publishes *On the Will in Bondage*

THE BIBLE AND HISTORY

When considering the claims of Christianity, one question must be asked immediately: Can we trust the Bible to tell us the truth about God's actions in history?

The first area we must explore when judging the historicity of the Bible is the question of authorship. Was the Bible written by eyewitnesses of historical events, or were some books written many years after the fact by men who had only heard vague accounts of the events they attempted to describe? For example, did one of Christ's apostles write the book of Matthew, or did some unknown scribe who had not known Christ write the book in an effort to strengthen the case for Christianity?

Today's scholars have little doubt that the books of the Bible were written largely by eyewitnesses. William F. Albright, a leading twentieth-century archaeologist, writes, "In my opinion, every book of the New Testament was written by a baptized Jew between the forties and the eighties of the first century (very probably sometime between about A.D. 50 and 75)."[2] Even H.G. Wells, a confirmed atheist, acknowledged that "the four gospels . . . were certainly in existence a few decades after [Christ's] death."[3] The evidence points to the conclusion that the history in the Bible was written by men living in that historical period.

However, a second objection arises. Perhaps, say the critics, the Bible was an accurate historical document as it was originally written—but it has been copied and re-copied for thousands of years, and so it has been warped by the inevitable mistakes of copyists. At first glance, this objection seems plausible. But one archaeological discovery made nearly half a century ago shattered this theory. Gleason L. Archer, Jr. explains: "Even though the two copies of Isaiah discovered in Qumran Cave 1 near the Dead Sea in 1947 were a thousand years earlier than the oldest dated manuscript previously known (A.D. 980), they proved to be word for word identical with our standard Hebrew Bible in more than 95 per cent of the text. The 5 per cent of variation consisted chiefly of obvious slips of the pen and variations in spelling."[4] That is, a manuscript one thousand years older than the oldest copy of the Bible previously known to exist proved the transmission over that time span to be virtually error-free.

> **[A]rchaeology has consistently supported the assertion that the Bible is a trustworthy historical document.**

In fact, archaeology has consistently supported the assertion that the Bible is a trustworthy historical document. "It may be stated categorically," says Nelson Glueck, "that no archaeological discovery has ever controverted a biblical reference."[5] Harvard's Simon Greenleaf (the greatest nineteenth-century authority on the law of evidence in the common law) believed "that the competence of the New Testament documents would be established in any court of law."[6]

One may conclude with confidence that the Bible is an accurate historical document; the events described in the Old and New Testaments did happen. But this poses a problem for every non-Christian, because the Bible states that God became man in Jesus Christ—and if this is true, no other worldview fits the facts of history. Some non-Christians at this point choose a rather illogical means of avoiding the seemingly unavoidable claims of the Bible, suggesting that while the Bible may be true, it does not accurately describe the man known as Jesus Christ. Indeed, some non-Christians go so far as to claim that Jesus Christ never existed. Therefore, we must turn our attention to this aspect of history.

THE HISTORICITY OF CHRIST

The obvious problem faced by people who deny that the Bible accurately describes the life of Jesus Christ is that archaeology and modern criticism have revealed the Bible to be historically accurate.. The atheist has no grounds for claiming that man cannot know what Christ did on earth, because the New Testament provides a historical account of His life. However, for the moment we will ignore this key point and touch upon two pieces of outside evidence that confirm the historicity of Christ.

Christ was treated as a historical figure by early historians other than Christians. Around A.D. 93, the great Jewish historian Josephus referred to Jesus at least twice in his *Antiquities of the Jews*. In one instance, he recorded that the high priest Annas "assembled the sanhedrim of the judges, and brought before them the brother of Jesus, who was called Christ, whose name was James . . ." (*Antiquities* XX.ix.1).

Another early historian, Cornelius Tacitus, wrote around A.D. 112 about "the persons commonly called Christians," and also stated, "Christus, the founder of the name, was put to death by Pontius Pilate, procurator of Judea in the reign of Tiberius: but the pernicious superstition, repressed for a time broke out again, not only through Judea, where the mischief originated, but through the city of Rome also."[7]

> "I consider that our present sufferings are not worth comparing with the glory that will be revealed in us."
>
> *Apostle Paul*

These references and others provide sufficient evidence for the historicity of Christ, even when the New Testament is ignored. Bruce Metzger writes that "the early non-Christian testimonies concerning Jesus, though scanty, are sufficient to prove (even without taking into account the evidence contained in the New Testament) that he was a historical figure who lived in Palestine in the early years of the first century, that he gathered a group of followers about himself, and that he was condemned to death under Pontius Pilate. Today no competent scholar denies the historicity of Jesus."[8]

THE RESURRECTION AND HISTORY

The Bible goes out of its way to place its message and major figures in history (see Luke 3:1-2). This is especially true with regard to Christ's resurrection. Luke mentions Pilate, Caesar, Herod, Barabbas, "Joseph, counsellor," "Arimathaea, a city of the Jews," and then describes Christ's resurrection as a real event in history (Luke 24:1-7).

The resurrected Christ was witnessed by more than 500 people (1 Corinthians 15:6), including Mary, Peter, and ten other apostles. These witnesses were so moved by the resurrection that they committed their lives to it and to the One whose divinity and righteousness it vindicated. The disciples did not abandon Christ, but instead were willing to die for the truth they were propagating. Indeed, the resurrection of Christ took "a group of scared (Mark 16:8; John 20:19) and skeptical (Luke 24:38; John 20:25) men" and transformed them "into courageous evangels who proclaimed the Resurrection in the face of threats on their lives (Acts 4:21; 5:18)!" If the disciples did not consider the resurrection a historical event, is it really conceivable that they would be willing to die for this kind of testimony?

The faith of modern-day Christians should be no less secure than that of the apostles, because it is grounded in historical fact. This fact forms the basis for the Biblical Christian worldview and the Christian philosophy of history.

Through the resurrection, God reveals His plan for mankind by conquering sin and guaranteeing a triumphant end to human history. D.W. Bebbington says that since the battle against evil was won by Jesus on the cross, "The outcome of world history is therefore already assured. God will continue to direct the course of events up to their end when the outcome will be made plain."[9] The Christian learns from history that Christ offered Himself up as a perfect sacrifice for mankind, and this is the most important revelation. But the Christian also discovers another important truth: God is active throughout history and plans to lead it to a triumphant conclusion.

While the course of history may seem tragic to some people, the Christian understands that all history is working together for good. Because God became man and died for man's sins, the final chapter of history will proclaim the conquering of sin. Thus, the Christian is prepared to face a difficult, sometimes pain-filled life, because he understands that the sin that causes pain has been erased from his future. The Christian holds no unreasonable expectations for his earthly lifetime—in fact, he anticipates persecution and trials—but he does expect to be

Snapshots In Time

A bit of mystery surrounds the discovery of the Dead Sea Scrolls in 1947. Some claim that the young man who found the first cave containing ancient Bible manuscripts was a simple shepherd; others suggest that he may have been involved in a smuggling operation. Regardless of his occupation, his discovery rocked the archaeological world.

One of the first Dead Sea Scrolls reproduced almost the entire book of Isaiah, in a manuscript more than 1,000 years older than what was previously thought to be the oldest manuscript. Incredibly, this ancient text was virtually identical to the modern Hebrew book of Isaiah!

This discovery, along with the subsequent discovery of fragments of almost every Old Testament book in nearby caves, reinforced the Christian assertion that the Bible is a trustworthy historical document that has not been corrupted by copyists. The Dead Sea Scrolls, and all relevant historical evidence, support the belief that the Bible provides an accurate account of actual people and events.

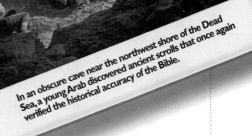

In an obscure cave near the northwest shore of the Dead Sea, a young Arab discovered ancient scrolls that once again verified the historical accuracy of the Bible.

triumphant in the end because God has come into history to save man from his own sinful inclinations.

From the Christian perspective history is a beautiful unfolding of God's ultimate plan for mankind. Does this mean, however, that only the future holds any value for the Christian? Does the Christian worldview destroy the role of the present in history? The answer is a resounding *no*. In the Christian view, God is active throughout history; therefore, this perspective creates more meaning for every moment of time than does any other worldview. "It is always a 'Now,'" writes Herbert Butterfield, "that is in direct relation to eternity—not a far future; always immediate experience of life that matters in the last resort—not historical constructions based on abridged text-books or imagined visions of some posterity that is going to be the heir of all the ages."[10]

The central difference between the Christian view of history and that of Marxism and Humanism comes down to this one point. Either human history was ordained by God and is directed by Him toward an ultimate conclusion, or human history began due to a random spark in a prebiotic soup and has only chance to thank for its present course.

PURPOSE IN HISTORY

This belief about God's actions in history has vast ramifications for mankind. If the Christian philosophy of history is correct, then not only is the overall story of mankind invested with meaning, but every moment that man lives is charged with purpose. "Where a God who is totally purposive and totally foreseeing acts upon a Nature which is totally interlocked," explains C.S. Lewis, "there can be no accidents or loose ends, nothing whatever of which we can safely use the word *merely*. Nothing is 'merely a by-product' of anything else. All results are intended from the first."[11]

Indeed, it is through understanding how God works in our individual lives that we can truly understand how God directs the course of history. Butterfield explains: "[T]here are some people who bring their sins home to themselves and say that this is a chastisement from God; or they say that God is testing them, trying them in the fire, fitting them for some more important work that he has for them to do. Those who adopt this view in their individual lives will easily see that it enlarges and projects itself onto the scale of all history . . ."[12] Purpose and meaning saturate both individual lives and the life of all mankind.

In order to speak accurately about purpose, however, the Christian must speak not only of God's activity throughout history but also of the ultimate goal toward which He is leading mankind. Purpose implies constant supervision by God, a direction for the course of human events, and an ultimate end or goal. For the Christian, history is moving toward a specific climax: the Day of Judgment (Acts 17:31; Romans 2:11-16). At this point, Christ's victory over sin will become apparent to all, and Christians throughout history will be allowed to share in His triumph. This is the good news of Christianity, the truth that makes all earthly trials bearable. Paul sums up this faith in 2 Corinthians 4:11-18, and also when he says, "I consider that our present sufferings are not worth comparing with the glory that will be revealed in us" (Romans 8:18).

The ultimate direction of history is toward a triumphant close. Even at this very moment, God is moving human history closer to that end—which, in a very real sense, is only the beginning.

THE LINEAR CONCEPTION OF HISTORY

This Christian belief about the direction of history is known as a linear conception of history. That is, Christians believe that human history had a specific beginning (creation) and is being directed by God toward a specific end (judgment), and that historic events follow a nonrepetitive course toward that end. To the individual living in the Western hemisphere, this may not seem to be a unique view of history. Doesn't everyone believe that human history had a beginning and moves along a linear path to its end?

Most of Western society has a linear view of history—but this view is founded on the Judeo-Christian perspective. Prior to this Christian description of history, Classical thought supported a cyclical view, in which historical events were repeated over and over by consecutive societies. Thus, the Christian view of history as directional did create a unique conception of the movement of mankind through time. "The importance of the Biblical conception cannot be overstressed," says John Warwick Montgomery. "Here for the first time Western man was presented with a purposive, goal-directed interpretation of history. The Classical doctrine of recurrence had been able to give a 'substantiality' to history, but it had not given it any aim or direction."[13] Direction, as always, comes from God.

CONCLUSION

Christian history centers in the reliability of the Bible. While we have focused on the most significant event in the Biblical Christian worldview (the resurrection of Jesus Christ), the history of the rest of the Bible is also open to close inspection. The Bible's history, as recorded in both Testaments, has stood the test of time.

Marxism/Leninism and Secular Humanism declare that man can save himself, but the Christian better understands human nature—and it is this perspective that allows him to form a consistent view regarding the past, the present, and the future. It also

History
At A Glance

Secular Humanism	Marxist/Leninist	Cosmic Humanist	Christianity
Historical Evolution	Historical Materialism	Evolutionary Godhead	Historical Resurrection

helps him to understand man's role in history. Man may freely choose to obey or disobey God, but it is only when he acts in obedience that he can affect history positively. Regardless of how man chooses to affect history, God will work through his actions to direct history toward His ultimate end: the Day of Judgment. This belief in a climactic conclusion causes the Christian to adopt a linear conception of history. This linear conception reflects the vast meaning with which God has endowed history.

If this historical perspective is correct, then the entire Christian worldview is proved to be true, and it follows that knowing, accepting, and following Jesus Christ as Savior and Lord is the most important thing anyone can do. Wise men still seek Him, and for good reason. He gives meaning to history, and to life.

FOUR WESTERN WORLDVIEW MODELS

SOURCES	SECULAR HUMANISM HUMANIST MANIFESTOS I AND II	MARXISM/LENINISM WRITINGS OF MARX AND LENIN	COSMIC HUMANISM WRITINGS OF SPANGLER, FERGUSON, ETC.	BIBLICAL CHRISTIANITY BIBLE
THEOLOGY	Atheism	Atheism	Pantheism	Theism
PHILOSOPHY	Naturalism	Dialectical Materialism	Non-Naturalism	Supernaturalism
ETHICS	Relativism	Proletariat Morality	Relativism	Absolutes
BIOLOGY	Darwinian Evolution	Darwinian/Punctuated Evolution	Darwinian/Punctuated Evolution	Creation
PSYCHOLOGY	Self-Actualization	Behaviorism	Collective Consciousness	Mind/Body
SOCIOLOGY	Non-Traditional Family	Abolition of Home, Church and State	Non-Traditional Home, Church and State	Traditional Home, Church and State
LAW	Positive Law	Positive Law	Self-Law	Biblical and Natural Law
POLITICS	World Government (Globalism)	New World Order (New Civilization)	New Age Order	Justice, Freedom and Order
ECONOMICS	Socialism	Socialism	Universal Enlightened Production	Stewardship of Property
HISTORY	Historical Evolution	Historical Materialism	Evolutionary Godhood	Historical Resurrection

Conclusion

"Come now, let us reason together," God says (Isaiah 1:18). "Be ready to give an answer to every man that asketh you a reason of the hope that is in you with meekness and fear," says the Apostle Peter (1 Peter 3:15). Acting in accordance with these exhortations, the Christian must meet the challenge posed by non-Christian worldviews that claim that Biblical Christianity is irrational, unscientific, and false. This chapter will demonstrate the power of the truth—the fact that Christianity works better in the real world because it is based on reality.

All non-Christian worldviews, of course, contain truth. Secular Humanism, for example, acknowledges the existence of the physical universe. Marxism acknowledges the significance and relevance of science. All three non-Christian views discussed in this text understand the importance of "saving" mankind. However, they differ radically with the Christian model of salvation: Christianity's message is that Jesus Christ is the key to reality—not Karl Marx, John Dewey, or Shirley MacLaine. Christianity views Jesus Christ as the way, the truth and the life (John 14:6). All other worldviews reject Jesus Christ—indeed, some deny His very existence. Thus, an insurmountable difference exists between Christianity and the false worldviews.

Did Jesus Christ live on this earth two thousand years ago? Was He God in flesh? Did He come to earth to reveal God's will for man and to save the human race from sin? These are important questions. Biblical Christianity lives or dies on the answers. "If Christ be not risen," says Paul, "your faith is in vain" (1 Corinthians 15:14).

Whether one chooses to accept Cosmic Humanism, Marxism/Leninism, Secular Humanism, or Biblical Christianity, that individual is accepting a worldview that describes the opposition as hopelessly distorted. Only one view depicts things as they really are; all other perspectives must be out of step with the nature of man and the universe. Indeed, the Marxists and the Humanists are quick to describe Christians as not only out of step but victims of serious delusion. Marx, of course, viewed all religion as a drug that deluded its adherents—an "opiate of the masses." Humanists

(Cosmic and Secular) often portray Christians as just plain crazy. For example, James J.D. Luce, the assistant executive director of Fundamentalists Anonymous, claims that "the fundamentalist experience can be a serious mental health hazard to perhaps millions of people."[1] His organization works to "heal" Christians of their "mental disorder"—Christianity. Harvard's Edward O. Wilson describes Christianity as "one of the unmitigated evils of the world."[2] Adherents to secular religious worldviews understand that, if their assumptions are correct, any worldview that postulates the supernatural must be dangerous to the health and safety of mankind. Cosmic Humanists hate Christianity because it promotes a God of justice and truth, and strips mankind of our purported godhood.

Likewise, the Biblical Christian must understand that his worldview excludes the possibility that foundational non-Christian assumptions might provide a helpful insight into reality. Such foundational assumptions are antithetical to Christian presuppositions. *No compromise can exist between the worldviews on this fundamental level.* Either the Christian correctly describes reality when he speaks of a loving, just, personal God and His incarnation and resurrection, or he is talking nonsense. We cannot blend the basic claims of the Bible with the non-Christian claims that man is inherently good and requires no savior other than himself. Only one view properly describes the cold hard facts of a universe that Christians believe was created by God.

Other worldviews paint a picture of reality so bleak that even their adherents, in their more lucid moments, recognize the need to cling to artificial hopes to avoid slipping into despair. Secular Humanist Herbert Tonne alludes to the atheist's willingness to abandon sanity at a crucial juncture in his worldview, claiming that

> a truly sane person would be socially insane. Functionally sanity means being deluded sufficiently to believe that life is worth living and that the human race is worth preserving. In our really sane moments we realize that life is but a "poor player that struts and frets his hour upon the stage and then is seen no more"; that "it is a tale told by an idiot full of sound and fury meaning nothing."[3]

The Christian position, of course, requires no delusion to convince its adherents that life is worth preserving. Scripture provides mankind with a view of reality that allows the individual to function cooperatively in society without deluding himself. The Christian treats man as "fearfully and wonderfully made" (Psalm 139:14) because his worldview describes man as such.

The Secular Humanist and the Marxist are aware of the complexity and value of mankind, without being able to account for its existence. This is a fundamental flaw of the secular religious worldviews, one that points up the fact that Christianity and other ideologies are mutually exclusive at ground level. We must discern which view is the proper attitude toward life and death, good and evil, design and chance, and then resign ourselves to a life of despair or welcome a life of joy, accordingly.

Because such differences exist, and because there can be no reconciliation between Christianity and opposing worldviews, men and women must examine the evidence and determine the truth. To this end, this chapter will focus on the fundamental concepts of these worldviews. We are not interested in hair-splitting. Cosmic Humanism, for example does not stand or fall according to its stance regarding gun control. It does stand or fall, however, on its theology, philosophy, ethics, and biology. Our emphasis will be foundational—we desire to examine the concepts on which each worldview is based. Here, in the heart of the ideologies, a student can test the character of the worldviews and separate wheat from chaff, truth from fiction. And here (we believe) Christianity stands tall, looming over its adversaries.

After working our way through a systematic analysis of the ten major components of the three worldviews, our studied conclusions are that:

in **theology,** the evidence for the existence of a personal and holy God, a designed universe, and an earth prepared for human life far outweighs any argument for atheism or pantheism;

in **philosophy,** the notion that mind (logos) precedes matter is far superior to the atheistic stance of matter preceding mind;

in **biology,** the concept of a living God creating life fits the evidence better than any hint of spontaneous generation and evolution;

in **ethics,** the concept that right and wrong are absolutes based on the nature and character of a personal, loving, just God is far superior both theoretically and practically to any concept of moral relativism;

in **law,** the notion that God always (absolutely) hates the perversion of justice is far superior to any theory of legal relativism or positive law;

in **psychology,** understanding man as an inherently sinful being in need of a Savior far outweighs expecting man to be inherently perfectible and guilt-free;

in **sociology,** the biblical family of father, mother, and child far transcends any experiments in homosexuality, trial marriages, etc.;

in **politics,** the Christian belief that human rights are a gift from God protected by government is more logically persuasive, morally appealing, and politically sound than any atheistic theory that maintains that human rights are a largess of the state;

in **economics,** the concept of stewardship of private property and using resources responsibly to glorify God is more noble than the notion of a society in which common ownership destroys individual responsibility and work incentives;

and in **history,** the veracity of the Bible and its promise of a future kingdom ushered in by Jesus Christ is far more credible than any vague, utopian, global schemes dreamed up by sinful, mortal men.

In other words, in every discipline, the Christian worldview shines brighter than its competition, is more realistic, better explains man and the universe, is true to the Bible, is more scientific, is more intellectually satisfying and defensible, and best of all, is in keeping with and faithful to the one person who has had the greatest influence in heaven and on earth—Jesus Christ.

Indeed, we cannot imagine one category in which the non-Christian worldviews outshine the Christian position. For example, putting Christian economics into practice results in prosperity and the avoidance of poverty, while all forms of socialism (including the welfare state) guarantee various levels of poverty. Putting Christian sociology into practice results in strong families that discourage societal trends toward drug-use, crime, unemployment, poverty, and disease, whereas non-Christian experimentation with the family unit (including Secular Humanism's self-proclaimed "important role in the sexual revolution") causes society to disintegrate. Putting Christian law into practice results in the Magna Charta and the U.S. Constitution, guaranteeing human rights as God-ordained, while the history of positive law—in France for two centuries, in the Soviet Union for seventy years, and in the U.S. for the last half-century—has been a history of blood baths. (Yes, blood baths in the United

States: 1.5 million unborn babies killed every year by abortion.) Most importantly, of course, putting Christian theology and philosophy into practice results in salvation of the soul (Matthew 16:26), enlightenment of the mind, and purpose in living.

SETTING THE STAGE

Most of the weaknesses inherent to the three non-Christian worldviews have been alluded to in the body of this text. When discussing Marxism and Secular Humanism, these allusions were rarely spelled out. Cosmic Humanism's flaws, on the other hand, were generally discussed at some length. This chapter, therefore, will focus almost exclusively on critiquing the Secular Humanist and Marxist/Leninist worldviews. Students interested in further criticism of the New Age movement should read *Unmasking the New Age* by Douglas Groothuis and *Apologetics in the New Age* by Norman Geisler and David K. Clark.

It should also be noted here that this critique does not treat Marxism and Secular Humanism as mutually exclusive, for the simple reason that, as Erich Fromm says, "Marxism is humanism." [4] The body of this text makes it obvious that most of Humanism's and Marxism's foundational or theoretical assumptions are virtually indistinguishable, with the notable exception that Marxism treats economics as primary, while Secular Humanism tends to concentrate on philosophy and biology. Both worldviews are, in the main, atheistic, materialistic, evolutionary, positivistic, monistic, utopian, and relativistic; but Marxism, thanks to its dialectic and well-developed economic theory, provides a better-defined perspective. Thus, there will be places in this critique where we address only the flaws of Marxist theory, but for the most part, our criticism will apply to both worldviews.

We contend that Marxism and Secular Humanism are incapable of describing the

Atheistic evolutionists, desperate for a universe that provides enough time for spontaneous generation to occur, have dared hope that our universe is up to 20 billion years old. Recent scientific observations suggest that such hope is unfounded.

Snapshots In Time

A recent discovery by astronomers using the Hubble Space Telescope once again demonstrates the difficulty in accurately estimating the age of the earth and the universe. In 1994, astronomers using the Telescope found evidence indicating that the universe is "only" eight billion years old. Other astronomers, working independently, estimated the universe to be only 7.3 billion years old.

Why quibble about an age of billions and billions? Because astronomers have long held that some stars are more than 16 billion years old! The obvious question arises: how can we claim that some stars are older than the universe itself? In other words, which estimates of age should we trust—or should we trust any at all?

Yet another problem arises for the atheist: how could spontaneous generation, and all the diversity of our biological world, occur in just 7.3 billion years? Even the most optimistic atheists would not assert that such a time frame is sufficient. Still, these atheists choose to cling to their irrational faith.

371

universe from start to finish. Therefore, we will contrast these views with Christianity using a model that begins with the beginning of time and works chronologically toward the future. This will reinforce what this text should make clear to all minds concerned with truth and intellectual integrity: only Biblical Christianity presents the proper view of the world and the things contained therein. "I now believe," says the former atheistic philosopher C.E.M. Joad, "that the balance of reasoned considerations tells heavily in favor of the religious, even of the Christian view of the world."[5]

GENESIS

In the beginning, one of two things existed: mind or matter. Either a supreme mind has always existed and created matter and the universe at a specific point in time, or matter is eternal and formed the universe by itself. *Either mind created matter, or matter created mind.*

The Bible, of course, declares that God is eternal and that He created the physical universe and its inhabitants (Genesis 1). It goes on to say that the physical universe was well thought out in the mind of God before creation ever took place (John 1:1-3). The Marxist and the Secular Humanist deny the very possibility that Scripture accurately accounts for the beginning of the universe. They therefore must hold that matter is eternal and has moved from a state of disorder to an ordered state as guided by chance. That is, matter previously packed into a mathematical point and scattered by an incredible bang ordered itself into such remarkable entities as supernovas, diamonds, beagles, DNA—and the mind of man. The non-Christian worldviews believe that the universe was once dead and yet brought forth life—that inorganic matter, given enough time and the proper recipe for primordial soup, brought forth amoebas and hummingbirds, squid and prairie dogs. Further still, the Marxist and the Secular Humanist believe that dead, disordered matter eventually organized man, a being capable of inventing bicycles, jokes, and *Hamlet*. The Christian's faith pales in comparison to the credulity required to believe that such diversity and complexity arose by chance.

> **Either mind created matter, or matter created mind.**

This is one of the most glaring flaws of Marxist and Secular Humanist theory—it asks man to believe that a reality that currently moves from order to disorder (according to the Second Law of Thermodynamics) moved in exactly the opposite direction for billions of years in the past. Of course, the Marxist and the Secular Humanist ignore, or at least downplay, the teleological nature of the universe and the wonder of man in an effort to mask this inconsistency—Stephen Jay Gould describes mankind as an "afterthought"[6]—but they cannot hope to sway any individual with an open mind about the mysteries and manifest intelligence of the universe.

Hillsdale College president George Roche provides an excellent example of the profound design manifested in our universe when he describes the special nature of human beings:

> Man is a very *strange* animal. . . . Not that there is anything particularly queer about our physical equipment; this is all quite reasonable. But gorillas have hands as we do, yet use them for very little, and never to play the piano or skip stones or whittle or write letters. Dolphins have bigger brains than we do, but you seldom hear them discoursing on nuclear physics. Chihuahuas are more hairless than we, but have never thought to wear clothes. . . . Man alone weeps for cause, and "is shaken with the beautiful madness called laughter," as Chesterton put it.[7]

Secular worldview adherents would like to ignore the unmistakably unique character of man, because their ideologies cannot adequately account for it. A worldview that asserts the primacy of matter has a difficult time explaining this unique creature so distant from the rest of the animal kingdom.

The Christian worldview, on the other hand, accounts for the unique character of man from the first chapter of Scripture. In Genesis 1:26, God declares, "Let us make man in our image, in our likeness, and let them rule over the fish of the sea and the birds of the air, over the livestock, over all the earth, and over all the creatures that move along the ground." Likewise, the Christian view accounts for the rest of the design found in nature, because it begins with a Designer. Whereas the Secular Humanist and the Marxist must rely on chance and matter to explain birds capable of astronomical navigation and bees that communicate through dance, the Christian posits an omniscient God who chose to order the universe into a beautiful symphony of light, life, sound, and color. "The heavens declare the glory of God; the skies proclaim the work of his hands" (Psalm 19:1). "Everywhere we look in nature (whether in living or non-living matter)," say Percival Davis and Dean Kenyon, "design and material organization are on display."[8]

It simply comes down to this: did life and intelligence and humor and design come from a living, intelligent God who loves order and joy, or did they arise randomly from dead matter? The Christian believes that a lawfully designed reality demands an origin that provides the groundwork for such attributes. Thus, the Christian finds the key in John 1:1-5:

> In the beginning was the Word, and the Word was with God, and the Word was God. He was with God in the beginning. Through him all things were made; without him nothing was made that has been made. In him was life, and that life was the light of men. The light shines in the darkness, but the darkness has not understood it.

MIND OVER MATTER?

The ultimate problem faced by the Secular Humanist and Marxist in the area of origins is the existence of mind (the overarching term we will use for all the supernatural qualities of man, including conscience, ideas, soul, and spirit). A naive student might be persuaded that life and order arose from non-living matter, but even the most gullible cannot swallow that the human mind, which has pierced the atom and conceived *The Brothers Karamazov,* came about by the chance workings of matter. It truly is a question of mind creating matter or matter creating mind—did the Supreme Mind instill in men reason, appreciation for aesthetic qualities, and a conscience, or did "eternal" nonliving matter?

Clearly, this is a fatal flaw of Marxist and Secular Humanist philosophy. While both secular worldviews claim that matter is primary or ultimate reality and mind is a pale reflection of this reality, they are faced again and again with the magnificent workings of the human mind. Further, experience suggests that mind acts creatively on matter, rather than vice versa. Warren Brookes speaks of the economy in mind as preceding the physical transfer of money, goods, and services. If men conceive things in their minds and then act creatively, doesn't it seem likely that the universe began in a similar fashion? Wouldn't we expect a supreme mind to precede matter?

Again, Roche provides us with an excellent example of an insurmountable problem created by the monistic attitude of Marxism and Secular Humanism. "Altruism," he writes, "is not a scientific concept. It is a metaphysical reality that is simply unaccountable to a materialist philosophy."[9] That is, the Christian expects heroism from his fellow man—after all, he is made in the image of the God who sacrificed His own life so that we might live. The secular religious worldviews, on the other hand, can only speak of self-preservation and species-preservation instincts, which provide a pretty poor explanation for a young man diving into an icy river to save an octogenarian. Indeed, the Secular Humanist and the Marxist had best ignore such non-material activity, since it demands more than a materialist explanation. No scientist, including the world's finest neurosurgeon, has ever held the idea of altruism in his hands for inspection or dissection.

The only time the secular worldviews care to treat the mind as important is in reference to the theories devised by their own minds. But as we have stressed throughout this text, it is irrational to consistently portray the mind as random chemical firings of synapses in the brain and a mere reflection of the physical universe, and then expect one's own mind to comprehend and process reality accurately. No less of an authority than Charles Darwin recognized the problem faced by adherents to atheistic, materialistic explanations of mind:

With me, the horrid doubt always arises whether the convictions of man's mind, which has been developed from the mind of lower animals, are of any value or at all trustworthy. Would any one trust in the convictions of a monkey's mind, if there are any convictions in such a mind?[10]

Furthermore, would anyone trust a mind whose ancestral roots trace back beyond monkeys' minds to mindless amoebas and even to mindless, inorganic, chaotic matter?

The answer is obvious. Naturalistic theologies and philosophies that begin with matter are incapable of explaining not only the teleological nature of the universe but also the capabilities of human minds and souls. Perhaps it sounds more manageable to simplify or reduce all reality to an ultimate material substance, but in the end this oversimplified worldview leads to hopeless complications because of its inability to explain reason. It is all well and good to declare, as Carl Sagan does in his book *Cosmos,* that matter (or nature, or the Cosmos) is all that has ever existed or ever will, but it leaves the Secular Humanist and the Marxist with a number of inexplicable phenomena to sweep under the rug.

> **Can man's mind, developed from an animal's mind, be of any value?**

What can a materialist do with mind, soul, altruism, creativity, rationality, conscience, song, and laughter? He may try to ignore them, but they face him every day. Indeed, he depends on them. It sounds learned to describe them as secondary, derivative, mere reflections of material reality, but how can the thought processes that formulated the notion of dialectical materialism be described as reflections, as cranial illusions, when they seem to be (at least for the Marxist) the most powerful facet of reality?

The questions of origins and ultimate substance provide an excellent starting point for a serious critique of Secular Humanism and Marxism, because they highlight the glaring weaknesses in both worldviews' theology and philosophy. The Christian expects man to be the most intricate part of an infinitely intricate creation, because he begins with a personal God, who specially created a world for male and female. The Secular Humanist and the Marxist should expect very little—should, indeed, be awed by ordered matter—and should recognize that man is completely inexplicable in materialist terms.

In *Does God Exist? The Great Debate*, Dallas Willard, a professor of philosophy at the University of Southern California, raises an important point. Every great philosopher—Plato, Aristotle, St. Augustine, St. Thomas, William of Occam, Rene Descartes, Baruch Spinoza, Gottfried von Leibniz, John Locke, George Berkeley, Immanuel Kant, and Georg W.F. Hegel—was a theist, in one form or another. Even David Hume, a man Secular Humanists embrace as one of their own, declared, "The whole frame of nature bespeaks an intelligent author; and no rational enquirer can, after serious reflection, suspend his belief a moment with regard to the primary principles of genuine Theism and Religion."[11] The conclusion for the Christian worldview is obvious: Christian theology and philosophy are more intellectually defensible than the secular worldviews' versions.

THE EVOLUTION OF EVOLUTION

Wait a minute. From the perspective of the Secular Humanist and the Marxist/Leninist, our discussion of mankind and all other life forms is premature. While the Biblical Christian can begin talking about mankind virtually from the beginning of time, the secular worldviews must postulate an immense amount of time (ca. 16 billion years) between the formation of the universe and the development of life and man. In order to do justice to Secular Humanism and Marxism's view of mankind and his institutions, we must back up and examine the cornerstone of their worldview: the theories of spontaneous generation and evolution.

> "If we conclude that the world is of a character that does not allow free will, we destroy our credentials for saying so."
>
> *George Roche*

We have, of course, discussed the theory of evolution at length in the section on biology. We have noted the scientific fact that no one has ever produced a new species by means of natural selection, and we have acknowledged microbiologist Michael Denton's charge that Darwinism lacks empirical verification: "Neither of the two fundamental axioms of Darwin's macroevolutionary theory . . . has . . . been validated by one single empirical discovery or scientific advance since 1859."[12] Indeed, we have highlighted most of the flaws in evolutionary theory already, because such commentary strengthens the Christian position of creationism (if Darwinian evolution and punctuated equilibrium are scientifically untenable, creation becomes more tenable). Evolutionary theory is marked with more inconsistencies and contradictions than can be discussed here. Thus, for the purpose of this critique, we will focus on two distinct aspects of the theory that were only touched on in the body of the text: the amount of faith required to believe in spontaneous generation, and the evolution of the theory of evolution.

One of the most fundamental beliefs that a Marxist or a Secular Humanist must cling to is that somewhere, somehow, sometime, life arose from non-life. Without spontaneous generation, something living must always have existed, namely an eternal God. Therefore, in order to be a consistent naturalistic atheist, the Secular Humanist and the Marxist must ignore the experiments of Francesco Redi and Louis Pasteur, which disproved spontaneous generation, and trust fervently in the ability of inorganic matter to self-organize toward life.

George Wald provides an excellent example of the dogmatic tenacity with which materialistic evolutionists cling to the concept of spontaneous generation. He speaks of believing in spontaneous generation as a "philosophical necessity" for the scientist and declares,

> Most modern biologists, having reviewed with satisfaction the downfall of the spontaneous generation hypothesis, yet unwilling to accept the alternative belief in special creation, are left with nothing. I think a scientist has no choice but to approach the origin of life through a hypothesis of spontaneous generation.[13]

In an effort to bolster their faith in spontaneous generation, proponents of the secular religious worldviews have encouraged numerous experiments in which sparks are introduced into carefully concocted primordial soups in an effort to duplicate the first jump from non-life to life. A.I. Oparin made these experiments famous and remains a darling of evolutionists. But the hard fact remains that neither Oparin nor any other scientist has succeeded in coaxing spontaneous generation in his primordial soup. Nor is such a miracle likely to occur. "The step from simple compounds to the complex molecules of life, such as protein and DNA, has proved to be a difficult one," say Davis and Kenyon, "thus far it has resisted all efforts by the scientists working on the problem."[14] Elsewhere these authors state, "Without intelligence using selected chemicals and control conditions, amino acids have not been collected in the laboratory. Doubtless the same is true in nature."[15] Besides, all of these experiments seeking to create life in a test tube were conducted in the absence of oxygen, since oxygen would destroy any organic compounds. "Yet scientists now know," say Davis and Kenyon, "that oxygen was present on the earth from the earliest ages."[16]

Fred Hoyle, for years a leading atheist spokesman, has seen the error of his thinking and now argues that there is a better chance of producing a Boeing 747 via an explosion in a junkyard than there is to arrive at life by accident. He believes there is no way of producing DNA by chance processes, noting that merely lining up the necessary enzymes by chance would consume 20 billion years. Three respected scientists— Charles Thaxton, Walter Bradley, and Roger Olsen—write in *The Mystery of Life's Origin: Reassessing Current Theories* that "the undirected flow of energy through a primordial atmosphere and ocean is at present a woefully inadequate explanation for the incredible complexity associated with even simple living systems, and is probably wrong."[17]

This conclusion is unacceptable for both the Marxist and the Secular Humanist. To admit that life cannot arise from non-life would shake their worldviews to the very foundations. Adherents of both secular worldviews are fond of labeling Christians as dogmatic, but they neglect to mention that the doctrine of spontaneous generation is every bit as sacred to the atheist as the doctrine of the Incarnation is to the Christian. Humanist Keith Parsons, for example, states, "With the environment operating to remove nonviable variations, the appearance of life on earth becomes a certainty rather than an extreme improbability."[18] Thus, we discover in Marxism and Secular Humanism a faith more profound and more unfounded than that of the most rudimentary religions.

Further, we find that this blind faith has been extended to encompass the entire discipline of biology. In the introduction to the 1971 edition of Darwin's *Origin of Species*, L.H. Matthews admits,

> The fact of evolution is the backbone of biology, and biology is thus in the peculiar position of being a science founded on an unproved theory—is it then a science or a faith? Belief in the theory of evolution is thus exactly parallel to belief in special creation—both are concepts which believers know to be true but neither, up to the present, has been capable of proof.[19]

In examining mankind's changing attitude toward evolutionary theory, it becomes obvious that evolution has been reduced to an insupportable dogma embraced by secular religions. But it wasn't always this way. Evolution began as just another scientific theory. Darwin even treated his theory as subject to falsification, believing that unless numerous transitional forms appeared in the fossil record, his theory broke down. He wrote, "The number of intermediate varieties which have formerly existed on the earth, [must] be truly enormous. Why then is not every geological formation and every stratum full of such intermediate links? Geology assuredly does not reveal any such finely graduated organic chain; and this, perhaps, is the most obvious and gravest objection which can be urged against my theory."[20] Darwin's embarrassment over his theory's conflict with the fossil record is evidenced by the fact that, in *The Descent of Man*, "Darwin did not cite a single reference to fossils in support of his belief in human evolution."[21] Despite Darwin's own reservations, however, atheists everywhere proclaimed evolution to be fact. Julian Huxley declared around 1960 that Darwin "rendered evolution inescapable as a fact . . . all-embracing as a concept."[22]

Perhaps in 1960 one could get away with such a rash claim. Perhaps more than three decades ago the evidence against evolutionary theory was not quite so damning. But today, as we have demonstrated in this text, it is generous to label evolution as a scientific theory, and one is sorely tempted to describe it as myth. In modern times, we have entered the third phase of the evolution of the theory of evolution: the theory has become a religious dogma that is counter-rational and therefore demands great resources of faith.

In the beginning, evolution was a theory; later (thanks to Secular Humanists and Marxists) it was championed as fact; today it is still touted as fact. But now it is such a remarkable fact that it can contradict all the factual findings of paleontology, homology, and molecular biology and still be labeled absolute truth. Atheists and pantheists cling to evolution *despite* the findings of modern science, using one of two methods: blinding themselves to all facts that contradict evolution, or abandoning Darwinian evolution and postulating a theory (punctuated equilibrium) that circumvents the absence of supportive facts (i.e., it explains away any need for evidence). The theory of punctuated equilibrium, of course, is the first "scientific" theory ever postulated that claims to be true not because any facts support it but because no fact can be conceived that disputes it. Clearly, this position has all the earmarks of blind faith, since it asks men to believe in occurrences of which no traces exist.

Modern Darwinists exhibit a similar blind faith. They must actually blind themselves to the entire fossil record in order to maintain their belief in evolution. For example, Secular Humanist Chris McGowan points to a few fossils and concludes, "These intermediate fossils falsify the creationists' claim that transitional fossils linking major groups do not exist, and provide compelling evidence for evolution."[23] The plain fact from which McGowan has shielded his eyes is this: the more honest members of his own camp—*evolutionists*—admit that not one transitional fossil exists. It would be one thing if only a few rabid creationists were proclaiming the absence of transitional fossils—but it is quite another when non-creationist paleontologists declare it. In fact, no less august an authority than Colin Patterson, a paleontologist with the London Museum of Natural History, admits that he does not know of any evidences, "fossil or living," that provide "direct illustration of evolutionary transitions."[24] Elsewhere he writes more definitely: "I will lay it on the line—there is not one such fossil [that is ancestral or transitional] for which one could make a watertight argument."[25]

The flaws in evolutionary theory have become so glaring that some reputable evolutionists are abandoning ship. Patterson is rapidly falling away from an evolutionary mindset, and his reasoning is sound:

> One of the reasons I started taking this anti-evolutionary view, or let's call it a non-
> evolutionary view, was that last year I had a sudden realization. For over twenty
> years I was working on evolution in some way. One morning I woke up and some-

thing had happened to me in the night, and it struck me that I had been working on this stuff for more than twenty years, and there was not one thing new about it. It's quite a shock to learn that one can be misled for so long. Either there was something wrong with me or there was something wrong with evolutionary theory. Naturally I know there is nothing wrong with me, so for the last few weeks I've been putting a simple question to various people and groups. Question is: can you tell me anything you know about evolution? Any one thing, any one thing that is true?[26]

It is startling to realize that evolutionists cannot point to even one aspect of their theory that they know to be true. Clearly, evolution must be abandoned. But few evolutionists can summon the courage to completely break away from their discredited theory. As the *Encyclopedie Francaise*, written in cooperation with the leading biologists of France, says, "It follows from this presentation that the theory of evolution is impossible. . . . Evolution is a kind of dogma in which its priests no longer believe but which they keep presenting to their people."[27]

It is our contention that this position will be dominant in the next century. To argue, as Sagan does, that we are the children of the stars may be good poetry, but it is terrible theology and even worse science. We agree with Soren Lovtrup's observation: "I believe that one day the Darwinism myth will be ranked the greatest deceit in the history of science."[28]

But the theory of evolution will die hard. Both the Humanists and the Marxists must trust in it blindly and defend it to the death. Their willingness to cling to such a poor explanation of life should not surprise us; G.K. Chesterton warned long ago that if man will not believe in God, the danger is not that he will believe in nothing, but that he will believe in anything. What should surprise us is that so much of the world and, tragically, so many Christians, swallowed the entire theory and allowed it to gain such ascendancy among worldviews. Even today, member institutions of the Christian College Coalition are accepting a text by Richard T. Wright that presents a Darwinian evolutionary point of view.

Christianity offers a worldview that really is capable of changing the world, and yet many Christians turned their backs on special revelation and bought into evolutionary theory, a theory that conflicts with the Bible and gradually is proving to conflict with science. This was a mistake, but it is not too late to turn from it.

Today, much damage has been done. Most of the basic premises of Secular Humanism and Marxism are founded on evolutionary theory (including those in law, ethics, and politics), and, ironically, they gained much of their credibility because of their close association with the "scientific" theory of evolution. Now the science is evaporating and the whole house of cards built on myth could crumble.

THE BUCK STOPS . . . WHERE?

Secular Humanist, Marxist, and New Age assumptions about human nature provide a prime example of the damage done by evolution. By accepting an erroneous explanation of man's origin, these worldviews also embrace a distorted view of human nature.

The Christian model of human nature is based on the book of Genesis. We believe that Adam and Eve lived in the Garden of Eden until they chose to disobey God, and that the human race has suffered the consequences of their disobedience ever since, including a universally shared sin nature. Ironically, Sagan acknowledges that the Genesis account explains a number of things, including the fact that "childbirth is generally painful in only one of the millions of species on Earth: human beings."[29] However, his evolutionary preconceptions will not allow him to accept the Bible as a trustworthy document; therefore he explains this phenomenon by postulating, "Childbirth is painful because the evolution of the human skull has been spectacularly fast and recent."[30]

It is our contention that Genesis provides a better over-all explanation for the way humans really are than does Marxism or Humanism (Secular or Cosmic). We stress this distinction because one's view of human nature colors one's attitude toward all the disciplines. In fact, Joad's conversion to Christianity resulted largely from his recognition that the Christian explanation of human nature better fits the facts of experience and allows a more comprehensible view of the world. He says his "changed view of the nature of man . . . led to a changed view of the nature of the world."[31] That is, once man understands himself to be sinful, he understands his need for Christ's sacrificial death, and the wonder of His resurrection. Man must first understand himself to be dead in Adam, before he can desire to be alive in Christ. But the theory of evolution, by doing away with Adam and Eve, makes nonsense of this central point of the gospel.

Secular Humanists, Marxists, and New Agers shudder at such a "guilt-ridden" description of man. They view man from an evolutionary perspective and believe that his gradual, tireless ascent implies that man is progressing toward perfection. The consistent evolutionist perceives human nature as morally perfect in its pristine state. Unfortunately for these evolutionists, they cannot deny that man acts immorally in the real world, so they must find a scapegoat for man's sinful actions. Their scapegoat is society and its institutions. They claim that man's environment encourages the wrong kind of actions in men and that men would stop doing the wrong thing if the right society was created for us.

This method of passing the buck—denying individual responsibility for individual actions—permeates virtually all non-Christian psychology. K. Platonov, a Marxist psychologist, provides an excellent example of how this attitude dehumanizes man, turning the individual into a machine that must be fine-tuned to fit into a particular set of circumstances extant in society:

> It should be constantly borne in mind that in administering psychotherapy we must consider the individual peculiarities of man, which spring from the enormous complex of intricate and socially conditioned temporary bonds and cortical dynamic structures of his life's experience. In restoring by methods of psychotherapy the normal state of the higher nervous activity which was disturbed by the ailment the physician must consider the basic peculiarities of the concrete social environment in which the person found himself before the ailment and will find himself after the treatment.[32]

Man is not responsible for his wrong-doings—he is only an automaton that responds to the stimuli forced on him by society.

For this reason, the Secular and Cosmic Humanist and the Marxist believe fervently that the most humane, noble thing they can do is to usher in the proper society. The most desirable goal for the proponents of these worldviews is the creation of a utopian society in which man's perfect nature can flourish. Toward this end, they call for major revisions of the traditional family unit. The *Communist Manifesto* derides the traditional unit of father, mother, and child as bourgeois, and communist Russia acted on this assumption for a long time, establishing free love associations and sanctioning lax divorce and abortion laws to break down family units based on Christian ideals. Secular and Cosmic Humanism have opted to move the same way, attacking the traditional family and encouraging experimentation, including bisexuality, homosexual marriage, open marriages, pederasty, and abortion as a means of birth control.

The Christian position is that just such attacks on the traditional family have formed the groundwork for many of our social ills, including AIDS, drug abuse, and crime. The family is the glue that holds society together. As the family goes, so goes society. Examples of the cause-and-effect role the family plays in society are everywhere: poverty is epidemic among families headed by single women; young men and women between 17 and 24 years old are far more likely to abuse drugs or commit crimes if they come from fatherless homes; legalized abortion has cheapened human life to the point that Americans are no longer shocked by euthanasia and child abuse rates have risen right along with abortion rates. These tendencies can only be righted in the home, according to the Biblical view. Thus, the Christian calls for a return to the traditional family unit of father and mother (married to each other for life) and children, and traditional family values including love, fidelity and respect.

Non-Christians cling to the hope that one day society will have evolved to the point where men and women are "free" of the constraints of such tradition. But the question arises: How does one know whom to trust as an architect of this perfect society, since all men are theoretically tainted by their present environmental stimuli? Can we trust Marx's conclusions, since his life work was influenced by his living in bourgeois society? Is Corliss Lamont's belief that the perfect society will be socialistic fostered by his inherent goodness, or a reflection of the negative impact American society has had on him? We cannot know. It is impossible to find a perfect man to shape a perfect society.

Why? Because when an individual is really honest with himself, when he asks himself whether his inclinations are really toward good or toward evil and if it is fair to blame society for his urge to steal a candy bar or tell a lie, that individual—each one of us—must face the fact that he has an inherent tendency toward sin. As Joad says,

> Is it not obvious that human arrogance and love of power, that human brutality and cruelty, that, in a word, man's inhumanity to man, are responsible for . . .
> [tragic events such as the Holocaust]; obvious, too, that it is precisely these characteristics that have
> written their melancholy record upon every page of human history?[33]

Deep down we all know it; we understand that "our righteous acts are like filthy rags" (Isaiah 64:6). A simple adherence to the ancient admonition "Know thyself" reveals the folly of the non-Christian view of human nature.

Marxism/Leninism, of course, provides some of the most powerful examples of sinful human nature in this century. The record stretches from Marx's consistent dishonesty and misrepresentation of facts in his writings to the slaughter of millions by Marxist/Leninist dictators. The *Moscow News* speaks of "the horrors of Stalinism" and admits that Joseph Stalin was responsible for the mass murder of

Dreams of a master Aryan race led Adolf Hitler to despise "weaker" members of German society, including Jews and the elderly. Hitler was responsible for the death of over 26 million during his reign as der Führer.

Snapshots In Time

The genocide initiated by Adolf Hitler was only one example of the incredible misuse of power by dictators in the 20th century. To date, governments in this century have murdered almost 170 million people—not including those killed in wars! "No other century," says professor R.J. Rummel "has seen a slaughter of such magnitude."

Men like Hitler, Joseph Stalin, Mao Tse–tung, and V.I. Lenin have consistently demonstrated the logical consequences of the secular reliance on government as redeemer. When the state is entrusted with absolute authority, the state is absolutely guaranteed to misuse its power.

Since 1949 alone, one out of every twenty Chinese citizens has been killed by their government. Similar examples can be found in North Vietnam, the former Soviet Union, Japan, and other countries where governmental power has gone unchecked. In the 20th century, countless people bought into the lie that God is dead and the state is sovereign— not coincidentally, our century has been the bloodiest century in history.

15,000 Polish officers in the Katyn forest. Robert Conquest documents Stalin's systematic annihilation of 14.5 million Ukrainians, and Ronald Nash mentions that Rumanian communist Nicolae Ceausescu ordered the deaths of some 60,000 people during his reign of terror.

Christianity expects man to be capable of such inhumanity. The Bible, in contrast to the world, never waxes romantic about human nature; instead, it graphically depicts the utter sinfulness of man (Jeremiah 17:9; Romans 3:10-23). The historical fruits of both Marxism/Leninism (e.g., Soviet and Chinese atrocities, the Cambodian killing fields) and Secular and Cosmic Humanism (e.g., the murder of 1.5 million unborn children in America alone every year) confirm the Bible's perspective. The Bible is right: the heart of man is deceitful and desperately wicked.

ANOTHER SOCIALIST EXPERIMENT

In their quest for the ultimate society, Marxists believe that economics and the forces of production play the primary role, while Secular Humanists trust world government to lead us to the promised land. Both worldviews want a world order based on atheism, evolution, and socialism.

The Marxist believes that the dialectic has worked throughout history to lead society through a series of syntheses, from primitive communism to slavery to feudalism to capitalism and, recently, to socialism. Socialism itself is a transition between capitalism and communism. Marxist theory trusts that the worker (the antithesis) will clash with the capitalist (the thesis), creating a revolution leading to world socialism and, eventually, communism. A dictatorship of the proletariat (under the guidance of the Marxist/Leninist party) will be necessary initially to enforce such a world order, but it will wither away with the advent of communism. Likewise, law is now necessary to move men toward communism, but eventually the need for law will disappear.

As with the rest of the Marxist worldview, there are a number of inconsistencies in its theories regarding civilization and her institutions. If man is but a helpless pawn of the dialectic, why bother to encourage workers to revolt—won't societal change happen inevitably when the dialectic demands it? Further, does the dialectic just stop working once the perfect society (i.e., communism) is attained? Or will communism draw a new antithesis to itself and clash to form another synthesis? In other words, since the synthesis is transitory, even utopia will be transitory and must logically give way to another social order.

A larger problem is created by the Marxist's insistence that socialism is an improvement over capitalism. Perhaps some credence might have been given to this claim a century ago, before the grand socialist experiment in Soviet Russia, but the constant failings of the Soviet economy unambiguously demonstrated the impracticality of socialism. As Biblical Christianity declared all along, socialism robs mankind of any incentive to better himself. It is contrary to human nature's built-in sense of justice. Those who are lazy and do not produce—whether grades in school or cars on an assembly line—should not receive an equal result. A student who studies hard and earns an "A" should not be required to share his or her grade with someone who studies little. Socialism discriminates against the competent, the hardworking, the productive, and encourages envy and laziness among poor men and women who might, in a capitalist society, achieve productivity and cultivate feelings of self-worth rather than jealousy.

Further, socialism does not hasten the abolition of class distinctions (as Marxists claim it will), but creates a new elite. Hoover Institute Research Fellow Arnold Beichman points out that socialism in the former Soviet Union created a class known as the *nomenklatura* (also referred to as the "state bourgeois" or the "class of privileged exploiters"). This class, according to Beichman, is the prime example of the inequality spawned by socialism. Its members "own everything, the auto factories, the dachas, the food markets, the pharmacies, the transport system, the department stores. Everything."[34] Instead of destroying class distinctions, socialism created a completely authoritarian class. Milovan Djilas says, "The Communist revolution, conducted in the name of doing away with classes, has resulted in the most complete authority of any single new class."[35] This elite, founded on political connections and applied communist ideology, ran the Soviet economic sector into the ground.

After being confronted with the tragic results of applied socialism, why would anyone be interested in attaining advanced socialism? The Marxist attitude toward private property removes the incentive to work and replaces it with governmental coercion—causing production to grind to a virtual halt—and then wants to remove the coercion! Somehow, we are told, the dialectic will lead mankind into a glorious society in which man works according to his ability, and takes according to his need. But the economies in China, Cuba and every other Marxist country in the world demonstrate that even the pale shadow of such a society (socialism) creates an environment in which man is less and less willing to demonstrate ability, and more and more willing to demonstrate need.

This is the same problem faced by the Secular Humanists who call for wealth redistribution. They ignore the fact that redistribution encourages recipients to work not to earn a living but to demonstrate need, to get the biggest piece of the redistributive pie. Further, both socialistic Secular Humanists and Marxists refuse to recognize that free enterprise and private property, a New Testament concept (Acts 5:1-4), actually work to produce wealth. In capitalism, property and skills can be used to produce more, thereby creating a wealthier society. In contrast, wealth redistribution programs merely spread wealth around, encouraging a consumptive, rather than productive, mindset. The question becomes not "How can I produce more?" but "How can I get more?" This is evident even in the United States, a country that should have learned from the practical failures of socialism around the world but instead is embracing more and more plans for wealth redistribution.

The greatest flaw in the socialistic schemes of both the Marxist and the Secular Humanist was pointed out by economist and social philosopher Ludwig von Mises years ago. Socialists expect to replace the precise free market mechanism with central planners. They trust that enough economists can make the proper decisions about what to produce and how much of it to produce, and assign various prices, as efficiently as the constant adjustments made by supply and demand. Not only does this claim appear unworkable in theory, it has been proven totally unworkable in practice in numerous socialist countries. There are not enough smart, moral people to know all the economic factors to make such decisions. Black markets thrive in such settings because they supply the goods and services people actually want— something the central planners have never shown themselves able to accomplish.

Trust in central planners, although impractical, is a logical extension of non-Christian thought. Because these worldviews believe that man is inherently good, they expect that, given enough control over his environment, man can create the perfect society. Central planners should work better than the free market, according to Marxist and Secular Humanist thought, because the free market is a part of the society that influences man to act improperly. By reshaping the economy to grant inherently good men more control, we should be moving toward a more desirable society.

The offshoot of such thought is obvious: we need only to grant men more power—to expand government a little more—before we have enough control over our environment to perfect it. One can imagine how bureaucracy swells in a socialistic society, when one considers all the necessary central planners. Then add the men and women responsible for social programs that create more "healthy" families (remember, the Marxists want to remove the burden of child-rearing from the parents), and social engineers such as mental health consultants and sociologists, and you are faced with an enormously complex system of government.

Naturally, both Marxists and Secular Humanists hesitate to discuss this aspect of their political theory, since *bureaucracy* is an unpopular term. The Marxist actually denies the major role that government plays in his worldview, claiming that the state will wither away in communist society. The question arises, then: When, exactly, can we expect to see the state begin to wither away? Which Marxist leader will show himself willing to abandon power rather than garner more?

These questions are unanswerable for the simple reason that no one who has tasted power is interested in abandoning it. Power, as Lord Acton said long ago, tends to corrupt. The more power one gets, the more it tends to corrupt him. And this problem is by no means restricted to the Marxist worldview—the Secular Humanists must answer variations of the same questions. When will government be big enough?

Until every problem faced by the human race—from famine to slander—is solved, Secular Humanists and Marxists will blame society and cry for more government to correct the flaws of our environment. Their move now is to establish one huge world government to control the whole human race in order to direct human evolution toward some unknown destination.

This call for world government is a cause for much concern among Christians. After witnessing Secular Humanists' systematic eradication of Christianity from the public square in America over the past thirty years, Christians are justified in opposing a world government that would surely work toward the same goal on a global scale. Such an order would be based on materialist, not Christian, values, since everyone promoting world government (Secular Humanists, Marxist/Leninists, New Agers, etc.) is anti-Christian. The roots of globalism smack of Psalm 2:1-3; its trunk and branches of Revelation 13.

The Christian recognizes the false assumptions that form the basis for bloated governmental power. He understands that the blame lies not on faulty societal structures but on the inherent sinfulness of every human heart. Thus, Christianity postulates a cure—the gospel of transformation by Christ—that actually treats the disease. By acknowledging man's responsibility for his actions, the Christian view grants every individual the opportunity to break the bonds of sin rather than saddling him with the quiet desperation of trusting the government to solve the world's problems. "Christianity," says John Warwick Montgomery, "asserts that man, being radically self-centered, can only be saved and transformed so as to treat his neighbor with proper dignity when he admits that he cannot 'do his duty' or save himself—and relies entirely on God in Christ for salvation."[36]

Marxism and Secular Humanism's false ideas of politics and economics trace back to their false assumptions of human nature, which in turn stem from their false beliefs about man's origins. By declaring that God does not exist and that matter organized itself into man, the secular worldviews strip sovereignty from God and find themselves

> **"All that a strict humanism has to say to most of the human race living and dead is 'Too bad you were born too early' and 'Too bad about your suffering.' The bulk of the world's pain is written off as a bad expense."**
>
> *William Kilpatrick*

forced to bestow sovereignty on the state. Secular Humanists and Marxists are usually unwilling to admit that their views grant sovereignty to government, but the simple fact remains that, barring anarchy, human beings require an absolute basis on which to judge individual actions, and if God is denied, the state must usurp His role. Thus, absolute power falls into the hands of politicians—men who are not, despite the claims of secular worldviews, infallible.

Ironically, one of the men Secular Humanists most frequently point to as a proponent of Humanist thought, Thomas Jefferson, strongly opposed big government. He believed that good government is government "which shall restrain men from injuring one another, shall leave them otherwise free to regulate their own pursuits of industry and improvement, and shall not take from the mouth of labor the bread it has earned."[37] This portrait of government is remarkably similar to the proper government described in Romans 13:1-5. It is also common sense, if one understands the true role of government and man's responsibility for his own actions.

THE EVOLUTION OF LAW

But Secular Humanists and Marxists don't understand, and thus they create another problem. When one denies man's responsibility and declares the state sovereign, one also destroys justice. This is perhaps the most dangerous aspect of the utopian vision. When government becomes the only guide for mankind, then only legal positivism can result. Legal positivism and the sovereignty of the state (statism) are inseparable—either theory assumes the other.

If we recall that the three most tyrannical dictators of the twentieth century, Adolf Hitler, Stalin, and Mao Tse-tung, all advocated statism and practiced positive law, we should find no comfort in knowing that the law on which the "new world order" will be founded is positivist. The legal structures proposed by world government proponents are based on the materialistic interpretation of man and government. Human rights are assigned according to the criteria of what will assist man in his evolutionary climb to perfection. The design of this whole legal and political superstructure, as Malachi Martin points out, "is built on the presumption that we ourselves are the authors of our destiny. Man is exalted. The God-Man is repudiated; and with him, the idea of man's fallenness is rejected. Evil is a matter of malfunctioning structures, not in any way a basic inclination of man."[38]

Why is the only law for Secular Humanists and Marxists positive law? Because God does not exist, and therefore neither does His law. Thus, man must either be a law unto himself or trust the sovereign state to manufacture law. Cosmic Humanists tend toward making every individual a law unto himself. But Secular Humanists and

Marxists understand that this leads to anarchy, and therefore choose to grant the state sovereignty.

Trusting the state as the absolute basis in law leads to legal relativism, since government is an ever-changing entity. For law to remain constant, for the word *justice* to mean anything in a rational sense, law must have an unchanging basis—i.e., Jesus Christ, "the same yesterday and today and forever" (Hebrews 13:8). Only such an absolute foundation can create absolute laws like "It is always unlawful and morally wrong for a judge to take a bribe." Other systems of law can only declare, "It is unlawful, in the present circumstances, to take a bribe" or "Thou shalt not commit bribery . . . ordinarily."

Legal positivism leads to rampant relativism, as demonstrated by Sidney Hook: "The rights of man depend upon his nature, needs, capacities, and aspirations, not upon his origins. Children have rights not because they are our creatures but because of what they are and will become. It is not God but the human community that endows its members with rights."[39] This is the height of relativism! Since man's nature is always in evolutionary flux and every individual differs from his fellow human beings in terms of needs and capacities, it naturally follows that each generation's and each individual's rights must vary in proportion to these differences. Does this mean, then, that I have fewer rights than a concert pianist, since he is more capable than I? Do I have more rights than the needy in Ethiopia? Clearly, it is no good founding rights on human characteristics or governmental policies. Rights and laws must be based on the character of God, or they will be arbitrary.

A prime example of this is provided by some Humanists' recently cultivated concern for animal rights. Kenneth L. Feder and Michael Alan Park write,

> [T]here is no objective rationale for elevating our species into a category separate from the rest of the animals with whom we share the presence of a nervous system, the ability to feel pain, and behaviors aimed at avoiding pain. Thus, the fundamental rights we accord ourselves must be equally applicable to any other organism with these same characteristics.[40]

Consistent with their evolutionary bias, these Secular Humanists see no distinction between humans and the rest of the animal kingdom—men and rats must be viewed as equals, with no favoritism displayed in the realm of rights. But this view strips man of his dignity as created in the image of God and denies God's will for mankind over His creation (Genesis 1:28), thus rendering human rights as transitory and meaningless as the rights we bestow on toads and tasmanian devils. We must seriously consider: will lions have the right, according to the Secular Humanist view, to pursue happiness, even if that entails depriving jackals of their right to life? Will we bestow rights on plants as well (after all, they are also living evolutionary relations), thereby starving the human race for fear of "murdering" a fellow organism? The absurdity is apparent—as obvious as the absurdity of animal rights advocates displaying more affection for bald eagles in the shell than for human babies in the womb. But the absurdity follows necessarily from worldviews that base human rights on temporal, changeable institutions and ideologies.

The danger of legal relativism should be obvious to all. It is no exaggeration to say that under positivist law, an individual might one day awaken to find that green eyes have been decreed illegal, and be executed that morning for his eye color. When the state is the only basis for law, any law may be conceived.

Examples of this truth may be seen throughout society. Hitler, Stalin, and many others used positive law to murder millions—passing laws to eliminate Jews, gypsies, the sick, landowners, Christians, or anyone they had an urge to destroy—which fundamentally means anyone who stood in the way of their absolute domination of every person and action in society. In America, laws that many people considered inconceivable a few years ago are now standards by which we must live. Abortion has been legalized because, suddenly, the state decided that a baby in the womb is not a baby. Perhaps, twenty years from now, infanticide will be legalized, because the state will have decided that a baby is not a human being until it can walk or talk. The distinction between right and wrong is tenuous in a society that subscribes to legal positivism.

Conversely, Christian law applied to society results in practical and just legal structures. Based on the character of God, a moral order, man created in the image of God, and the coming of Jesus Christ in flesh, Christian law has produced the concept of common law, the Magna Charta, the Declaration of Independence, and the Constitution of the United States.

The Magna Charta resulted in a just government in England; likewise, the application of Christian law to the U.S. Constitution positively shaped America. Because her founding fathers read the nature of man correctly and divided power properly, America instituted a system of law that protects human rights and human dignity and is the envy of the world. "There is no country in the whole world," said Alexis de Tocqueville, "in which the Christian religion retains a greater influence over the souls of men than in America; and there can be no greater proof of its utility, and of its conformity to human nature, than that its influence is most powerfully felt over the most enlightened and free nation of the earth."[41]

Contrast such legal history with the history of positive law in the first half of the twentieth century: "No half-century ever witnessed slaughter on such a scale," said

Robert Jackson, "such cruelties and inhumanities, such wholesale deportations of peoples into slavery, such annihilations of minorities." Ideas have consequences. And the consequences of legal positivism are tragic.[42]

DOUBTING THOMASES

Politics, economics, and law—all closely related disciplines—are aspects of Marxist and Secular Humanist worldviews that do not adequately take into account the workings of the real world. Adherents to both worldviews try to circumvent the problems of statism by claiming that the real basis for the state's guidance of society lies in the scientific method. That is, man is able to use science to discern the proper direction for society, and science provides a foundation that is not subject to the whims of man. Science becomes the force that will lead man to utopia. Paul Kurtz says bluntly, "Science (reason in the community) is the ultimate source of our knowledge of value. . . . It discovers and creates ideal systems which contribute to the homeostatic expansion of life. Therefore, the extension of science is perhaps the chief practical good for humankind to achieve."[43]

This discussion naturally leads us back to philosophy. When one speaks of science as the means of discerning knowledge, values, and guidance, one is making an epistemological claim. Both the Secular Humanist and the Marxist rely on science (conveniently ignoring the science of archaeology when it confirms Biblical veracity) as their method of knowing. In this, they believe, they rely on an epistemology far superior to that of the Christian. They claim to believe only in things that can be observed and tested, whereas the Christian believes even in things he cannot physically see.

For this reason, secular worldviews label Christians unscientific and claim science as their exclusive property. But is it fair to stake such a claim? Indeed, could science even exist today if the Marxist and Secular Humanist descriptions of reality were correct?

Of course not. If the atheistic, materialistic assumptions of these two worldviews were correct, we would live in a disorderly universe that followed no discernible pattern and subscribed to no unalterable laws. We would neither have seasons nor the law of gravity nor swallows that migrate to the same area year after year. Only in the Christian model of the universe—a universe created by a rational, personal God—can one expect to find such magnificent order. And only an ordered and intelligible universe allows room for science.

The fact that science arose at all is powerful testimony to the truth of Christianity. As Louis Victor de Broglie says, "We are not sufficiently astonished by the fact that any science may be possible." [44] This is especially true of the Marxist and the Secular Humanist. They do not understand that science could never have been conceived in a society dominated by their worldviews. Historian and philosopher of science Stanley Jaki says that "the belief in a personal rational Creator . . . as cultivated especially within a Christian matrix . . . supported the view for which the world was an objective and orderly entity investigable by the mind because the mind too was an orderly and objective product of the same rational, that is, perfectly consistent Creator." Man believed science possible because man believed in a God of reason and order.[45]

Secular Humanists and Marxists were certainly not responsible for the founding of science and, in fact, could not have been. The supreme irony is that modern science classrooms, using the arbitrary power of positive law, bar the Christian worldview while welcoming both the Marxist and the Secular Humanist perspectives. It is an irony that Jefferson would have been quick to spot:

> Was the government to prescribe to us our medicine and diet, our bodies would be in such keeping as our souls are now. Thus in France the emetic was once forbidden as a medicine, and the potato as an article of food. Government is just as infallible, too, when it fixes systems in physics. Galileo was sent to the Inquisition for affirming that the earth was a sphere; the government had declared it to be as flat as a trencher, and Galileo was obliged to abjure his error. This error, however, at length prevailed, the earth became a globe, and Descartes declared it was whirled round its axes by a vortex. The government in which he lived was wise enough to see that this was no question of civil jurisdiction, or we should all have been involved by authority in vortices. In fact, vortices have been exploded, and the Newtonian principle of gravitation is now more firmly established, on the basis of reason, than it would be were the government to step in, and to make it an article of necessary faith. Reason and experiment have been indulged, and error has fled before them. It is error alone which needs the support of government. Truth can stand by itself.[46]

Atheist worldviews have, of course, expanded on the concept of science to the point of distortion, assigning it the ability to grant man knowledge of everything, including value and truth. Tonne declares, "Seeking the nearest approximation to truth that we can attain is an endless struggle. It is probably the most important study we undertake. That is what 'science' is all about."[47] The secular worldviews have invested science with an almost supernatural quality—even speaking of its "omnipotence"—trusting the scientific method to provide them with the correct answer to virtually any question.

But such attitudes toward science are false. Science has natural limits, including the fact that it can only provide us with knowledge about the material, observable universe. Any attempt to expand science beyond these natural limits leads not to better science but to scientism. Trusting science for one's entire epistemology leads either to frustration or to methods of obtaining knowledge that are labeled scientific but are unfounded. Humanists and Marxists are usually guilty of the latter error, describing utopian social programs and ethical codes with no basis in science as "scientific." This approach actually hinders true scientific progress. Jaki explains, "Scientism is never a genuine reverence for science but a harnessing of science for a nonscientific purpose. Since that purpose is fixed, science can only serve it by remaining fixed, namely, by remaining in its supposedly final stage."[48]

Scientism is yet another flaw that taints both Marxist and Secular Humanist theory. It is unreasonable to demand that science provide mankind with all knowledge. Even Julian Huxley, in one of his more candid moments, recognized the limited nature of the scientific method:

> Science has removed the obscuring veil of mystery from many phenomena, much to the benefit of the human race: but it confronts us with a basic and universal mystery—the mystery of existence in general, and of the existence of mind in particular. Why does the world exist? Why is the world-stuff what it is? Why does it have mental or subjective aspects as well as material or objective ones? We do not know.[49]

EXPERIMENTING WITH THE TEN COMMANDMENTS

Unfortunately, Secular Humanists and Marxists ignore Huxley's startling admission and cling tenuously to their scientism. Without science for their epistemology, they would have to revert to the "trust the voice within you" mentality of Cosmic Humanism. That is, their theory of knowledge could only be based on individual experience. But by clinging to science, they find themselves trusting an epistemology unqualified to speak to a number of disciplines, including ethics.

Marxists and Secular Humanists apply the theories of evolution and the dialectic to morality and conclude that ethics develops as humanity progresses and that we have not yet established the perfect ethical code that will govern man in utopian society. Indeed, the Marxist goes so far as to declare all present moral codes bourgeois and therefore sinister. Given these beliefs, proponents of Marxism and Secular Humanism must perceive ethics as relative. They must reject all ethical absolutes, and even view claims of unchangeable ethical codes as horrible deceptions. Tonne warns that "the notion that there is an absolute truth etched into the eternal heavens as so many of us were brought up to believe is not only a falsehood, it is a menace to human development."[50]

In reality, Tonne's ideas are the menace to human development. Trusting science and evolution to provide one with the proper conclusions about modern-day ethics can lead one down a number of paths—all of which are hopelessly twisted. If ethics can be shown to be relative and based on evolutionary theory, then Hitler, Stalin, and Tse-tung are twentieth-century saints. Hitler applied the theory of evolution, especially Darwin's idea of natural selection, to morality and concluded, "There is absolutely no other revolution but a racial revolution. There is no economic, no social, no political revolution. There is only the struggle of lower races against the higher races."[51] Marx and Frederick Engels applied science to ethics and concluded that the ends justified the means, which justified Stalin's conclusion that "the dictatorship of the proletariat is the domination of the proletariat over the bourgeoisie, untrammeled by the law and based on violence and enjoying the sympathy and support of the toiling and exploited masses."[52] Mao's first lectures to villagers following his 1949 conquest of China were not about Marxist theory; they were about Charles Darwin. Nowadays, most Marxists and Secular Humanists are quick to condemn Hitler, Stalin, and Mao, but they are hard pressed to explain why. If ethical relativism is true and each culture determines its own moral conduct, Hitler, Mao, and Stalin were morally correct in doing what they did best. And if they moved the evolutionary timetable forward a notch or two, then Secular Humanists and Marxists should applaud them.

Still another frightening conclusion that Secular Humanists must accept when attempting to base their ethics on scientism is summed up by Harry Elmer Barnes. He assumes that an individual with enough brains can use the scientific method to establish morals, and he draws the logical conclusion that

> one can probably say that there is no truly or completely intelligent person who is not at the same time moral in the scientific sense of that term. . . . It should be absolutely clear to any thoughtful and informed person that morality, far from being divorced from intelligence, depends more thoroughly and completely upon intelligence and scientific information than any other phase of human thought.[53]

This theory takes on a sinister character when one realizes that it grants those men and women labeled "intelligent" by society free reign in morals. Further, it allows such persons to dictate right and wrong for every member of society with a lower IQ. Barnes admits as much: "Wide variations in capacity appear to be the most important single fact about the human race. . . . It would seem to follow that there will be certain kinds of conduct which will not be harmful for the abler members of society; which, indeed, may be positively desirable and beneficial."[54]

This belief that some men will always know better than others, regardless of actual concern with morality, has already severely wounded our world. It allowed dictators

394

to commit unspeakable acts of violence. It encouraged the attitude in America that the mother knows what is right for her unborn baby, even if it means abortion, that doctors know when a fatally ill person would like to die, and that Planned Parenthood knows the proper means of sex education for our children (which doesn't happen to include the biblical admonition to abstain from sex until marriage). The results of such morality are the slaughter of Ukrainians and the unborn and a raging AIDS epidemic. "The new morality," says William Stanmeyer, "makes it quite possible to be a passionate lover of humanity, like a . . . Marx or a Lenin, and to be a passionate hater of actual human beings."[55] According to such an ethical vision, it makes sense to kill millions of bourgeois or millions of babies, since they are obstacles to mankind's march toward utopia.

Naturally, Secular Humanists and Marxists do not like to talk about the devastating consequences of their ethics. When discussing morality, they prefer positive terms like *justice, love,* and *courage.* But when asked for the specific basis for such concepts, they flounder. Science can no more reveal a meaningful foundation for these terms than it can explain a man and a woman falling in love. So, despite railing against absolute codes and traditional morality, the secular worldviews must fall back on some form of Christian ethics when postulating specific moral suggestions. Secular Humanist H.J. Eysenck warns, "In rejecting religion altogether, Humanism may be throwing out the ethical baby with the supernatural bathwater."[56] Lamont also tries to borrow Christian ethics while snubbing their foundation: "Any humane philosophy must include such New Testament ideals as the brotherhood of man, peace on earth and the abundant life. There is much ethical wisdom, too, in the Old Testament and its Ten Commandments. Without accepting any ethical principle as a dogmatic dictum never to be questioned, the Humanist certainly adheres in general to a Biblical commandment such as, 'Thou shalt not bear false witness against thy neighbor.'"[57]

That sounds nice, of course, but Lamont surely knows that if God is missing, everything is permissible. Without its foundation in the absolute nature of God, morality flounders. Will Durant admits, "[W]e shall find it no easy task to mold a natural ethic strong enough to maintain moral restraint and social order without the support of supernatural consolations, hopes and fears."[58] Francis Schaeffer responds: "It is not just difficult, it is impossible."[59]

Did science have anything to do with forming the foundation for biblical morality? Certainly not. God's character is the foundation for Christian law and ethics—and as a result, Christian legal and ethical systems fit the facts of reality and provide genuine guidance for the man seeking to act rightly. Schaeffer remarks that one of the distinctive things about God is that "He is a God with character. Everything is not equally right before God, and because of this we have our absolutes."[60] God is opposed to ethical systems that encourage evil men to destroy human value and dignity, giving rise to Tiananmen Square, Buchenwald, Katyn Forest, and the gulag. Whereas Marxists and Humanists have built their ethical systems on shifting sand and therefore tolerate any action that supposedly causes the human race to progress toward utopia, the Christian bases morality on the unchanging nature of God, a moral order reflecting God's character, and understands that man's highest calling is to servanthood (Mark 10:43-45; Romans 7:4-6).

"I Couldn't Help Myself"

Ethics, however, is not the only realm in which the secular worldviews' scientism creates unsolvable problems. Marxists and Secular Humanists' psychology is also distorted by their theoretical assumptions. Because both worldviews assume that science is the only means of discerning truth, both must abandon all "unscientific" notions like mind, idea, conscience, soul, and spirit. Wilson declares, "A scientific humanist ... is someone who suggests that everything in the universe has a material basis. And that means everything, including the mind and all its spiritual products."[61] Humanist psychology is ontological monism since mind and brain are considered materialistic events or entities.

We noted many of the inconsistencies of such a belief when discussing man's origins, but the full ramifications can only be examined in the context of the twentieth century, when men like I.P. Pavlov and B.F. Skinner carried the secular worldviews to their logical conclusion. Before then, or at least before Darwin's *Origin of Species,* mankind would have scoffed at the completely behavioristic theories of Pavlov and Skinner. Many early atheists, of course, had suggested that mind and soul did not exist, but none had the audacity to draw the logical conclusion: without mind, man's actions are but a series of responses to various external stimuli; therefore, they are completely determined.

Such a conclusion shouldn't shock us. Behaviorism is the logical extension of naturalism. What should shock us is that the Marxist and the Secular Humanist expect us to believe that this model accurately describes reality. A model that strips man of free will can only lead to nonsensical conclusions. As Roche points out, it "means you literally have no choice about reading this book at this moment; your doing so was, as it were, determined by the stars. Nor have I any choice in what I'm writing, being, as it were, merely a stenographer for what is dictated by the dance of the atoms. Consequently, if I were to write that all naturalists were ugly useless cockroaches, the naturalist would have to agree that Nature herself forced me to say so."[62]

That is, the naturalist could not blame Roche for such a statement, because behaviorism absolves man of responsibility for his actions. Of course, in real life, Secular Humanists and Marxists do hold people responsible for their actions (when someone steals their car, they demand prosecution), but when they do so they are acting inconsistently. True adherence to secular philosophy, theology, psychology, and biology requires never blaming (or praising) an individual for his actions.

Further, true adherence to a behavioristic view of man negates the meaningfulness of the behaviorist's findings. "We must use our will," says Roche, "to study the world. If we conclude that the world is of a character that does not allow free will, we destroy our credentials for saying so."[63] Only if our mind is more than a receptor and processor of stimuli can we trust it to devise meaningful theories. Only if our will is our own, and not slave to the changeable winds of society, can we arrive at a rational conclusion.

Marxists and Secular Humanists are embarassed by these problems—thus, they presently downplay the behavioristic aspect of their worldviews. This works to their advantage in a related area as well, because both secular worldviews like to treat man as if he possesses free will when they encourage him to choose to support their particular revolution or utopian vision. In a very real sense, Secular Humanists and Marxists want to have their cake and eat it, too. They desire a universe without God, made entirely of matter, and evolving toward perfection, but they wish to retain concepts negated by these presuppositions, including mind, ideas, and free will. Secular Humanist Wayne L. Trotta provides the perfect example of this mentality: "It may be prudent to assume that all behavior is governed by causal laws. But reducing human conduct to a set of mechanistic—'if this happens then that happens'—formulae would ultimately reduce therapy to nothing more than a set of techniques."[64] Basically, Trotta is saying that he still thinks Humanism's behaviorist assumptions are true, but Humanism should ignore them in practice since they don't work. This is the height of inconsistency! Why retain a theory that doesn't fit the facts? If behaviorism doesn't explain the way things really are, then get rid of it—along with its foundational assumptions of atheism, naturalism, evolution, and monism.

In a sense, this is what Marxists and Secular Humanists are forced to do when coping with the real world. Their worldviews describe the universe one way, but they cannot *live* in accordance with their views. Secular worldview proponents leave their atheism and materialism on the shelf and embrace the concept of absolutes and free will when interacting with the community.

One wonders why the Marxist and the Secular Humanist would continue to cling to worldviews that must be abandoned when faced with cold, hard facts. If, as 1 Timothy 1:5 tells us, love "comes from a pure heart and a good conscience and a sincere faith," why do secular worldviews insist on denying the existence of the supernatural? Why, when Marxist regimes are crumbling throughout the world, do American professors still believe that Marxism is a workable worldview? Why do Secular Humanists deny the existence of the conscience and the divinity of Christ and then proclaim, as Bertrand Russell does, that the world needs more "Christian love"? The answer is that both secular worldviews are religions that require an unreasonable faith. The reason people are willing to accept worldviews that require such faith will become clear as we turn our eyes toward the future.

THE KINGDOM OF HEAVEN OR UTOPIA?

Both the Secular Humanist and the Marxist base their attitudes toward history and the future on the belief that evolution is a fact. Accordingly, all of life is on a grand march forward, progressing toward perfection (Marxism makes doubly sure of this progress by postulating a near-divine, teleological dialectic that moves men through various means of production toward the most desirable society). This belief that evolution virtually guarantees the eventual perfection of life is as old as Darwin, who suggested that since "natural selection works solely by and for the good of each being, all corporeal and mental endowments will tend to progress towards perfection."[65]

Clearly, Marxist and Secular Humanist worldviews offer incentives for their faithful. Not only do they promise an "inevitable" ascent into paradise; they also promise a heaven without the uncomfortable concept of a holy, just God. Man does not have to be responsible for his actions; he can still achieve paradise! This belief about history and the future provides the incentive for men and women to cling to worldviews that are otherwise untenable.

Sadly, even the paradise that provides hope for so many Secular Humanists and Marxists is a pale and inadequate thing. Since nothing supernatural exists, the individual dies when his body dies. Thus, paradise becomes a fleeting state, and all men who have already died will never experience it. William Kirk Kilpatrick points out,

> What good does it do to the billions who have already passed through this life in wretchedness, that scientific humanism will one day create a world without suffering? For that matter what good does it do to those who are right now dying miserable and lonely deaths all over the world? All that a strict humanism has to say to most of the human race living and dead is "Too bad you were born too early" and "Too bad about your suffering." The bulk of the world's pain is written off as a bad expense. [66]

Such a callous, tenuous paradise could hardly be described as paradise at all.

As one might expect, some Secular Humanists and Marxists try to circumvent man's mortality in an effort to create a more appealing notion of utopia. By granting the evolutionary process a state of wisdom usually reserved for God, they claim that progress will one day guide man to an evolutionary form that fosters immortality. For example, Victor Stenger claims that computers are the next step in the evolutionary ladder and says that since their memory banks are basically immortal, mankind *"also can become immortal.* It should be possible in the future to save the accumulated knowledge of an individual human being when he or she dies. Perhaps even those thoughts which constitute consciousness will also be saved, and the collective thoughts of all human beings will be continued in the memory banks of computers."[67]

Even ignoring Stenger's inconsistent belief that it is possible to discuss an immortal consciousness and still deny the existence of the supernatural, one must be appalled by the naivete of his faith in evolution. Such a trust that change always denotes progress is completely unfounded in reality. As Roche says,

> We have to sweep away the trashy modern superstition that history is on some sort of grand, unstoppable march to human betterment. . . . In its thrall, we automatically assume that "new" is better. The ceaseless anti-heroic murmur for "change" is a statement that everything past is evil, and any change is better. This is not only idiocy but moral defection. Does anybody really believe Germany was the better for Hitler? Change for the worse, both personal and social, is more the rule than the exception. Humans are born backsliders.[68]

This is one of the biggest flaws in the view of history founded on evolution and the dialectic: there is no evidence that mankind and society are moving toward perfection. In fact, the evidence is to the contrary. Twentieth-century Nazism, communism, world wars, abortion, homosexuality, hedonism, perversion of culture, etc. are examples not of evolution but of devolution. The human race has not produced a playwright the equal of William Shakespeare in 400 years. More significantly, no man has come close to duplicating the moral character of Jesus Christ, who lived almost 2,000 years ago.

Secular Humanists and Marxists cannot dispute this, but neither can they accept the logical implication: the truth of the Biblical Christian worldview. Because they begin with the assumption that God is not, they must ignore all evidence to the contrary and make not one but numerous irrational leaps of faith to cope with their theology, philosophy, ethics, biology, etc. This necessarily distorts their entire perspective and causes them to discount the one historical Figure who really holds the key to a paradise in mankind's future—"the kingdom of God's dear Son" (Colossians 1: 13), open to anyone who accepts the Lord Jesus Christ (Acts 16:31; Matthew 7:21;

Ephesians 2:8-10). By opting for a paradise that does not require man to be responsible to God, the Marxist and the Secular Humanist turn their backs on the One who said He was the Way, the Truth and the Life (John 14:6).

They also turn their backs on reality. They choose to deal in distortions and shadows, advancing theories that deny the most important aspects of existence: God, the soul, mind, conscience, ideas, free will, and altruism. Such denial leads to inhuman theories and concepts, including "survival of the fittest" and the morality of violence against an entire class of people (the bourgeoisie). It leads to moral nonsense like "Thou shalt not commit murder . . . ordinarily," and a whole host of sexual perversions.

A CALL TO DEDICATION

The acceptance of many of these distortions by the Christian community is our greatest shame. Countless Christians, thanks to books like *Biology Through the Eyes of Faith*, have accepted evolutionary theory, many so firmly that they treat creationists as unwelcome brethren or worse. Many Christian colleges that have finally recognized the scientific weaknesses of theistic Darwinian evolution still shun special creationism, moving instead toward punctuated equilibrium. Other Christians are embracing various forms of Marxism and socialism, calling it "Liberation Theology." Some have bought into concepts like ontological monism, self-actualization, behaviorism, feminism, abortion, Eastern meditation, and world government.

Why do Christians so easily accept inconsistencies into their worldview? In this sense, non-Christians are much more consistent. There are no Marxist/Leninist creationists. There are no New Agers who believe in ethical absolutes. The Christian, who trusts the Scriptures and therefore has access to the one worldview based on eternal truth, should be the first person to recognize the bankruptcy of secular religious views. Yet all too often he is the first to embrace them!

It is our position that too many Christians ignore Paul's admonition that they not be taken captive "through vain and deceitful philosophy" (Colossians 2:8).

This text is an attempt to amend that situation. The superiority of the Christian position in theology, philosophy, ethics, economics, politics, law, biology, history, psychology, and sociology has been elucidated again and again. The non-Christian worldviews have, in their own words, declared their position to be irreconcilable with Christianity. The battle lines have been drawn. As Christians armed with the truth—indeed, armed with the revelation of Truth Himself (John 14:6)—we are more than equipped to shatter the myths of all opposing worldviews,

For though we walk in the flesh, we do not war after the flesh: (for the weapons of our warfare are not carnal, but mighty through God to the pulling down of strongholds;) casting down imaginations, and every high thing that exalteth itself against the knowledge of God, and bringing into captivity every thought to the obedience of Christ (2 Corinthians 10:3-5).

And yet we are not doing the job. The Christian worldview is in retreat in nearly every arena of American life—including our universities, media, arts, music, law, business, medicine, psychology, sociology, public schools, and government. "The humanistic system of values has now become the predominant way of thinking in most of the power centers of society,"[69] claim James C. Dobson and Gary L. Bauer. According to Dobson and Bauer, the Christian worldview has only two power centers remaining in America—the church and the family—and both of them are under tremendous pressure to surrender.

What are we to do?

Go on the offensive! Light a candle. Pray (2 Chronicles 7:14; Colossians 1:9-14). Study (2 Timothy 2:15). Understand the times (1 Chronicles 12:32). Rebuild the foundations (Psalm 11:3). Spread the word. Truth is our greatest weapon. Philosophy students at Charles University in Prague, Czechoslovakia, told their professors they had had enough of Marxist/Leninist dialectics. American students can do the same—casting Secular, Marxist and Cosmic Humanism out of the classroom. But such a stand will not come easy; it will take a rebirth of morality, a revival of spiritual interests, a renewal of intellectual honesty, and a recovery of courage. It will take a shoring up of the family and a reawakening in our churches. It will take blood, sweat, and tears to re-establish the influence of Christianity on our culture, but it can be done.

Perhaps most importantly, Christians must shore up our worldview and teach it to young people. We must immerse ourselves and our children in *Christian* theology, *Christian* philosophy, *Christian* ethics, *Christian* politics, *Christian* economics, *Christian* psychology, *Christian* sociology, *Christian* biology, *Christian* law, and *Christian* history.

Some progress has been made in this direction. Alvin Plantinga, a leading Christian philosopher, has challenged the Christian community to discover its worldview. Philosophers like Plantinga, Henry, Willard, J.P. Moreland, William Lane Craig, and Geisler have gone to great lengths to defend Christianity from its Secular Humanist opponents.

Henry Morris, Duane Gish, Ken Cummings, A.E. Wilder-Smith, and a whole host of Christian men of science have demonstrated the veracity of the creationist position. Wendell Bird's *Origin of Species Revisited* contains enough scientific data to sink evolutionary theory. Thaxton, Bradley and Olson's *The Mystery of Life's Origins* and Davis and Kenyon's *Of Pandas and People* encourage the position that science and Christianity are allies. Still, much more needs to be accomplished to remind the world of the truth of Christianity and give encouragement for the future.

We need Christian young people, strong in the faith, to follow Cal Thomas and Fred Barnes into the media, to take charge of the universities, to run for Congress and school boards, and to espouse Christian sociology (with a strong emphasis on traditional family values). We need Christian artists challenging us with something that feeds the spirit and fuels the imagination (instead of art, literature, and music fit for the cultural sewer).

Christians can reclaim law, history, politics, economics, and all other disciplines. Understanding themselves to be men and women created to serve God, they can feel the call to excellence more profoundly than proponents of any other worldview (especially because most other worldviews strip man of his dignity and free will). Thus, we join Roche in issuing this challenge:

> If you take the anti-heroic view that there is nothing the individual person can do to control his own destiny, then stand aside. Be the helpless pawn of fate you say you are. But if you long for the sense of life and purpose our era denies; if your mind hungers and your spirit thirsts for something far better than the pursuit of things, or power, or politics, or self, then the time to change is now.[70]

The first and last words Christ spoke to Peter were, "Follow me." He speaks them to us still. To follow Christ entails, at the minimum, taking every idea captive for Christ (2 Cor. 10:5) and not allowing humanistic worldviews to take us captive (Col. 2:8).

ENDNOTES

Chapter 1

[1]James C. Dobson and Gary L. Bauer, *Children at Risk: The Battle For the Hearts and Minds of Our Kids* (Dallas, TX: Word, 1990), p. 19.

[2]Ibid., pp. 19-20.

[3]Ibid., p. 20.

[4]Carl F.H. Henry, *Toward a Recovery of Christian Belief* (Westchester, IL: Crossway Books, 1990), p. 113.

[5]L. Neff, "Christianity Today Talks to George Gilder," *Christianity Today*, March 6, 1987, p. 35.

[6]C.E.M. Joad, *The Recovery of Belief* (London: Faber and Faber, 1955), p. 22.

[7]Ibid., p. 240.

[8]Bertrand Russel, *Human Society in Ethics and Politics* (New York: Mentor, 1962), p. viii.

[9]Alexis de Tocqueville, *Democracy in America*, two volumes (New Rochelle, NY: Arlington House, n.d.), vol. 1, p. 294. Elsewhere he declared, "The Americans combine the notions of Christianity and of liberty so intimately in their minds, that it is impossible to make them conceive the one without the other" (p. 297).

[10]Francis A. Schaeffer, *A Christian Manifesto* (Westchester, IL: Crossway Books, 1981), p. 17.

[11] Ibid.

[12]"No One Here But Us Church Mice," *National Review*, December 31, 1989, p. 15.

[13]Reed Irvine, "Soviet Religious Propaganda, "*The Washington Times*, April 3, 1984, p. 9A.

[14]David B. Richardson, "Marxism in U.S. Classrooms," *U.S. News and World Report*, January 25, 1982, pp. 42-5.

[15]Georgie Anne Geyer, "Marxism Thrives on Campus," *The Denver Post*, August 29, 1989, p. B7.

[16]Ibid.

[17]Herbert London, "Marxism Thriving on American Campuses," *The World and I*, January 1987, p. 189.

[18]*Accuracy in Academia Campus Report*, April 1987 p. 1.

[19]Roger Kimball, *Tenured Radicals* (New York: Harper and Row, 1990), p. xiii. Christian young people should read Kimball's book, then Allan Bloom's *The Closing of the American Mind: How Higher Education has Failed Democracy and Impoverished the Souls of Today's Students* (New York: Simon and Schuster, 1987), and finally Ronald Nash's *The Closing of the American Heart* (Brentwood TN: Wolgemuth & Hyatt, 1990) to grasp what Christian students face in America's colleges and universities.

[20]Kimball, *Tenured Radicals*, p. xiv

[21]Newsletter of the Christian Anti-Communist Crusade, P.O. Box 890, Long Beach, California 90801; February 1, 1988.

[22]Cal Thomas, "Turner's Takeover Tender," *The Washington Times*, November 6, 1989, p. F2.

[23]Julie Lanham, "The Greening of Ted Turner," *The Humanist*, Nov./Dec. 1989, p. 6.

[24]Jonathan Adolph, "What is New Age?" *New Age Journal*, Winter 1988, p. 11.

[25]Johanna Michaelsen, *Like Lambs to the Slaughter* (Eugene, Oregon: Harvest House, 1989), p. 11.

[26]Marilyn Ferguson, *The Austrian Conspiracy* (Los Angeles: J.P. Tarcher, Inc., 1980), p. 23.

[27]Jonathan Adolph, "What is New Age?" *New Age Journal*, Winter 1988, p. 11.

[28]Ray A. Yungen, *For Many Shall Come in My Name*, (Salem, Oregon: Ray Yungen, 1989), p. 34.

[29]John Randolph Price, *The Superbeings* (Austin, TX: Quartus Books, 1981), pp. 51.

[30]Marx and Engels, *Karl Marx-Frederick Engels: Collected Works*, 40 volumes (New York: International Publishers, 1976), vol. 3, p. 296.

[31]Paul Kurtz, *The Fullness of Life* (New York: Horizon Press, 1974), p. 36.

[32]Carl F.H. Henry, *Twilight of a Great Civilization* (Westchester, IL: Crossway Books, 1988), p. 94.

Chapter 2

[1]H. Burtness, "Bonhoeffer, Dietrich," in *Baker's Dictionary of Christian Ethics*, ed. Carl F.H. Henry, (Grand Rapids, MI: Baker, 1973), p. 67.

[2]Whittaker Chambers, *Witness*, (Lake Bluff, IL.: Random House, 1952), p. 17.

[3]Alexander Solzhenitsyn, Harvard Lectures

[4]Gustav A. Wetter, *Dialectical Materialism* (Westport, CT: Greenwood Press, 1977), p. 558.

[5]Bertrand Russell, *Understanding History* (New York: Philosophical Library, 1957), p. 95.

[6]Paul Kurtz, ed., *Humanist Manifestoes I and II* (Buffalo: Prometheus, 1980), p. 3, emphasis added.

[7]John Dewey, *A Common Faith* (New Haven: Yale University Press, 1934), p. 87.

[8]Kurtz, ed., *Humanist Manifestoes I and II*, p. 16.

[9]United States v. Seeger, 380 U.S. 163. Also see Welsh v. United States, 398 U.S. 333 (1970).

[10]See American Education on Trial: Is Secular Humanism a Religion? (Cumberland, VA: Center for Judicial Studies, 1987), p. 34.

[11]Ibid., p. 34.

[12]Paul Kurtz, "Is Secular Humanism a Religion?" *Free Inquiry*, Winter 1986/87, p. 5.

[13]Kurtz, *Eupraxophy: Living Without Religion* (Buffalo: Prometheus, 1989). p. 80.

[14]Richard A. Baer, "They Are Teaching Religion in Public Schools," *Christianity Today*, February 17, 1984, p. 15.

[15]Albert Ellis, "The Case Against Religiosity," from a section reprinted in "Testament of a Humanist," *Free Inquiry*, Spring 1987, p. 21.

[16]W.E.H. Lecky, *History of European Morals* (from Augustus to Charlemagne), two volumes (New York: George Braziller, 1955), vol. 2, pp. 8-9.

[17]W.R. Bird, *The Origin of Species Revisited*: *The Theories of Evolution and of Abrupt Appearance*, two volumes (Nashville, Thomas Nelson Publishers, 1991), vol. 2, p. 367.

[18]Ken Adelman, "Beyond Ideology," *The Washington Times*, December 25, 1989, p. D4.

[19]Cited in Charles Colson, *Kingdoms in Conflict* (Grand Rapids, MI: Zondervan, 1987), p. 225.

Chapter 3

[1]Paul Kurtz, "Is Everyone a Humanist," in *The Humanist Alternative*, ed. Paul Kurtz (Buffalo: Prometheus Books, 1973), p. 177.

[2]Bertrand Russell, "My Mental Development," in *The Basic Writings of Bertrand Russell*, ed. Robert E. Egner and Lester E. Denonn (New York: Simon and Schuster, 1961) p. 40.

[3]Russell, "Why I Am Not a Christian," in *Basic Writings of Bertrand Russell*, p. 586.

[4]Miriam Allen deFord, "Heretical Humanism," in *The Humanist Alternative*, p. 82.

[5]Corliss Lamont, *The Philosophy of Humanism* (New York: Frederick Ungar Publishing, 1982), p. 145.

[6]Ibid., p. 14.

[7]Ibid., p. 22.

[8]Ibid., p. 123.

[9]Ibid., p. 145.

[10]*Humanist Manifesto I* (Buffalo: Prometheus Books, 1980), p. 8.

[11]*Humanist Manifesto II* (Buffalo: Prometheus, 1980), p. 16.

[12]Isaac Asimov, " An Interview with Isaac Asimov," *Free Inquiry*, Spring 1982, vol 2, no. 2 p. 9.

[13]Paul Kurtz, " Is Everyone a Humanist?" *The Humanist Alternative*, p. 178.

[14]Paul Kurtz, "Marxism as a Religion," *The Fullness of Life* (New York: Horizon Press, 1974), pp.35-6.

[15]Ibid., pp. 35-6.

[16]Julian Huxley, *Religion Without Revelation* (New York: Mentor, 1957), p. 32.

[17]Norman Mailer, cited in Warren Allen Smith, "Authors and Humanism: A Classification of Humanism, and Statements," *The Humanist*, no. 5, 1951, p. 201.

[18]Harold H. Titus, "Humanistic Naturalism," *The Humanist*, no. 1, 1954, p. 33.

[19]Ibid., p. 30.

[20]John Dewey, *A Common Faith* (New Haven, CT: Yale University Press, 1934, renewed 1962), p. 84.

[21]Ibid., p. 31.

[22]Ibid.

[23]Ibid.

[24]Ibid.

[25]Chris Brockman, *What About Gods?* (Buffalo: Prometheus Books, 1978).

[26]Peter Angeles, ed., *Critiques of God* (Buffalo: Prometheus books, 1976), p. xiii.

[27]"A Secular Humanist Declaration," *Free Inquiry*, vol. 1, no. 1 (Winter 1980/81), p. 5.

[28]Ernest Nagel, "Philosophical Concepts of Atheism," in *Critiques of God* (Buffalo: Prometheus Books, 1976), p. 17.

Chapter 4

[1]V.I. Lenin, *Complete Collected Works*, forty-five volumes (Moscow: Progress Publishers, 1978), vol. 10, p. 83.

[2]See James D. Bales, *Communism: Its Faith and Fallacies* (Grand Rapids: Baker Book House, 1962), p. 37.

[3]Karl Marx and Frederick Engels, *On Religion* (New York: Schocken Books, 1974), p. 15.

[4]See Richard Wurmbrand, *My Answer to the Moscow Atheists* (New Rochelle, NY: Arlington House, 1975), p. 16.

[5]Marx and Engels, *Karl Marx-Frederick Engels: Collected Works*, 40 volumes (New York: International Publishers, 1976), vol. 3, p. 175.

[6]Ibid., vol. 3, p. 182.

[7]Marx, Theses on Feuerbach, in Marx, *On Historical Materialism* (New York: International Publishers, 1974), p. 13.

[8]Marx and Engels, *Collected Works*, vol. 3, p. 175.

[9]Ibid., vol. 3, p. 463.

[10]Lenin, *Collected Works*, vol. 15, p. 402.

[11]Ibid., p. 405.

[12]Ibid., vol. 10, p. 86.

[13]Ibid., vol. 35, p. 122.

[14]The Great Soviet Encyclopedia (Moscow: 1950), cited in Bales, *Communism: its Faith and Fallacies*, p. 37.

[15]Young Communist League's "Ten Commandments of Communism," cited in Bales, *Communism: its Faith and Fallacies*, p. 37.

[16]Nikita Khrushchev, speech, September 22, 1955, cited in Bales, *Communism: Its Faith and Fallacies*, pp. 165-6.

[17]*The Atheist's Handbook*, [Sputnik Ateista], (Moscow: 1959), reproduced in English by U.S. Joint Publications Research Service (Washington, D.C.), p. 117.

[18]Ibid., p. 69.

[19]Paul Kurtz, "Militant Atheism Versus Freedom of Conscience," *Free Inquiry*, Fall 1989, p. 28.

[20]Robert Conquest, *Harvest of Sorrow*, p. 209. Many of the facts concerning the closing of the churches are found in Conquest's chapter *"The Churches and the People."*

[21]Whittaker Chambers, *Witness* (New York: Random House, 1952), p. 712.

Chapter 5

[1]Kevin Ryerson, *Spirit Communication: The Soul's Path* (New York: Bantam Books, 1989), p. 106.

[2]David Spangler, *Reflections on the Christ* (Scotland: Findhorn Publications, 1982), p. 73.

[3]Science of Mind, October 1981, pp. 40-2, cited in Yungen, *For Many Shall Come in my Name, p.*

164.

[4]John White, "A Course in Miracles: Spiritual Wisdom for the New Age," *Science of Mind*, March 1986, p. 10.

[5]John Bradshaw, *Bradshaw on the Family* (Pompono Beach, Florida: Health Communications, 1988), p. 230.

[6]Ruth Montgomery, *A World Beyond* (New York: Ballantine/Fawcett Crest Books, 1972), p. 12.

[7]John White, ed., *What is Enlightenment?* (Los Angeles: J.P. Tarcher, 1984), p. 126.

[8]Meher Baba, cited in Allan Y. Cohen, "Meher Baba and the Quest of Consciousness," in *What is Enlightment?*, ed. White, p. 87.

[9]Cited in F. LaGard Smith, *Out On a Broken Limb* (Eugene, OR: Harvest House, 1986), p. 181.

[10]Cited in Francis Adeney, "Educators Look East," *Spiritual Counterfeits Journal*, Winter 1981, p. 29. SCP Journal is published by Spiritual Counterfeits Project, P.O. Box 4308, Berkeley, CA 94704.

[11]Cited in Benjamin B. Ferencz and Ken Keyes, Jr., *Planethood* (Coos Bay, OR: Vision Books, 1988), p. 92.

[12]Cited in Smith, *Out on a Broken Limb*, p. 12.

[13]Gary Zukav, *The Seat of the Soul* (New York: Simon and Schuster), p. 29.

[14]Mathew Fox, in an interview with Laura Hagar, "The Sounds of Silence," *New Age Journal*, March/April 1989, p. 55.

[15]Shakti Gawain *Living in the Light* (San Rafael, California: New World Library, 1986), p. 69.

[16]Etan Boritzer, *What is God* (Willowdale, Firefly Books Ltd., 1990), p. 26.

[17]Marilyn Ferguson,*The Aquarian Conspiracy* (Los Angeles: J.P. Tarcher, Inc., 1980), p. 383.

Chapter 6

[1]Roy Wood Sellars, "The Humanist Outlook," in *The Humanist Alternative*, ed. Paul Kurtz (Buffalo: Prometheus, 1973), p. 135.

[2]James Orr, *The Christian View of God and the World* (Edinburgh: Andrew Elliot, 1897), p. 111.

[3]Millard J. Erickson, *Christian Theology*, three volumes (Grand Rapids, MI: Baker Book House, 1983), vol 1, p. 153.

[4]Carl F.H. Henry, *God, Revelation and Authority*, six volumes (Waco, TX: Word Books, 1976ff), vol. 2, p.11.

[5]Ibid., p. 15.

[6]Charles Darwin, *Autobiography* (New York: Dover Publishing, 1958), p. 59.

[7]C.S. Lewis, *Broadcast Talks* (London: 1946), pp. 37-8.

Chapter 7

[1]Roy Wood Sellars, "The Humanist Outlook," in *The Humanist Alternative*, ed. Paul Kurtz (Buffalo: Prometeus, 1973), p. 135.

[2]*Humanist Manifesto II* (Buffalo: Prometheus, 1980), p. 16.

[3]Corliss Lamont, *The Philosophy of Humanism* (New York: Frederick Ungar,1982), p. 28.

[4]Sellars, "The Humanist Outlook," p. 133.

[5]Henry Miller, as cited in *The Best of Humanism*, ed. Greeley, p. 149.

[6]Corliss Lamont, as cited in *The Best of Humanism*, ed. Greeley, p. 149.

[7]Carl Sagan, *Cosmos* (New York: Random House, 1980), p. 4.

[8]Robert Green Ingersoll, as cited in *The Best of Humanism*, ed. Greeley, p. 162.

[9]Lamont, *The Philosophy of Humanism*, pp. 170-1.

[10]Roy Wood Sellars, *Evolutionary Naturalism*, (Chicago: Open Court, 1922), p. 5.

[11]*The Humanist Manifesto II*, p. 16.

[12]Carl Sagan, *UFO's-A Scientific Debate* (Ithaca, NY: Cornell University Press, 1972), p. xiv.

[13]Corliss Lamont, *The Illusion of Immortality* (New York: Frederick Ungar, 1965), pp. 124-5.

[14]Corliss Lamont, *Voice in the Wilderness* (Buffalo: Prometheus, 1975), p. 82.

[15]Lamont, *The Philosophy of Humanism*, pp. 82-3.

[16]Ibid., 82.

[17]Victor J. Stenger, *Not By Design* (Buffalo: Prometheus, 1988), pp. 188-9.

[18]Edwin Arthur Burtt, *Types of Religious Philosophy* (New York: Harper and Brothers, 1939), p. 353. Clearly, the Humanist has no patience with the Anthropic Principle, which contends that the world was tailored for man's existence. For an excellent defense of this principle, see Roy Abraham Varghese, ed., *The Intellectuals Speak Out About God* (Dallas, TX: Lewis and Stanley, 1984), pp. 102ff.

[19]Clarence Darrow, as cited in *The Best of Humanism*, ed. Greeley, p. 154.

Chapter 8

[1]Frederick Engels, Anti-Duhring, cited in V.I. Lenin, *The Teachings of Karl Marx* (New York: International Publishers, 1976), p. 14.

[2]Karl Marx, Letter to Engels, December 12, 1866, cited in Lenin, *The Teachings of Karl Marx*, p. 15.

[3]Engels, cited in Joseph Stalin, *Dialectical and Historical Materialism* (New York: International Publishers, 1977), p. 15.

[4]V.I. Lenin, *Materialism and Empirio-Criticism* (New York: International Publishers, 1927), p. 21.

[5]Ibid., p. 145.

[6]Lenin, *Materialism and Empirio-Criticism*, p. 252.

[7]Ibid., p. 81.

[8]Ibid., p. 102.

[9]Maurice Cornforth, *The Open Philosophy and the Open Society* (New York: International Publishers, 1968), p. 82.

[10]V.I. Lenin, *Collected Works* (Moscow: Progress Publishers, 1977), vol. 7, p. 409.

[11]Gustav A. Wetter, *Dialectical Materialism* (Westport, CT: Greenwood Press, 1977), p. 4.

[12]Frederick Engels, *Ludwig Feuerbach* (New York: International Publishers, 1974), p. 44.

[13]Engels, *Anti-Duhring*, p. 27.

[14]Frederick Engels, *Socialism: Utopian and Scientific* (New York: International, 1935), p. 48.

[15]Engels, *Dialectics of Nature*, p. 13.

[16]Jean L. McKechnie, et al., ed., *Webster's New Twentieth Century Dictionary of the English Language*, 2d ed., unabridged (usa: Collins & World, 1977), p. 1132.

[17]Fundamentals of Marxism-Leninism, p. 15. Cited in *A Lexicon of Marxist-Leninist Semantics*, ed. Sleeper, p. 168.

[18]Alexander Spirkin, *Dialectics and Materialism* (Moscow: Progress Publishers, 1983), p. 66.

[19]Engels, *Dialectics of Nature*, p. 337.

[20]Karl Marx, *Introduction to Capital* (London: 1889), vol.1.

[21]Lenin, *Materialism and Empirio-Criticism*, p. 66.

[22]Maurice Cornforth, *The Theory of Knowledge* (New York: International Publishers, 1963), p. 22.

[23]*The Fundamentals of Marxist-Leninist Philosophy*, chief ed. F.V. Konstantinov (Moscow: Progress Publishers, 1982), p. 78.

[24]Karl Marx, Theses on Feuerbach, in *Collected Works*, forty volumes (New York: International, 1976), vol. 5, p. 8.

Chapter 9

[1]Joseph Campbell, *The Power of Myth* (New York: Doubleday, 1988), p. 49.

[2]David Spangler, *Emergence: The Rebirth of the Sacred* (New York: Delta/Merloyd Lawrence, 1984), p. 12.

[3]Fritjof Capra, *The Turning Point* (Toronto: Bantam, 1982), pp. 77-8.

[4]Shakti Gawain, *Living in the Light* (San Rafael, California: New World Library, 1986), p. 69.

[5] Joseph Campbell, *The Power of Myth*, p. 6.

[6]Jack Underhill, "My Goal in Life," *Life Times Magazine*, Winter 1986/1987, p. 90.

[7]Dean C. Halverson, *Crystal Clear: Understanding and Reaching New Agers* (Colorado Springs, CO: NavPress, 1990), p. 91.

[8]Robert Mueller, *The New Genesis: Shaping a Global Spirituality* (New York: Image Books, 1984), p. 189.

[9]Spangler, *Emergence: The Rebirth of the Sacred*, p. 83.

[10]Gary Zukav, *The Seat of the Soul* (New York: Simon and Schuster), pp. 85-6.

[11]Marilyn Ferguson, *The Aquarian Conspiracy* (Los Angeles: J.P. Tarcher, Inc., 1980), p. 383.

[12]Marianne Williamson, *A Return to Love: Reflections on the Principles of "A Course in Miracles"* (New York: Harper Collins, 1992), p. 22.

Chapter 10

[1]*Select Writings of Francis Bacon*, ed. Hugh G. Dick (New York: Random House, 1955), p. 44.

[2]C.E.M. Joad, *The Recovery of Belief* (London: Faber and Faber Limited, 1955), p. 16.

[3]Ibid., p. 22.

[4]Carl F.H. Henry, *God, Revelation and Authority*, six volumes (Waco, TX: Word Books, 1976), vol. 1, p. 169. Henry mentions W.J. Neidhardt's work *"Faith, the Unrecognized Partner of Science and Religion"*: as the source for his comments.

[5]Edward T. Ramsdell, *The Christian Perspective* (New York: Abingdon-Cokesbury Press, 1950), p. 42.

[6]Warren C. Young, *A Christian Approach to Philosophy* (Grand Rapids, MI: Baker, [1954] 1975), p. 37.

[7]Young, *A Christian Approach to Philosophy*, p. 182.

[8]Joad, *The Recovery of Belief*, p. 107.

[9]*An Anthology of C.S. Lewis*, ed. Clyde S. Kilby (New York and London: Harcourt, Brace & World, 1968), p. 240.

[10]Francis A. Schaeffer, *How Should We Then Live?* (Old Tappan, JN: Fleming H. Revell, 1976), p. 134.

[11]Ibid., p. 134.

[12]Stanley L. Jaki, *The Road of Science* (South Bend, IN: Regnery Gateway, 1979).

[13]*A Mind Awake*, ed. Kilby, p. 234.

[14] Henry, *God, Revelation and Authority*, vol. 5, p. 336.

[15]Young, *A Christian Approach to Philosophy*, p. 37.

[16]Ibid., p. 120.

[17]James Oliver Buswell, Jr. *A Christian View of Being and Knowing* (Grand Rapids, MI: Zondervan, 1960), p. 8.

[18]Ibid., p. 142.

[19]*A Mind Awake*, ed. Kilby, p. 205.

[20]D. Elton *Trueblood, Philosophy of Religion* (Grand Rapids, MI: Baker Book House, 1957), p. 206.

[21]Young, *A Christian Approach to Philosophy*, pp. 228-9.

Chapter 11

[1]Max Hocutt, "Toward an Ethic of Mutual Accommodation," in *Humanist Ethics*, ed. Morris B. Storer (Buffalo: Prometheus Books, 1980), p. 137.

[2]Paul Kurtz, ed., *The Humanist Alternative* (Buffalo: Prometheus, 1973), p. 50.

[3]Kurtz, ed., *The Humanist Alternative*, p. 179.

[4]Paul Kurtz, ed. , *Humanist Manifestoes I & II* (Buffalo: Prometheus, 1980), p. 3.

[5]Storer, "Preface," *Humanist Ethics*, ed. Storer, p. 3.

[6]Paul Kurtz, "Does Humanism Have an Ethic of Responsibility?" in *Humanist Ethics*, ed. Storer, p. 13.

[7]Ibid., p. 22.

[8]Mihailo Markovic, "Comment by Max Hocutt on Hannay Article," in *Humanist Ethics*, ed. Storer, p. 33.

[9]Ibid., p. 35.

[10]Max Hocutt, "Comment by Max Hocutt on Hannay Article," in *Humanist Ethics*, ed. Storer, p. 191.

[11]Hocutt, "Toward an Ethic of Mutual Accommodation," p. 137.

[12]Annual General Meeting of the British Humanist Association, July 1967.

[13]Lamont, *The Philosophy of Humanism*, p. 253.

[14]Cited in Bolton Davidheiser, *Evolution and Christian Faith* (Philadelphia, PA: Presbyterian and Reformed, 1969), p. 352.

[15]Mason Olds, "Ethics and Literature," *The Humanist*, Sept./Oct. 1985, p. 36.

[16]Arthur E. Gravatt, cited in William H. Genne, "Our Moral Responsibility," *Journal of the American College Health Association*, vol. 15 (May 1967), p. 63.

[17]Joseph Fletcher, "Humanist Ethics: the Groundwork," in *Humanit Ethics*, ed. Storer, p. 255.

[18]Herbert W. Schneider, "Humanist Ethics," in *Humanist Ethics*, ed. Storer, pp. 99-100.

[19]Kurtz, ed., *The Humanist Alternative*, p. 55.

[20]Paul Kurtz, "Does Humanism Have an Ethic of Responsibility?" in *Humanist Ethics*, ed. Storer, p. 15.

[21]Kurt Baier, "Comment by Kurt Baier on Schneider Article," in *Humanist Ethics*, ed. Storer, p. 81.

[22]Lamont, *The Philosophy of Humanism*, p. 248

[23]Lena Levine, "Psycho-sexual Devlopment," *Planned Parenthood News*, Summer 1953, p. 10.

[24]Corliss Lamont, *Voice in the Wilderness* (Buffalo NY: Prometheus Books, 1974), p. 97.

Chapter 12

[1]V.I. Lenin, *Collected Works*, forty-five volumes (Moscow: Progress Publishers, 1982), vol.31, p. 291.

[2]Ibid.

[3]Karl Marx and Frederick Engels, *Collected Works*, forty volumes (New York: International, 1977), vol. 6, p. 503.

[4]Lenin, *Collected Works*, vol. 31, p. 291.

[5]G.L. Andreyev, *What Kind of Morality Does Religion Teach?* (Moscow:1959), cited in *A Lexicon of Marxist-Leninist Semantics*, ed. Raymond S. Sleeper (Alexandria, VA: Western Goals, 1983), p. 174.

[6]Nikita Khrushchev, "The Great Strength of Soviet Literature and Art," *Soviet Booklet no. 108*, March 1963 (London: Farleigh Press Ltd., 1963), p. 30. Cited in Bales, *Communism and the Reality of Moral Law*, p. 5.

[7]Marx and Engels, *Collected Works*, vol. 6, p. 494.

[8]Lenin, *Collected Works*, vol. 31, p. 293.

[9]*Scientific Communism: A Glossary*, (Moscow: 1975), pp. 131-2, cited in *A Lexicon of Marxist-Leninist Semantics*, ed. Sleeper, p. 106.

[10]Selsam, *Socialism and Ethics*, p. 98.

[11]S.O. Pidhainy, ed., *The Black Deeds of the Kremlin* (Toronto: The Basilian Press,1953), p. 14. Robert Conquest in *The Harvest of Sorrow*, p. 305, places the figure at 14.5 million.

[12]Lenin, *Collected Works*, vol. 36, pp. 255,265.

[13]Andreyev, What Kind of Morality Does Religion Teach?, cited in *A Lexicon of Marxist-Leninist Semantics*, ed. Sleeper, p. 175.

[14]Marx and Engels, *Collected Works*, vol. 6, p. 519.

[15]Nikita Khrushchev, Ukrainian Bulletin, August 1-August 15, 1960, p. 12 Cited in Bales, *Communism and the Reality of Moral Law*, p. 121.

[16]Lenin, *Collected Works*, vol. 28, p. 72.

[17]Joseph Stalin, speech delivered April 24, 1924 (New York: International Publishers, 1934).

[18]Robert Conquest, *The Harvest of Sorrow: Soviet Collectivization and the Terror-Famine* (New York: Oxford University Press,1986) p. 117.

Chapter 13

[1]Shirley MacLaine, quoted by F. LaGard Smith in *Out On a Broken Limb*, (Eugene, Oregon:Harvest House, 1986), p. 33.

[2]Cited in William Goldstein, "Life on the Astral Plane," *Publishers Weekly*, March 18, 1983, p. 46.

[3]Marilyn Ferguson, *The Aquarian Conspiracy* (Los Angeles: J.P. Tarcher, Inc., 1980), p. 327.

[4]Vera Alder, *When Humanity Comes of Age* (New York: Samuel Weiser, Inc., 1974), pp. 48-9.

[5]Shakti Gawain, *Living in the Light* (San Rafael, California: New World Library, 1986), p. 128.

[6]Marilyn Ferguson, *The Aquarian Conspiracy*, p. 331.

[7]Ibid., p. 192.

[8]Marianne Williamson, *A Return to Love: Reflections on the Principles of "A Course in Miracles"*, (New York: Harper Collins, 1992), p. 22.

[9]Randall N. Baer, *Inside the New Age Nightmare* (Lafayette, LA: Huntington House, Inc., 1989), p. 88.

[10]Gawain, *Living in the Light*, p. 60.

[11]Shirley MacLaine, *Out On a Limb* (Toronto: Bantam, 1984), pp. 96, 111.

[12]Ferguson, *The Aquarian Conspiracy*, p. 381.

[13]David Spangler, *Reflections of the Christ*, (Scotland: Findhorn, 1977), pp. 40-44.

[14]Kevin Ryerson, *Spirit Communication: The Soul's Path*, (New York: Bantam Books, 1989), p. 84.

Chapter 14

[1]John Warwick Montgomery, *Human Rights and Human Dignity* (Dallas, TX: Probe Books, 1986), p. 113.

[2]C.S. Lewis, *The Abolition of Man* (New York: Macmillan, 1973), p. 56-7.

[3]Calvin D. Linton, "Sin," in *Baker's Dictionary of Christian Ethics*, ed. Carl F.H. Henry (Grand Rapids, MI: Baker, 1973), p. 620.

[4]Francis A. Schaeffer, *How Should We Then Live?* (Old Tappan, NJ: Fleming H. Revell, 1976), p. 145.

[5]Lewis, *The Abolition of Man*, p. 78.

[6]W.E.H. Lecky, *History of European Morals (from Augustus to Charlemagne)*, two volumes (New York: George Braziller, 1955), vol. 2, pp. 8-9.

[7]Norman L. Geisler, *Ethics: Alternatives and Issues* (Grand Rapids, MI: Zondervan, 1979), p. 156.

[8]Carl F.H. Henry, *Christian Personal Ethics* (Grand Rapids, MI: Eerdmans, 1957), pp. 221-2.

[9]Geisler, Ethics: *Alternatives and Issues*, p. 179.

[10]William Young, "Moral Philosophy," in *Baker's Dictionary of Christian Ethics*, ed. Henry, pp. 432-3.

[11]Henry, *Christian Personal Ethics*, p. 209.

[12]Ibid., p. 172.

[13]D. James Kennedy, *Why I Believe* (Waco, TX: Word Books, 1980, p. 91.

[14]Ibid., p. 90.

[15]C.S. Lewis, *God in the Dock* (Grand Rapids, MI: Eerdmans, 1972), p. 286.

[16]Joan Winmill Brown, ed., *The Martyred Christian* (New York: Macmillan, 1985), p. 157.

Chapter 15

[1]George Gaylord Simpson, *The Meaning of Evolution* (New Haven: Yale University Press, 1971), p. 345.

[2]*Humanist Manifesto I* (Buffalo: Prometheus Books, [1933] 1980), p. 8.

[3]*Humanist Manifesto II* (Buffalo: Prometheus Books, [1973] 19800, p. 17.

[4]Julian Huxley, Evolution: *The Modern Synthesis* (New York: Harper and Brothers Publishers, 1942), p. 457.

[5]Isaac Asimov, in *Science and Creationism*, ed. Ashley Montagu (Oxford: Oxford University Press, 1984), p. 183.

[6]Carl Sagan, *Cosmos* (New York: Random House, 1980), p. 27.

[7]Julian Huxley, "At Random", a television preview on Nov. 21, 1959. Also, Sol Tax, *Evolution of Life* (Chicago: University of Chicago Press, 1960), p. 1.

[8]Antony Flew, "Scientific Humanism," *The Humanist Alternative*, ed. Kurtz, p. 110.

[9]Darwin, *The Origin of the Species*, cited in Sagan, *Cosmos*, p. 23.

[10]Carl Sagan, *The Dragons of Eden* (New York: Random House, 1977), p. 6.

[11]Charles Darwin, *The Origin of the Species* (London: John Murray, 1859), p. 84.

[12]Corliss Lamont, *The Philosophy of Humanism*, rev. ed. (New York: Frederick Ungar, [1949] 1982), p. 120.

[13]Isaac Asimov, *The Wellsprings of Life* (London: Abelard-Schuman, 1960), p. 57.

[14]Charles Darwin, as cited in Norman Macbeth, *Darwin Retried,* (Boston: Gambit, 1971), p. 73.

[15]Julian Huxley, *Essays of a Humanist* (New York: Harper & Row, 1964), p. 67.

[16]Sagan, *The Dragons of Eden*, p. 6.

[17]Julian Huxley, *Man in the Modern World*, (New York: Mentor, 1944), p. 168.

[18]Chris McGowan, *In the Beginning. . .* (Buffalo: Prometheus Books, 1984), p. 29.

[19]Darwin, *Origin of Species*, p. 189, cited in Macbeth, Darwin Retried, p. 76.

[20]Julian Huxley, "At Random," a television preview on Nov. 21, 1959.

Chapter 16

[1]Karl Marx and Frederick Engels, in a letter to Lassalle dated Jan. 16, 1861, *Selected Correspondence* (New York: International Publishers, 1942), p. 125.

[2]Karl Marx, cited in Charles J. McFadden, *The Philosophy of Communism* (Kenosha, WI: Cross, 1939), pp. 35-6.

[3]John Hoffman, *Marxism and the Theory of Praxis* (New York: International Publishers, 1976), p. 69.

[4]Karl Marx, *Capital* (Lawrence and Wishart, 1970), vol. 1, p. 341.

[5]Frederick Engels, *Selected Works* (1950), vol. 2, p. 153, cited in R.N. Carew Hunt, *The Theory and Practice of Communism* (Baltimore: Penguin Books, 1966), p. 64.

[6]V.I. Lenin, *Collected Works*, forty-five volumes (Moscow: Progress Publishers, 1977), vol. 1, p. 142.

[7]Marx, *Selected Correspondence*, p. 125.

[8]F.V. Konstantinov, ed., *The Fundamentals of Marxist-Leninist Philosophy* (Moscow: Progress Publishers, 1982), p. 42.

[9]Karl Marx, Economic and Philosophical Manuscripts, cited in Francis Nigel Lee, *Communism Versus Creation* (Nutley, NJ: The Craig Press, 1969), p. 68.

[10]M.V. Volkenshtein, *Biophysics* (Moscow: Mir Publishers, 1983), p. 565.

[11]A.I. Oparin, *The Origin of Life* (Moscow: Foreign Languages Publishing House, 1955), p. 101.

[12]Karen Arms and Pamela S. Camp, *Biology*, 2d ed. (New York: CBS College Publishers, 1982), p. 293. Arms and Camp then turn to Oparin and Haldane for confirmation of spontaneous generation: "In 1924 a Russian, Alexander Oparin, published a theory of how life could have arisen from simple molecules on the early earth. An Englishman, J.B.S. Haldane, published a paper in 1929 that said essentially the same thing. . . . Research since then has largely borne out the predictions made by Oparin and Haldane. Scientists have simulated prebiotic (before life existed) conditions in their laboratories; surprisingly, the nonliving systems formed in these artificial environments exhibit many properties that we consider characteristic of life" (p. 294). Haldane, wrote the preface and notes for Engels' Dialectics of Nature, 1940 edition. See Frederick Engels, *Dialectics of Nature* (New York: International Publishers, 1976).

[13]Frederick Engels, *Dialectics of Nature* (New York: International, 1976), p. 189.

[14]Karl Marx, Gesamtausgabe, sect. 2, vol. 3, p. 396, cited in McFadden, *The Philosophy of*

Communism, p. 36.

[15]Engels, *Dialectics of Nature*, p. 13.

[16]Frederick Engels, *Ludwig Feuerbach* (New York: International, 1974), p. 54.

[17]Lenin, *Collected Works*, vol. 24, pp. 54-5.

[18]G. Plekhanov, *Fundamental Problems of Marxism* (London: Lawrence, 1929), p. 145.

[19]Michael Denton, *Evolution: A Theory in Crisis* (Bethesda, MD: Adler and Adler, 1985), pp. 192-3.

[20]Niles Eldredge and Stephen J. Gould, *Paleobiology*, vol. 3 (Spring 1977), pp. 145-6, cited in Sunderland, *Darwin's Enigma*, p. 108.

[21]Volkenshtein, *Biophysics*, p. 617.

[22]Ibid., p. 618.

[23]T.D. Lysenko, Iarovizatsiia (1939), No. 1, cited in David Joravsky, *The Lysenko Affair* (Cambridge, MA: Harvard University Press, 1970), p. 211.

[24]T.D. Lysenko, *Agrobiologia* (1949), p. 486, cited in Joravsky, *The Lysenko Affair*, p. 210.

[25]Frederick Engels, *Socialism: Utopian and Scientific* (New York: International, 1935), p. 21.

Chapter 17

[1]Pierre Teilhard de Chardin, *The Phenomenon of Man* (New York, Harper and Row, 1955), pp. 219, 221.

[2]Dean C. Halverson,*Crystal Clear: Understanding and Reaching New Agers* (Colorado Springs, CO: NavPress, 1990), p. 77.

[3]Marilyn Ferguson, *The Aquarian Conspiracy* (Los Angeles: J.P. Tarcher, Inc., 1980, p. 70.

[4]David Spangler, *Emergence: The Rebirth of the Sacred* (New York: Delta/Merloyd Lawrence, 1984), p. 18.

[5]Ferguson, *The Aquarian Conspiracy*, p. 70.

[6]Randall N. Baer, *Inside the New Age Nightmare* (Lafayette, LA: Huntington House, Inc., 1989), p. 47.

[7]Armand Biteaux, *The New Consciousness* (Oliver Press, 1975), p. 128.

[8]John White, "The Second Coming," *New Frontier Magazine*, (December 1987), p. 45.

[9]Pierre Teilhard de Chardin, *The Phenomenon of Man* (New York, Harper and Row, 1955), p. 310.

[10]Peter Russell, *The Global Brain* (Los Angeles: J.P. Tarcher, 1983), p. 99.

[11]Joseph Campbell, *The Power of Myth* (New York, Doubleday, 1988), p. 230.

Chapter 18

[1]Australian Broadcasting Co., June 10, 1976. Cited in Morris, *The Long War Against God* (Grand Rapids, MI: Baker, 1990), p. 58.

[2]Stanley L. Jaki, *The Road of Science and the Ways to God* (Chicago: The University of Chicago

Press, 1980), p. 11.

[3]Langdon Gilkey, *Maker of Heaven and Earth* (Garden City, NY: Doubleday, 1959), p. 110.

[4]Michael Denton, *Evolution: A Theory in Crisis* (Bethesda, MD: Adler and Adler, 1986), p. 340.

[5]Paul Davies, *Superforce* (New York: Simon and Schuster, 1984), p. 223.

[6]Denton, *Evolution: A Theory in Crisis*, p. 250.

[7]Charles Thaxton, "In Pursuit of Intelligent Causes: Some Historical Background," an unpublished essay presented at an Interdisciplinary Conference in Tacoma, Washington, June 23-26, 1988, p. 13.

[8]Walter T. Brown, Jr., *In the Beginning* (Phoenix: Center for Scientific Creation, 1986), p. 6.

[9]Ibid.

[10]Ibid., p. 5.

[11]A.E. Wilder-Smith, *Man's Origin, Man's Destiny*, (Wheaton, IL: Harold Shaw, 1968), p. 55.

[12]Ibid., pp. 57-8.

[13]Brown, *In the Beginning*, p. 9.

[14]Wilder-Smith, *Man's Origin, Man's Destiny*, p. 72.

[15]Pierre Paul Grasse, *Evolution of Living Organisms: Evidence for a New Theory of Transformation* (New York: Academic Press, 1977), p. 87.

[16]Edward S. Deevey, Jr., "The Reply: Letter from Birnham Wood," *Yale Review* vol. 61, p. 636.

[17]Charles Darwin, *The Origin of Species*, reprint of sixth edition (London: John Murray, 1902), pp. 341-2.

[18]Brown, *In the Beginning*, p. 3.

[19]David Raup, "Conflicts Between Darwin and Paleontology," *Field Museum of Natural History Bulletin* , January 1979, p. 25.

[20]Brown, *In the Beginning*, p. 3.

[21]Ibid.

[22]Charles Darwin, *The Origin of Species* (London: John Murray, facsimile printed by Harvard University Press, 1966), p. 189.

[23]N. Barlow, *Autobiography of Charles Darwin* (London: Collins, 1958), pp. 235-7.

Chapter 19

[1]Carl Rogers, "Notes on Rollo May," *Journal of Humanistic Psychology*, Summer 1982, p. 8.

[2]Abraham Maslow, in *Humanistic Psychology*, ed. Welch, Tate, and Richards, p. 11.

[3]Rogers, "Notes on Rollo May," p. 8.

[4]Paul Kurtz, et al., "Credo," *The Humanist*, July/Aug. 1968, p.18.

[5]Erich Fromm, *You Shall Be as Gods* (New York: Holt, Rinehart and Winston, 1966), p. 7.

[6]Wendell W. Watters, "Christianity and Mental Health," *The Humanist*, Nov./Dec. 1987, p. 32.

[7]Ibid., p. 10.

[8]Maslow, in *Humanistic Psychology*, ed. Welch, Tate, and Richards, p. 189.

[9]Rogers, "Notes on Rollo May," p. 8.

[10]Rollo May, "The Problem of Evil: An Open Letter to Carl Rogers," *Journal of Humanistic Psychology*, Summer 1982, p. 12.

[11]Harold P. Marley, "First Know the Self," *The Humanist*, Nov./Dec. 1954, p. 258.

[12]Abraham Maslow, *Toward a Psychology of Being* (New York: Van Nostrand Reinhold, 1968), p. 149.

[13]Rogers, in *Humanistic Psychology*, ed. Welch, Tate, and Richards, p. 223.

[14]Abraham Maslow, *Motivation and Personality* (New York: Harper and Row, 1987, pp. 127-8.

[15]Maslow, *Toward a Psychology of Being*, p. vi.

[16]Maslow, *Motivation and Personality*, pp. 140-1.

[17]Ellis G. Olim, in *Humanistic Psychology*, ed. Welch, Tate, and Richards, p. 219.

[18]Erich Fromm, *Man for Himself* (New York: Holt, Rinehart and Winston, 1964), p. 17.

[19]Mildred Hardeman, "A Dialogue with Abraham Maslow," *Journal of Humanistic Psychology*, Winter 1979, p. 25.

[20]Maslow, *Toward a Psychology of Being*, p. 169.

[21]Rollo May, *Psychology and the Human Dilemma* (Princeton: D. Van Nostrand Company, 1967), p. 188.

[22]Arthur Koestler and J.R. Smythies, ed., *Beyond Reductionism* (New York: Macmillan, 1970), p. 252.

[23]Rogers, in *Humanistic Psychology*, ed. Welch, Tate, and Richards, p. 45.

Chapter 20

[1]Ivan P. Pavlov, *Lectures on Conditioned Reflexes* (New York: International Publishers, 1963), p. 41.

[2]B.F. Skinner, *Beyond Freedom and Dignity* (New York: Bantam Books, 1972), p. 96.

[3]Ibid., p. 16.

[4]B.F. Skinner, *Science and Human Behavior* (New York: Macmillan, 1953), p. 447.

[5]Pavlov, *Lectures on Conditioned Reflexes*, p. 42.

[6]Ibid., p. 391.

[7]Ivan Pavlov, in a statement to his assistants on Feb. 21, 1936, according to W.H. Gantt in the *Introduction to Conditional Reflexes and Psychiatry* (New York: International Publishers, 1963), p. 34.

[8]Joseph Nahem, *Psychology and Psychiatry Today*: A Marxist View (New York: International Publishers, 1981), p. 13.

[9]Ibid., p. 48.

[10]Karl Marx, "The Third Thesis on Feuerbach," *Gesamtausgabe* (Frankfurt, 1927-1932), sec. 1, vol. 5, p. 534.

[11]Nahem, *Psychology and Psychiatry Today: A Marxist View*, p. 9, citing Pavlov's Selected Works (Moscow: Foreign Languages Publishing House, 1955), p. 537.

[12]Ivan Pavlov, *Selected Works* (Moscow: Foreign Languages Publishing House, 1955), p. 537.

[13]Nahem, *Psychology and Psychiatry Today: A Marxist View*, p. 45, citing Marx's Theses on Feuerbach, p. 84.

[14]L.P. Bueva, *Man: His Behaviour and Social Relations* (Moscow: Progress Publishers, 1979), p. 28.

[15]Ibid., p. 179.

[16]Karl Marx, "The Eighteenth Brumaire of Louis Bonaparte," *Collected Works* (New York: International Publishers,1979), vol. 11, p. 103.

[17]Nahem, *Psychology and Psychiatry Today*: A Marxist View, p. 46.

Chapter 21

[1]Ken Carey, in a speech at Whole Life Expo, (Los Angeles), Feb. 1987.

[2]John White, *Frontiers of Consciousness* (New York: Julian Press, 1985), p. 7.

[3]Marilyn Ferguson, *The Aquarian Conspiracy* (Los Angeles: J.P. Tarcher,1980), p. 248.

[4]Shakti Gawain, *Living in the Light* (San Rafael, California: New World Library, 1986), p. 156.

[5]Vera Alder, *When Humanity Comes of Age* (New York: Samuel Weiser, Inc., 1974), p. 82.

[6]Ferguson, *The Aquarian Conspiracy*, p. 257.

[7]Shirley MacLaine, *Out on a Limb* (Toronto: Bantam, 1984), pp. 96.

[8]"The Joys and Frustrations of Being a Healer," *Life Times Magazine*, vol. 1, no. 3, p. 61.

[9]Kathleen Vande Kieft, *Innersource: Channeling Your Unlimited Self*, (New York: Ballantine Books, 1988), p. 114.

[10]John Randolph Price, *The Superbeings*, (Austin, Texas: Quartus Books,1981), pp. 51-2.

[11]Etan Boritzer,*What is God?* (Ontario: Firefly Books Ltd., 1990), p. 30.

[12]Marianne Williamson, *A Return to Love: Reflections on the Principles of "A Course in Miracles"*, (New York: Harpers Collins, 1989), p. 208.

[13]Ibid., p. 209.

Chapter 22

[1]William Kirk Kilpatrick, *Psychological Seduction* (Nashville: Thomas Nelson, 1983), p. 14.

[2]Kilpatrick, *Psychological Seduction*, pp. 15-16.

[3]Charles L. Allen, *God's Psychiatry* (Westwood, NJ: Revell, 1953), p. 7, emphasis added.

[4]Paul Weiss, in *Beyond Reductionism*, eds. Koestler and Smythies, pp. 251-2.

[5]Wilder Penfield, *The Mystery of the Mind* (Princeton, NJ: Princeton University Press, 1975) is a valuable resource.

[6]Francis Schaeffer, True Spirituality, in *The Complete Works of Francis Schaeffer*, five volumes (Westchester, IL: Crossway Books, 1982), vol. 3, p. 329.

[7]Paul Vitz, *Psychology as Religion* (Grand Rapids MI,: Eerdmans, 1985), p. 43.

[8]Schaeffer, *True Spirituality*, p. 322.

[9]Ibid.

[10]Jay E. Adams, *Competent to Counsel* (Grand Rapids, MI: Baker Book House, 1970), p. 28.

[11]Ibid., p. 29.

[12]Karl Menninger, *Whatever Became of Sin?* (New York: Hawthorn Books, 1974), p. 48.

[13]Adams, *Competent to Counsel*, pp. 32-33.

[14]Lawrence Crabb, Jr., *Basic Principles of Biblical Counseling* (Grand Rapids, MI: Zondervan, 1975), p. 102.

[15]Vitz, *Psychology as Religion*, p. 103.

[16]Kilpatrick, *Psychological Seduction*, p. 181.

[17]Menninger, *Whatever Became of Sin?* p. 95.

[18]Schaeffer, *True Spirituality*, p. 334.

[19]Kilpatrick, *Psychological Seduction*, p. 233.

Chapter 23

[1]Robert Tannenbaum and Sheldon A. Davis, "Values, Man and Organizations," in *Humanistic Society*, eds. John F. Glass and John R. Staude (Pacific Pallisades, CA: Goodyear Publishing, 1972), p. 352.

[2]Read Bain, "Scientific Humanism," *The Humanist*, May 1954, p. 116.

[3]Patricia Hill Collins, "Perspectivity and the Activist Potential of the Sociology Classroom," *Humanity and Society*, August 1986, p. 341.

[4]Cited in Mark Schoofs, "International Forum Debates Treatment of Homosexuality," *Washington Blade*, December 18, 1987, p. 19.

[5]Erich Fromm, *Escape from Freedom* (New York: Holt, Rinehart, and Winston, 1969), p. 12.

[6]Erich Fromm, *The Sane Society* (New York: Holt, Rinehart and Winston, 1955), p. 362.

[7]Walda Katz Fishman and C.George Benello, *Readings in Humanist Sociology* (Bayside, NY: General Hall, 1986), p. 3.

[8]Robert Rimmer, "An Interview with Robert Rimmer on Premarital Communes and Group Marriages," *The Humanist*, March/ April 1974, p. 14.

[9]Sol Gordon, "The Egalitarian Family is Alive and Well," *The Humanist*, May/June 1975, p. 18.

[10]Paul Kurtz, "Fulfilling Feminist Ideals: A New Agenda," *Free Inquiry*, Fall 1990, p. 21.

[11]Ibid.

[12]Lawrence Casler, "Permissive Matrimony: Proposals for the Future," *The Humanist*, March/April 1974, p. 6.

[13]Ibid., p. 7.

[14]Collins, "Perspectivity and the Activist Potential of the Sociology Classroom," p. 341.

[15]John J. Dunphy, "A Religion for a New Age," *The Humanist*, January/February 1983, p. 26.

[16]*Humanist Manifesto II* (Buffalo: Prometheus Books, 1980), p. 19.

[17]Fromm, *The Sane Society*, p. 20.

[18]Maurice R. Stein, "On the Limits of Professional Thought," in *Humanistic Society*, eds. Glass and Staude, p. 165.

[19]John F. Glass and John R. Staude, "Individual and Social Change," in *Humanist Society*, eds. Glass and Staude, pp. 271-2.

[20]Erich Fromm, *Beyond the Chains of Illusion* (New York: Simon and Schuster, 1962), cited in Ross Ellenhorn, "Toward a Humanistic Social Work: Social Work for Conviviality," *Humanity and Society*, May 1988, p. 166.

[21]Fromm, *The Sane Society*, p. 277.

[22]Curtis W. Reese, "The Social Implications of Humanism," *The Humanist*, July/August 1961, p. 198.

Chapter 24

[1]Karl Marx and Frederick Engels, *Collected Works*, forty volumes (New York: International, 1976), vol. 6, p. 502.

[2]Frederick Engels, *The Origin of the Family*, Private Property and the State (New York: International, 1942), p. 67.

[3]Karl Marx and Frederick Engels, *The Individual and Society* (Moscow: Progress, 1984), p. 193.

[4]Ibid., p. 194.

[5]Karl Marx and Frederick Engels, *The Individual Society* (Moscow: Progress, 1984), p. 162.

[6]Joseph Stalin, *Problems of Leninism* (Moscow: 1947), p. 579. Cited in Wetter, Dialectical Materialism, p. 217.

[7]V.I. Lenin, *The State and Revolution* (New York: International, 1932), p. 73.

[8]Fundamentals of Marxism-Leninism (Moscow: 1959), p. 310, cited in *A Lexicon of Marxist-Leninist Semantics*, ed. Raymond S. Sleeper (Alexandria, VA: Western Goals, 1983), p. 36.

[9]Madan Sarup, *Education, State and Crisis* (London: Routledge and Kegan Paul, 1982), p. 91.

[10]People's Education (Moscow), April 1949, cited in *A Lexicon of Marxist-Leninist Semantics*, ed. Sleeper, p. 101.

[11]Aleksandra M. Kollontai, *Communism and the Family* (New York: 1920), p. 10. Cited in H. Kent Geiger, *The Family in Soviet Russia* (Cambridge: Harvard University Press, 1970), p. 51.

[12]Engels, *The Origin of the Family*, Private Property and the State, p. 67.

[13]V. Yazykova, *Socialist Life Style and the Family* (Moscow: Progress, 1984), p. 7.

Chapter 25

[1]Gary Zukav, *The Seat of the Soul*, (New York, Simon and Schuster Inc. 1989), p. 162.

[2]Marilyn Ferguson, *The Aquarian Conspiracy* (Los Angeles: J.P. Tarcher, Inc., 1980), p. 104.

[3]David Spangler, *Emergence: The Rebirth of the Sacred* (New York: Delta/Merloyd Lawrence, 1984), p. 82.

[4]Vera Alder, *When Humanity Comes of Age* (New York: Samuel Weiser, 1974), pp.83-4.

[5]Shakti Gawain, *Living in the Light* (San Rafael, California: New World Library, 1986), p. 110.

[6]Ibid., p. 3.

[7]Kevin Ryerson, *Spirit Communication: The Soul's Path* (New York: Bantam Books, 1989), p. 172.

[8]Ferguson, *The Aquarian Conspiracy*, p. 280.

[9]John Dunphy, "A Religion for the New Age," *The Humanist*, January/February 1983, p. 26.

[10]Zukav, *The Seat of the Soul*, p. 164.

Chapter 26

[1]William A. Stanmeyer, *Clear and Present Danger* (Ann Arbor, MI: Servant Books, 1983), p. 161.

[2]Rousas John Rushdoony, *Politics of Guilt and Pity* (Fairfax, VA: Thoburn Press, 1978), p. 1.

[3]Francis A. Schaeffer, *Death in the City* (Downers Grove, IL: Intervarsity Press, 1976), p. 21.

[4]C.S. Lewis, *God in the Dock* (Grand Rapids, MI: Eerdmans, 1972), pp. 109-110.

[5]S.D. Gaede, *Where Gods May Dwell* (Grand Rapids, MI: Zondervan, 1985), pp. 75-6.

[6]Rockne McCarthy, Donald Oppewal, Walfred Peterson, and Gordon Spykman, *Society, State, and Schools* (Grand Rapids, MI: Eerdmans, 1982), p. 151.

[7]Dietrich Bonhoeffer, *Ethics* (New York: Macmillan 1959), p. 207.

[8]Ibid.

[9]Dobson and Bauer, *Children at Risk*, p. 112.

[10]Ibid., p. 55. For an in-depth look at what is transpiring in such classroom instruction we recommend Dobson and Bauer's book, Phyllis Schlafly's *Child Abuse in the Classroom* (Alton, IL: Marquette Press, 1985), and Judith A. Reisman and Edward W Eichel's *Kinsey, Sex and Fraud* (Lafayette, LA: Huntington House, 1990).

[11]Francis A. Schaeffer, *The Church at the End of the 20th Century* (Downers Grove, IL: InterVarsity Press, 1974), p. 73.

Chapter 27

[1]Frederick Edwords, "The Human Basis of Laws and Ethics," *The Humanist*, May/June 1985, p. 12.

[2] Julian Huxley, "Evolution and Genetics," in *What is Science?* ed. J.R. Newman (New York: Simon and Schuster, 1955), pp. 278

[3]Paul Kurtz, "Humanism and the Moral Revolution," in *The Humanist Alternative*, ed. Kurtz, p. 50.

[4]Edwords, "The Human Basis of Laws and Ethics," p. 11.

[5]V.M. Tarkunde, "Towards a Fuller Consensus in Humanistic Ethics," in *Humanist Ethics*, ed. Morris B. Storer (Buffalo: Prometheus Books, 1980), p. 156.

[6]Cited in John W. Whitehead, *The Second American Revolution* (Elfin, IL: David C. Cook, 1982), p. 46.

[7]Richard Hertz, *Chance and Symbol* (Chicago: University of Chicago Press, 1948), p. 107.

[8]Morris B. Storer, "A Factual Investigation of the Foundations of Morality," in *Humanist Ethics*, ed.Storer, p. 291.

[9]Paul Kurtz, *Eupraxophy: Living Without Religion* (Buffalo: Prometheus Books, 1989), p. 158.

[10]Julian Wadleigh, "What is Conservatism?" *The Humanist*, Nov./Dec.1989, p. 21.

[11]Ibid

[12]Delos B. McKown, "Demythologizing Natural Human Rights," *The Humanist*, May/June 1989, p. 22.

[13]Paul Kurtz, *The Fullness of Life* (New York: Horizon Press, 1974), p. 162.

[14]Paul Kurtz, *Forbidden Fruit* (Buffalo: Prometheus Books, 1988), p. 196.

[15]John Herman Randall, Jr., "What is the Temper of Humansim?" in *The Humanist Alternative* , ed. Kurtz, p. 59.

[16]Kurtz, *The Fullness of Life*, p. 162.

[17]Ibid.

[18]Max Hocutt, "Toward an Ethic of Mutual Accommodation," in *Humanist Ethics*, ed. Storer, p. 137.

[19]McKown, " Demythologizing Natural Human Rights," pp. 23-24.

[20]Ibid, p. 34

[21]Kurtz, *The Fullness of Life*, p. 163.

[22]Roscoe Pound, *An Introduction to the Philosophy of Law* (New Haven: Yale University Press, 1969), p. 3.

[23]Tibor R. Machan, "Are Human Rights Real?" *The Humanist*, Nov./Dec. 1989, p. 28.

[24]Alastair Hannay, "Propositions Toward a Humanist Consensus," in *Humanist Ethics*, ed. Storer, p. 187.

Chapter 28

[1]Karl Marx and Frederick Engels, *Collected Works*, forty volumes (New York: International Publishers, 1976), vol.6, pp. 494-5.

[2]V.I. Lenin, *On Socialist Ideology and Culture* (Moscow: Foreign Languages Publishing House), pp.51-2, cited in James D. Bales, *Communism and the Reality of Moral Law* (Nutley, NJ: The Craig Press, 1969), p. 2.

[3]L.S. Jawitsch, *The General Theory of Law* (Moscow: Progress Publishers, 1981), p. 160.

[4]Lenin, *On Socialist Ideology and Culture*, pp. 51-2.

[5]Frederick Engels, *The Origin of the Family, Private Property and the State* (Chicago: Kerr, 1902), p. 206.

[6]V.I. Lenin, *The State and Revolution* (New York: International Publishers, 1932, p. 9.

[7]Marx and Engels, *Collected Works*, vol. 6, p. 501.

[8]Maurice Cornforth, *The Open Philosophy and the Open Society* (New York: International Publishers, 1976), p. 290.

[9] Frederick Engels, *The Condition of the Working Class in England* (Moscow: 1973), p. 168. Cited in R.W. Makepeace, *Marxist Ideology and Soviet Criminal Law* (Totowa, NJ: Barnes and Noble, 1980), p.30.

[10] Jawitsch, *The General Theory of Law*, p. 46.

[11] V.I. Lenin, *Collected Works*, forty-five volumes (Moscow: Progress Publishers, 1981), vol.28, p. 236.

[12] Jawitsch, *The General Theory of Law*, p.160.

[13] Howard Selsam, *Socialism and Ethics* (New York: International Publishers, 1943), p. 13.

[14] E.B. Pashukanis in a 1930 speech regarding the Soviet State and the Revolution of Law (Moscow).

[15] V.I. Lenin, *Works*, 4th ed. (Moscow: 1949-50), vol. 25, p. 155. Cited in John Hazard, *Settling Disputes in Soviet* Society (New York: Columbia University, 1960), p. 3.

[16] Jawitsch, *The General Theory of Law*, p.290.

[17] Andrei Y. Vyshinsky, *Judiciary of the USSR*, 2d ed. (Moscow: 1935), p. 32. Cited in Berman, *Justice in the USSR*, pp.42-3.

[18] Cited in John Hazard, *Law and Social Change in the USSR* (London: Stevens and Sons, 1953), p. 79.

[19] Andrei Y. Vyshinsky, The Law of the Soviet State (New York: 1948), p. 13. Cited in *A Lexicon of Marxist-Leninist Semantics*, ed. Raymond S. Sleeper (Alexandria, VA: Western Goals, 1983), p. 147.

[20] J. Plamenatz, *Man and Society*, (London: 1966), vol. 2, p. 374. Cited in Makepeace, *Marxist Ideology and Soviet Criminal Law*, p. 35.

Chapter 29

[1] Marianne Williamson, *A Return to Love: Reflections on the Principles of "A Course in Miracles"*, (New York: Harper Collins, 1989), p. 37.

[2] Shakti Gawain, *Living in the Light* (San Rafael, California: New World Library, 1986), p. 110.

[3] Ibid., p. 37.

[4] Ibid., p. 3.

[5] David Spangler, *Revelation: The Birth of a New Age* (Middleton, Widconsin: Lorian Press, 1976), pp. 65.

[6] Shirley MacLaine, *Out on a Limb* (New York: Bantam Books, 1989), p. 204.

[7] Ibid.

[8] Mark Satin, *New Age Politics* (New York, Dell Pubishing Co., 1978), p. 103.

[9] Joseph Campbell, *The Power of Myth* (New York: Doubleday, 1988), p. 118.

Chapter 30

[1] Russell Kirk, "The Christian Postulates of English and American Law," *Journal of Christian Jurisprudence* (Tulsa, OK: O.W. Coburn School of Law/Oral Roberts University, 1980), p. 66.

[2]Carl F.H. Henry, *Twilight of a Great Civilization* (Westchester, IL: Crossway Books, 1988), p. 147.

[3]John W. Whitehead, *The Second American Revolution* (Westchester, IL: Crossway Book, 1988), p. 80.

[5]John Warwick Montgomery, *The Law Above the Law* (Minneapolis: Dimension Books, 1975), p. 26.

[5]A.E. Wilder Smith, *The Creation of Life* (Costa Mesa, CA: TWFT Publishers, 1970),p.ix.

[6]John W. Whitehead, *The Second American Revolution* (Westchester, IL: Crossway Books, 1988), p.21.

[7]Ibid.,p.73.

[8]WIlliam Blackstone, Commentaries on the Laws of England, in *Blackstone's Commentaries* with Notes of Reference to the Constitution and Laws of the Federal Government of the United States and of the Commonwealth of Virginia, five volumes, ed. St. George Tucker (Philadelphia: William Young Birch and Abraham Small, 1803; reprint, South Hackensack, NJ: Rothman Reprints, 1969), vol. 1, pp. 38-9.

[9]John Eidsmoe, *Christianity and the Constitution* (Grand Rapids: Baker Book House, 1987), p.58.

[10]Whitehead, *The Second American Revolution*, p. 76.

[11]Ibid., pp.87-8.

[12]Montgomery, *The Law Above the Law*, p.47.

[13]Schaeffer, "Joshua and the Flow of Biblical History," *The Complete Works*, Vol. 2, p.249.

[14]Gary T. Amos, *Defending the Declaration* (Brentwood, TN: Wolemuth and Hyatt, 1989), p. 109.

[15]Ibid., p. 117.

[16]Rousas John Rushdoony, *The Politics of Guilt and Pity* (Fairfax, VA: Thoburn Press, 1978), p. 135.

[17]John Eidsmoe, *God and Caesar* (Westchester, IL: Crossway Books, 1985), p. 197.

[18]Simon Greenleaf, A Treatise on the Law of Evidence (1824), Part V, Section 29, n. 1, cited in Herbert Titus, *God, Man, and Law*: The Biblical Principles (2d temporary ed., 1983), p. 85.

Chapter 31

[1]Lucile W. Green, "The Call for a World Constitutional Convention," *The Humanist*, July/August 1968, p.13.

[2]Paul Kurtz, "Is Everyone a Humanist?" in *The Humanist Alternative*, ed. Paul Kurtz (Buffalo: Prometheus Books, 1973), p. 179.

[3]Rudolf Dreikurs, "The Impact of Equality," *The Humanist*, Sept./Oct. 1964,p. 143.

[4]Corliss Lamont, *The Philosophy of Humanism* (New York: Frederick Ungar, 1982), p.262.

[5]Dreikurs, "The Impact of Equality," p. 143.

[6]Julian Huxley, "The Humanist Frame," in *The Humanist Frame*, ed. Huxley (New York: Harper and Brothers, 1961), p.15.

[7]Ibid.,p.7.

[8]Walt Anderson, *Politics and the Humanism* (Pacific Palisades, CA: Goodyear Publishing

Company, 1973), p. 83.

[9]Timothy J. Madigan, "Humanism and the Need for a Global Consciousness," *The Humanist*, March/April, 1986, pp. 17-18.

[10]Paul Kurtz, *Forbidden Fruit* (Buffalo: Prometheus Books, 1988), p. 146. Among these forces are Marxism/Leninism, the New Age movement, Secular Humanism, and various Internationalist and Transnationalists organizations including the Council for Foreign Relations, Club of Rome, Bilderburgers, Trilateral Commission, and the United Nations. Biblical Christianity constitutes one major opposition to one-world government; Revelation 13 declares that the head of a man-made world government will be the Beast or Anti-Christ. For a fairly complete list of organizations and movements striving for a world order, see Malachi Martin, *The Keys of This Blood* (New York: Simon and Schuster, 1990), pp.275f.

[11]Paul Kurtz, "A Declaration of Interdependence: A New Global Ethics," *Free Inquiry*, Fall 1988, p. 6.

[12]*Humanist Manifeto II* (Buffalo: Prometheus Books, 1980), p. 23.

[13]Erich Fromm, *May Man Prevail?* (Garden City, NY: Double Day, 1961), p. 248.

[14]Linus Pauling, "Humanism and Peace," *The Humanist*, 1961, no 2, p.75.

[15]William G. Carleton, *Technology and Humanism* (Nashville: Vanderbilt University Press, 1970), p. 22.

[16]Corliss Lamont, *Voice in the Wilderness* (Buffalo: Prometheus Books, 1975), p. 318.

[17]*Humanist Manifesto II*, p. 22.

[18]Dreikurs, "The Impact of Equality," p. 146.

[19]Huxley, "The Humanist Frame," p. 16.

[20]Julian Huxley, cited in *Humanist Ethics*, ed. Morris B. Storer (Buffalo: Prometheus Books, 1980), p. 2.

[21]Huxley, "The Humanist Frame," p. 107.

[22]Sidney Hook, *Religion in a Free Society* (Lincoln: University of Nebraska Press, 1967), p. 36.

[23]Mark Reader, "Humanism and Politics," *The Humanist*, Nov./Dec. 1975, p. 38.

[24]James R. Simpson, "Toward a Humanist Consensus on International Development," in *Humanist Ethics*, ed Storer, p. 130.

[25]V.M. Tarkunde, "An Outline of Radical Humanism," *The Humanist*, July/Aug. 1988, p. 13.

[26]Walt Anderson, *Politics and the New Humanism* (Pacific Palisades CA: Goodyear Publishing Company, 1973), p. 141.

[27]Lamont, *The Philosophy of Humanism*, p. 267.

[28]*Humanist Manifesto II*, p. 22.

[29]Tarkunde, "An Outline of Radical Humanism," p. 13.

[30]Kurtz, *Forbidden Fruit*, p. 176.

Chapter 32

[1]Karl Marx, *Civil War in France* (New York: International, 1937), p. 19.

[2]Karl Marx, *A Contribution to the Critique of Political Economy* (Chicago: C.H. Kerr, 1911) p. 11.

[3]Karl Marx, Frederick Engels, and V.I.Lenin, *On the Dictatorship of the Proletariat* (Moscow: Progress Publishers, 1984), p. 243.

[4]Ibid., p. 124.

[5]Ibid., p. 59.

[6]V.I. Lenin, *The State and Revolution* (New York: International, 1932), p. 9.

[7]Marx, Engles, and Lenin, *On the Dictatorship of the Proletariat*, p. 122.

[8]Lenin, "O lozunge 'razoruzheniia," October 1916. Cited in Elliot R. Goodman, *The Soviet Design for a World State* (New York: Columbia University Press, 1968), p. 287.

[9]Claire Sterling, *The Terror Network: The Secret War of International Terrorism* (New York: Berkley Books, 1982), p. 203.

[10]V.I. Lenin, *Selected Works* (New York: International Pulishers, 1938), vol. 7, p. 81.

[11]V.V. Zagladin, ed., *The World Communist Movement* (Moscow: Progress Publishers 1973), p. 159.

[12]Joseph Stalin, "Beseda s pervoi amerikanskoi rabochei delegatsiei," Sept. 9, 1927. Cited in Goodman, *The Soviet Design for a World State*, p. 191.

[13]Frederick Engels, *The Origin of the Family, Private Property and the State* (Chicago: Kerr, 1902), p. 206.

[14]Marx, Engles, and Lenin, *On the Dictionary of the Proletariat*, pp. 249-50.

[15]Ibid., p. 256.

[16]Ibid., p. 251.

[17]Georgi Shakhnazarov, *The Coming World Order* (Moscow: Progress Publishers, 1981), p. 18.

[18]Ibid., p. 201.

[19]R.J. Rummel, *Death by Government*, (New Brunswick, Transaction Publishers, 1994), p. 9.

Chapter 33

[1]Mark Satin, *New Age Politics*, (New York: Dell Publishing, 1978), p. 22.

[2]Donald Keys, *Earth at Omega: Passage to Planetization* (Boston: Branden Press, 1982), p. iii.

[3]David Spangler, *Emergence: The Rebirth of the Sacred* (New York: Delta/Merloyd Lawrence, 1984), p. 42.

[4]Randall N. Baer, *Inside the New Age Nightmare* (Lafayette, LA: Huntington House, Inc., 1989), p. 34.

[5]Mark Satin, *New Age Politics* (New York, Dell Publishing Inc., 1978), pp. 20-21.

[6]Marilyn Ferguson, *The Aquarian Conspiracy* (Los Angeles: J.P. Tarcher, Inc., 1980), p. 240.

[7]Mark Satin, *New Age Politics* (New York, Dell Publishing Co., 1978), p. 106.

[8]Robert Muller, *The New Genesis: Shaping a Global Spirituality* (New York: Image Books, 1984), p. 164.

Chapter 34

[1]James Madison, *The Federalists Papers*, no. 51 (New York: Pocket Books, 1964), p. 122.

[2]E. Calvin Beisner, *Prosperity and Poverty: The Compassionate Use of Resources in a World of Scarcity* (Westchester, IL: Crossway Books, 1988) p. 45.

[3]Rousas John Rushdoony, *Politics of Guilt and Pity* (Fairfax, VA: Thoburn Press, 1978), p. 239.

[4]Charles Colson, *Kingdoms in Conflict* (Grand Rapids, MI: Zondervan, 1987), p. 226.

[5]Francis A. Schaeffer, *A Christian Manifesto* (Westchester, IL: Crossway Books, 1982), p. 34.

[6]Charles Colson, *Who Speaks for God?* (Westchester, IL: Crossway Books, 1988) p. 144.

[7]Colson, *Kingdoms in Conflict*, p. 77.

[8]Schaeffer, *A Christian Manifesto*, p. 93. An example of the proper time for disobedience recently arose when the American government (through its public health services) advised churches to amend their attitude toward homosexuality. The Bible clearly dictates the proper Christian response to homosexuality (see Romans 1 and Jude 1), and the church must stand firm in her commitment to obey God's dictums even when they must conflict with those of the state.

[9]Colson, *Kingdoms in Conflict*, p. 291.

Chapter 35

[1]Erich Fromm, *On Disobedience and Other Essays* (New York: Seabury Press, 1981), p. 90.

[2]Robert Scheaffer, "Socialism is Incompatible with Humanism," *Free Inquiry*, Fall 1989, p. 19.

[3]Marvin Zimmerman, "Hooked on Freedom and Science," in *Sidney Hook: Philosopher of Democracy and Humanism*, ed. Paul Kurtz (Buffalo: Prometheus Books, 1983), p. 80.

[4]Scheaffer, "Socialism is Incompatible with Humanism," p. 19.

[5]Sidney Hook, *Out of Step* (New York: Harper & Row, 1987), pp. 600-601.

[6]Corliss Lamont, *Voice in the Wilderness* (Buffalo: Prometheus Books, 1975), p. 163.

[7]John Dewey, *Liberalism and Social Action* (New York: G.P. Putnam's Sons, 1935), pp. 356-7.

[8]Fromm, *On Disobedience and Other Essays*, p. 74.

[9]John Kenneth Galbraith, *Economics, Peace and Laughter* (Boston: Houghton Mifflin, 1971), p. 101.

[10]Hook, *Out of Step*, p. 30.

[11]Lamont, *Voice in the Wilderness*, p. 164.

[12]Dewey, *Liberalism and Social Action*, p. 88.

[13]Ibid., p. 90.

[14]Fromm, *On Disobedience and Other Essays*, pp. 75-6.

[15]Ibid., p. 62.

[16]Lamont, *Voice in the Wilderness*, p. 166.

[17]Ibid., p. 169. Lamont is clearly confused about economic theories. In reality, fascism is more closely akin to socialism than to capitalism, for while fascism leaves titular ownership of produc-tive property in private hands, it insists that only the central government should control produc-tive property. Capitalist philosophy has always held that control was an essential element of own-

ership. Therefore capitalism regards fascism as allowing private ownership of the means of productions in name only, and not in substance. The only difference between fascism and socialism is that the former allows people to hold legal title to capital; neither allows them to control it. It is no wonder, therefore, that of the two major fascist movements in this century, one in Italy under Mussolini and the other Germany under Hitler, the latter called itself National Socialism, i.e., Nazism.

[18]Dewey, *Liberalism and Social Action*, pp. 79-80.

[19]Hook, *Out of Step*, p. 600.

[20]John Dewey, *Individualism, Old and New* (New York: 1930), p. 119.

Chapter 36

[1]V.I Lenin, *Selected Works* (New York: International Publishers, 1937), vol. 9, p. 479.

[2]Karl Marx and Frederick Engels, *Collected Works*, forty volumes (New York: International Publishers, 1976), vol. 6, p. 487.

[3]Karl Marx, *Capital* (London: Sonnenschein), pp. 660-1, cited in Laidler, *History of Socialism*, pp. 152-3.

[4]Frederick Engels, *Socialism: Utopian and Scientific* (New York: International Publishers, 1935), p. 69.

[5]Political Dictionary (Moscow: 1940), p. 245, cited in *A Lexicon of Marxist-Leninist Semantics*, ed. Raymond S. Sleeper (Alexandria, VA: Western Goals, 1983), p. 30.

[6]Ibid., p. 249.

[7]Lenin, *Selected Works*, vol 9, p. 479.

[8]Marx and Engels, *Collected Works*, vol. 6, p. 350.

[9]Karl Marx, The Gotha Program, cited in *Cameron, Marxism: the Science of Society*, p. 97.

[10]V.I. Lenin, *Collected Works*, forty-five volumes (Moscow: Progress Publishers, 1980), vol. 30, p. 107.

[11]Marx and Engels, *Collected Works*, vol. 6, p. 351.

[12]Harry W. Laidler, *History of Socialism* (New York: Thomas Y. Crowell, 1968), p. 384.

[13]*Pravada*, Nov. 7, 1921.

[14]Lenin, "Concerning the Food Tax," cited in Laidler, *History of Socialism*, p. 390.

[15]Lenin, *Collected Works*, vol. 26, pp. 414-15.

[16]G.A. Kozlov, ed., *Political Economy: Socialism* (Moscow: Progress Publishers, 1977), p. 55.

[17]Fundamentals of Marxism-Lenin (Moscow:1961), p. 741. Cited in *A Lexicon of Marxist-Leninist Semantics*, ed. Sleeper, p. 302.

[18]Kenneth Neill Cameron, *Marxism: the Science of Society* (Massachusetss: Bergin & Garvey, 1985), p. 85.

[19]John Strachey, *The Theory and Practice of Socialism* (New York: Random House, 1936), title page.

Chapter 37

[1]Marianne Williamson, *Return to Love: Reflections on the Principles of "A Course in Miracles"* (New York: Harper Collins Inc., 1989), p. 168.

[2]Vera Alder, *When Humanity Comes of Age* (New York: Samuel Weiser, Inc., 1974), pp. 48-9.

[3]Marilyn Ferguson, *The Aquarian Conspiracy* (Los Angeles: J.P. Tarcher, Inc., 1980), pp. 326-7.

[4]Shakti Gawain, *Living in the Light* (San Rafael, California: New World Library, 1986), p. 110.

[5]Ibid., 142.

[6]Randall N. Baer, *Inside the New Age Nightmare* (Lafayette, LA: Huntington House, Inc., 1989), p. 140.

[7]Marianne Williamson, *Return to Love: Reflections on the Principles of "A Course in Miracles"*, p. 158.

[8]Ibid., p. 171.

[9]Kevin Ryerson, *Spirit Communication: The Soul's Path* (New York: Bantam Books, 1989), p. 160.

[10]Shirley MacLaine, *Out on a Limb* (New York: Bantam Books, 1989), p. 291.

[11]Marianne Williamson, *Return to Love: Reflections on the Principles of "A Course in Miracles"*, p. 158.

Chapter 38

[1]Ronald Nash, *Poverty and Wealth: The Christian Debate Over Capitalism* (Westchester, IL: Crossway Books, 1987), p. 63.

[2]Irving E. Howard, *The Christian Alternative to Socialism* (Arlington, VA: Better Books, 1966), p. 43.

[3]E. Calvin Beisner, *Prosperity and Poverty: The Compassionate Use of Resources in a World of Scarcity* (Westchester, IL: Crossway Books, 1988), p. 66.

[4]Ibid., pp. xi-xii.

[5]Ibid., p. 52.

[6]Ibid.

[7]Michael Novak, *The Spirit of Democratic Capitalism* (New York: Simon and Schuster, 1982), p. 15.

[8]Nash, *Poverty and Wealth*, p. 71.

[9]George Gilder, *Wealth and Poverty* (New York: Basic Books, 1981), p. 63.

[10]Ibid, p. 245. For further discussion of the role of mind in economics, see Warren Brookes' excellent work *The Economy in Mind* (New York: Universe Books, 1982).

[11]P.T. Bauer, *Equality, the Third World, and Economic Delusion* (Cambridge, MA: Harvard University Press, 1981), p. 18.

[12]Beisner, *Prosperity and Poverty*, p. 54.

[13]Karl Marx and Frederick Engels, *Collected Works*, forty volumes (New York: International Publishers, 1976), vol.3, p. 399.

Chapter 39

[1]Julian Huxley, *Essays of a Humanist* (London: Chatto and Windus, 1964), p. 77.

[2]*Humanist Manifesto II* (Buffalo: Prometheus Books, 1980), p. 13.

[3]Ibid., p. 14.

[4]Roger E. Greeley, ed. *The Best of Humanism* (Buffalo: Prometheus Books, 1988), p. 174.

[5]Huxley, *Essays of a Humanist*, p. 33.

[6]Ibid., p. 78.

[7]Robert E. Egner and Lester E. Denon, eds., *The Basic Writings of Bertrand Russell* (New York: Simon and Schuster, 1961), p. 685.

[8]Paul Kurtz, *Eupraxophy: Living Without Religion* (Buffalo: Prometheus, 1989), pp. 33-4.

[9]Harry Elmer Barnes, *The New History and the Social Studies* (New York: Century, 1925), p. 21.

[10]Harry Elmer Barnes, *Living in the Twentieth Century* (Indianapolis: Bobbs-Merrill, 1928), p. 32.

[11]Corliss Lamont, *The Philosophy of Humanism* (New York: Frederick Ungar, 1982), p. 282.

[12]*Humanist Manifesto II*, p. 16.

[13]Huxley, *Essays of a Humanist*, p. 76.

[14]Lamont, *The Philosophy of Humanism*, p. 283.

[15]Erich Fromm, *You Shall Be as Gods* (New York: Rinehart, and Winston, 1966), p. 88.

[16]Ibid., p. 123.

[17]Lamont, *The Philosophy of Humanism*, pp. 107-8.

[18]Victor J. Stenger, *Not By Design* (Buffalo: Prometheus Books, 1988), p. 186.

[19]Ibid., p. 188.

Chapter 40

[1]Joseph Stalin, *Dialectical and Historical Materialism* (New York: International, 1977), p. 29.

[2]Karl Marx, *A Contribution to the Critique of Political Economy* (New York: International, 1904), p. 11. Marx's view here is identical to that of the existentialists, who insist that existence precedes essence. Little wonder that so many existentialists have also been Marxist.

[3]Marx, *Contribution to the Critique of Political Economy*, p. 12.

[4]Marx and Engels, *The Communist Manifesto*, p. 5.

[5]Karl Marx and Frederick Engels, *On Historical Materialism* (New York: International, 1976), p. 120.

[6]Karl Marx, *The Poverty of Philosophy* (New York: International, 1936), pp. 152-3.

[7]Lenin, *On Historical Materialism*, p. 461.

[8]Stalin, *Dialectical and Historical Materialism*, p. 19.

[9]V.I. Lenin, *Selected Works*, forty five volumes (Moscow: Progress Publishers, 1980), vol. 2, p. 57, cited in *A Lexicon of Marxist-Leninist Semantics*, ed. Raymond S. Sleeper (Alexandria, VA: Western Goals, 1983), p. 121.

[10]Maurice Cornforth, *The Open Philosophy and the Open Society* (New York: International, 1976), p. 159.

[11]Maurice Cornforth, *Historical Materialism* (New York: International, 1972), p. 68.

[12]Lenin, *Collected Works*, vol. 11, p. 71.

[13]Marx, *On Historical Materialism*, p. 135.

Chapter 41

[1]Marilyn Ferguson, *The Aquarian Conspiracy* (Los Angeles: J.P. Tarcher, Inc., 1980), p. 71

[2]Benjamin B. Ferencz and Ken Keyes, Jr., *Planethood* (Coos Bay, Oregon: Vision Books, 1988), p. 141.

[3]Ibid., p. 33.

[4]Paul Davies, *The New Scientist*, December 17, 1987, pp. 41-2.

[5]Joseph Campbell, *The Power of Myth* (New York: Doubleday, 1988), p. 18.

[6]Ibid.

[7]M. Scott Peck, *The Road Less Traveled* (New York; Simon and Schuster, 1978), pp. 269-70.

[8]Marianne Williamson, *A Return to Love: Reflections on the Principles of "A Course in Miracles"* p. 71.

[9]Dean C. Halverson, *Crystal Clear: Understanding and Reaching New Agers* (Colorado Springs, CO: NavPress, 1990), p. 77.

[10]Donald H. Yott, *Man and Metaphysics* (New York: Weiser, 1980), p. 74.

[11]Levi, *The Aquarian Gospel of Jesus the Christ* (Los Angeles: DeVorss & Co., 1970).

[12]Shakti Gawain, *Living in the Light* (San Rafael, California: New World Library, 1986), p. 179.

[13]David Spangler, *Emergence: The Rebirth of the Sacred* (New York: Delta/Merloyd Lawrence, 1984), p. 12.

Chapter 42

[1]Ronald H. Nash, *Christian Faith and Historical Understanding* (Dallas, TX: Probe Books, 1984), p. 112.

[2]W.F. Albright, "Toward a More Conservative View," *Christianity Today*, Jan. 18, 1963, p. 4.

[3]H.G. Wells, *The Outline of History* (Garden City, NY: Garden City Publishing, 1921), p. 497.

[4]Gleason L. Archer, Jr., *A Survey of Old Testament Introduction* (Chicago: Moody Press, 1968), p. 19.

[5]Nelson Glueck, *Biblical Archaeologist*, vol. 22 (Dec. 1959), p. 101.

[6]John Warwick Montgomery, *Human Rights and Human Dignity* (Dallas, TX: Probe Books, 1986), p. 137.

[7]Cornelius Tacitus, Annals XV. 44; cited in McDowell, *Evidence that Demands a Verdict*, p. 84.

[8]Bruce M. Metzger, *The New Testament: its Background, Growth, and Content* (Nashville: Abingdon Press, 1965), p. 78.

[9]D.W. Bebbington, *Patterns in History* (Downers Grove, IL: InterVarsity Press, 1979), p. 169.

[10]Herbert Butterfield, *Christianity and History* (New York: Charles Scribner's Sons, 1950), p. 66.

[11]C.S. Lewis, *Miracles: A Preliminary Study* (London: Geoffrey Bles, 1952), p. 149. Norman Geisler says of Lewis's work on miracles, "The best overall apologetic for miracles written in this century;" *Miracles and Modern Thought*, p. 167.

[12]*God, History, and Historians*, ed. C.T. McIntire, (New York: Oxford University Press, 1977), p. 201.

[13]John Warwick Montgomery, *The Shape of the Past* (Minneapolis: Bethany Fellowship, 1975), p. 42.

Conclusion

[1]James J.D. Luce, "The Fundamentalists Anonymous Movement," *The Humanist*, Jan/Feb 1986, p. 11.

[2]Edward O. Wilson, "The Relation of Science to Theology," *Zygon*, Sept/Dec 1980, cited in Henry M. Morris, *The Long War Against God* (Grand Rapids, MI: Baker Book House, 1990), p. 34.

[3]Herbert A. Tonne, *Scribblings of a Concerned Secular Humanist* (Northvale, NJ: Humanists of North Jersey, 1988), p. 39.

[4]Erich Fromm, *On Disobedience and Other Essays* (New York, The Seabury Press, 1981), p. 24.

[5]C.E.M. Joad, *The Recovery of Belief* (London: Faber and Faber, 1955), p. 22.

[6]Cited in Daniel S. Levy, "Interview: Evolution, Extinction and the Movies," *Times*, May 14, 1990, p. 19.

[7]George C. Roche, *A World Without Heroes* (Hillsdale, MI: Hillsdale College Press, 1987), p. 103.

[8]Percival Davis and Dean H. Kenyon, *Of Pandas and People* (Dallas, TX: Haughton, 1989), p. 55.

[9]Roche, *A World Without Heroes*, p. 245.

[10]Francis Darwin, ed., *The Life and Letters of Charles Darwin* (London: J. Murray, 1888), vol. 1, p. 316.

[11]Cited in Dallas Willard, "Language, Being, God, and the Three Stages of Theistic Evidence," in *Does God Exist? The Great Debate*, ed. J.P. Moreland and Kai Nielsen (Nashville: Thomas Nelson, 1990), p. 211. Willard cites Hume's Introduction to *The Natural History of Religion*.

[12]Michael Denton, *Evolution: A Theory in Crisis* (Bethesda, MD: Adler and Adler, 1986), p. 345.

[13]George Wald, "The Origin of Life," *Scientific American*, August 1954, p. 33.

[14]Davis and Kenyon, *Of Pandas and People*, p. 3.

[15]Ibid., p. 56.

[16]Ibid., p. 4.

[17]Charles Thaxton, Walter Bradley, and Roger Olsen, *The Mystery of Life's Origin: Reassessing Current Theories* (New York: Philosophical Library, 1984), p. 186. Students particularly interested in biological origins should also read Davis and Kenyon, *Of Pandas and People: The Central Question of Biological Origins*.

[18]Keith Parsons, "Is There a Case for Christian Theism?" in *Does God Exist: The Great Debate*, ed. Moreland and Nielsen, p. 185.

[19]L.H. Mathews, "Introduction," in Charles Darwin,The Origin of Species (London: J.M. Dent and Sons, 1971), pp. x-xi. Cited in Luther D. Sunderland, *Darwin's Enigma* (San Diego: Master Books, 1984), pp. 30-31.

[20]Cited in Davis and Kenyon, *Of Pandas and People*, p. 94.

[21]Ibid., p. 108.

[22]Julian Huxley, *Essays of a Humanist* (London: Chatto and Windus, 1964), p. 9.

[23]Chris McGowan, *In the Beginning* . . . (Buffalo: Prometheus Books, 1984), p. 141.

[24]Cited in Sunderland, *Darwin's Enigma*, p. 89.

[25]Cited in Davis and Kenyon, *Of Pandas and People*, p. 106.

[26]Cited in Roche, *A World Without Heroes*, p. 277.

[27]Carl Sagan, *The Dragons of Eden* (New York: Random House, 1977), p. 93.

[28]Soren Lovtrup, Darwinism: *The Refutation of a Myth* (London: Croom Helm, 1987), p. 422.

[29]Carl Sagan, *The Dragons of Eden* (New York: Random House, 1977), p. 92.

[30]Ibid., p. 93.

[31]Joad, *The Recovery of Belief*, p. 46.

[32]K. Platonov, *The Word as a Physiological and Therapeutic Factor* (Moscow: Foreign Languages Publishing House, 1959), p. 223.

[33]Joad, *The Recovery of Belief*, p. 64.

[34]Arnold Beichman, "Immune from the Shortages," *The Washington Times*, December 31, 1990, p. G3.

[35]Cited in Ibid.

[36]John Warwick Montgomery, *Human Rights and Human Dignity* (Dallas, TX: Probe Books, 1986), p. 123.

[37]Cited in Roche, *A World Without Heroes*, p. 186.

[38]Malachi Martin, *The Keys of This Blood* (New York: Simon and Schuster, 1990), p. 656.

[39]Sidney Hook, "Solzhenitsyn and Secular Humanism: A Response," *The Humanist*, Nov/Dec 1978, p. 6.

[40]Kenneth L. Feder and Michael Alan Park, "Animal Rights: An Evolutionary Perspective," *The Humanist*, July/August 1990, p. 44.

[41]Alexis de Tocqueville, *Democracy in America*, two volumes (New Rochelle, NY: Arlington House, n.d.), vol 1, p. 294.

[42]Cited in Montgomery, *Human Rights and Human Dignity*, p. 107.

[43]Paul Kurtz, *Philosophical Essays in Pragmatic Naturalism* (Buffalo: Prometheus Books, 1990), p. 163.

[44]Cited in Roche, *A World Without Heroes*, p. 289.

[45]Stanley L. Jaki, *The Road of Science and the Ways to God* (Chicago: University of Chicago Press, 1978), p. 242. We also recommend Norman L. Geisler and J. Kerby Anderson, *Origin Science: A Proposal for the Creation-Evolution Controversy* (Grand Rapids, MI: Baker Book

House, 1987), and J.P. Moreland, *Christianity and the Nature of Science* (Grand Rapids, MI: Baker Book House, 1989).

[46]Thomas Jefferson, Notes on Virginia, cited in *The Jeffersonian Cyclopedia*, two volumes, ed. John P. Foley (New York: Russell & Russell, [1900] 1967), vol. 1, p. 386.

[47]Tonne, *Scribblings of a Concerned Secular Humanist*, p. 40.

[48]Jaki, *The Road of Science and the Ways to God*, p. 218.

[49]Huxley, *Essays of a Humanist*, p. 107.

[50]Tonne, *Scribblings of a Concerned Secular Humanist*, p. 40.

[51]Cited in Roche, *A World Without Heroes*, p. 248.

[52]Joseph Stalin, speech delivered April 24, 1924 (New York: International Publishers, 1934).

[53]Harry Elmer Barnes, *The New History and the Social Studies* (New York: Century, 1925), p. 543.

[54]Ibid., p. 539.

[55]William Stanmeyer, *Clear and Present Danger* (Ann Arbor, MI: Servant Books, 1983), p. 167.

[56]H.J. Eysenck, "Reason With Compassion," in *The Humanist Alternative* ed. Paul Kurtz (Buffalo: Prometheus Press, 1985).

[57]Corliss Lamont, *A Lifetime of Dissent* (Buffalo Prometheus Books, 1988), p. 55.

[58]Cited in Francis A. Schaeffer, A Christian Manifesto, in *The Complete Works of Francis A. Schaeffer: A Christian View of the West*, five volumes (Westchester, IL: Crossway Books, 1982), vol. 5, p. 439. Schaeffer cites Durant's article from *The Humanist*, February 1977.

[59]Schaeffer, *Complete Works*, vol. 5, p. 439.

[60]Ibid., vol. 4, p. 30.

[61]Edward O. Wilson, "Biology's Spiritual Products," *Free Inquiry*, Spring 1987, p. 14.

[62]Roche, *A World Without Heroes*, p. 116.

[63]Ibid., p. 106.

[64]Wayne L. Trotta, "Why Psychotherapy Must Be, and Cannot Be, a Science," *The Humanist*, Sept/Oct 1989, p. 42.

[65]Cited in Roche, *A World Without Heroes*, p. 238.

[66]William Kirk Kilpatrick, *Psychological Seduction* (Nashville, TN: Thomas Nelson, 1983), p. 185.

[67]Victor Stenger, *Not By Design* (Buffalo: Prometheus Books, 1988), p. 188.

[68]Roche, *A World Without Heroes*, p. 87.

[69]James C. Dobson and Gary L. Bauer, *Children at Risk* (Dallas, TX: Word, 1990)p. 22.

[70]Roche, *A World Without Heroes*, p. 358.

FOR FURTHER READING

Anderson, Martin. *Impostors in the Temple: American Intellectuals Are Destroying Our Universities and Cheating Our Students of Their Future.* New York, NY: Simon and Schuster, 1992.

Ankerberg, John, Craig Branch, and John Weldon. *Thieves of Innocence.* Eugene, OR: Harvest House Publishers, 1993.

Behe, Michael J. *Darwin's Black Box: The Biochemical Challenge to Evolution.* New York, NY: Free Press, 1996.

Bernstein, Richard. *Dictatorship of Virtue: Multiculturalism and the Battle for America's Future.* New York, NY: Alfred A. Knopf, 1994.

Bork, Robert H. *Slouching Towards Gomorrah: Modern Liberalism and American Decline.* New York, NY: Harper Collins, 1996.

Breese, David A. *Seven Men Who Rule the World from the Grave.* Chicago, IL: Moody Press, 1990.

Brown, William E., and W. Gary Phillips. *Making Sense of Your World.* Chicago, IL: Moody Press, 1991.

Collier, Peter, and David Horowitz. *Destructive Generation.* New York, NY: Summit Books, 1989.

Craig, William Lane. *Reasonable Faith: Christian Truth and Apologetics.* Wheaton, IL: Crossway Books, 1994.

Davis, Percival, and Dean H. Kenyon. *Of Pandas and People.* Dallas, TX: Haughton Publishing, 1989.

Dobson, James C., and Gary L. Bauer. *Children at Risk: The Battle for the Hearts and Minds of our Kids.* Dallas, TX: Word Publishing, 1990.

Gilder, George. *Men and Marriage.* Gretna, LA: Pelican Publishing Co., 1986.

Jaki, Stanley L. *The Road of Science and the Ways of God.* Chicago, IL: The University of Chicago Press, 1978.

Jaki, Stanley L. *The Savior of Science.* Washington, D.C.: Regnery Gateway, 1988.

Johnson, Paul. *Intellectuals.* New York, NY: Harper and Row, 1988.

Johnson, Philip E. *Darwin on Trial.* Downers Grove, IL: InterVarsity Press, 1991.

Johnson, Philip E. *Reason in the Balance: The Case Against Naturalism in Science, Law and Education.* Downers Grove, IL: Inter Varsity Press, 1995.

Kilpatrick, William. *Why Johnny Can't Tell Right from Wrong.* New York, NY: Simon and Schuster, 1992.

Kimball, Roger. *Tenured Radicals.* New York, NY: Harper and Row, 1990.

Kreeft, Peter. *Back to Virtue.* San Francisco, CA: Ignatius Press, 1992.

Kreeft, Peter. *Three Philosophies of Life.* San Francisco, CA: Ignatius Press, 1989.

LaHaye, Tim. *The Battle for the Mind.* Old Tappen, NJ: Fleming H. Revell, 1980.

Marsden, George M. *The Soul of the American University: From Protestant Establishment to Established Nonbelief.* New York, NY: Oxford University Press, 1994.

Moreland, J.P. *Christianity and the Nature of Science.* Grand Rapids, MI: Baker Book House, 1989.

Moreland, J.P., ed. *The Creation Hypothesis: Scientific Evidence for an Intelligent Designer.* Downers Grove, IL: InterVarsity Press, 1994.

Moreland, J.P. *Scaling the Secular City.* Grand Rapids, MI: Baker Book House, 1987.

Morris, Henry M. *The Long War Against God.* Grand Rapids, MI: Baker Book House, 1989.

Nash, Ronald. *Worldviews in Conflict.* Grand Rapids, MI: Zondervan Publishing House, 1992.

Noebel, David A. *Understanding the Times: The Religious Worldviews of Our Day and the Search for Truth.* Eugene, OR: Harvest House Publishers, 1994. Unabridged.

Overman, Christian. *Assumptions That Affect Our Lives.* Chatsworth, CA: Micah 6:8, 1996.

Pearcey, Nancy R., and Charles B. Thaxton. *The Soul of Science: Christian Faith and Natural Philosophy.* Wheaton, IL: Crossway Books, 1994.

ReMine, Walter James. *The Biotic Message: Evolution Versus Message Theory.* St. Paul, MN: St. Paul Science, 1993.

Schaeffer, Francis A. *A Christian Manifesto.* Wheaton, IL: Crossway Books, 1982.

Schaeffer, Francis A. *The Great Evangelical Disaster.* Wheaton, IL: Crossway Books, 1984.

Stanlis, Peter J. *Edmund Burke and the Natural Law.* Shreveport, LA: Huntington House, 1986.

Van der Heydt, Barbara. *Candles Behind the Wall.* Grand Rapids, MI: William B. Eerdmans Publishing, 1993.